ELYSIAN FIELDS

V. S. Yanovsky

ELYSIAN FIELDS

A Book of Memory

V. S. YANOVSKY

Translated by Isabella Yanovsky and the Author

Foreword by Marc Raeff

Northern Illinois University Press

DeKalb, Illinois 1987

Library of Congress Cataloging-in-Publication Data
ÎAnovskiĭ, V. S. (Vasilii S.), 1906–
Elysian fields.
Translation of: Polĩa Eliseĭskie.
1. ÎAnovskiĭ, V. S. (Vasiliĭ S.), 1906–
2. Russians—France—Paris—Biography. 3. Soviet Union—
History—Revolution, 1917–1921—Refugees. 4. Refugees,
Political—France—Paris. 5. Russians—France—Paris—
Intellectual life—History—20th century. 6. Paris
(France)—Intellectual life. I. Title.
DC718.R8I26413   1987   944'.3610049171024
[B]   86-21677

Translated from the Russian *Polya Eliseyskie*
(New York: Silver Age Publishing, 1983)

Aux Morts on ne Doit que la Vérité.—Voltaire

I Must Warn You Not to Be Surprised if I Speak about the Dead as
if They Were Alive.—V.S.Y.

Contents

Foreword *by Marc Raeff*   ix

1   Boris Poplavsky   3

2   Felsen   26

3   G. Fedotov   43

4   I. Fondaminsky   62

5   Adamovich, Khodasevich *et al.*   84

6   Sundays at the Merezhkovskys'   105

7   Our Philosophers   131

8   Mother Marie   153

9   The Union of Writers and Poets   174

10   Meetings   191

11   Newspapers and Journals   212

     Notes   233

     Persons Mentioned in the Text   239

     Journals and Literary Groups of the Emigration   295

     Index   299

Foreword

Marc Raeff

How many cities was Paris in the 1920s and 1930s! The capital of France and of its empire, the center of avant garde plastic arts and music, the curator of West European cultural traditions, the residence of expatriate writers, painters, and musicians, the refuge of political exiles from all corners of the world, not to speak of the mecca for tourists and pleasure seekers. This protean Paris also contained a "Russian Paris," the "capital" of about a million Russian emigrés who had left their homeland as a consequence of the Revolution and Civil War. This entire million of Russians of course did not settle in Paris, or even largely in France; most emigrés lived elsewhere, scattered all over the globe—and Germany, Yugoslavia, Czechoslovakia, Manchuria, and the countries bordering on the Soviet Union (Baltic states, Poland, Romania) were the major areas of refuge. But from the middle 1920s, through that decade and the next, Paris was the common cultural and political focus from which they drew their intellectual and spiritual sustenance.

What distinguished the Russian emigrés from all the other groups of exiles that made of Paris their temporary abode? First of all was the sad fact, eventually acknowledged by both the Russians and their French hosts, that their emigration was permanent, at least as far as one could foresee. There seemed no practical prospect of going back home to Russia (even on a visit). To do so was to face a most uncertain fate, even if, in some few individual cases, they received the necessary permissions to return. Second, they represented a group numerous enough, educated enough, concerned enough to maintain their cultural traditions, and to make the necessary efforts to support intellectual, literary, and artistic creativity. Third, the very dispersion of the Russian emigration meant that Paris served not only Russian Paris but a much larger audience outside Paris or France; and it also meant that there were still a number of emigrés who—with the help of foreign organizations and donations—could pay for manifestations of emigré culture. Finally, since it was quite difficult to integrate into French society, the Russian emigrés wanted to raise their

children in the knowledge of Russian literature, history, and religion (independent of the fact that they also had to receive a French, German,
Czech, or whatever education) in the hope, however vague and unlikely,
that eventually these children and their knowledge might be useful to the
land of their ancestors as well. To this end there were organized educational institutions, cultural events, scholarly enterprises, and publications
that addressed themselves specifically to the preservation of Russian literature and culture. The long and short of it was the cardinal fact that there
was little prospect of assimilation; the Russians were political emigrés,
they were not immigrants who would in due course merge into the society
that had given them asylum. It is what distinguished the Russians of Paris
(and elsewhere) between the two world wars from subsequent waves of
refugees after 1945; it also explains why Russian Paris came to an abrupt
end with the fall of France in June 1940.

Paris was not the first cultural capital of the Russian diaspora. Berlin
had played this role in the first half of the 1920s but had to relinquish it
because of its own economic and political developments. It should be
noted, however, that Russian Berlin had been quite different from Russian Paris—and not only because of the two European capitals' diver-
gent cultural traditions and climates. The main reason for the difference
lay in the fact that during the Berlin period there had been much lively
contact between the emigrés and the Sovieticized homeland. Indeed,
until about 1926 or 1928, it was possible for Soviet writers, artists, and
scholars to travel abroad and meet with emigrés. And for a variety of
reasons Berlin was the focal point for such encounters. Furthermore,
literature published abroad (mainly in Berlin) did find its way—albeit in
abridged and expurgated form—into the Soviet Union. In the Berlin
era, then, the line dividing emigré from Soviet cultural life was not
sharply drawn; the two cultures were not yet separated into distinct
watertight compartments. With the end of the New Economic Policy,
the onset of collectivization and the first Five Year Plan, and even more
so with the introduction of a rigid political and aesthetic orthodoxy
(socialist realism), heavy-handedly enforced by Stalin's despotism, the
emigrés were virtually cut off from Russia and had to fall back on their
own resources. Thus began an independent creative cultural life, with a
distinctive Parisian "note," that manifested itself in literature, the arts,
and social, philosophic, and religious thought. The culture of the Great
Russian Emigration must be identified with Russian Paris—it is what
gave it its individual *cachet*, as V. S. Yanovsky's reminiscences abundantly illustrate.

Russian Paris—even in its cultural aspects—was far from homogene-

ous. Besides the obvious socioeconomic stratifications, we may identify
a plethora of groups, clubs, unions, associations, church and military
fraternal organizations—each catering to a specific political, professional,
or cultural commitment. But it is also important to note that individual
emigrés in Paris—like members of a normal Western democratic
society—held several roles: for example, one might be politically active
while also deeply involved in literary or philosophic concerns; committed to a professional life and also devoted to charitable, religious, or
intellectual endeavors. This variety made it difficult to maintain the de-
sirable degree of independence and integrity in all one's activities, for
political preferences (or dreams) and philosophic or religious commit-
ments easily encroached upon literary, artistic, or educational pursuits.

Quite naturally, too, earning a living was the paramount emigré concern; and that was no simple matter. For the contemporary reader it may
be hard to realize the simple fact that in the interwar years a foreigner,
especially one without a country to return to or a diplomatic mission to
protect him, had almost no legal rights. He had to solicit permission to
be gainfully employed, even as a simple laborer, and this permission was
granted grudgingly and was always subject to revocation. It was even
more difficult, if not completely impossible, to obtain permission to
practice a profession. Nor could an emigré travel abroad easily. Most
Russians were stateless and therefore, instead of holding ordinary national passports, had to make do with a Nansen Office document that
required a special visa. No comprehensive social welfare legislation existed in France before the advent of Léon Blum's Front Populaire government (1936), so that everyone—but especially the emigré—was without
protection against unemployment, disability, sickness, and old age.
When the Great Depression hit France, in about the mid-thirties, unemployment rose; naturally, the unprotected and legally discriminated
against emigrés were its first mass victims. Needless to say, since it is so
vividly described by V. S. Yanovsky, intellectuals without a special
marketable skill, in particular the young writers, had the hardest time
making a living. Some did not even try; for almost all of them, a regular
family and creative life was out of the question. No wonder that they
displayed acute insecurity, touchiness, desperation, and bitterness in
everything they did or wrote. Yanovsky correctly remarks that a writer
needs readers even more than publishers—and the potential pool of
readers depended on the material security and well-being of the Russian
emigrés in Paris, France, and elsewhere.

In a generational sense, too, the cultural milieu of Russia was hardly
uniform: two quite distinct, albeit related, generations vied with each

other for the public's attention. The older one, the "fathers," had achieved recognition at home before the revolution. Naturally, when they emigrated, they brought along a fully matured technique and artistic outlook. They could not, and would not, adapt to new circumstances, revise their values, and accept the new that Western Europe, as well as their own experience, offered them. They also believed, sometimes not without justification, that their reputation entitled them to special consideration, priority of publication, and critical recognition. They viewed newcomers with suspicion and incomprehension—sentiments that easily might be translated into near-hatred in the ennervating competition for artistic, and perhaps also physical, survival. But while their reputations ensured many a permanent readership, the numbers of readers inexorably declined as the emigration aged; this too contributed to insecurity, jealousy, and anxiety.

The younger generation, on the other hand, consisted mainly of those who had been caught up in the Civil War (drafted, volunteered, or evacuated along with the White Armies). Most had not managed to finish their higher (sometimes even secondary) education in Russia, and they arrived in Paris traumatized by what they had seen and experienced during the Revolution and Civil War. Quite naturally, too, they were more open to new trends, fashions, and experimentation; they were eager to discover and absorb what was new in European literature and art. To them, the West was full of meaningful revelations since, unlike their elders, they had had no direct experience of prewar European cultural trends. We should speak not so much of the "children" of the "fathers" but of "stepchildren" (or waifs) whose relationship to their elders was ambiguous and ambivalent, fraught with conflict and scorn.

The gulf separating the two generations had an intellectual—aesthetic, moral, philosophic—aspect as well. The writers of the older generation who found themselves in emigration in Paris belonged, by and large, to the realistic (or naturalistic) tradition of the nineteenth century. Even those who had witnessed the heady years of the Silver Age had been sobered by the destructive forces unleashed by war, revolution, and civil war. The older writers (and their intellectual supporters) in Paris tended to dwell on a nostalgic "remembrance of things past" (without its Proustian psychological and aesthetic dimensions)—those things that were mere words for the younger. On the other hand, some of the younger writers and the representatives of the religious and philosophic renaissance of the Silver Age had great affinity. They had experienced and witnessed so much human moral, physical, and material deprivation and suffering that they had become conscious of the social service function of the Church; the philosophic—spiritualist and idealist—renaissance answered more adequately than nineteenth-century positivism and materialism the difficult ethical and metaphysical questions that were raised by their existential predicament.

The search for a deeper religious and spiritual foundation for human existence ran counter to the social and political traditions of the liberal and socialist intelligentsia whose representative leaders held many key positions in the publishing, journalistic, and cultural institutions of the Russian emigration. It resulted in additional grounds for tension and a still greater drawing apart of the older and younger generations that has not been paid sufficient attention. Yanovsky's reminiscences go a long way toward redressing the balance in this respect. And in so doing he establishes the importance of religion for the younger generation, underpinning their acute awareness of the antinomies of civilization and the threats of humanity brought about by science and technology as well as by secular ideologies and political conflicts. In fact, the younger generation of Russian Paris pioneered in the elaboration of the major tenets of postwar Christian socialism.

The material difficulties experienced by emigré littérateurs in Paris as they sought outlets for their works in print—and the need to communicate with one another, to experience a companionship that their isolation from French society precluded—drove them to associate informally in cafés, clubs, or circles. Some of these gatherings were rather formally organized, with their own particular intellectual—aesthetic or moral—physiognomy. Such was the Circle (Krug) so often referred to and described by V. S. Yanovsky. Others were rather occasional and informal affairs. Emigré culture was thus also very much an oral culture, and as such left fewer documentary traces than one would wish, besides the poetry and fiction published in journals and almanacs. To recapture Russian Paris—if only in outline—we must depend on memoirs of participants as our most promising source. V. S. Yanovsky's is a specially significant source on the younger generation of emigré authors.

At this point the reader may well ask about the nature of the emigrés' relationship to the French ambient society and culture. It was very slight indeed. The Russian Paris lived almost in total isolation from the Paris of the French. To be sure, the Russians, especially the younger emigrés, kept themselves informed about what was happening in contemporary French literature, arts, ideas. Avant garde modernism attracted the younger generation of emigré writers and artists—and Paris was indeed the place to study and soak up this international movement. But it is quite striking—as most memoirs make clear—that there were almost no personal contacts between the Russian emigrés and their French hosts (or most expatriates and exiles of other nationalities). The French evinced little interest in such contacts, and their social traditions and institutional arrangements precluded interaction between themselves and most foreigners (especially emigrés) in their midst. Of course, there were exceptions—but they were rare and limited to the most prominent and lucky few. After the defeat of 1940 and the occupation of France by the Germans, the situation changed dramatically. Many Russians joined the ranks of the French Résistance, and the survivors—and especially their children—were largely integrated into French postwar society, another factor in the demise of the Russian Paris of the interwar years.

A friend of V. S. Yanovsky, the writer V. S. Varshavskii, entitled his memoir-study of Paris in the 1920s and 1930s "The Unnoticed Generation"—a most apt characterization of his cohort. The generation of the younger Russians in Paris went unnoticed by the French and by other Europeans; it was even barely noticed as a creative and innovative force by other Russian emigrés, not to speak of the Soviets. Little wonder that bitterness, cynicism, and despair put a deep stamp on their outlook and work; and with that went frustration, envy, and lack of charity toward others. Yanovsky perceptively captures this mood in his portraits and retrospective reflections on his friends and acquaintances in those years. Today, however, this generaton can no longer be called "unnoticed." The Russian Paris has been rediscovered since the arrival of the "Third Wave" of Russian emigrés from the Soviet Union in recent decades, the rise of the dissident movement inside the USSR, and as a consequence of the growing interest in the Russian avant garde. In the last few years, moreover, a mini-Russian Paris has been created by the emigrés of the Third Wave. Like its ancestor, it publishes an ever-growing list of journals and books, organizes discussions, lectures, conferences, and exhibitions. But there is a profound difference: the Third Wave emigration is not so isolated from the ambient milieu, and it is recognized by its hosts. Many of its members have obtained a place in the educational and cultural institutions of France and other Western countries. Not surprisingly, however, the Third Wave emigrés—as well as their Western friends—have become interested in their predecessors of a generation ago. Emigré writings of the 1920s and 1930s are republished, the scholarly and philosophic accomplishments of Russian Paris are studied: in short, the Elysian fields of Yanovsky's memoirs enter, albeit belatedly, into the history of Russian culture.

Nor does the rediscovery seem limited to the West and the Third Wave of Russian emigrés. There is some evidence of what might be called a feedback to the Soviet Union. The works of the older generation of emigré writers, as well as those deemed ideologically inoffensive, are republished—albeit selectively—in the Soviet Union. News has been received recently that even emigré martyrs at the hands of the Nazis and participants in the French Résistance have been posthumously honored by the Soviet government. The ideas of emigré thinkers, especially those with a spiritualist religious orientation, circulate underground and are the subject of lively discussion among Soviet intellectuals. Should this trend continue and expand, cultural life in Soviet Russia will surely respond to the Russian Paris of the 1920s and 1930s.

In the rediscovery of the "unnoticed generation," the lively reminiscences and combative judgments and opinions of V. S. Yanovsky will play a central role. His is a very personal picture, but also a very compassionate and insightful one. Memoirs are, after all, subjective; and it is precisely this quality that makes for their importance as historical source and their fascination as literature.

Acknowledgments

The author wishes to acknowledge Catharine Theimer Nepomnyash-chy's indispensable work on notes and transliteration and to thank managing editor Wanda H. Giles for her great interest in and respect for the text.

ELYSIAN FIELDS

Chapter 1 · Boris Poplavsky

Мыс Доброй Нацежды!Мы с доброй надеждой тебя покидали. Но ветер крепчал . . . —Борис Поплавский

(Cape of Good Hope! We Left You with Good Hope. But the Wind Got Stronger . . .")—Boris Poplavsky

The great Russian emigration is dying out. One after the other, classics and epigones depart, vanish: the cemeteries have opened wide their brotherly embrace. Some have come to rest around Paris or Nice, others in New York or California.

The bugle resounds:

> . . . and whose fate it is
> to fall in the steppes,
> Almighty God will remember. . . .

Here is Berdyaev, a blue beret over his grey lion's mane, convulsively biting on a stubby empty cigarholder; there Khodasevich, nervously dealing the cards with his forever ailing, bandaged, greenish fingers; Fedotov, tweezing his small professorial beard, holding forth in a soft, guttural, yet convincing voice; Fondaminsky, looking like a Georgian, with gusto inviting us to comment on the paper that has just been read; the greying Bunin, gaunt, in tails, with difficulty making himself understood in French.

Where are they?

And yet, inside myself, I see and hear and recognize them all. True, I can no longer press their warm hands, touch them in the flesh, converse with them. But is this necessary? After all, the tenderness I now feel, the pain and pity, I did not then, while we were "in touch," detect in myself. Thus, death and time, while taking away one dimension, have added another . . . and the impact of the present image of our former companions is by no means less real or less full.

What is there left to do for the artist who is carrying on his never-ending struggle with irreversible processes? What is there, but to reincarnate
in his work these departed friends, adding the newly acquired feelings of
tenderness and regret.

Let these be distorted portraits, distorted according to the laws of a
subjective perspective. The more there will be of such candid, involved
witnesses, the more solid, if roughhewn, a picture will emerge. So do
two eyes—looking separately from a somewhat different angle—each on
its own perceive an object as flat, but, in the end, together, reproduce it
objectively, plastically, and three-dimensionally.

There was a time when, on Sundays, young writers would gather
around the Merezhkovskys' table for tea. At about five o'clock we would
all leave together and sit down for an hour or so at a taxi drivers' bistro,
continuing the discussion or, more often, simply gossiping.

"Did you notice how the former commander-in-chief grabbed me by
the button and wouldn't let go?" Ivanov asked, flattered by Kerensky's
attention but at the same time deeming fit to emphasize his independence.

"And Zakovich kissed Merezhkovsky's hand by mistake!"

"But Merezhkovsky wasn't a bit surprised," picked up Poplavsky, a
past master at this kind of repartee.

Vildé and I might settle down to a game of chess; Kelberin kibitzed, a
concern which however did not prevent him from participating most
intensively in the chatter. At the miniature billiard table with pockets
(called "moscow") Alfyorov and Yury Mandelshtam vied with each
other: the latter played all games with equal passion and badly. Felsen,
reserved as always, lights a "yellow" cigarette* in a holder and, with the
smile of a schoolboy who is fooling around during class, whispers something into his neighbor's ear. Chervinskaya absolutely has to know what
he has told Adamovich as the latter was getting ready to leave. Adamovich, who has a long way to his home at Metro Convention,** has
already run off: tonight he is entertaining some young men for dinner.

As I behold again in my mind's eye this mirror-lined place, brightly lit
but at the same time hazy with tobacco clouds, reverberating with
laughter, exclamations, and the knock of billiard balls, as I now contemplate all this, I am amazed at how signals of general doom abounded. We
were wont to boast about our intellect, perspicacity, talents—but that the

---

*The Gauloise jaune (yellow cigarette) was a better cigarette than the less-expensive Gau-
loise bleu.
**Station of the fifteenth *arrondissement*.

ground was giving way beneath our feet, that Paris, France, Europe, were tumbling into a dark hole, this we chose not to see!—even though the blotches of steam settling high up on the mirrors were assuming strangely suspicious letterlike shapes.

"In a room with many mirrors one always feels as if there were a draft," Bunin said, savoring again this old Moscow *trouvaille* of his. (Such observations were his forte.)

With the last remnants of enthusiasm we quoted the early Blok, his mutinies, blizzards, and masks, admiring his prophecies but not recognizing in time the new conflagration that was gathering over Christian Europe. Though now it seems we did know without being conscious of it.

For decades we sat in cafés, the same groups, in the same poses, repeating almost the same speeches, as if giving fate a chance to take good aim. And hit us it did. Brutally.

There is no doubt that life treated the older generation and its epigones with much more forebearance. Most of them managed to get a slice of the sweet Russian pie, to snatch a share of success, recognition, even affluence. Later on, in emigration, they were considered high-ranking officers (of tsarist vintage) and received loans and subsidies from various funds, Czechoslovak, Yugoslav, American YMCA. "Ah, Teffi, ah, Zaitsev, of course, of course!"

In the winter of 1961 I met at the house of W. H. Auden a nice, cultured lady, a member of the Soviet literary mission, well versed in all the secrets of Anglo-Saxon poetry. To my eternal question—what do you know about Russian emigré literature?—she replied politely: "Why, of course, you had Averchenko, Igor Severyanin."

Bunin and Shmelyov, after some weeding out, are now published in editions of hundreds of thousands in the Soviet Union. For a long time to come Russia will be feeding on nothing but epigones. She seeks children's literature, fit for primitives.

A century may pass, before the USSR again becomes European. Only then will Russia discover those "enthusiastic lads" who never severed their inner links with Europe and their native land. (For emigré *poetry* this may happen sooner.)

At around seven the more venerable left the taxi drivers' café . . . Time for dinner! But some of us still did not feel like parting: thus we might lose the kingdom of heaven, continuing forever those tangled debates, in the certainty of doing something important (as, perhaps, we were).

In the early thirties, Poplavsky, Felsen, and I, sometimes joined by

Charchoune, made a habit of finishing these Sunday evenings at Remizov's who lived in the same, the 16th, *arrondissement*. We crossed a square
shrouded in fog. There, at a corner, one could hear the rushing of water
in the rusty "Vespasian" for two.* Toward it we resolutely directed our
steps. Felsen entered first (as the oldest, and perhaps also for other reasons). Then I, ahead of the hesitating Boris. He remained outside, drum-
ming on the resounding tin of our shelter, jokingly yet insistently cursing; only a moment ago he had courteously let me go in before him, and
there he was, already clamoring for his rights!

Now Felsen and I are waiting for Poplavsky: his laughter and curses,
the noise of rushing water and of gas light, of chestnut trees rustling (in
the spring) or naked branches creaking (in the fall)—all this has formed a
knot, is ripening in me and will, any moment now, sprout fresh, transfi-
gured shoots.

Usually Felsen vanished for an hour (to have supper at his wealthy
sister's place). Boris and I restored ourselves with a cup of chocolate and
croissants at a counter, then strolled about, avidly absorbing the living,
creative Paris sky. We talked. Of love, of Marcion, of Proust, and the
early Zoshchenko—all this spiced with poems, bon mots, and, above all,
literary gossip.

Toward nine we converged at Remizov's. Aleksei Mikhailovich, one
of the truly great emigré writers, we considered completely old hat. (For
a short time it had been thought good taste to be fascinated by his
appearance, his toys, and, of course, his prose.) But now this was the
only place in the sixteenth where we could gather again at night. I repeat:
at times we found it insufferable to separate. (As if we already knew how
ephemeral our intellectual bliss was to be and sensed its approaching
end.)

After all, at the conclusion of such a Sunday, was it that difficult to
perceive that the Merezhkovskys-and-Ivanovs would remain consistent
with themselves and grovel before the German colonels; that our "patriots," the Ladinskys-and-Sofievs, would at the first opportunity leave for
the Soviet Union? That Mother Marie, Felsen, and Mandelshtam would
perish, each in his own way? And that the first to depart would be
Poplavsky? This, as a matter of fact, was easy to predict.

As I said, we considered Remizov old hat and did not like him, though
we only gradually (in tune with our overall passivity) broke the bonds
and habits we had formed. A tense, false, pseudoclassical atmosphere

---

*Public urinal.

reigned in their house; Aleksei Mikhailovich pretended to be a lame hunchbacked eccentric; he coined his sentences in a such a crisp whisper that one could not help looking around to all sides in search of another, secret, meaning to his statements. It was accepted as incontrovertibly proven that Remizov had many enemies, was published very little, and was abused by everyone.

Aleksei Mikhailovich poured from an enormous teapot covered with a dirty cozy. His spouse, Serafima Pavlovna—a pathologically obese creature, drowning in layers of fat, with a childish little nose—awkwardly towered over the table, breathing laboriously, constantly chewing, ever so often smiling in a housewifely (shrewd) way. In addition to the tea came a platter with fragments of stale French bread, croissants, or rolls, all hard as stone.(Poplavsky, ever fond of gossip, claimed that he had once been treated to pastries in their house, which however were taken away precipitately when the doorbell rang. Khodasevich also told something remotely resembling this story.)

Boris's anecdotes and inventions were remembered; they "stuck," even if they did not quite correspond to reality. His apocrypha about Merezhkovsky gained special fame: three Magi from the East supposedly came to Dimitry Sergeevich's apartment (ll, bis Colonel Bonnet) and involved him in a conversation:

"What is the first truth?" the Magi inquired. And Merezhkovsky, without batting an eyelash, revealed the mystery.

"What is the second truth?" the wise men continued their investigation. Once more the Russian thinker easily satisfied their curiosity.

"And where does the money collected at the Green Lamp[1] galas go?"

Here, Merezhkovsky could not answer and broke into tears.

Evil had an aesthetic fascination for Poplavsky. In this sense he was demonic. Participating in an obscure spiritualist séance (or only watching, as an outsider) he would smile a proud, tender smile full of suffering, as if possessing a particular knowledge, a revelation all his own.

His exterior would have been quite ordinary, almost plain, if not for his eyes—the eyes of a person blind from birth (there are such psaltery players). Incidentally, he always complained of some discomfort "as if sand had gotten into my eyes." But this was no ordinary sand, for it could not be washed away. And he wore dark glasses, which gave him the air of a mystical conspirator.

They say that he was a puny child, something of a crybaby. Working with hysterical stubbornness on different exercise machines, Boris soon developed heavy biceps and shoulder muscles which, in combination with his sunken chest, gave him a somewhat cumbersome appearance.

When enraged, he would swear like a trooper, utterly indignant—yet not convincing. He himself could be rude but, at the same time, lacked, as it were, a protective skin and would scream at the slightest touch.

Poplavsky's influence on the Russian Montparnasse during the first half of the thirties was enormous. Whatever heresy he uttered, one could always sense through it a creative fabric. Listening to him, one also, for a while, began to think creatively (even if disagreeing with him). The time may come when some researcher will determine to what extent the work of the Parisian critics and philosophers lost its luster after Poplavsky's death.

He was disliked by many (or so it seemed) during his lifetime. People constantly argued with him, jabbed at him, fell upon him in a pack, enviously pursued him (as was the custom in good old Russia). But he, like a strong draft horse harnessed to a lightweight gig, leaned to with his mighty shoulders and pulled everything out of the bog: an unsuccessful meeting, a boring lecture, even a dismal party. It might end in a scandal, but nevertheless in many a mind the next morning—as in a park after a thunderstorm—fresh creative shoots would sprout up.

When Poplavsky took the floor at a meeting, he spoke in a nasal monotone, all but choking toward the end of a long sentence and, when starting to choke, speeding up his speech and raising his voice, so as to make the thought clear before he was obliged to catch his breath. However, this acceleration and raising of his voice somehow always coincided with his most poignant thoughts (or did they perhaps seem so *because* of this cleverly hampered breathing?).

He read his poems in a singsong voice (as if through a reed) with the same sudden accelerations. However, at the beginning of a stanza his voice could sound like that of a schoolboy. I used to be good at imitating him, but with the years I lost the knack. In those days "Chornaya Madonna" (The Black Madonna) and "Mechtali Flagi" (The Flags Dreamed) were recited ad infinitum, not only in Paris but also on the Parnassi of Prague, Warsaw, and Revel.

Poplavsky was one of my earliest acquaintances on Montparnasse. From our first meeting we adopted the familiar "thou," which, in Russian Paris, was not at all the custom. For the next ten years he probably remained my only "thou." This was typical of Boris.

In a stuffy basement on the Place St. Michel, whither we had repaired after a meeting at La Bollet, I once witnessed how Boris for an entire night addressed Felsen as "thou" while the latter politely but firmly replied with "you." Many years later Felsen defended himself by explaining that he did not like to be *forced* into anything. (How he must have suffered in the clutches of the Germans!) That night the hours dragged on endlessly as in a bad dream. Poplavsky seemed on the verge of a seizure: as if his eternal life depended on whether Felsen would return the brotherly "thou."

In those days, Felsen was still a newcomer to Montparnasse; all that was known was that Adamovich, Khodasevich and several wealthy patrons of the arts thought highly of him. This might have influenced Boris in the beginning, but the struggle that ensued no longer concerned their careers.

The topics, incidentally, did not at all suit the Felsen of that period. We spoke of Saint Sophia, of the thief on the cross, of the Roman patrician condemned to death and so afraid to face it that his concubine pierced her breast with the dagger and said, smiling, "You see. It's not that hard." This was Boris's favorite story. And into all this talk, wherever possible, he injected the intimate "thou," expecting an immediate response, an echo, a miracle.

He used to drop in on me (often at unusual hours) at the rue Boutebris to read my new short stories. He found them "full of tension." After the publication of my novel *Mir* (The World), he repeatedly said that I reminded him of an elephant cramped for space and constantly stepping on everybody's toes.

In his *Apollon Bezobrazov*, Poplavsky's Lazarus, after rising from his grave, exclaims, "*Merde!*" There is something similar in *Mir*, and Poplavsky accused me of having plagiarized from him. When I proved on the basis of the manuscript that there could be no question of direct stealing, he sadly agreed: "Yes, we are all stewing in the same juice and are getting to be alike."

Quarrels with him were always followed by stretches of unadulterated friendship. We strolled through the endless Paris markets and fairs, through zoos and botanical gardens; bargained for an old musket or telescopes dating back to the time of the Armada. Occasionally we rested in a movie house or refreshed ourselves with the eternal coffee and croissants. I believed in medicine, then, and as a prevention against bronchitis during the ice cold spells of February would drink scalding hot sweetened milk. Boris made fun of me, invented different amusing (but also nasty) situations, and later passed them on as actually having taken place.

Once, after a meeting with Boris I went the following Saturday to see our mutual friend Protsenko, one of those Ukrainian Socrateses, a "teacher of life" who, although he did not distinguish himself with any particular talents, had, nevertheless, a lasting influence on many of us. As I entered his place, Protsenko, before even offering me a glass of wine, asked with feigned sternness:

"What is this, Vassily Semyonovich, I hear that the protagonist in one of your stories drinks horse urine?"

Rumors about this latest of Boris's fabrications had already reached me.

"It says, 'The smell of horse urine made his throat tickle'; that's all," I disgustedly defended myself.

One of Boris's favorite inventions was a conversation he claimed to have overheard in Monte Carlo:

"Are you, too, a mystic?"

"No, I am simply an unhappy man."

Another story he loved to tell concerned a monk who during his prayers was constantly tempted by the vision of a ravishingly beautiful woman. "What does this anchorite want?" Jehovah finally inquired. "He wants a w-o-o-o-o-man," the guardian angel informs Him. "Then give him a w-o-o-o-o-man."

Poplavsky knew the secrets of many of his friends, but he always managed to present them casually, even indulgently. To my question whether the name of one of our literati was indeed a pure Italian one, he explained with a sweet and pained frown: "He's a Caucasian Armenian. He changed his name from something similar to Ter-Abramyanets, you know." And the smile of a fallen angel lit up his ashen-pale inspired face with the dark wheels of its sunken eyes. He gave similar explanations about several of our artist friends. (By the way, Boris had studied painting and knew a great deal about art, certainly no accident in his life.)

One felt that he had an enormous reserve of vital forces, that he could easily shove aside anyone who stood in his way. But suddenly he would lose his grip, unexpectedly, yet clearly, for all to see. A mainspring snapped, and he would freeze in full run, a spellbound medium, smiling a sleepy smile. And he conceded, agreed, gave in, "left."

His metaphysical life could overflow with frightening contradictions and at such times, dark, saturated forces gathered around him. I always thought: he won't hold out, he won't win (obviously, this concerned another plane, for nobody questioned his talent, his genius, even). Inwardly too he was in a hurry, endeavoring to develop his spiritual muscles, just as he had formerly trained his body.

Relationships with Poplavsky never operated on an even keel. He was the only one amongst the Paris writers with whom I ever came to blows. In a dark alley, behind Protsenko's *atelier* (where demipoets and demichauffeurs and their ladies were having fun).

That evening Boris was from the beginning full of resentment; Adamovich's arrival excited him even more. He was oversensitive to critical reviews and never tried to hide the fact. Even an article by a notoriously stupid or worthless colleague mesmerized him.

This trait, typical of Russian literati in general, became hideously distorted in the emigration, because of the senselessness and sterility of our existence. Even if one or the other praised you, there could be none of the normal consequences: no reprints, no royalties, no respect. It was nothing but scratching each others' backs. Reviews were considered the ultimate reward, since the higher authority, the reader, was missing!

That there could be another relationship between writer and critics I understood only later, in Anglo-Saxon countries, where independent gentlemen consider it their duty to be indifferent to what other gentlemen are obliged to write about them. (In the annals of American literature there is not one article along the lines of what, let us say, Saltykov-Shchedrin wrote about his contemporary, Dostoevsky.)

A most astonishing admission of Bunin's (there were very few of them) concerned precisely this problem. Once, in Dominique,★ late at night, having missed the last metro, he confided: "Even now—and how much there has been of it—even now, whenever I see my name in print, I feel here" (and he put his hand on the pit of his stomach) "I feel here something akin to orgasm."

Can one blame Poplavsky? No one had taught him any better. To the west of the Rhine the idea gradually took hold that, as long as true Christian relationships have not yet become part of our society, one must at least behave decently. While the Russian interpretation of *comme il faut* pertained mainly to well-shined shoes and clean gloves, it by no means extended to fair play. And yet, man is not born with a knowledge of it: fair play must be inculcated.

Why not admit it? In our dear Russia, people experience a very special

---

★Russian cafe near Montparnasse.

kind of satisfaction if they succeed, unexpectedly, in hurting someone or
in behaving basely. As a Dostoevsky hero might say: "Here we have
been debating the most subtle matters and have behaved in a thoroughly
civilized way, and now, ha, ha, ha, I'm going to do something really
nasty, hee, hee, hee." (According to reports of reliable witnesses, Stalin
derived ecstatic delight from feasting with a comrade whom he had
already sentenced to arrest and torture.)

"Overly offensive or overly flattering." Thus Poplavsky defined his
own malady. A more correct appraisal would be: overly offensive *and*
overly flattering, simultaneously!

G. Ivanov, who was on an intimate footing with all kinds of existential
baseness, but a good poet and a very clever man in his own way, used to
repeat with glee Gumilyov's words: "To get into literature is like squeezing into an overcrowded trolley car. And, once inside, you do your best
to push off any new arrival who tries to hang on."

Alas, these "trolley car manners" extended beyond literature. In Russian politics (be it of the Right or the Left) the same sort of gymnastics
was practiced.

These vestiges of cave culture are characteristic of the entire East, but
they are especially disheartening in Russia where the vocation of writer is
inordinately respected, almost on a par with that of prophet, saint, or
holy warrior. In the West, the attitude toward literature is different.
Hemingway wrote good short stories, but he would not have dreamed
of advising his contemporaries on which presidential candidate to vote
for. Proust invested his money in a bordello and, living on the income,
was able to devote himself to writing his great novel.

What a revelation it was for me when, at the age of twenty, I learned
that it was permissible for a writer to play the stock market or chase after
boys . . . and that it was by no means necessary to preach, to suffer, to
condemn, and be sent off to Siberia (or to pretend that you suffered and
made sacrifices). Paradoxically, those civilized writers who play the
stock market never indulge in backbiting aimed at their colleagues (nor
do they scour their works for errors).

There were a few true gentlemen among the Paris writers: Osorgin
and Felsen, for instance. What a miracle of peace and harmony it was to
associate with them: paradise, an island of benevolence in a sea of
hooliganism.

"Here," said Poplavsky, boastfully handing me a note. "If you do
something, do it right!" It was a letter from Mark Aldanov to Zeeler, the
secretary of our Union of Writers and Journalists (a man who looked a
lot like Sobakevich in *Dead Souls*). Aldanov was recommending Poplav-

sky as a talented poet and backing his request for a subsidy of 100 francs. Aldonov liked this kind of philanthropy and never refused anyone his support. He once gave me a list of his foreign translators. "All dead souls," Ivanov warned me with a malicious cackle, when I told him about it.

I think our attitude toward other peoples' money and their favors calls for an explanation. In those years it was considered a compliment to receive a handout. I well remember the tantrum Smolensky threw when Felsen, as the chairman, denied him a share of a certain collection, explaining that Smolensky was working and not in great need. Smolensky howled tragically: "Am I a poet or not? Am I worse than Kelberin? And if I'm not worse, then I too have a right to the money." Grants and alms, in our offended consciousness, assumed the importance of rank and medals in Chekhovian Russia. There were hardly any instances of refusing such gifts. However, we all knew that Osorgin and Aldanov never sought and never accepted any subsidies, whether from organizations or private sources; but this only elicited some cynical remarks from Ivanov, who indiscriminately fleeced timid lambs as well as lecherous wolves.

Only later, in the United States, when I saw modest, good-humored people of different social strata lining up on Friday at the payroll window and with dignity receiving their check for a week's work, only then was something revealed to me. These naive Americans had yet to settle with the IRS, but they liked to repeat on suitable and unsuitable occasions that they were beholden to no one and did not ask anything of anybody . . . This is a certain deep-rooted ideal (as was the fight for the exploited in old Russia), an ideal equally obligatory for dishwashers and for poets teaching creative writing in colleges, for black elevator men and graying, gold-conscious dentists.

In childhood, we were told over and over again about heroes who plugged up machine guns with their fingers and threw bombs at governors-general or of holy men dividing their mortgaged estates among the little *muzhiks*. But about working for a whole week and on Friday, having received one's check and paid all the bills, announcing proudly, "Thank God, I don't owe anyone anything and don't ask for any favors"—such a variant of civic virtue had never been brought to our attention. And this is a pity.

On the other hand, in the United States, people appear somewhat confused if you start talking to them about the mystery of the fall, the national soul, the community of arts, or of Tolstoi's flight from Yasnaya polyana.[2] And this too, of course, is also a pity.

Thus, at the party in Protsenko's workshop (where ties and scarves were dyed during the day) Boris was in a particularly irritable mood. Adamo-vich's article, which had hurt his feelings; the wine, which Beck, a former submarine crew member and now a taxi driver, had brought along from his new stock; or his steady girlfriend, who dogged his every step—all or any of these could have a depressing effect on him. Incidentally, this girlfriend spoke Russian with a deplorable southern accent: about her Boris repeatedly said to me, with a malicious and long-suffering frown, "She feeds on my offals."

It began when I got to talking with Adamovich, who was convinced that he had praised Poplavsky (in the Thursday issue of *Poslednie novosti* [The Latest News]). In general, a critic in the emigration did not have an easy life: we were all thrown closely together, exposed to each other, meeting and shaking hands daily. If you panned A., you had to criticize B. even more severely; if you praised B., you must needs give even more favorable attention to G. Every word was immediately weighed on ever so sensitive and accurate, if not material, scales; and complaints were promptly registered. Besides, there were the publishers, old profession-als, extinct species (aurochs), influential snobs, and radicals. How could a critic possibly keep his balance and remain popular? In addition , it must be remembered that a writer is never satisfied.

On this particular occasion, Adamovich had singled out Poplavsky's line "The City slept, dreamless like Lethe," pointing out that the last two words—*kak Leta*—sounded very much like "kotleta."* Very witty in-deed. But Boris, in hysterics, had announced that he had been disgraced forever. ("Oh, you can't understand," he kept repeating, almost in tears. "I'm a poet, and we experience things in a special way.")

My tête-à-tête with the critic did not please Poplavsky, who had quite a strain of jealousy. Around midnight he walked out with his girl into a dark alley (next to métro Censier Daubenton). Yes, as far as sex was concerned, things were not too well arranged for us. The sad fact was that, beyond the realm of literary ladies (not created for vulgar relation-ships), no one paid any attention to us. And no wonder—we were poorly dressed, penniless, and above all not geared to an easy life and pleasant liaisons. Paris abounded in excited foreign females who had come there eager to get rid of their hateful chastity—precisely what we were after; but, alas, it seemed to us that these women were meant for a different kind of men, successful men (an expression which, for some reason, stood for vulgar, graceless fellows). Yet another trait of the Eastern

---

*Hamburger.

Hamlet: the cult of failure, the vengeful contempt of success! (Judging by the DPs, the Bolsheviks have put an end to that.) But once in a while we came upon an alarming paradox: successful successes! Talented, intelligent, metaphysically well developed—and still, the Firebird is within their reach! In such cases we did not know how to behave. We invented all kinds of explanations, floundered from one extreme to the other: overly offensive or overly flattering! (This, actually, was the basis for the ugly persecution of the "Berliner" Sirin-Nabokov by the contributors of the Paris *Chisla* [Numbers].)

So Boris went out with his girl into the dark alley, where they made themselves comfortable in Beck's taxicab, standing in wait of its master. (Later Beck complained that they had thrown up all over the upholstery. "And I still had to work that night!") There, in the backseat, Poplavsky was reclining with his paramour when I, too, appeared. Out of sheer mischief I honked the horn a couple of times: it seemed a witty and even endearing gesture. But suddenly, Poplavsky, with the clumsiness of a bear, tumbled out of the car and, wildly cursing, jumped me. "Oh, what a brute, oh, what a brute!" In his suffering voice there was a note of true despair. For a few minutes we wrangled, concentratedly and to little avail; for some reason he was tearing at my shirt collar and even grabbed my hair. Our mutual friend Protsenko happened to be relieving himself at the fence. He was taken completely by surprise and, since he loved both of us, remained literally paralyzed, at a loss as to what to do (so he later explained to me). The wine, of course, also played its part.

Attracted by the rumpus, more men of letters, chauffeurs, and their ladies streamed out, Vsevolod Poplavsky, Boris's brother, shouting in a joyful burr, "I adore the Russian tongue!" Beck pulled us apart. Later he declared that only out of respect for a great poet did he not punish Boris for the damaged upholstery. (This, of course, flattered Poplavsky.)

"Could it be that some day we'll enter a large assemblage as real, acclaimed celebrities?" he asked me very seriously.

Inwardly he was in a hurry, too much of a hurry.

We walked a lot during those decades; to stroll at night from Montparnasse to Châtelet, where Poplavsky then lived, was a joy as well as an economy. On the way he would stop at a café-tabac to purchase some hollow French candles. They cost a pittance, and I was sometimes able to help him out. (Incidentally, these hollow Paris candles aroused the ire of our super-patriots. "Look at that," they would yell. "How can such a nation think of fighting the Germans!")

In farewell, Boris would say with affected rudeness: "Now you're

hitting the sack, while I'm going to work on my novel." The Poplavskys' old apartment still had gas light, which his mother turned off for
the night, not only as a safety measure and for reasons of economy but
also (so it seemed to me) to spite her son.

We usually left the literary meetings together. I remember one evening
at La Bollet when Gorgulov read to us for the first time. We were treated
to a poem about a black tomcat who kept wanting to screw something or
somebody; Pavel Bred (his literary pseudonym) envisaged this poem as
an opera and claimed to have already found a suitable composer. The
backroom of the cafe, on one wall the phony plaque engraved with the
names of great men who formerly had met here (Verlaine, Oscar
Wilde)—this small squarish room literally shook with the jeers and
laughter of contemporary Russian poets.

Dryakhlov, a member of the board, happened to be presiding. A very
Russian man with all the proper Russian merits and shortcomings—
usually tactless and clumsy—he could become inordinately gentle and
genuinely aristocratic where the underprivileged and dejected were concerned. (And a minute later he would again show his teeth in an obscene,
unpleasant smile.) There he was, my friend Valerian Fyodorovich, a poet
with whom I had frequent and entirely unnecessary arguments about a
game of chess or a book by Blavatsky, pounding his small bony fist on
the medieval oaken table, calling the members to order. Then Gorgulov
rose to his full, epic height, and those sitting close became scared. This
was a giant, a weight lifter who could easily grab one of the heavy
benches and smash us all to pieces. And yet, how ridiculous, how incon-
gruous: a model of physical fitness with an obvious flaw in the brain.
Why in the world was he writing poetry?

That night, Gorgulov, Poplavsky, and I roamed for hours through the
Tuileries garden. This was the trend in our Paris: immediately to try and
conquer a new arrival. Boris was particularly tenacious in this respect.

Gorgulov, several years our senior, had finished medical school in
Prague. It was only natural that he try to get information from me about
hospitals, exams, and opportunities for foreigners to practice medicine.
While blithely ignoring our achievements, he had no doubt of his own
literary vocation. However, some of his questions confused me. Who
performs abortions here? What kind of girls do you have here? Why
weren't there any pretty ones there tonight?

Alas, my answers obviously did not satisfy him. It was becoming quite
sad: he was simply a man of a different conformation. We had nothing to
say to each other.

Suddenly Poplavsky stopped underneath the most beautiful arch in
Paris (the Carrousel) and began to relieve himself. Gorgulov and I imme-

diately caught on and approvingly followed suit. There was the Royal park, and the Louvre with all its treasures, and above it the overcast sky of an inimitable dawn. It smelled of fields and a river . . . But we, the three Magi from the East, were relieving ourselves in the center of the civilized world. That was our answer to Europe. (*Lordam po mordam!*) Poplavsky was a superb medium. He readily fell under the influence of alien rays and vibrations: unconsciously he had evaluated Gorgulov— and yielded.

Gorgulov had an overabundance of strength. But what to do with it— that was the question. A few months later he killed the president of the republic, innocent, gray-haired old Doumer.

Strolling through the historic *faubourgs,* we had often tried to imagine what the aristocrats felt as they were driven across Paris to the guillotine. And now it had happened: one of us, a member of the Paris Association of Russian Writers and Poets, was mounting the scaffold. A career entirely the opposite of—but in its brilliance almost equaling—that of Sirin-Nabokov.

The crowd on Boulevard Arago was softly rumbling; the bistros stayed open through the night. The excited and exciting laugh of garishly painted women (no telling who is a whore and who a society lady); the wild outcries of worried Corsicans unsure of their own destiny . . . An atmosphere of solemnity (as in church) and of reckless hazard (as at the races).

It was already getting light when they finished him off. From afar, watching the movement of the crowd (which had become as one body), we could guess that things were not proceeding according to schedule. The last minutes dragged on forever. In a whisper, people passed on the rumor that the knife of the guillotine had jammed and that they had had to start all over again. But the morning papers told what had happened: Gorgulov's huge body had not fit into the guillotine; the Cossack's neck had been too big for the frame beneath the blade.

Not long ago, in New York, I had to place a heavyweight truck driver, who would not start breathing normally after the operation, inside an iron lung. It was impossible to fit his gigantic body into something vaguely resembling the guillotine. Then I remembered my contemporary, Gorgulov. The fact is that our instruments and appliances—for execution as well as resuscitation—are calculated for the "average" man.

Gorgulov died, surrounded by a crowd of strangers, in the manner of Gogol's Ostap Bulba* ("Do you hear me, father?"). In other times, under

---

*Of *Taras Bulba.*

different stars, in familiar surroundings, he might have become a hero. If society nowadays accepts the theory that our living conditions—our childhood, parents, sicknesses—are greatly responsible for the crimes we commit, the same must be true with regard to our heroic feats. That is, we have to admit that many heroes deserve neither rewards nor honors, for they too were propelled along their glorious paths by "objective conditions." Either a man is personally responsible for his wrongdoings, or he does not deserve personal praise for his achievements.

I say this with regard to Russian history of the last hundred years: what a heroic epoch! Every youth a revolutionary; every revolutionary a saint, a victim, a shining martyr. Did they not all go to Siberia—for their ideals, for the people? Those selfsame characters who now chase about New York trying to grab away from one another an advance payment for some subsidized government "project." Former heroes, changed into something resembling the contractors of the era of the Crimean War, about whom the horrible Saltykov-Shchedrin wrote with such insight.

"They slice off your soles while you're on the run," admiringly noted a DP who himself manifested powerful elbows, "and yet they were supposed to be delicate intellectuals!" Who knows, perhaps it is the era, the epoch, the eon that often dictates one's behavior, and not personal initiative or effort, particularly if one is by no means original and easily falls under the sway of prevailing fashions.

Spring and autumn in Europe are magnificent. In Paris, the summer too can be great, despite the smog and heat (Poplavsky even sang the praises of this congealed hell). Filled with youthful enthusiasm, we roamed the markets and boulevards in search of the ideal incarnation, the brilliant exploit or sin.

All of a sudden Boris became deeply impressed with the Orthodox liturgy (he did not follow fashions but established them himself). He fasted and prayed, swam and lifted weights to the point of exhaustion, worked out on gymnastic machines that would mortify his flesh (but also, o wonder, develop his muscles). He invented a sort of hairshirt for himself, and on his way to Montparnasse he constantly exercised with a handgrip. He fasted seriously for an entire Lent and therefore was hardly seen in the cafés. "Hell," he remarked with satisfaction, "to stand through a long Russian service, that's not like those Roman Catholic genuflections."

By that time we had all fallen under the spell of the Paris School of Orthodoxy (as somewhat later many went to the Masons). There was a poet, Pusya or, rather, Boris Zakovich, a friend, disciple, and slave of Poplavsky and author of a few enchanting poems. (Poplavsky dedicated his second volume of poetry to him—a generous gift to a loyal companion.) If I addressed Zakovich as Pusya, he firmly objected (it was comical: he seemed such a musically yielding creature, as if of quicksilver). "For you I am Boris, not Pusya!"

Pusya played an abominable game of chess and, since I never played gratis with weak partners, lost what seemed to me at that time considerable sums. And he often refused to pay up, citing Poplavsky: "Bob says I don't have to pay. It's dishonest to play for money with me."

Zakovich too became fascinated with the liturgy of St. Basil the Great; this, however, did not prevent him from very soon joining the Masons in the company of other men of letters.

Poplavsky had always been intrigued by Freemasonry. He preached that we were living in an era of secret societies and had to unite before the onset of utter darkness. But the "generals" did not trust him: he didn't have the right character. His many attempts and hysterics notwithstanding, the Masons never accepted him. Meanwhile, Pusya and a dozen other enthusiasts easily became Masons.

Sofiev and Terapiano had been Masons, of different lodges, long before that; Osorgin organized a lodge he called, if I'm not mistaken, Northern Brothers. The theosophists and anthroposophists* had their own cells. Little by little, all united: the arch-rightists swamped the variety of lodges in the hope of conquering Troy from the inside. (In France, unlike Russia, Freemasonry of course is legal.)

There were rumors that a recently arrived "Berliner" was trying to become head of the Russian Masons (supposedly supported by Avksentiev). All this greatly perturbed Poplavsky, and it probably was then that he began to sniff cocaine. (Pusya's father, a dentist, had left behind, after his death, a heap of the most suspicious-looking little packages.) "Perhaps he wasn't a simple dentist," joyfully explained Poplavsky, with a beautiful, meditative, and evil smile.

Furthermore, he had fallen unhappily in love. The young lady was to join her fiancé in the Soviet Union but before leaving, quite unaccountably, secluded herself with Vildé, thereby almost causing a duel.

At that time, Felsen and I were starting a publishing venture. Under the aegis of our young writers' association, we organized at the Roerich Museum[3] an exhibit of Russian books published in the emigration; the monies from the sales and entrance fees and from a yearly subscription fee were supposed to provide for the publication of new books.

---

*A branch of theosophy founded by Rudolph Steiner.

Poplavsky handed us the manuscript of his big novel *Domoi s Nebes* (Home from Heaven), hoping that we would publish it. He wrote in the tempestuous, powerful, lyrical prose of a great poet, with all the virtues and infelicities of the manner (from Andrei Bely to Pasternak inclusive).

When voices were raised on Montparnasse, criticizing us, "the editorial board," for publishing our own works first of all—Felsen's *Pisma o Lermontove* (Letters about Lermontov) and my novel *Lyubov vtoraya* (The Other Love)—Boris staunchly defended us. "Why not? Aren't they writers too?" he demanded, loud and clear. He would often visit our exhibition and curse "those bores."

However, we were unable to tackle his novel: it was too big and there were not enough subscribers. This was a blow for Boris. The following year we brought out, instead, Ageev's *Roman s kokainom* (Novel with Cocaine). It goes without saying that our authors did not receive any money.

Now I simply cannot understand how we could have rejected his work for trivial financial reasons. Later T., who had married Poplavsky's girlfriend and who also became his literary executor, supposedly tried hard to find a publisher for the novel, but he did not succeed (psychoanalysts would diagnose his condition as a subconscius block). Be that as it may—in any case Felsen and I failed to bring out the book.

One other typical failure of ours . . . About that time, Fondaminsky, having buried his spouse, decided to organize the Circle (Krug): literary-philosphical-religious discussions which were to bring together for the first time the growing new generation with the slowly aging bonzes of the emigré intelligentsia. Fondaminsky earnestly consulted with all of us, in private as well as in group meetings, painstakingly establishing a list of acceptable members. He made inquiries, compared the information, and finally, on the basis of the general concensus, made his decision. It was then that we all, separately and collectively, managed to paint Poplavsky in such a way that he was not accepted into the Circle. Later on, as the meetings developed vigorously, he probably would have been asked to join, for he would have fitted perfectly into the atmosphere of the group. But the fact remains that, initially, he was rejected. In the fall of that year Boris died.

The parable about the stone which the builders rejected is one of the most "existential" in the New Testament. We have to remember it time and time again.

After two successful seasons we had the idea of selecting an inner circle of the Circle, something akin to a new Order. This circle was to unite those of us who were not only eager to discuss our dreams and beliefs but were also ready to act upon them. Under such conditions, friendship and love amongst the members of the Order would become obligatory. But when Vildé was proposed for this inner circle, there were objections; we said there was something obscure, something puzzling about him, that we first had to sort out matters—was he perhaps a Captain Kopeikin (from *Dead Souls*)? No such objections were made about anyone else: only once were they expressed and only about Vildé, the one and only man of our milieu who was soon to become a leader in the Resistance and be executed, actively fighting the forces of evil.

Two bad jokes! I learned a lot from them. Vildé, incidentally, was accepted into the "inner circle of friends" after all. Another member and I were given the task of meeting with him initially in order to "clarify things." What could we possibly have dug up? We dutifully accomplished our mission: we met with him at an unusual hour in a café, had a drink together and thus felt out the ground. As a result of our report (given at Fondaminsky's apartment), Vildé was accepted into the Inner Circle (but about that, later).

In the spring, much to the detriment of my examinations, I suddenly started writing a story about the devil (ostensibly about chess). I sent my piece to *Sovremennye Zapiski* (Contemporary Annals) and immediately left for Calvados* on what I considered a well-deserved vacation; swimming and bicycling there to the point of exhaustion would then keep me going all winter.

In August, I received a letter from V. Rudnev, the most punctual of men, together with the manuscript of my *Dvoinoi Nelson* (Double Nelson), which had by then lost its virginal freshness. The story was not good enough for *Sovremennye zapiski*.

Rudnev was the kindest, the most honest and warmhearted of the Russian "intelligenty," a nobleman, a county doctor, and an SR; like almost everyone with his background, he was not very versed in the arts and never expressed opinions about painting or poetry. But prose he considered a simple, straightforward matter. In general, 75 percent of literature in Russia is merely an appendage to the suppressed forces waging war against tyranny. And this most honest of aurochs was the editor of the only "thick" literary emigré journal.[5] (Of the other editors only the poet M. Zetlin was in the right place.)

When, some years later, my story was published in *Russkie zapiski*

---

*In Normandy.

(Russian Annals), Khodasevich invited me, under memorable circumstances, to his house: he was very conscientious about his duties as a critic
and, before writing about the story for *Vozrozhdenie* (Renaissance),
wanted to clear up several points. When he learned that *Sovremennye
zapiski* had once rejected *Dvoinoi Nelson,* he fell into a rage. "Why do
they meddle with art? Why, oh why do they meddle with art?" he
repeated with disgust.

I know that on different occasions Khodasevich wrote polite letters to
Vishnyak and Rudnev, and perhaps also to Milyukov. He probably
started out, "My dear. . ." and concluded, "Most respectfully
yours. . . ." But only narrow minds might deduce from this that Khodasevich loved or respected these public figures.

His wrath, in those days, was mainly directed at Vishnyak, who incidentally served as a scapegoat for many people, as if he alone or he above
all others had been responsible for all the historical farces of our era.
Which, of course, is not true. But there are people who for no particular
reason crystallize around them the anger of the public. I have met many a
thoughtful person who felt deep contempt for the Russian Constituent
Assembly[6] simply because M. Vishnyak identified himself with this
noble but more or less fictitious institution.

Thus, in Calvados, I received my story back—a fillip in the nose! I
thought highly of *Dvoinoi Nelson.* (In the end, Adamovich and Khodasevich both, in rare unanimity, unreservedly praised it.) And for the first
(and last) time in my life I wrote a letter of complaint to the editor . . .
Did these heroes with great principles realize what they were doing? Did
they know that in our fantastic reality, approval and recognition might
perhaps save a writer from self-destruction? Did they not understand that
the creative process in the emigration had nothing in common with the
rural movement of the intelligentsia?

Back in Paris at the beginning of September, I went on the first Sunday
to the taxi drivers' bistro, counting on meeting my friends there. But it
turned out that many were still away (or had over the summer lost the
habit of going there). To save money I decided not to occupy a table.
Poplavsky escorted me to the door. I then noticed his unnatural pallor
(but only later became aware of the cause of it): his ashen face, like a
buckwheat pancake, with a dark, narrow, unpleasant mustache he had
grown over the summer.

He was taciturn, reserved, somehow oddly conventional. *Chisla* had
stopped publication; *Sovremennye zapiski* had rejected his novel; anyway,
he was now mainly interested in spiritualism: on Tuesday (I believe it

was Tuesday) he was invited to a lady's place for a séance. If I cared to, I could join him.

"Come at five. We'll take a walk before we go," were his last words.

On that we parted. He froze on the threshold, as if a pallid mask with the mustache of an Inca or an Aztec were hanging suspended at head level. I later realized that the drugs must have transformed the color and texture of his skin. I will remember forever his taut and deathly immobile face, without glasses.

Boris's game with narcotics was no coincidence; it had started early in life. He had always been attracted to beauty, the beauty of dreams or the beauty of evil. (Evil is a dream, a dream is beautiful.) He was repulsed by the coarseness and ugliness of life (to act means to contribute to the ugliness of life). The struggle against life's distortions only multiplied these distortions. O, to go away, to just go away.

The story of the devil is complex literature. And Poplavsky knew this better than anyone. The devil is beautiful, and beauty is a whirlpool. Yes, the saints are great. But precisely because of the devil's jealous interference.

"In general, sailors are great, but let's not talk about that . . ." he loved to repeat the line of his favorite "stoic," Aleksandr Ginger.

Death is inevitable and beautiful (though it is evil). Let us die like new Romans, in bathing suits, on a rock by a swimming pool with chlorinated water, falling asleep, smiling through the pain. ("To return to familiar dreams.")

I frequently met Boris at the house of mutual friends (Protsenko, Dryakhlov), where we would eat, drink wine, play belote or chess, yell and argue, berate, curse, and hurt each other. (These agapes, I'm afraid, were much more pleasant when one of us, Boris or I, was not present.) And I have seen him drunk on more than one occasion.

Some people experience a deadly languor as they become intoxicated and try to overcome or resist it by any and all means, often ugly ones. They moan and sigh, run to the bathroom, hang out of the window, stick a finger down their throat, in short, as Poplavsky would say, they raise metaphysical Cain. Others fall into a dead calm. Docile and in their way beautiful, they settle down: on the floor, in an armchair, against the wall. Immobile, uncomplaining, barely breathing. (Thus, both these psychological types will behave in their last agony.) Poplavsky belonged to the latter group.

That Tuesday I did not attend the spiritualistic séance. (Had I not forgotten about it, everything might have turned out differently.) Boris too must have changed his mind; instead of going to the esoteric lady, he joined a new friend of his, a repulsive Russian-Parisian who peddled a mixture of heroin and cocaine indiscriminately to anyone, thus making enough to support his own habit. There were rumors that this wretched creature had been contemplating suicide for a long time and was only waiting for a suitable companion; it is a specific trait of certain degenerates to pick up a fellow traveler. For his purpose he had simply to double or triple the regular dosage.

I do not believe Boris was aware of his forthcoming journey. He was, after all, a professional and would, at the last minute, have remembered his diaries and unfinished manuscripts and left them in some sort of order.

In the evening they both came to the Poplavskys' apartment. (The family lived next door to the Russian Zemgor[7] where, incidentally, *Sovremennye zapiski* had found shelter in a cubicle). They behaved oddly: both were excited and irritable and took frequent trips outside to the toilet, returning each time gay and rejuvenated. The old folks went quietly to bed and did not hear anything further. In the morning they found two cold bodies.

Boris's portrait appeared in *Poslednie novosti* and, for the first time, I realized that our life too (not only the battle of Borodino)[8] is a matter of history and should be thoroughly studied, since there can be two opinions about it.

When I arrived at the apartment of the deceased, a crowd had already assembled there; Charchoune and Knut were rummaging like beetles in batches of papers. The old Poplavsky, yellow and puffy with unbuttoned collar, was for some reason holding up Boris's pants against the light to demonstrate how threadbare they were. (I later heard that he had shown these pants to others too, as if they presented some metaphysical argument.)

Then there was the funeral, with heaps of costly flowers: the roses did indeed "smell of death." The small Russian church was filled to bursting. Young girls were sobbing; the many members of other religions stood with strained faces. (Poplavsky liked Jews, and, imitating Rozanov, knew how to improvise on the theme of Christ, blood, and circumcision.)

Father Bakst (of Protestant background, I believe) officiated. He gave a "biting and tactless" sermon denouncing narcotics, which angered some of the ladies, who then attempted to leave the overcrowded church. Especially furious was the one who, according to the words of the departed, had fed on his offals.

During the war I met Father Bakst in Marseilles. I am grateful to him for a peaceful tea and gentle Russian conversation amidst a world beleaguered by barbarians. (On the infamous Sunday of 22 June 1941,* after the liturgy, my dear compatriots in Marseilles, and as well in Nice, exchanged kisses, congratulating each other on this Easter of the Spirit.)

Poplavsky's death, though logical, was yet not all that characteristic of him: several variants were possible. Had *Chisla* been continued or had another such enterprise, capable of absorbing Boris, been in preparation, he would not have perished. With the same ease he might have gone to Spain a year later. And, under the Germans, he would undoubtedly have joined the Resistance, with hysterical ups and downs (perhaps even with failures, like Lydia Chervinskaya).

He has left behind a number of mysteriously beautiful poems, but Poplavsky's value goes beyond these volumes. He wrote dozens of pages of inspired prose—but his novels too do not tell all! Poplavsky undoubtedly had "a certain vision" and struggled to remember and incarnate it (often losing his way, despairing, and taking recourse in false shortcuts). Best of all, perhaps, he expressed himself in essays such as "Christ and His Acquaintances," and of course in those endless (immortal) conversations.

Even now, a quarter of a century later, I still detect in the brilliant improvisations of some of our emigré prima donnas grains of that golden sand, scattered so generously, carelessly, and persistently by Boris Poplavsky.

---

*The date of the German surprise attack on the Soviet Union.

Chapter 2 · Felsen

LAISSONS LES BELLES FEMMES AUX HOMMES SANS IMAGINATION.
—MARCEL PROUST

I met Yuri Felsen—pseudonym for Nikolai Berngardovich Freiden-stein—at Kochevie (The Nomads) at the high point of this literary circle, the end of the twenties and of NEP.[1]

How wrong first impressions can be! On closer acquaintance and over the years even his looks changed for the better, despite the fact that his color faded. There he was, dry, getting thinner, stooped, benevolently listening to you, never losing his own train of thought, grasping between his strong bony fingers the eternal Gauloise jaune in a cheap holder. If I had to define his essence in a short phrase, I would call it "the opposite of a traitor"—in relation to his neighbor as well as to himself.

He suffered from a disease of the spine or, rather of the ligaments of the vertebrae, so that he could no longer fully straighten up, a position that emphasized his lordly immobility and courteous attentiveness.

His first short story was published in the *Novy Korabl* (New Barque) and he read it several times, at different meetings: he would undo a neatly rolled-up package, put the small magazine in front of him and distinctly, calmly, yet with great inner fire, deliver his strangely constructed, artful sentences.

He wrote about love, spiced with suicidal jealousy, and in this respect followed in the "way" of Proust; there, however ended his connection with the latter. He composed long and difficult sentences, but there were none of the Proustian comparisons between two subjects taken from entirely disparate realms. Felsen's world was linear. Here is a typical sentence:

> Lola no longer needed me, and all her feelings of friendship van-ished, as formerly, with the end of her love quandaries and con-scious struggle for me, her irritability had vanished; I simply be-

came superfluous, but, soberly realizing it, out of weakness I could
not refrain from going to see her, and Lola, ecstatic, overflowing
with joy, generously presented me with the alms of her so very
life-giving presence.

I mention Proust because Felsen often suffered from his stylistic (and
typographical) resemblance to this, his beloved, great, and fashionable
writer. Thus he recounted with a smile that, after a reading of his at the
Union of Young Writers (Denfert-Rochereau),* G. took the floor and
declared that this was sheer Proust, although a few years later he confessed to Felsen that at the time he had not yet read Proust.

In general, at the end of the twenties, many legends sprang up about
Proust, but only very few had read him—just as, during the time of the
Russo-Japanese war, submarines were blamed for everything, although
no one had ever seen a submarine with his own eyes.

Felsen's prose is colorless: a grey drawing with a sharp pencil, marked
by boring precision. As Poplavsky put it: "Who can listen to an entire
concert for just one flute!" To appreciate such literature one had to elbow
one's way through a thicket. In this task Felsen was miraculously aided
by various influential people, many of them hostile toward one another.
Adamovich, Khodasevich, Gippius, Weidlé—each of them made sure to
praise him, even inordinately, at least once a year. Which sometimes
seemed unjust! It should be noted that, after the fall of Paris and Felsen's
tragic death, not one of the surviving venerable critics devoted an article
to his novels. Considering their former compliments, this failure is almost indecent. I believe that Felsen's talent expressed itself mainly not in
his books but in his ability to bring to life the best traits inherent in those
with whom he came in contact. This is a great and rare human gift, and
all of us, unconsciously, were grateful to him for it. Practical, clever and
sharp-eyed, he always played his cards honestly while never missing a
trick. Or so, at least, it seemed.

Bridge he played better than any other one of us, at chess he was
weak. Thanks to his skill at cards, he reconciled such inveterate enemies
as Adamovich and Khodasevich. It was especially pleasant to have him
for a partner, against any opponents, even professionals. Wherein lay
the secret?

Khodasevich was usually nervous during bridge; he fidgeted and grim-
aced when his partner went down. Felsen always smiled triumphantly,

---

*Street and metro station.

like a schoolboy who had got away with some mischief, and raked in his tricks. At the end, to tease us, he would say: "Mind you, I won without any cards. I've never had a more miserable hand." And then he looked like the star pupil in the class, praised by all teachers. But this was only outward appearance. Independent, in many ways obstinate, informed, sober, and honest even in trifles, he could, when circumstances demanded it, very well defend his opinions, which often seemed bland against the background of our colorful inventions. He did this without compromise, and he answered with a slap in the face—even if only a symbolic one—every boorish lout (and there were compatriots who began to raise their rudimentary ancient reptiles' heads).

Felsen, the son of a St. Petersburg physician, graduated from law school in 1912. After the revolution the family emigrated to Riga, where the father continued to practice medicine. In the Russian capital, Felsen's uncle had been the owner of a big tailoring establishment which furnished brilliant uniforms to gilded youth. These clients of his uncle, it seems to me, played a decisive role in Felsen's development.

In the emigration, he himself became involved in commercial dealings; first, successfully, in Berlin, later, with less success, in Paris. I imagine that there his writing began to get in the way.

For some reason he was often cheated by his partners. He frequented the stock exchange but without much profit, losing his entire capital in some transaction. Luckily, one of the above-mentioned partners had married his sister, and in their house Felsen henceforth resided for free.

The stock exchange and West European commerce put a special stamp on his writing: the result was a novel mixture, unique in Russian literature. He transferred commercial honesty into his private life and his novels.

I mention all this also for the reason that Felsen perished in connection with some shady affairs of his friends and relatives. Of course his sister and her husband would be best able to shed light upon these matters. I understand they are both living in Switzerland or Italy; they did not return to France for fear of prosecution, since they conducted business with the Germans during World War II.

In Felsen's novel, the hero, accustomed to a good life, continues his commercial activities, but without much success; from volume to volume he is in love with the same, never-aging Lola (the object of constant jokes in Montparnasse).

Felsen explained proudly that the portrait of Lola was "pure chemistry." In other words, to the prototype, who lived in Riga, he had added the traits of diverse ladies with whom fate had brought him together.

His many books were supposed to be parts of a single novel. Felsen searched for but could not find a unifying title which would equal in significance *À la Recherche du temps perdu*. Besides this creative occupation he had yet another: falling in love. In his real-life love affairs he invariably arrived at the same situation and found himself in the role of a suffering, jealous victim. Like Proust, he was sensually attracted to such tortures and relished the role of the witness who, from a corner of the drawing room, watches his Lola as she flirts with other men.

We met the original Lola in Montparnasse when she visited Paris. Later, she perished under the Nazis in Riga, a fact which of course adds a new dimension to her image. When I saw her at Dominique, she was a somewhat large woman with (as Felsen expressed it) "advantageous legs," about whom one could say that she had a fine figure, that she was practical and apparently of strong character. The mystery of a personality is revealed in creative work, in suffering and in love! This topic interested Felsen and myself equally, and we often were inspired by it.

In fact, in such intimate conversations lay the main charm of communion with Felsen. With Poplavsky one wanted to argue, call each other names and, after parting, in revenge, create yet one more new mystical variant of the universe. With Felsen it was the opposite: the quiet, concrete exchange of ideas created immediate, productive, spiritual comfort. Listening to him talk, it seemed natural to recall something parallel from one's own past and to share it with him. He knew how to listen, and he understood everything. Not in a flash (not seizing the meaning at once) but by posing questions, sensibly and to the point. Then he would think for a moment and nod his head; he had accepted it and placed it next to his own experience.

In the thirties, we met almost daily. I had just finished *Lyubov vtoraya* (The Other Love); *Sovremennye zapiski* (Contemporary Annals) had published an excerpt under the title *Preobrazhenie* (The Transfiguration). And this seemed to be the end of my relations with the *Annals*. How could I get the book published?

Meanwhile, Russian Paris rejoiced, celebrating Bunin's Nobel Prize with him. He started the day with champagne: this produces a special sort of tipsiness—not without belching. Vera Nikolaevna Bunin, departing with her husband for Stockholm, declared before witnesses: "Believe me, I sense it in my heart, I shall go there once more for the prize." (The idea being that Zurov would become the second laureate.)

Be that as it may, we had no way of getting published. This, at that time, seemed to be the most important obstacle to a writer's career. Now it has become clear that emigré literature is perishing for lack of a cultivated readership.

Our books were sold in all the Russian limitrophes. But we did not take full advantage of it. The authors' negligence and the crookedness of the publishers ruined the market.

At this point I had a truly Napoleonic brainstorm and chose Felsen as a partner for its realization. Having just finished his *Pisma o Lermontove,* he immediately caught on to all the implications.

The idea was to organize an exhibit of emigré books; the various publishers would be glad to provide books for display and additional copies for sale at reduced prices. Simultaneously, we would solicit visitors to the exhibition to subscribe to our future publications: for ten francs they would, at the end of the year, receive one or two or three newly published books—depending on the number of subscribers—for all moneys collected would be used for printing expenses. There would be no overhead.

Felsen fully appreciated this plan, but in his own practical way. While I was mainly looking for subscribers and the sacrificial impulse, he was interested in the entrance fee, a percentage from sales, and so on.

"Everything sounds all right, but where are we going to find decent premises for free?"

I had thought of this too! The Roerich Museum, where Prince Shirinsky-Shikhmatov's Post-Revolutionary Club[2] met once a week. An exhibit of emigré literature would be good publicity for the museum, which stood empty all year round, decorated with Roerich's Tibetan paintings. In those years, Roerich tried to create an organization similar to the Red Cross for the conservation of works of art of coming wars. Collaboration with emigré writers could be a help—but of course only if our exhibit did not appear to be a private undertaking.

We decided to act in the name of the Union of Writers and Poets and were granted formal authorization. We founded a committee, consisting of Felsen and myself, and the three books brought out and sent to the subscribers within the next two years carried the imprint of this committee as the legitimate publisher.

In the course of the ensuing vicissitudes of preparation and liquidation, Felsen and I spent entire days, if not weeks and months, together, all without any of the irritation so usual in such ventures. His thinking was always clear, practical, and constructive, especially in details. He delighted and amazed me with his savoir faire. When I ordered chicken in a restaurant and soup for the first course, he admonished me: "Rather order an hors d'oeuvre! They give you only a quarter of a chicken, you need something substantial before." Although I have since been to places where they bring a whole capon to the table, I always order hors d'oeuvres with it.

Saturday night, in Montparnasse, people were wont to drink too much; they quarrelled and one or the other might start a fight. On such occasions, Felsen acted the peacemaker. "I'm in charge here," he announced firmly, separating the adversaries. And since many loved and almost all respected him; it worked. "Yes, Nikolai Berngardovich, you be the judge!" And, like Solomon, he judged to everyone's satisfaction.

Once, however, a newcomer, the captain of a sailing vessel, whom the poet Dovid Knut had brought to Montparnasse, protested: "No, you are *not* in charge here!" And for the moment, to general consternation, all that Felsen had built up over the years collapsed like a house of cards.

We went back to Dominique (the brawl had taken place on the sidewalk next to Métro Vavin) and ordered a vodka each, for consolation. Felsen valiantly downed his glass and winked. Dissecting a Russian herring, he laughingly explained to me the absurdity of what had happened. And I, who had also tried to interfere, joyfully listened to another truly hilarious story.

A certain semi-Maecenas and semi-Dane, an acquaintance of Felsen, had come down to Paris in the company of a young 100 percent Danish woman with rose-colored hair. The quarrel started when the Maecenas, having had his fill of drink, decided to take his girl to their hotel. But the above-mentioned captain and his friend Kuba thought they could not leave such a splendid, and quite tipsy, blonde alone to this half-baboon.

"Imagine," Felsen said chuckling, as he listlessly picked at the rest of his herring, "he brought her down from Copenhagen, they are in one room at the hotel . . . Isn't it absurd?"

He had a particularly well-developed respect for the rules of the game. *Les règles du jeu* he saw as autonomic values whose disruption would lead to utter chaos.

In Montparnasse, critical situations were apt to arise. Often someone had to be "rescued," bailed out, pacified. One day it was Georgy Ivanov who got into hot water with Burov, another it was Otsup who threatened to strike Khodasevich, or Chervinskaya who smashed several cups and saucers. And trying to calm down Lydia Chervinskaya at times led to a complete clarification of *all relationships* among those involved, a process which, after midnight, required an iron constitution.

Thus I once came upon Felsen in a dark alley behind the Monocle or the Sphinx: he was dragging the vigorously resisting *poetesse* by the arm. Recognizing me, he sat down heavily on a stoop, took a deep breath and then said calmly and fiercely, "I can't, I simply can't any more . . ." and, without waiting for an answer, vanished into the shadows, as if swept away by the early morning breeze.

Once, entering the Café du Dôme* on business of my own, I was confronted by a scene which I promptly and accurately sized up: a heap of dishes on the floor, waiters in threatening attitudes, and Lydia Chervinskaya, tall, slightly stooped, resembling Greta Garbo, standing at the bare table, as if waiting for a verdict.

In a stutter, I immediately explained that things could very simply be set right. Since I didn't have a penny, this declaration of mine bordered on heroism. Luckily, Kuba, who was the cause of Lydia's tantrum and who had been hiding somewhere in the back, stepped forward and handed us the needed cash.

Legends sprang up about the Russian Montparnasse, but as a matter of fact, our lives proceeded in an exceptionally proper, almost dull way, except for the only important basic entertainment: passionate, inspired talk.

As a rule the writers would sit around in a café with one cup of coffee until the last Métro, at 12:30 A.M. Sometimes, having missed it, we would move on to Dominique. There we would be welcomed by the sturdy Pavel Tutkovsky, with whom I supposedly conversed in Latin, using all the familiar proverbs. Tutkovsky, a general prosecutor of the old Russian school, knew and loved his Latin.

"*Vita nostra brevis est,*" I would say for an opening.

"*Brevi finietur,*" he readily replied. "Will you have the usual?"

People with money ordered vodka. Smolensky was sometimes treated by a female companion. But even if you could pay, it was embarrassing to drink while some hungry soul sat next to you—and there were such amongst us.

Marya Ivanovna, the darling wife of Stavrov, liked to repeat: "They say there are orgies going on in Montparnasse," and she would grimace most amusingly, in imitation of imaginary gossips. "What orgies? They make love. Big deal!"

And indeed, nothing preternatural went on in Montparnasse. Our lives were staid and moral in comparison with local customs. In order to

---

*A café on Boulevard du Montparnasse, frequented by writers and artists.

survive, one had to work, somehow. And write! This too is hard labor, especially prose writing. In addition, some of us regularly trotted to the Sorbonne.

"I don't know *when* I write my poems," Ivanov said, crinkling his drowned man's face. "I write them while washing or shaving. I don't know when I write my poems." Alas, prose writers knew that they needed time and a special place, and they suffered from the abnormal conditions.

Felsen and his current lady usually came late to Montparnasse, feeling in fine fettle after having dined somewhere with vodka.

"Are you before or after?" I would joke.

Laughing, they would reply: "After, after."

The talk around, about the good thief on the Cross or about Blok, mingled with the latest literary gossip while the bridge players, settling down at the next table, asked not to be disturbed.

"Why didn't you take the queen?" Khodasevich inquires biliously.

"With what? With my fingers?" Yanovsky's voice.

Between two deals, Adamovich hastily relates a recent dream: He is playing against M. and R.N. He opens his hand and discovers one entire solid suit. His heart begins to beat as before a grand slam, but suddenly he realizes that he is holding a completely unfamiliar suit of a green color, and he has no idea what to bid. . . .

"Ha, ha, ha, and now let's play!" Khodasevich is getting nervous.

That these two most celebrated emigré critics were peacefully sitting at the same bridge table had to be considered a miracle. A miracle performed by Felsen, who had brought the two adversaries together.

There were many reasons, metaphysical and practical, for the inveterate enmity: different esthetic philosophies, different life stories, different temperaments and tastes.

According to his theoretical elaborations, Adamovich should have established a definite hierarchy of values: most important, let us say, evangelical love, then philosophy or science, then play, sex, and finally, in the last place, art—a modest but by no means shameful activity. But here was the paradox! As soon as a man, in tune with the above order, devoted himself to "creative work," he immediately started the quest for what is "most important" or of the "greatest depth," thus turning the whole pyramid of values upside down and proving with his entire being that precisely art was the most important thing in life—that art is meant to transfigure, explain, and save everything! Otherwise it would make no sense to get involved with it at all.

This is the kind of contradiction to which, if I am not mistaken,

Khodasevich tried to draw our attention. His logic fitted perfectly between Aristotle and Newton.

Apart from philosophical differences there were of course also petty
reasons for the enmity. Adamovich was the critic for the better and more
decent paper; Khodasevich naturally could not find recognition among
most of the collaborators of *Vozrozhdenie*. Yet *Vozrozhdenie* and *Poslednie novosti* were competitors, and their contributors were involved in
group polemics.

Khodasevich could eventually have forgiven Adamovich his inordinate praise of Charchoune's novels (let the man be happy!). But eulogies
of the poet Ivanov—that was outrageous! Ivanov, according to Khodasevich, derived from Fet (and not from the best of Fet). Besides, Georgy
Ivanov's moral proclivities flew in the face of Adamovich's entire esthet-
ics of "what would Tolstoi have said . . ." Georgy Ivanov, in his turn,
was not caught napping and whispered, whispered, whispered in his
friend's, Adamovich's, ear.

Khodasevich, who was for a time completely isolated, made do as well
as he could and even put into circulation the witty gossip about the rich
old lady murdered in Petrograd by Adamovich and Ivanov. Eventually
this incensed the capricious Adamovich. But the years and Felsen's tact-
fulness did their work; by the beginning of the thirties and the *front
populaire*[3] both arbiters started friendly relations in Montparnasse, from
which all of us profited greatly.

In the morning, before the opening hour of the exhibit, Felsen and I met
at a café. We invariably had a hot chocolate; he would light his Gauloise
jaune ("the most affordable among the better cigarettes") and slowly sip
the hot concoction. Viewing the passersby, he gave me the latest news in
detail. The evening before, on his way home, he had dropped in at the
Murat,★ where the "professionals" were playing bridge. He had just sat
down next to Khodasevich, when Otsup appeared in the basement, began hurling abuse, and was about to start a fight, so that someone had to
interfere. (In his latest article Khodasevich had written that Otsup was a
wheeler-dealer, living "off" *Chisla.*)

"Strangely enough, Otsup seemed to have expected that we would
support him," Felsen continued, smiling pensively and casting attentive
glances at the couples sitting near our table. "He's only been away for a
few months, but he has completely lost touch with reality."

★Café on Boulevard Murat near Porte d'Auteuil.

I could have heard from a dozen witnesses about the scene at the Murat. But that last remark, that Otsup had counted on our goodwill and help, was very typical of Felsen. His whole literature was based on "psychologism"; he seemed not yet to know any higher values. That's why he cared so much for Lermontov, in whose prose he perceived the beginnings of the Russian psychological novel.

It was even more amusing to listen to Felsen recount adventures from the past. Such stories lived in him as an autonomous reality; this I felt then as I feel it today, but I still do not understand wherein consists their true value. That there is such a value, of this I am certain.

"I had been interested in her for some time," Felsen might begin. "We met occasionally at the house of mutual friends; her husband traveled on business, and she often came alone. Once, as we were about to part, I said: 'Please, listen to me and don't get angry. It's late, at home no one is expecting you. How about spending the rest of the night together?' and without any hypocrisy she accepted! Very nice, but at her doorstep she suddenly changed her mind: 'No, it's embarrassing. It's no good in our apartment. And the neighbors might notice.' Well, it happens," Felsen went on. "But I knew a certain hotel in the vicinity. I hailed a taxi and off we went. We had just entered the room, when again she got into a flurry. On the verge of tears she declared that this was the first time she had dared do anything like this. 'What is it anyway? A woman in her thirties has to know what she wants.' I gave her a smart slap," Felsen continued, "and imagine, she immediately calmed down. Everything went splendidly and later she admitted that I had been absolutely right, and we established an excellent relationship."

Another episode, for juxtaposition:

"In general it's not my way to jump on a woman. On the contrary, I even used to be quite timid. One day, sitting in the Rotonde,* leafing through a magazine, I noticed that the young woman at the next table kept looking at me. I got into conversation with her. Her husband was a musician, constantly on tour. They lived near Métro Muette. She liked Scriabin and loved Russian ballet. Before parting we exchanged telephone numbers. I did not pay much attention to our conversation, but a week later, as I was having dinner, the phone rang: 'Have you had your coffee?' 'Not yet.' 'Come over to my place.' I bought a bottle of Courvoisier and was on my way. Well, coffee, cognac, kisses. Finally she excused herself and, after a minute reappeared in nothing but a thin robe. Quite unexpect-

---

*Café on Boulevard du Montparnasse, frequented by writers and artists.

edly everything turned out well, despite the fact that, at the time, I was involved in another, for me quite important, relationship. But listen to what happened then . . ." he stopped me; I had assumed that this was the end of his story. "Suddenly she started a very serious, even sad, conversation. She was by no means reproaching me, no one could have foreseen it, but that's how things happen. 'I beg you to forget everything! It won't happen again! Should we accidentally meet, then only as old friends. Please, forgive me, but don't insist!' I acquiesced." Felsen made an ironic gesture. "Actually, I had no claims in this case." After a pause he continued triumphantly: "But imagine, a few days later there was another call: 'I have to see you.' We made a date at the Rotonde. Long explanations. She hasn't lived with her husband for a long time, has been thinking a lot about me. If it suited me, she was ready to continue our relationship."

"Wow!" I exclaimed, glad and bewildered, not knowing how one should behave in such a situation. "What did you do?"

Felsen smiled condescendingly.

"I said that I had already become accustomed to our break-up and that now I would find it difficult to change again."

"Wow!" I uttered, feeling that that was precisely the right answer.

One more story:

A young, middle-class couple, childless but with a poodle, occupied the villa next to the one where Felsen and his sister were living in the summer. The two families became friendly and spent a great deal of time together; in the fall everyone left, and they did not see each other again in Paris.

"Can you imagine, the other day I found out that they were not married and never lived together in the city. My sister ran into her by chance: she lives alone, there's no villa, no husband, even the poodle did not belong to her . . ."

Felsen repeated this last sentence several times, as if it hurt to touch upon the mystery of human relations which so fascinated him. The very fact that he mentioned this couple only now, several years later, when he heard that "even the poodle did not belong to her," was characteristic.

Felsen was usually the first to arrive for an appointment at a café and immediately extracted from his pocket some folded pages covered with his small, even, clear handwriting: his draft! Where and when he wrote it I do not know. Above the lines of this draft he entered more and more new words with a very sharp pencil. He would think for a second, erase what he had just written and on that same spot put something different. Thanks to the exceedingly sharp pencil, his corrections turned out to be neat and legible. That's why he availed himself every other minute of one of those tiny sharpeners that schoolchildren use. These pauses also gave him a chance to size up passersby and to think. Although artificially inverted, Felsen's sentences gave an impression of finely carved precision.

During the "phony" war,[4] he was working on a new book which he had in mind to call *Repetition of the Past:* "I told Adamovich the title and he said: 'It's original.' "

Of course, he was not lying, but I realized that if Adamovich had disapproved of the title, Felsen would not have mentioned it. He never repeated an unflattering remark made about him; while we, the post-revolutionary generation, relished such disclosures. Felsen only looked at us in astonishment and pity.

When the person he was expecting came toward his table, Felsen would smile distractedly and amiably, rise, shake hands and say hello. Immediately after that he put his papers back into his pocket to rest there until the next opportune moment. On-and-off rumors had it that Adamovich was writing a big article about Felsen; or that Gippius, Adamovich, Khodasevich, and Weidlé were organizing an evening when he would read his work. Such rumors, of course, did not arise spontaneously. Not for nothing did Khodasevich make up his frivolous four-liner about how ladies make careers in Paris (and elsewhere).

I'm trying to say that Felsen had somehow to work on all these people, prepare them. And this indeed he did, but unobtrusively, subtly, with great dignity. As a result, Gippius would in the most miraculous way take a seat on the dais next to Khodasevich and second Adamovich in his analysis of the new writer.

Such arrangements used to outrage me. I was no more envious than any other Russian writer, but the irresponsibility of these undertakings depressed me. It seemed to me as ugly as fascism or communism. In Adamovich's beloved Pushkin quotation, "literature will pass but friendship will remain." I found an affinity to the *Gavriliada!*[5] In both there is a sin against the Holy Ghost. On top of this, it is sheer nonsense. I have no idea where Pushkin's friendship with Delvig and the latter's poetry now dwell, but Pushkin's poems—*literatura*—apparently endure.

"In literature it's like in high school," Felsen explained benevolently. "The first impression is very important. If you happen to get a bad mark at the beginning of the school year, you may well be stuck with it until the next grade. And maybe even up to the final examinations. That's how difficult it is to change one's teachers' opinions."

Felsen must often have felt uneasy in the Circle. He seemed to be an *areligious* person, utterly devoid of theological intuition and with no interest whatsoever in ecclesiastical discussions. He supported a formal democracy, considering it a lesser evil and, in an era when myths were built around Hitler's Thousand-Year Reich, was always guided by sober, honest reasoning. In social questions he tried to follow our lead, but his heart was not in it; he simply could not believe that as a consequence of hunger and exploitation human beings started hating and killing their own kind. He hardly ever took part in our disputes about Christianity. To me he confessed that Natasha's love for Prince Andrei in *War and Peace* revealed to him almost the entire gospel message. I was astonished and delighted by this declaration.

Despite these formal limitations, Felsen was loved and respected in the Circle and wielded a measure of authority. He was with us on the general and editorial boards. But he was not asked to join the Inner Circle. The editorial board of *Krug* (Circle) consisted of all the members of the general board plus Adamovich, who was not a member of the latter.

At the crowded editorial meetings, from which Adamovich was usually absent, where Gershenkron quoted the ancient Greeks and I quarrelled with Terapiano, precisely there, Felsen, unhurriedly and soberly, dealt with the business at hand. Organized, intelligent, practical, of refined taste, he could, under different circumstances, have become the outstanding editor of an important magazine. Instinctively he followed his own line, defended his understanding of art in prose as well as in poetry, and also kept his personal interests in mind. Thus, during the preparation of the first issue the question arose in what order to print the material: alphabetizing was good for price lists and epigones; we did not have to be afraid to point out once more *what* we considered important!

Felsen suggested starting with an excerpt from the late Poplavsky's work and grouping the other pieces according to their kinship with it. This resulted in placing Felsen himself directly after Poplavsky, although it is hard to imagine greater opposites than these two writers in their interpretation and transfiguration of life.

After those editorial meetings at 130 avenue de Versailles, I often landed in the cafe Murat, where serious bridge was played. A constant visitor there was Aldanov's mother-in-law, a vivacious, kind old lady. It was she who revealed to me the great secret that it is not advantageous to open with three aces and no other support. I accepted her advice gratefully, as I do any revelation based on personal experience.

In that ruthless basement, Felsen nevertheless managed to hold his own and sometimes to win. "Strange, I won again," he would announce with a smile of satisfaction. "And what's more, I did it completely without cards!" He once said to me, reminding me of Tolstoi's Ivan Ilich, that it was embarrassing to win too much. Khodasevich lost constantly, although he could ill afford it; he enjoyed the game in his own way.

Aware that writers congregated there, Bunin and Aldanov, after having dined, sometimes came down into the basement, animated by the duck and the wine, voluble in the way of old people, and quick to take offense.

"Tolstoi's plays are rather weakish," I once told them (after I had lost). Aldanov's awe was something to behold! "Everything Tolstoi wrote is good!"

Their boundless love for Tolstoi was becoming harmful in that it turned into indifference and even loathing for everything that came afterward in world literature.

"They kept bending my ear: 'Proust! Proust!' " Bunin would cut straight from the shoulder. "What's in your Proust? I've read him. He's nothing special! I still have to look into Kafka, I'm sure it's equally nonsensical." He reminded me of a character in a story by Zoshchenko: "The theatre? I know it. I've been on the stage."

And, in the meantime, Felsen was making his tricks, slapping down one card after another, saying, "Spade, spade, and one more spade!" mischievously but not irritatingly.

What a curious thing: gambling, games, cards. In Montparnasse there were poets and writers who adored any game of chance, and next to them there were others, just as talented, who never participated.

Tolstoi and Dostoevsky, so different otherwise, shared almost the same obsession about cards. Bunin, Aldanov, Zaitsev were absolutely sterile in their attitude toward gambling; others, like Felsen, played only "commercial games." Adamovich, Khodasevich, Vildé, Stavrov, Varshavsky, and Yanovsky played at anything, even three-card Monte. Ivanov and all our ladies never touched cards.

Since Felsen's family always left for the summer, I slept several times at his house, in his niece's room. In the morning, the maid served hot chocolate and croissants. I then realized that the whole family had been accustomed to this drink from childhood (from their Russian past, perhaps).

Thanks to the exhibit of emigré books, we were regarded as some kind of specialists. Thus the secretary of the *Archives Internationales de Danse* proposed to us to organize (for a small salary) an exhibit of books devoted to the ballet. I was inordinately surprised by such a success; but

Felsen, after thinking it over, said, "It's always like that in business; you have to get onto the rails, then you'll be pushed ahead." I liked his comparisons and generalizations, sensing that they were based on authentic experience. Such experiences were highly valued by us, perhaps too highly.

Sometimes he arrived in Montparnasse carrying a parcel of tiny sandwiches: black caviar, cheese, pâté—leftovers from his sister's latest party. It gave him pleasure to see how we appreciated these crumpled delicacies. In such acts there was probably more Christian love than in many of our eschatological discussions.

At that time I was assisting Dr. Z., an elderly Russian physician recently arrived from Berlin, in opening his practice in Paris. A highly intelligent man and a failure, very experienced, slightly cynical, Dr. Z. attempted to combine diverse and opposing therapeutic measures into one system. His patients were kept busy all day long with exercises, salads, and scraped apple, so that they had no time for moping around. I sent him his first patients: a few of our writers and philanthropists.

Felsen consulted Z. once and then brought his sister to him. As a consequence she began to leap stark naked through the apartment, flogging herself with wet towels. It was then that Felsen coined his famous witticism: One has to have an iron constitution to be treated by Dr. Z.

Late in the night, when we were leaving the Select* for Dominique, two writers, Charchoune and Emelianov, usually stayed behind. Grinning like a naughty schoolboy, Felsen would whisper with a wink: "Jolly fellows!" And this was very funny, for whatever else these "fellows" were, they certainly were not "jolly."

For some reason, washrooms played an important role in Parisian life. In the course of the evening, everybody went down a couple of times— to wash up, comb his hair, perhaps even to accost some striking girl. In the Metro toilets, beggars, vividly reminiscent of those in the Scriptures, lay curled up on the tiles and on the grating (from which heat arose). Above them the water murmured softly. In these early morning hours, after a wasted night, one sought to pray; but such a mood was decidedly alien to Felsen.

Loved by all of us, even the "Generals," he never lost his former stock-exchange connections. He was, of course, a rare bird among them, but there too he was treated with respect. Some heavyset, strange types sometimes came up to Felsen's table, grinning broadly and speaking to

---

*The Select Café was in Montparnasse, opposite the Café de la Rotonde.

him in German. Some of them he would ask to sit down, and a bottle of cognac would materialize: the waiters were by then accustomed to the fact that visitors from abroad ordered whole bottles. Lydia Chervin-skaya, one of our better poets, would enthrone herself in the center, the others settled modestly at the side—but with full glasses.

It was in connection with these speculators and his relatives that Felsen perished. Soon after the outbreak of the war, his sister and her husband ran off to Switzerland. In order to liquidate his brother-in-law's affairs, Felsen stayed on in Paris with his old deaf mother. He was supposed to receive some millions or billions of francs and bring them to Geneva. But he never got the money: the racketeers kept procrastinating. Here it has to be noted that, during the years of the occupation, foreigners partici-pated as vigorously in the sell-out of France as in the heroic deeds of the Résistance. The French did not know how or refused to have any deal-ings with the Germans, at least in the beginning. The paintings Goering seized for his thousand-year collection passed through many quite unex-pected middlemen.

In the spring of 1941 I met Adamovich in Nice; he showed me a postcard from Felsen. "I no longer go to the Merezhkovskys," Felsen sadly told him. "They now have completely different visitors." At this same meeting, Adamovich mentioned a postcard that Bunin had recently received from B. in Paris, urging him to return from the free zone and assuring him that "now unification of the entire emigration has become possible." What a bitch, we both decided. She even puts it on an ideo-logical basis. But Felsen's letter had a very somber ring.

According to some, Felsen managed to collect part of the monies and was promised the rest in Lyon. He installed his mother with a kind soul and himself traveled to Lyon, where he lost further precious time waiting for contact with the racketeers. Perhaps there were still other reasons why he lingered, but no one has yet told of them.

Finally, Felsen left for Switzerland, with all of the cash or part of it—I don't know. Less than a hundred years before, Herzen had fled along the same route in a stagecoach.

Felsen was expected for tea in Geneva, as E. Kuskova asserts in her dispute with me (*Novoe Russkoe Slovo* [New Russian Word], 1955). But he never arrived. No trace of him has ever been found. Apparently the German border guards detained the entire group. If Felsen had been taken to an internment or concentration camp, he would have been able to send at least one message. I believe that he perished right there, at the border.

Before the war, at the Salle Lascaze, a meeting of the National Workers

Union,[6] where Georgy Ivanov had found a niche for himself, was for some reason devoted to literature. At that meeting they heaped fierce abuse on Adamovich, honoring him with all the epithets so dear to their hearts, from Smerdyakov to Judas. From the back rows they also hurled "kike" and "bastard." It was then that Felsen asked for the floor and launched into a defense, not so much of Adamovich as of our new literature, which was entirely indebted to him. He spoke softly, firmly, and with his usual moderation, so that he impressed even this rather mixed, uncultivated crowd.

If Yury Felsen had tried to conceal his Jewish background from the Germans, he would undoubtedly have succeeded. I do not know where and under what circumstances he died, but I am convinced that he did not betray his inborn courage and dignity, did not show either weakness or fear and, above all, did not ask the enemy for mercy.

Chapter 3 · G. Fedotov

PUSHKIN IS: THE EMPIRE AND FREEDOM.—G. FEDOTOV

A thin, youngish face, heavy Byzantine eyebrows, a professor with a beard à la Lenin and an ingratiating, soft, persuasive voice with the gutteral "r" of a Russian nobleman. The general impression is one of compliance and delicacy, yet, at the same time, his every word is like a nail, fastening down a clear, definite, courageous thought.

In his articles, Georgy Petrovich Fedotov was overly literary and florid, often irritating his readers, particularly those who did not know him personally. But if the words were supported by that soft musical voice with its irregular breath (the heart!)—soft and musical but insistent when it came to the ultimate truths—then another dimension, as it were, was added to Fedotov's writing. And whether we agreed with him or not, he aroused in us a patriotic pride thanks to this wonderful mixture of the new and the thoroughly familiar—of Russia and Europe.

Men like him, combining musical pliancy with prophetic wrath and hatred with love for their country, could be found mainly in that Russia which always counted itself a part of Europe. These were men like Pecherin,* Chaadaev, Herzen and, perhaps, Solovyov.

Incidentally, despite its colossal historical perversions, Germany has not produced a single thinker of stature who had the courage to confess his country's sins and expose the national canker.

Everything in Fedotov appeared fluid, contradictory, unstable, everything except his universal Orthodoxy and formal democratic convictions. The somewhat unusual combination of these two principles created one more seeming contradiction, repelling potential allies (but also attracting adherents from the opposite camp).

I often, almost nightly, saw Georgy Petrovich in the thirties—at the

---

*Vladimir Sergeevich Pecherin, professor of Greek, emigrated to Ireland, where he became a Jesuit priest.

meetings of the Circle or the board of the Circle and at the Inner Circle, the Post-Revolutionary Club, and so on. He was the only religious philosopher among my close acquaintances who courageously acknowledged the responsibility of the Orthodox Church in Russia's difficult history. And with what joy he did cling to anything new and beautiful that blossomed around us in the emigration. "Now, with Mother Marie," he thrilled, "the social task has forever entered into the Orthodox Church. It will merely have to be continued by others."

Fedotov's belief in the ideals of democracy was another rare phenomenon. For the first time in Russian thought, Orthodoxy united its ideals with formal democracy, thus proving *de facto* that there are no canonical reasons for clinging to a caesar, a sultan or any other kind of autocratic ruler. How such an Orthodoxy could have further evolved is testified by the fact that in the Paris of those years very many eagerly joined the Russian Church, among them not only formerly indifferent classical sceptics but also French Catholics, Russians of the Jewish faith, and even militant atheists.

It has become the custom to speak about the "special note" in Parisian Russian literature (or poetry), but this is inadequate. The special Parisian note could also be found in philosophy and theology, in political activity and in the arts. Even in chess. The entire spirit was "special"; a miraculous metamorphosis was taking place under our very eyes. The Latin graft onto the semi-wild maximalistic Russian root turned out to be a creative success. In this respect, Father Bulgakov, Mother Marie, and Fedotov were just as life-giving for the future European Russia as our young literary generation.

French white bread and red wine nourished everyone equally, and the Roman perception of nationality as a legal attribute—without racial or religious criteria—turned out to be nothing less than a revelation.

Georgy Petrovich played his role in this creative flowering perhaps precisely because of his external ambiguity. He stood in the middle between philosophy and theology, between history and poetry, literature and politics. Equally cherishing the Russian rennet apple and the French "duchesse" pear, the past and the future, everyday life and existential potentialities, he was loath to give up anything that fell within the framework of Western Christianity.

Poplavsky once said to him by way of reproach: "Even if your convictions demanded it, you would never agree to blow up Chartres Cathedral." And Merezhkovsky, who was sitting next to us, gleefully seconded: "Yes, that's exactly the point!"

I don't remember Georgy Petrovich's answer. I think he was indeed incapable of blowing up Gothic cathedrals—and not necessarily from pusillanimity. However, in the days of the Spanish civil war he wrote an article about La Pasionaria, declaring that she represented historical justice. This expressed the feelings of the majority of us at the time.

The Spanish campaign was the turning-point in the life of many Europeans. We awakened from a marvelous religious-poetic dream. The civil war knocked with its hideous fist at our windows, and we had to ally ourselves with the lesser evil. That was the only choice. Some immediately left for Madrid, others were endlessly preparing to go there. By tradition and ideology most of us felt intimately linked with the legal republican government. History was again repeating itself; again it was neither Lenin nor Kolchak! And once again democracy fouled up its chances. If *they* had in good time limited the freedom of the citizens, arrested the generals, communists and anarchists, directed the economy with an iron hand and given work and bread to the populace, then the regime could perhaps have been saved. But what would have remained of democracy? Here was the age-old problem of how to square the circle. Christianity plus Democracy! became the motto of Fondaminsky's and Fedotov's *Novy grad (New City),* seconded from Germany by Professor Fyodor Stepun. What, however, would it have meant in practice? Where and when had such a regime ever come into existence? If police and sanitation workers are needed, isn't it better to install them independently of the Scriptures and the Holy Trinity?

Fedotov's words on La Pasionaria emotionally answered many of our "accursed" problems and reconciled the most blatant contradictions. Many things around us became, if not clearer, at least more acceptable. Not for nothing did one "exemplary personality," a professor at the Orthodox Institute, where Fedotov taught, demand the latter's exclusion as "a covert Free Mason and Marxist." Since the institute was supported by Anglican philanthropists, it was easy to silence this "exemplary Christian." But the fight cost Fedotov a lot of inner energy. On the other hand, the incident drew him closer to us, the young writers.

Every day or so Fondaminsky was wont to organize a new emigré group. The task of giving it an ideological frame was always poor Georgy Petrovich's duty, including anniversary speeches and congratulatory addresses. It was pathetic to behold how he coped heroically with it all. But his soul grew visibly tired from the never-ending round of "banquets" under the aegis of Fondaminsky. On top of it, he had to feed a family, another drain on his vital forces.

In the summer, the Fedotovs rode off on women's bicycles to the Loire and along the valley with its knightly castles and great cathedrals.

Georgy Petrovich adored the Gallic soil, its impressionistic vegetation and severe Gothic, its white bread, acidulous wine, its cheeses, and the temperamental, hot-blooded but extraordinarily sensible French people, where the logic of Pascal and Descartes might find an echo in a concierge or a pimp. Bunin would drink a glass of Veuve Clicquot* and boisterously swear that in Moscow even the champagne was better! And the sturgeon, and the caviar, and the Volga . . . after which followed the entire culinary nonsense à la Kryuchkov the Cossack.[1]

Fedotov knew the grandeur of French history; he did not argue when I declared that civilization was started around the Mediterranean by brown-eyed people. But he always, with unshakable, soft stubbornness, pointed out to us the horrors of the revolutions that had taken place in the Latin world. The question of whether there had ever been a revolution in England very seriously occupied us at that time. It all came down to this: is it possible to humanize a filthy regime, avoiding fratricidal mutations?

Came the fatal days of the autumn of 1938 which ended, after a partial mobilization, with the complete defeat at Munich.** Immediately, a great many vipers began to stir in different emigré corners, preparing to climb onto Hitler's bandwagon. Fedotov was the only one in our circle who defended Munich. This we could not forgive him.

La Pasionaria and Munich! These two halves are equally important for an understanding of Fedotov. His reasoning went more or less along the following lines: regardless of who emerged victorious, a modern global war would lead to the final destruction of the old, inimitable Europe. Therefore it was better to lie low behind the Maginot Line[2] and continue praying, building cathedrals, and writing poems as long as there was still the slightest chance.

We countered: "Even if the Maginot Line fulfills its purpose, the fetid stench of living and dead corpses will reach us from across the border. Creative freedom will be smothered, inspired prayer stifled, and the greatest architectural marvels will lose their convincing power."

In the winter we organized the Inner Circle, a sort of order meant to exist clandestinely and to continue the struggle in the approaching long night. Unanimously we voted against Fedotov's candidacy.

"It's to laugh!" howled Fondaminsky. "You accept Zhaba and reject Georgy Petrovich! It's to laugh," he repeated his favorite expression.

---

*A champagne.
**The decision to partition Czechoslovakia.

"You disagreed with Fedotov on one point. But Munich is over, it's already in the past. New problems are arising in areas where Georgy Petrovich may be ahead of us all."

Indeed, it was absurd, and Fedotov and his wife were invited to join the Inner Circle. At the first meeting of this new organization, Mrs. Fedotov inquired bluntly: "Shall we again do nothing but talk here, or shall we perhaps begin throwing bombs? That's what I'd like to know." It was indicative of our mood at the time.

Later, already in New York toward the end of the war, I was supposed to "examine" Fedotov. Irma Manziarli, Helen Iswolsky, Arthur Lourié, and I were starting the *Third Hour,* a magazine of ecumenical and post-revolutionary character. In every issue there were articles by Berdyaev; but Fedotov, who was here, near to us, we did not even invite to our meetings. This is how we punished him for his hostile attitude toward the Soviet Union, even at the time of Stalingrad.

I remember how once, in the middle of the day, he came to Iswolsky's place; she and I were apparently supposed to decide whether he fitted into the *Third Hour*—whether he was good enough. Fedotov had just suffered another heart attack and was very sick; he spoke unevenly, with a failing voice, while taking quick small sips of the red wine the *Third Hour,* loyal to the old Parisian tradition, always served. With a mirthless laugh, Fedotov said: "You don't accept me but you publish Kasem-Bek." And I could hear Fondaminsky's familiar, "It's to laugh!" On leaving, Fedotov sadly summarized our talk: "Right now there are no real disagreements between us. You want a German defeat and the triumph of democracy. I want the same. Our disagreements will begin the day after victory."

Like Churchill, only significantly earlier, Fedotov asserted that Soviet Russia had to be kept away from Europe, and the latter temporarily frozen, lest all its rotted parts crumble to pieces. I argued with him. But now I have to admit that his basic intuition was right. I gather that he never dared to express fully his comprehensive vision of Russia, her history, her church, and even her people.

"Russia must come back to Europe and stay a long time as her pupil, as her younger sister, or she will be strangled, thrown back to the East and dismembered." So I often understood his speeches and they seemed to me the ravings of a madman. But in the light of the latest Chinese historical moves, Georgy Petrovich's prophecies became reality. And no sputniks will help, just as the V1 and V2 did not help the Germans. He who fights against the entire world on two fronts is bound to perish.

The burden of the ideological struggle within the *Novy grad* lay on Fedotov's shoulders. I. I. Fondaminsky was primarily a planner and organizer; Georgy Petrovich was supposed to make fresh water run through the laid-out pipes.

Among the Socialist Revolutionaries, I. I. Fondaminsky was considered a brilliant orator. This, like Kerensky's highly praised eloquence, is one of the myths of the era. We listened to Fondaminsky with a smile. When once, before an important debate, I advised him to keep his speech short, definitely not longer than forty minutes, he was genuinely surprised: "I used to speak for hours without stopping, and yet everyone listened." he said in timid self-commendation.

And, of course, he was not lying. Before the summer attack of 1917, Kerensky intoxicated the soldiers at the front with his speeches; and the sailors of the Black Fleet carried their commissar, Fondaminsky, on their arms. And there also was Chkheidze. At that time they were all considered Jaurèses of the Russian Revolution. Magic? Stupidity? The stupidity of single individuals or of an entire epoch?

I felt embarrassed listening to Kerensky and Fondaminsky, as if in the presence of the naked emperor—another moment, and the people would see the truth. They were both highly endowed emotionally, but each in his own way was limited or simply not intelligent enough. I always suffered during their orations and waited impatiently for the end, as if I were responsible for their childish babble.

Pavel Nikolaevich Milyukov sounded a wholly different note: alien, three-dimensional, but solidly grounded, protected, if not from a hurricane than at least from an occasional downpour.

Fondaminsky frittered away his strength by trying to penetrate the maximum number of groups and organizations, to teach everyone about Russian humanism, democracy, and the great order of the intelligentsia. Presumably, if he—or we—were asked to come, it meant yet one more victory for the forces of good.

I persistently pointed out to him that beyond the confines of his apartment at 130 ave. de Versailles, there was not one place where we could count on 51 percent of the votes—a fact that called into question the wisdom of our tactics. Also, for us as men of letters, it was absurd to affiliate ourselves with so many groups and organizations while we ourselves had no organ of our own. Fondaminsky could not see the point; besides, he naturally felt reluctant to enter into competition with the *Sovremennye zapiski*. Being a "professional optimist," he always repeated: "Wait, just wait a while, and we'll take over the *Sovremennye zapiski.*" But Fedotov supported me, as did my contemporaries, notably

Sofiev, who was versed in diplomatic negotiations. I do not remember the details, but at the next meeting of the Board, Fondaminsky announced that there would be a new journal, *Krug (The Circle)*.

On Fedotov's initiative we began to assemble once a month for "agapes," as we called them. Tables were set up in Fondaminsky's study, covered with tablecloths and heaped with bottles of red wine, sandwiches, and fruit. Instead of the usual lecture and debate, there was spontaneous, undirected, friendly conversation lasting deep into the night. At moments it seemed that indeed love, *caritas,* was floating around, transfiguring us . . . Meanwhile, however, horrible times were approaching. Many of those present were already marked by fate: Mother Marie, Fondaminsky, Vildé, Felsen, Yury Mandelshtam . . . each in his own way. Alas, others, like Judas, having secured for themselves a place in Hitler's *baggage,* were already jingling their new bright silver pieces.

As I, in my mind, contemplate all those faces, inspired with future suffering or stamped with the seal of Cain, I am mainly struck by the utter lack of surprises in our groups. The cards had been dealt long ago and lay open-faced on the table: in this sense, the game was played almost honestly.

Once a week, I believe on Tuesdays, the Fedotovs received in their "studio." There, surrounded by young girls—daughter Nina and her friends—young seminarians of the Orthodox Institute boomed with as yet unsteady voices; we Montparnassians also dropped by, most frequently Sofiev.

Georgy Petrovich made a point of acting the fatherly professor and only for rare moments permitted himself to get involved in the conversation, soon to fall silent again, his Byzantine eyes continuing to shine under bushy beetle brows.

Sofiev would sing romances and declaim poetry; he behaved like a young officer or student and was a great success with the ladies. Thanks to him, the future priests also became imbued with romantic proclivities. One young woman, the mother of two children, was a frequent visitor and so was the seminarian Zh., already in a monk's habit. Zh. avidly longed for an ascetic career and wrote his dissertation on the subject of monkhood, comparing it to the Lord's bride of the Song of Songs. So, Zh. fell in love with the pretty mother, who promptly left her husband for him. But later, Zh. became the victim of yet another temptation: he went to England, married the daughter of an Anglican clergyman, and himself became a priest in the "High" Church of England.

The host did not interfere with this atmosphere of flirtatious youth. If anything, he stimulated it in some esoteric way. With his trim beard, Fedotov presented the aspect of a middle-aged professor, a serious thinker or publicist. And he did not dress at all romantically. As a matter of fact, he dressed badly, untidily. Very rarely did any of us acquire brand-new garments. The mainstay for procuring clothes was the *marché aux puces*,* where one could chance upon wonderful bargains from the great houses of sports *couture*. But Georgy Petrovich spurned even this source. And the suits that well-intentioned philanthropists passed on to him were all, as if especially chosen, dark, boring, and of the wrong size.

I would say that, in general, in our circles the style of "voluntary poverty" (or something close to it) reigned. Even those who had money behaved as if they were ashamed of being well-off. No one in Russian Paris doubted that "Money is a sin!" Thus, when Fondaminsky one fine day showed up in a new tweed suit, he guiltily and at length explained that certain friends had insisted that he order it. "I don't need it at all. But they say it's disgraceful how I'm showing off my rags."

Poplavsky liked to say with some malice: "Give a Russian intellectual a belt for his pants and he'll still put on suspenders. He has no respect for his own belly, no faith in it." Indeed, when Fedotov took off his jacket in the heat of summer, he proudly exposed a belt *plus* suspenders. But the reason for it was that the pants, never having been intended for him, did not fit. At one of the first meetings in New York, Fedotov enfolded himself in an overcoat of such infinite breadth that it amazed us all.

And yet, despite his accentuated appearance of an untidily dressed middle-aged professor, certain definitely erotic, soft, soothing, feminine fluids flowed abundantly and tangibly from Georgy Petrovich. There is a Russian line of eroticism, stemming from Dostoevsky, Solovyov, and Rozanov, which holds that ancient gods can be in harmony with Byzantium, the Church, and the Old Testament. Such a magnetic field clearly made itself felt around Fedotov.

My impression is that he was never quite in his place, that he was a man who could not or did not dare to fully express himself. I think he always heaved a sigh of relief when he finally remained alone, with his books and a cup of tasteless tea.

I remember how once, on the west side, two burly moving men invaded Fedotov's apartment to carry away or bring to another floor Nina Fedotov's piano (she used to practice assiduously in her youth). Deliberations began between the ladies and the muscular blacks. Certain

---

*Flea market.

formalities had not been observed, and minor difficulties arose. The professor, meanwhile, in one rather discreditable motion, gathered up the tea, the book, and the folds of his robe, planning to sneak discreetly into his den. But mother and daughter cried out in one voice, "Oh, you coward!" thereby attracting my attention to this memorable scene. At different times I had occasion to observe this whirlabout "treacherous" movement of his, away from one or another everyday vicissitude. This was not mere cowardice: he was fully aware of his utter helplessness in practical matters.

The terrible fall of 1939 was approaching. In August, the finest specimens of Scandinavian blondes were still thronging Paris. The old-timers claimed that not in years had Montparnasse experienced such *joie de vivre* and thirst for sin. The Luxembourg Gardens were suffocating under the weight of flowers and lust.

Finally, the radio announced the friendly meeting of Stalin and Ribbentrop in Moscow. And soon we could watch in the newsreels as the Poles sent their cavalry against Krupp's heavy tanks. The horsemen, in uniforms like those of the Russian Akhtirka Hussars, flung themselves against the fire-spitting steel towers and immediately turned into smoking flesh. Only fools like Stalin and Hitler could think that they had succeeded in liquidating this immortal nation.

And then, on 1 September, I believe, an enigmatic sentence flashed in the paper: "England and France are in a state of war with Germany. . . . *dans un état de guerre. Mobilisation générale.*"

Once again there were the posters with two crossed tricolors. Everything went into motion: men streamed out with rifles on makeshift holders and no clips, dressed in the sky-blue cotton uniforms of 1918. Chalked onto the wooden shutter of the neighborhood bistro: closed— *pour la durée.*

There is a fountain in the Luxembourg Gardens, stocked with fat fish in the fall. On moonlit nights this toy body of water could supposedly become a reference point for enemy aircraft. (The government anticipates everything!) It was ordered drained immediately, the first public execution (of fish) followed. Soldiers from an anti-aircraft battery installed in the bushes in front of the Senate waded into the tiny basin. In puttees and heavy boots and armed with nets, they inspiredly caught the shocked fish. The men's backs were sweatsoaked under the sun, the long, youthful necks tanned. But their profiles, the slightly aquiline nose of Gauls and Franks, testified that this was Europe, the West, France, the first daughter of the Catholic church and not patriarchal Orthodox Russia, herded together from the villages by clever officials to fight their historical enemy. Meanwhile the fish, taken out of the water, suffered, opening their mouths reproachfully, pitifully contemplating the cloudless sky: the unforgettable, blessed Roman sky of *Lutèce*.

I was rushing to a meeting of the presidium of the Circle and it was getting late; but I could not tear myself away from this crowd, this exemplary garden, this magically shining, alien, blessed, impressionistic picture. (Later, however, when misfortune gripped these people in earnest, the same crowd began playing its role according to classical patterns; the day before the Germans entered, I had an experience at the Convention métro station somewhat similar to the scene of Vereshchagin's execution in *War and Peace*.)

So I was in a hurry for the meeting of the Circle, but I never got there—I was carried off by the general, heroic, festive whirlwind. Directly facing the barrel of an anti-aircraft gun was the branch of a young tree: they were about to saw it off when one of the soldiers had an inspiration and hastily tied up the branch so that it was no longer obstructing the muzzle. (Even the slender young sergeant smiled happily, glad that the innocent tree had been spared.) Where are you, dear *poilu* from the Landes or Provence? Who, within a year, will throw your frozen body into a crowded German grave? Or did you perhaps escape from a prisoner-of-war camp to become a hero of the black market, assuring your neighbors that it wasn't worth fighting for Jews and foreigners?

From the very beginning of the war we moved, spellbound, in circles. Our personal and professional lives changed radically. Many of us were mobilized or volunteered; others were waiting to be called up and already felt like true recruits. Working conditions were turned topsy-turvy, families shuffled about like cards, and new romantic possibilities opened up. Intellectual encounters became rarer and less meaningful: the muses fall silent when machine guns speak.

Fondaminsky, nevertheless, organized a new group, a Franco-Russian one, in which emigré "generals" were supposed to debate with French *intellectuels*. Of the latter I knew only Gabriel Marcel, soon to become the leader of the Catholic existentialist movement. We, the young generation, were not invited (for lack of space). I considered this an affront and appeared, uninvited, at the first meeting. Fondaminsky only sighed as he let me in. When I complained to Fedotov about the arrangement, he said with a knowing laugh: "That's how he acts with me too. Ilya Isidorovich rates each of us differently. You, for instance, get a nine, I an eleven. That's the whole difference."

These particular meetings, however, did not fulfill my expectations; and I soon stopped attending them. Berdyaev spoke about the national

soul; Marcel (and someone else from the Sorbonne) countered very soberly: "All this is very nice and interesting, but right now we are at war
with a merciless enemy, and we have to defeat him at any price."

Such practical speeches made a bad impression—too simple and shallow. Although all of us welcomed the war and considered it sacred, no
one envisaged a concrete victory. The overall mood was utterly apocalyptic. Schooled by bitter experience, the entire spectrum of the Russian
emigration subconsciously expected a catastrophe and could not believe
in victory. "Yes," many among us thought, "the sun will rise again one
day, but in the meantime a long night is setting in and we have to plod
through it."

The winter of the "phony" war was starting, in which nothing
"phony" could be observed. I celebrated New Year's Eve 1940 at the
Fedotovs. Of the older generation there was only Mother Marie. Fondaminsky had promised to drop by but got waylaid. The Oldenburg
family came, including daughter Zoe, then a modest pupil at the lycée
(now a famous French writer). My wife and I brought along a young
Montparnassian, "for the girls." There was vodka, wine, herring, vinai-
grette, ham, salads, everything as it ought to be. But there was no joy.
That New Year's Eve resembled a wake. We attempted to make the
customary noises, to be gay, sing, pronounce patriotic speeches, and
clink glasses, but something was amiss: our insides knew a truth which
reason refused to accept.

For many this was the last year in Paris and for some the last year of
life. We were burying the old, splendid, poverty-stricken, creative,
Gallo-Russian past and, with it, glorious European humanism. Striding
toward us were neo-cannibals, neo-Cains, neo-primitives. History
moves in spirals: Herzen describes the New Year's Eve of 1852 in similar
terms: "At midnight, the usual toast was offered—we smiled tensely;
inside us was death and horror, we all felt ashamed to make any wish
whatsoever for the New Year. To look ahead was more frightening than
to look back."

At our gathering, Fedotov forced himself, at midnight, to deliver a
speech with conventional fervor. Then Mother Marie spoke. Wrapped in
a black shawl, with sickly-red cheeks, snub-nosed, very Russian, she
nevertheless resembled Teresa of Ávila. I do not remember what she
said, but I know that she did not evince any particular optimism.

Somehow we floundered through this "phony" winter and managed
to pay the spring rent. In Paris lilacs bloomed as usual, lanterns cast their
greenish light in the evening, life triumphed, and the prostitutes ceased
carrying their awkward gas mask containers.

And, on 10 May, the Germans broke though the lines at notorious

Sédan and pushed toward the sea. A couple of days later all Frenchmen realized that the war was lost: Paris would be abandoned. In a garage near Métro Pasteur there were already fugitives from Lille sleeping on straw . . . how it all resembled the lice-ridden Russian railroad stations or the *centres d'accueil* of the time of the Spanish civil war. One could say that in misfortune, nations resemble each other. It is only success and wealth that develop new traits in them.

After a long interruption, I was once again on my way to Fondaminsky. I needed information. After all, these veterans of catastrophes had connections; they ought to know exactly what we should prepare ourselves for. It was daytime, and Fondaminsky's dining room was lit by the rays of the spring sun. There I found Solovechik, Ivanovich and others engrossed in a strange occupation. They were checking off names, mostly of the older generation, against a list lying before them. From what followed I gathered that, at the beginning of May, Kerensky had gone to the precinct of the 16th *arrondissement* to make an application for exit from Paris for the entire "group." (After the beginning of the war, foreigners were of course forbidden to travel without special permit.) Solovechik was about to go to the police to get the certificates; but since some of the members of the group had left long ago on their own, it seemed appropriate to go over the list once more.

It had not even occurred to Fondaminsky to include some of the younger ones. Later, when America sent "special" visas, again only the famous, respected figures were considered. Incidentally, at precisely that moment I was trying to get my pregnant wife legally out of the capital but was unable to secure a *sauf conduit* for her. (I did not even bother about one for myself.)

Fondaminsky asked me with restrained solicitude: "And you, what do you plan to do?"

On Monday, 10 June, I dropped by at the Fedotovs in the evening. If I'm not mistaken, I tried to include my wife in a caravan of friends who were leaving Paris. It turned out that Georgy Petrovich had not yet managed to get hold of his permit and planned to retrieve it the next day from Fondaminsky. I advised them to take the very first train in the morning, to forget about official documents, and not to lose precious time.

"Just go out into the empty streets and smell the air," I said, "and you'll understand that the gates of the city are wide open."

This evaluation appealed to Mrs. Fedotov. "Yes, just go out and smell the air! No certificates are needed!" she repeated eagerly.

On this we separated. The next day I managed to put my wife on a train. I left a day later, on 12 June. Toward the evening of 13 June, the Germans were at the gates of Paris.

Many Russians left the train at Poitiers. We didn't really know what was going on. I still vaguely hoped that there would be resistance at the Loire: new armies would take over the south bank, and we would all do our duty. This wrong appraisal of the situation probably cost many good people their lives.

In Poitiers, the Grjebine family, with whom I traveled, and I lost a couple of precious days (during which the "optimists" got transit visas and crossed the Spanish border at Irun). There, in the *centre d'accueil*, I ran into Gershenkron, one of the most valued collaborators in the Circle; he had planned to seek refuge at a famous monastery near Poitiers and had lost his way. Always highstrung, he was now extremely upset; he too did not realize what was going on. Actually, we could not reconcile ourselves to the thought that France was about to capitulate. Besides, we all were badly off as far as finances were concerned. Gershenkron almost immediately began to voice complaints about Mother Marie: they had bumped into each other in the crowd at the Gare de Lyon, where she was seeing off Mochulsky and her son Yury. (She herself had decided to stay on in Paris.) They had all previously acquired tickets and Kerensky's permits. But Yury did not want to leave and beseeched his mother to let him stay. So it happened that poor Gershenkron bought Yury's ticket, for cash.

"What did I need this ticket for?" he said plaintively, having apparently spent his last francs in Poitiers. "After all, you made it without any tickets."

There, in the big square of Poitiers, where the refugees rested at noon in the café, general attention was suddenly attracted by a strange cavalcade consisting of three women's and one man's bicycles: the Fedotovs, followed by Nordic, blond, dishevelled Nina, and by Vadim Andreev, who resembled an Algerian. Having missed the last train, they had made the entire journey from Paris on their bicycles, pedalling for four or five days straight. Luckily they had found a sensible companion in Andreev.

The roads of France are wonderful in the summer; nevertheless, Michelin maps abound in arrows indicating "steep slopes." This bicycle trip—not undertaken in order to admire ancient castles—was Professor Fedotov's last sporting achievement. In New York he soon developed the coronary thrombosis from which he was later to die.

There, in Poitiers, we once again took leave of one another. Fedotov rushed into a liquor store and emerged, turning an oddly shaped bottle round in his hands, his face reflecting amazement. Nina made a snide remark, apparently not approving the purchase.

They had decided to go west, toward the Channel, not southwest, where Fondaminsky had settled near Bordeaux. Andreev's family and the Sosinskys now lived on the Ile de Ré, and in that direction, toward the very foundation of Hitler's future Atlantic Wall, the women's bicycles were now headed.

This meeting of ours seemed to be something out of a nightmare. Indeed, during those marvelous June days, all of France resembled an evil dream, while Charles de Gaulle painfully and slowly underwent the metamorphosis from provincial colonel to legendary leader.

All around us there were weary crowds from the cities—old people and children—sleeping on the ground, on straw, on the grass. From the nearby *chaussée* came the rustling of biblical locusts—thousands of citizens trudging south, dragging their suitcases and arthritic limbs.

For the young and sturdy ones it was easy: stepping on those who lagged behind, they advanced! A comforting thought: we simply have to calculate things so that political, social, and geological upheavals occur during the period in our lives when we are at our biological and spiritual best.

Despite the deprivations, these weeks would remain in the memories of many of us as a blissful period of freedom, a vacation, a liberation from the captivity of the city. Having a snack at a fountain from Gallo-Roman times, sipping warm wine in the company of practical, intelligent southerners, it was still possible to bless the sun, France, and life! But I truly pity people who had to undergo this kind of trial in Poland, Belgium, or Manchuria. What injustice in the fate of nations, assuming that the basic sins—greed, lust, stupidity, anger, envy—are about the same everywhere.

In fact, what can rival the landscape of Latin Europe, its climate, which not only makes it possible to indulge in painting all the year round but also to reap two or three harvests of potatoes? (On such soil there cannot be chronic, endemic hunger as, remember, has always existed in Russia—be it Tartar, tsarist, or socialist.)

And let's allow snow and ice for winter sports, one month a year. Even Tatiana,* the owner of a couple of hundred "souls,"** could not explain why it was she so loved the frosts of Russian Christmas. I have a sneaking suspicion that if she could have managed to get away and end up under Pushkin's "eternally blue sky," she, too, perhaps would have defected. (Pushkin was unconditionally refused a passport to travel abroad; in this respect, Gogol and Turgenev were lucky.)

---

*Tatiana Larina, from Pushkin's *Eugene Onegin*.
**Serfs.

A year later the Fedotovs turned up in Marseilles to receive their American visas. From Marseilles they sent me a long letter to Montpellier, giving all sorts of practical advice and promising their help.

Special boats traveled rarely; Mrs. Fedotov, anxious about her husband's fate, put him on the first available ship, from which he landed directly in a concentration camp at Dakar.

My wife, who was at that time again in Paris, told me later that Fondaminsky, who had also returned to Paris, continued to rush from one meeting to another and quite often joked: "Fedotov ran away to Africa and landed in a camp. Think of it, in Africa! Yet we are still here. Here we can still work."

In July 1942, when I finally reached New York with my family, Mrs. Fedotov greeted us on the pier and handed me twenty dollars which she had collected from among friends. In this first year of our second exile we still met frequently. But there was no longer any special closeness. As if we all felt ashamed of some hastily uttered, superfluous words. And of hasty, superfluous words there had been many.

In the United States all of us had to pass yet one more test. The problem consisted in preserving one's personal status in an atmosphere of a general "revaluation of values." For the first time I had no social circle, group, or other uniting force backing me. Here, the Russians had their own prophets and "generals" demanding respect and even reverence. The reigning literary style seemed to be in the vein of Riga; now that the "Europeans" were arriving en masse, the number of the dissatisfied and offended grew from day to day. Fedotov, of course, became associated with the *Novy zhurnal* (New Journal); but there was no Fondaminsky there, and Fedotov couldn't but feel as out of place as a white crow.

His articles and lectures worried me. I had left France when the first artillery volleys were sounding at Stalingrad, and all of Europe was once again listening to the thunder of battle on that latter-day Kulikovo Field.[3] Every one of us knew that the fate of the humanistic heritage was being decided there. Unwittingly, Stalin was defending Jerusalem, Athens, Rome, as well as Jewish refugees from Austria. At the American consulate in Marseilles I met some who asked with horror and hope: "What do you think, will they hold Sevastopol?"

It so happened that the naive American government, fearing provocation or blackmail, had introduced a new rule according to which persons born on territory already taken over by the Germans could not be issued a visa. As a result, factories for the production of false birth certificates and other documents sprang up and blossomed; and the Austrian who wanted to know whether the Russians would be holding the Crimea—

his newly acquired place of birth—had a vital interest in an affirmative answer.

It was not only Sevastopol or Russia that the Soviet people were defending at that time but all that was being abused or persecuted in the world. And the prayers of saints as well as of weak and sinful victims or heroes were at that time with Russia, with that Russia which was again saintly and great, that Russia which, in a last passionate burst, had once again corrected her mistakes, atoning for her guilt by brotherly alliance with the enlightened Western nations.

So it was during the times of the Tartars and of Karl of Sweden who set out to conquer the world. The same happened to Napoleon and twice in our memory to the Germans. In each instance Russia, at the last moment, straightened out, supported by an angel or archangel, to assume its responsible place at the side of the traditionally Christian, humanitarian nations. (In particular, smaller incidents, the princes, tsars, and commissars, alas, sinned, and sinned very badly indeed.) What happened then will repeat itself tomorrow, perhaps in a decisive confrontation with the Chinese or with the combined armies from Venus and Mars.

At night I walked through the deserted streets of Montpellier, swept by a harsh breeze from the sea. I was on my way home from the café where I played chess with refugees from Spain. The East was brightening, and the sky seemed to pulsate with innumerable explosions of heavy artillery. I all but felt those distant blows, and the air funnels stopped my breath. I seemed to distinguish in the sky an enormous, rearing mare, snarling and neighing, and with her forelegs fighting off a pack of wolves on the snow-covered steppe. She gingerly retreats toward the Volga, and the face of the mare is awesome, with fire blazing from her nostrils.

In such a mood we sailed off to the New World. Yet Fedotov, as at the time of Munich, permitted himself to hold fast to his opinion. The disagreement, of course, was not about the present, in which we had to fight and, by all means, to win. This he did not deny. The divergences began in connection with the future which, according to Fedotov, would be ugly and shameful.

We imagined that after her saintly effort in concert with Europe, something would have to shift, inadvertently change, even in Stalin's Russia. The USSR would return, by right, to Europe, and Europe would again accept Russia.

It was precisely this that Fedotov bitterly denied. He implored, threatened, and cursed. As I already said, Russia, according to his prophetic words, should be kept out of Europe at any price, should not be allowed to cross its historical borders, lest it put an end to Western culture.

Fedotov claimed that even the ethnic type of the urban Russian had already changed, judging by newsreels and photos in magazines. Asia was transforming Russia from the inside, devouring parts of Europe. Such arguments, at a time when our friends were dying in the camps, in prison, or on the front, aroused our anger and even hostility.

I lived on the same street as Georgy Petrovich, on West 122nd Street, next to Union Theological Seminary, where he taught and had his quarters. By then he was very sick and often stayed for weeks in his small room that resembled a monk's cell, except for the eternal sordid left-over tea.

At about that time, the I.s arrived from Munich. Fedotov got involved in helping them to settle down, and they quickly became friends. He took I. under his wing, introduced him to the important Russian public figures, stayed out late, and obviously exhausted himself.

This sudden spurt of activity can only be explained by his great need for disciples. In Russia, two generations of students would have listened to Fedotov, thus according him what constitutes the secret of success of any spiritual leader. From his Parisian friends Fedotov could not expect this degree of recognition. Our relationships—whether with Berdyaev, Shestov, or Merezhkovsky—were always based on an exchange of views: each of us had his own opinions and tried to put them across. The result was a healthy circulation of ideas, proof of a living creature: a give-and-take. Some gave less and took more, but all participated in the sharing. I. became Fedotov's pupil, and this must have been a comfort to the professor in the last stage of his life.

Fedotov had found a panacea for Russia: Pushkin! "Pushkin stands for the Empire and Freedom." And his adepts repeated enthusiastically: "The Empire and Freedom!"

Once, in Paris, I had asked him: "What if the Empire fights Freedom? 'To the Slanderers of Russia,'⁴ *The Gavriiliada,* what are we to do about such trash?" However, with respect to Poland he responded unwaveringly: "That is our sin."

Occasionally I would meet Fedotov in the evening as he trotted, alone, toward Amsterdam Avenue to a cheap restaurant and on to a dark, half-black movie house (now razed). We would talk for a while on my stoop, as if on the Boulevard St. Michel.

Fedotov: "It's good that you find some elements of gnosticism in St. Paul. If there were many, it would be bad."

I pointed out that there was more Manichean heresy in St. Augustine than Montanist heresy in Tertullian.

"What's important is the direction. The former moved from heresy to the Church while the latter moved from the Church to heresy," explained Georgy Petrovich and laughed when I remarked: "As far as I'm concerned all those Africans remind me of Dzerzhinsky."

At that time my *Amerikansky opyt* (American Experience) was being published in the *Novy zhurnal* and torn to pieces by all the mediocrities in our emigration. Georgy Petrovich was one of my few defenders.

In the name of the editors of the journal, Maria Zetlin always invited the contributors to her drawing room for a discussion of the latest issue. I, the author of a big controversial novel, was not invited, an ommision that might be expected from true democrats.

In the absence of Yanovsky, the honorable and childless dinosaurs were free to act without embarrassment. Poor Mikhail Mikhailovich Karpovich, the editor-in-chief, was forced to hold up further printing of my *Amerikansky opyt* for an issue or two. The attacks against me were made mainly in the name of American patriotism. I was accused of being a Fascist sympathizer. Thanks to Fedotov and a few other benevolent souls—I believe Helene Iswolsky and Aleksandrova—Karpovich managed to carry the series through to the end. I must say that with the death of my old acquaintance M. O. Zetlin, it became easier to conduct business with the *Novy zhurnal,* that is, with M. M. Karpovich alone.

"That's because of our *printsipialnost,"* Fedotov explained with a mirthless smile. "That's our curse, the Russian intelligentsia's reliance on principles. It transforms civilized, good people into censors and gendarmes. But Karpovich comes from a completely different milieu."

At the very beginning of my stay in New York I dropped in at a reception given by the Club of the New Arrivals from Europe; at the end of the meeting we all got stuck at the cloakroom on account of Fedotov.

"Are you looking for your galoshes?" I asked facetiously. (According to Nina Fedotov, the first thing her father did upon his arrival in the New World was to purchase a pair of galoshes, which reminded him of the old Russian ones sold under the brand name of Treugolnik.)

It turned out that Georgy Petrovich had lost his check and was unable to describe his overcoat. We had to wait until the crowd dispersed; and even then he eyed his garment doubtfully: he had just that very morning received it from a philanthropic society and had not yet had a good look at it. Anecdotes about his clothes abound in the life of Fedotov. They hounded him to his grave. This is why I keep mentioning them.

Because of his deteriorating health, Georgy Petrovich frequently had to skip his lectures at the Theological Seminary. His direct superior was Father Florovsky, the only great contemporary Russian theologian; coming from a background of generations of priests, he was neither a former member of the intelligentsia nor a writer or social philosopher. A jaundiced man, offended by all Berdyaevs, he somehow did not believe in Fedotov's illness or, in any case, did not show any particular compassion and threatened to fire him. Because of this, altercations occurred between the two that were in no way connected with patristics. As a result, when Florovsky celebrated the liturgy at Fedotov's funeral, some people regarded it as a temporary triumph of Florovsky.

The yearly meeting of the Christian Students' Movement, I believe, was taking place at Sea Cliff. I went there in the hope of meeting many old friends. It was a hot summer day, and I stopped at a little restaurant on the Sound. At the table next to me sat V. G. Terentiev, also refreshing himself with a cold drink. He was the one who told me that, the night before, Fedotov had died in a hospital.

Of all the participants at the meeting, Karpovich seemed to be the most depressed, even confused, by this news. He was to follow Georgy Petrovich in the not so distant future.

That same day, in Sea Cliff, I made the acquaintance of one of Fedotov's former Paris pupils, Father Alexander Schmemann. Later, we were to meet often in a religious-philosophical circle which we founded together. Thus the cultural succession had become established.

According to Fedotov's last letters to his wife, he had gone from the place of some friends with whom he was staying during the summer to the small local hospital. "Thanks to Blue Cross, it's almost for free, and it's cozy, clean and quiet," he wrote. The nurse recounted later that in the evening he would sit on the sofa in the recreation room with a book and the inevitable cup of tea.

This was a wondrous and complicated rite in Fedotov's life: book and tea, inseparable. The nurse saw him the last time precisely like that: drinking with eyes and lips, bent down in his robe. When she returned a few minutes later, Georgy Petrovich was dead.

All that remained was to transfer the body to New York and to bury him. Prince Zubov, one of his new friends, ignorant of the basic facts of Fedotov's biography, assumed this task. The tiny room in which Fedotov had lived at the Union Theological Seminary turned out to be locked up, and the key had gone astray among the departed's belongings. Meanwhile the funeral bureau insisted he be attired in a black suit ("dignified," as they call it). On the spot, unhesitatingly, Fedotov's friend bought a brand-new dark suit for the deceased. According to the American custom, rouge was applied to his lips and cheeks.

In his coffin, in the center of the Cathedral on East Second Street, Fedotov half-reclined, almost unsubstantially, as if hovering. I knew that for the last quarter of a century Georgy Petrovich had not once acquired a new garment for himself. And it was painful to see the fine suit in which he was about to be buried.

Chapter 4 · Fondaminsky

Write So That Every Word Emits a Fragrance.—I. Fondaminsky

In the twenties I seldom ran across Fondaminsky. It was said about him that, although an editor of the *Sovremennye zapiski,* he did not undertake to judge fiction—did not consider himself qualified. And this I liked.

As a rule, the conviction reigned in reputable emigré publications that the appraisal of poetry demanded a special knack and culture; as for prose, any honest public figure could read and reject it. Emigré poetry obviously profited from this point of view: poems were passed on to experts or published "on trust," based on the opinion of the leading critics. Then the rhymed stanzas were squeezed in like vignettes between fragments of prose. Without question, the main advantage of poetry lies in its brevity. Verses take up little room and thus do not interfere with keeping an exact account of Soviet iniquities.

But prose, I beg your pardon, prose the Vishnyak-Rudnevs (*Sovremennye zapiski*) or a Slonim (*Volya Rossii* [The Will of Russia]) are quite able to do justice to on their own, without the help of consultants. No one can fool them! The results turned out to be most pitiful in the case of *Volya Rossii;* in the *Sovremennye zapiski* this approach was gradually subverted by the continuous pressure of the young writers, and also thanks to Fondaminsky, who, not relying on his own personal taste, heeded public opinion.

The truth is that the men of their generation (quite extraordinary on another plane) completely lacked adequate organs for the evaluation of artistic works. It always seemed to me that if one of those editors were to keep on smelling a manuscript for a long time, he would understand it much better than he could have done merely by reading it.

On Fondaminsky's heavy, dark-complexioned face the nose with its soft, flaring nostrils occupied a prominent place; his entire appearance was somewhat sensual, colorful, resembling that of a Circassian highlander—tall, with scarlet lips and dark, burning eyes beneath black arched brows. In later years, when he coaxed us to contribute to *Novy grad* or *Novaya Rossiya* (New Russia), he never failed to add, "But write so that every word has its fragrance," and he would bring his fingers close to his lively, beautiful nostrils, inhaling deeply, as if already relishing the aroma of our future creations.

The other editors of the *Sovremennye zapiski* were skeptical and expected nothing useful from us. Rudnev was more delicate than Vishnyak, more careful and profound; but he suffered from the same general sickness, an infallible, stubborn "adherence to principle" (*printsipialnost*). He had only a softer touch and would listen without immediately interrupting the speaker; but when he declared, "This I don't understand," no further explanations were possible. By and large, as a generation, these people were exceptionally limited; yet they relied mainly on their reasoning powers. What Zenzinov "didn't understand" did not and could not exist in respectable literature or philosophy.

Rudnev was the most honest, the most decent of Russian intellectuals, a socialist and a county doctor. I happened to detect on his face traces of genuine suffering as he returned a manuscript to a young writer whom he considered talented. But alas, "this I don't understand . . ." Duty above all and, particularly, in one's personal interpretations, without amendments or compromises.

V. Rudnev had traditional leanings towards Orthodoxy; he loved the Russian church and observed the major feasts. But how one could argue about religion or become involved in theological subtleties was beyond him. Religion was a citizen's private affair, strictly personal! It had to be separated from the state and from one's life in public. Difficult to imagine more criminal nonsense, although it seems to have its historic justifications.

In such a climate, the appearance of Berdyaev, Fedotov and young writers of mystical inclination in the bosom of the *Sovremennye zapiski* could be considered a miracle. This, of course, was where Fondaminsky's influence made itself felt.

Time, incidentally, worked in our favor (unfortunately not for long). And toward 1936 some issues of the magazine appeared without any of the "old men," nothing but the younger generation. Articles by "mystics and obfuscators"—no Shmelyovs, not even an Aldanov. Imperceptibly, the topic of the Constituent Assembly was replaced by the mystique of democracy, the equality of God-created souls and the coming millennium. So that Rudnev and Vishnyak could not help but feel passed over.

At the beginning of the thirties, Fondaminsky rarely showed up on our Montparnasse. His wife, Amalia Osipovna, was painfully dying of tuberculosis and needed his full attention. When, in 1933 I believe, her condition seemed hopeless, it was decided to turn for help to Dr. I. I. Manukhin, whose treatment consisted of X-ray irradiations of the spleen. (He was supposed to have saved Gorky and ruined Katherine Mansfield.) The organism reacts to these rays with such violence that the patient either collapses or improves. After a few sessions, Mrs. Fondaminsky deteriorated altogether and soon died.

V. M. Zenzinov had been living with the Fondaminskys as an old friend of the family. Platonically in love with Amalia Osipovna, he had been nicknamed "the old spinster" Both he and Fondaminsky suffered their loss deeply, but in different ways.

Zenzinov retreated into his room to write his memoirs—"the memoirs of a terrorist in love," as we jokingly referred to them—while Fondaminsky crashed like a rhino into the social jungle, indiscriminately keeping busy with a multitude of superfluous duties and assignments. Little by little, being an impressionable and gregarious person, he became genuinely involved in these activities, which originally had been meant to serve as occupational therapy.

It was then that he started the Circle: a meeting ground for fathers and sons—where we would talk and argue about religion, philosophy and literature.

In connection with this new undertaking, I frequently met with him in the spring of 1935 on the terraces of pleasant cafés. He would come running, looking worried and crumpled, and arrange pages filled with notes on the table before him; he would call out a name and listen attentively to our comments, every so often, however, averting his eyes. In the end he placed a mark, next to other such signs, by the name of yet another potential candidate for the Circle. Thus he conferred with many friends, comparing their opinions and preferences, critically weighing them and, in the end, making his own decision. In the main, our judgments seemed to coincide: without consulting each other, we unanimously rejected Poplavsky.

At the time I believed that any congenial person, even if not sparkling with special talents, should be invited into the Circle. For of talent there is more than enough in Russia, but there is a dearth of amiable companions. This point of view Fondaminsky could not understand, although he did not argue with me. Only much later did I realize how naive or stupid my approach must have seemed to him. He firmly believed in "talent," "mission," "work," "merit," "rank."

About the Merezhkovskys there were no arguments either: no one wanted them in the Circle. G. Ivanov was invited to join—without his wife, I. Odoevtseva; for some reason his reactionary ideology was never taken seriously.

By the end of the summer the Circle was ready. Incidentally, no one ever invented this name; it came about spontaneously and proved ideal. In the fall we began to meet every other Monday in Fondaminsky's apartment at 130 ave. de Versailles.

So, there was the Circle. Also the journal of the same name and the Inner Circle; there were also the *Sovremennye zapiski, Russkie zapiski,* and *Novaya Rossiya.* And Fondaminsky had many other interests: the Orthodox Cause,[1] the Round Table of the Mladoross[2] and former Mladoross, the *Novy grad,* the Post-Revolutionary Club of Prince Shirinsky-Shikhmatov, the Russian emigré theater. Any exile association of acceptable character, that is, which did not foster pogroms nor wish to present the Germans or the Japanese with chunks of old Russian territory, applied to Fondaminsky for moral and material support. And he helped them all, to different degrees—at the very least confining himself to organizational and practical advice. He addressed innumerable meetings, enlightening, persuading, advising, sowing "the rational, the good, the eternal"; he even "went to the people,"[3] traveling around the provinces with his naive lectures, propagating the traditional Russian national, humanistic ideals.

I do not know when exactly his love for Orthodoxy started, but by that time he already attended Russian services. The group known as Orthodox Cause, which centered around Mother Marie and a former Catholic abbé who had become an Orthodox priest, met regularly at 130 ave. de Versailles and probably gave Fondaminsky more comfort than all the other organizations and clubs.

By education and vocation he was a historian; his *Russia's Historical Ways* has preserved a certain value up to this day. However, "actual" history interfered throughout his life with his scholarly pursuits. At first it was the underground, the Land and Freedom Party[4] that overshadowed the subject of history. At the time of the *Potemkin* uprising* he was sent to one of the rebelling cruisers and produced a fitting harangue—for which he was court martialled and only by a miracle escaped the gallows. (He told us that, waiting for death in solitary confinement, he experienced for the first time the presence of the living God and, he believes, actually prayed.)

In the emigration, social and political activities again prevented him

---

*Mutiny on the battleship *Potemkin* on the Black Sea off Odessa, 14–25 June 1905.

from engaging in his beloved history. "I know I'm of more use in what I'm doing," he said with a sigh. "Do you think I enjoy dealing with actors and philanthropists? Now you, you are a writer, but sometimes one has to make sacrifices, go to unfriendly, antagonistic people and try to teach, to enlighten them." Thus he urged us on and even instituted a sort of social "conscription."

Fondaminsky was an incorrigible optimist. "Wait, just wait, there will be everything: a magazine, and a publishing house, and readers, and even a government."

Financially he was well off; this of course nourished his optimism but also troubled his traditional Russian sense of guilt. He was closely connected with the Vysotsky tea business but never meddled in office matters, for which, it was rumored, the firm provided him with a handsome sinecure. Coming up day and night against emigré needs, even amongst his closest associates, Fondaminsky must have often felt ill at ease. So, willy-nilly, we pitied him. (According to the wise words of Chaliapin to a poor, aged widow: "You think that it is hard to ask. No, to refuse is even harder.")

For himself Fondaminsky no longer wanted anything, and the fact that he did not look for personal benefits placed him in the role of an almost impartial arbiter. We in the Circle and other groups inevitably elected him president; it was evident beyond any doubt that without this extraordinary man all of us would immediately have begun to quarrel and proudly disperse, each to his own lair, as happened after the last war, when all feeble attempts at a creative unification collapsed under the pressure of dissent, intrigues, and the ambitions of different leaders.

Only now has Fondaminsky's worth become clear. Such people are indispensable for the foundation of a cultural milieu with a definite hierarchy and responsible leadership. We need such people perhaps more than Berdyaevs or Herzens.

Incidentally, about Herzen . . . Fondaminsky adored this great nineteenth-century emigré and deplored the fact that "no Herzen had turned up in our midst." When Solonevich came out with his first documentary novel, Fondaminsky, always in a hurry, immediately announced: "Yes, a Herzen has appeared. But in *their* camp."

"Their camp" was the extreme right, for which, however, Fondaminsky did not bear any blind hatred: he was ready to argue with any honest adversary. I have seen him in the most unsuitable, semi-pogromist company; he behaved with utter dignity and was obviously delighted to confront an opponent whom he understood so well. Adherence to principle in the old Russian interpretation of *printsipialnost,* the fear of "dirtying one's cassock" so characteristic of the dodos of the intelligentsia—all this he despised and, in this respect, influenced a number of his contemporaries. He was able to bring with him an entire group of old and new friends to the Round Table dinners of Kazem-Bek, the originator of the "Tsar and Soviets" movement.*

This all-consuming, unselfish activity apparently gave him the right to treat people like building blocks or chess men: he placed us all on the board and endeavored to use us for the common weal, in accordance with the qualities, influence and, above all, the established reputation of each collaborator.

Every person had his place in Fondaminsky's scale of values. One rating for Berdyaev, another for Fedotov and Stepun, a third for Adamovich and Sirin-Nabokov, and finally one for us, the young. Some he rated low on the Russian plane but high on the British or French. All this made for very complex bookkeeping, which only he himself—without accounting to anyone—could understand. Basically, he did not negate the possibility of tranferring someone from one category to another, but he did not like such untidiness and only grudgingly yielded if there was an about-face in public opinion. (*Au fond,* the Russian radicals and rebels are very conservative souls.)

This at times merciless treatment of friends and collaborators by a revolutionary, almost a terrorist, this habit of judging according to exterior success, rank, honors, medals, newspaper reviews, seems to me to underline the essential paradox which characterizes this last generation of Russian public figures. A heroic, an honest generation, but at the core without a spark, lacking originality and independence of thought, even in microscopic doses.

Although imperceptibly to outsiders, the Christian Church was transforming Fondaminsky. He traced the roots of his religious experience far back into his past (the isolation cell!). In our discussions, where "mystics" argued with agnostics and skeptics, he was invariably on the side of the believers (with emphasis on social justice). A couple of times he spoke of his first "encounter" with God: He had not realized it then, but time but, as a matter of fact, he had walked out of the fortress a new man.

Yet he still needed another quarter of a century to understand and explain it all to himself. His stories were touching but not interesting: I believe he lacked theological intuition.

Mladorossy.

He held forth at great length and with gusto on political and social topics which were not really the main concern of the Circle. Soon, however—between the Anschluss and Danzig—geopolitics hit us hard. Again, reptiles were rustling nearby, raising their ancient heads. There was the smell of blood in the air, the blood of friends, brothers, neighbors, of the insulted and of heroes . . . Fondaminsky, the optimist, never doubted that democracy would win out.

He also liked to expound on specific historical subjects. He had studied in depth the era of Nicholas I, had submerged himself in it all his life, and had gradually fallen in love with the emperor "of the dim, leaden eyes," who was equally hated by Herzen and Tolstoi.

From Fondaminsky I learned that the reign of Nicholas Palkin ("the Stick") had to be viewed from a psychological point of view. During the first days of his monarchy, the Decembrist Conspiracy[5] shocked the "anointed of God," whose life, from then on, would be the psychological answer to the sacrilegious uprising of 14 December 1825. (The behavior of contemporary dictators and even presidents might become more plausible if we were to pay attention to their personal traumas rather than to sociology and geopolitics.)

But Fondaminsky's main genius lay in his organizational talent. If he had been meant to become a saint, he would not have chosen for a model a philosopher such as Thomas Aquinas, or such a mystic as John of the Cross, but rather a manager and builder like Stefan of Perm, the enlightener of the Zyrians in Siberia.

He was one of the founders and editors of *Sovremennye zapiski*. Rudnev and Vishnyak could read manuscripts and write letters, but to establish the material basis for an emigré publication and to unite all the active forces from literature, philosophy, religion, and science (and not only those of the conventional left persuasion) was a far more serious and difficult task. First of all, the magazine had to be distributed, not allowed to languish in some obscure warehouse; and then one had to discover new people, new talents; sniff them out; look and listen without preconceived opinions. This is what Fondaminsky did. And if, toward the mid-thirties, *Sovremennye zapiski* became the most valuable "thick" journal, the best in the history of the Russian culture—not only of the emigration—it is mainly because of I. I. Fondaminsky. He invited Berdyaev and Father Bulgakov to contribute, defended the prose of Tsvetaeva (which Fedotov read for him), patched up conflicts created by Rudnev and Vishnyak, who kept forever bringing up gendarme-like objections based on their unshakable adherence to principles (*printsipialnost*). Fondaminsky would even have published the chapter from Nabokov's *Gift* concerning Chernyshevsky, but Vishnyak went into hysterics. It should be noted that Fondaminsky respected Chernyshevsky no less than Vishnyak did. "A typical member of the intelligentsia, a member of the Order," he proclaimed with elation of the author of *What Is to Be Done.*

When patrons of the arts arrived from the provinces, ready to start a new publication, Fondaminsky invariably encouraged them, while the other editors feared possible competition. After the first issue of *Russkie zapiski,* Rudnev asked smugly: "What work of genius did they publish that could not have come out in *Sovremennye zapiski?*"

"My *Dvoinoi Nelson,*" I countered. "You rejected it!" At that moment I felt that this kindest, most honorable and honest of men was my enemy.

All kinds of barriers prevented us new writers from breaking into *Sovremennye zapiski.* These difficulties had nothing to do with intrigues or ill will, but only with the fact that those of the older generation, people of the Rudnev-Vishnyak type who were educated on the ideals of Gorky's *Burevesnik* (Stormy Petrel) and other nonsense, were receptive to only one kind of literature, which in substance did not differ much from that of Plekhanov and Bukharin. Kuprin, Shmelyov, or Zaitsev also did not deem our work worthy of attention (voicing this opinion in whispers more than once). In any case, they never supported anyone.

Bunin singled out Zurov amongst all the young writers in exile; the latter, naturally, wrote in the same key as Bunin. About Sirin-Nabokov, who was older than we were, Bunin, to the best of my knowledge, never expressed a definite word of praise in print.

Prose came up slowly on foreign soil; such is the nature of prose. But our poets had already achieved their deserved success in the thirties. Poplavsky, Chervinskaya, Ladinsky, Steiger, Knut, let alone the older ones, Khodasevich, Tsvetaeva, G. Ivanov, Otsup, Adamovich. Bunin could have learned something from them. But Ivan Alekseevich stubbornly protected his sovereignty; he would have nothing to do with such "novelties," just as in the past he had scorned Blok and Bely. Herein lies the dialectic not of an epigone but of a fossil: unable to accomplish complex mutations, he autonomously dies out. Bunin liked to boast that no "Kafkas or Prousts" had influenced him. Indeed, they had not.

"Ivan Alekseevich," Stavrov once said to him in Montparnasse, "we love you, but not for your verses."

"I don't love you for your verses either," Bunin countered adroitly. (For what, then, did he love the Montparnassians?)

Bunin's poems are now being successfully republished in the Soviet Union. Poor socialist realism!

Like all emigré publications, *Sovremennye zapiski* lost money, for sub-scriptions could not cover expenses. The editorial board was choking under the mass of contributions submitted for the three yearly issues. Aldanov alone had, for twenty years, appeared in every single one of them. Slowly, he was joined, and even edged out, by Nabokov.

Of course, people of means, like Fondaminsky and Zetlin, could give money, but this would not solve the basic problem: to put the magazine on a commercial basis, find an active readership, sell it, and not have the volumes rot in the warehouse.

So, Fondaminsky founded yet one more "order"—of ladies, this time—for the sale of tickets to monthly lectures under the aegis of *Sovremennye zapiski.* These ladies, in furs, couldn't be dealt with once and for all: one had to meet with them regularly for tea, talk to them, keep up an intellectual relationship. Besides, every month a lecture hall had to be hired and a suitable, interesting speaker enlisted. And the seats in the Salle Lascase had to be numbered (and the tags afterwards collected for the next *soirée*). Later on we had to listen to the reproaches of the "furred" ladies concerning Zhabotinsky or Professor Rostovtsev (who seemed to be leaning toward fascism).

After one such meeting, sacrificing pleasant company in Montpar-nasse, I offered to help Fondaminsky, who was sweating over the chairs, put things in order while Zenzinov was counting up the proceeds. Fon-daminsky accepted gratefully but, after a minute or so, with a sidelong glance at me he said: "Run along, I know you want to be with your friends." And I ran away from a social duty: my generation was never good at social tasks.

On such occasions, Zenzinov was always at Fondaminsky's side: taci-turn, often sullen, of a skeptical frame of mind. I think that had he still been in France at the time of Marshal Pétain's shameful Brest-Litovsk type of peace,[6] Fondaminsky's fate would have been different.

The Circle met every other Monday. Fondaminsky's apartment was on the *rez-de-chaussée:* one entered a small foyer leading into the dining room where, in preparation for the meeting, we drank tea and ate sweet rolls at a long table. (A staircase led down to the kitchen and maid's room in the basement.) The dining room communicated with Zenzinov's den: a bed, a desk, a typewriter, and a pack of American cigarettes. On this Remington, Zenzinov, during the day, typed his memoirs of unfulfilled love or, perhaps, of an altogether unfulfilled life. A couple of times I ravaged his supply of sweetish Lucky Strikes, after which he no longer left the pack in view.

I, a writer, did not own a typewriter in Paris. (Aleksei Tolstoi took along Mrs. Zetlin's Underwood to the USSR, in the twenties.) Usually when I had finished a novel or a story, I went to Prince Y. A. Shirinsky-Shikhmatov, the head of the Post-Revolutionary Club and editor of *Utverzhdeniya* (Affirmations). His wife, Evgenia Ivanovna, was the widow of Boris Savinkov. In their house I spent many thrilling and enlightening hours, days and nights, immersing myself in the living past of double-headed Russia.

Yury Alekseevich's father had been chief procurator of the Holy Synod[7] of the Russian Orthodox Church and also a member of the government council: he liked to say, "To the right of me—there is only the wall!"

Yury Alekseevich, a former *"pravoved"** and officer of the royal guard, made a turn of a hundred and eighty degrees: from the extreme monarchical right wing to the left, postrevolutionary, national maximalistic movement;[8] Evgenia Ivanovna, Princess Savinkova as we sometimes called her, was a living legend of the era of dynamite and governor-generals. Names like Khomyakov, Leontiev, Kalyaev, Sazonov,[9] rolled off their tongues as easily as the nicknames of cousins.

This couple had always been glad to lend me their typewriter. Now that I came so frequently to Fondaminsky's place, it seemed only natural to ask for the loan of his typewriter for a day or two.

"What's the matter with you?" Fondaminsky said. "Don't you know that no one ever lends anyone a camera, a bicycle, or a typewriter?"

Luckily, I didn't know that. Besides Prince Shirinsky's typewriter, I also frequently borrowed Dr. Z.'s bicycle (for cameras I felt a certain aversion). Apparently such reverence for the products of industry was typical of socialists from agrarian countries.

Crossing Zenzinov's room, one came into Fondaminsky's spacious study: there he slept on a leather divan which he made up with a sheet every night. The study had a separate exit through which one could leave the apartment without using the front door. This came in handy at times, since different, often hostile, factions met at the apartment.

I usually came by bicycle—since youth I had craved independence, and now I could not put up with petit-bourgeois last-métro transportation. Dressed in a sweater and knickerbockers, flushed, looking active and enterprising, I brought my bike into the tiny foyer. Several times, Ilia

---

*Graduate of the Shkola pravovedenie, an elite aristocratic institution for the study of law.

Isidorovich greeted me with the same exclamation: "How do you manage to look always so energetic!" For him it was an enigma how anyone
could bear without complaining a kind of life that was so full of deprivations. I sometimes think that if he had arrived in exile a poor and lonely
man, he would not have withstood the tribulations and probably would
have committed suicide.

Two Siamese cats, the darlings of the late Amalia Osipovna, were
living out their days in his apartment. Spoiled to the core, mysteriously
depraved, aristocratic creatures, they were obviously useless but claimed
special attention. I have always been familiar with all kinds of animals,
domestic and otherwise; I love and understand them. But I am for a strict
hierarchy: no democracy here. A dog or a cat must not usurp the best
seat in a room; I even would go so far as to say that they should willingly
accord us priority.

The amazement, nay the outrage, of these Siamese majesties was
something to behold when I brushed them off a comfortable armchair
and settled myself in it . . . Felsen, laughing like a mischievous schoolboy, said in his low, firm, yet friendly voice: "Probably no one in their
whole life has treated them so rudely." As more people arrived, the
Siamese would vanish into the kitchen downstairs.

Zenzinov poured the tea. They had a tiny samovar suspended above a
spirit lamp. The samovar was constantly being refilled with boiling
water from a kettle: the spirit lamp maintained the temperature so that
the water kept purring. Fondaminsky anxiously addressed me or Sofiev:
"You like it strong, of course?" This surprised me until I gradually
solved the riddle: for the Russian intelligentsia, from the Petroshevsky
circle[10] to the SRs, strong tea was something akin to hashish. And Fondaminsky imagined that, were we in Russia, we would be drinking strong
tea. Alas, I did not fit into the tradition and in the evening liked to drink
only wine or cognac. (Cognac, according to our *gourmands,* Bunin included, smelled of bedbugs.)

Little by little the members arrived; those who had already finished
their tea passed on through Zenzinov's room into the study filled with
the books so dear to our heart. (Later, a charming German colonel would
wheedle them out of Fondaminsky.) Most of the regular members of the
Circle had their favorite armchair or corner on a sofa and settled there.

"Berdyaev has to leave in an hour and a half," Fondaminsky informed
us from his chairman's seat at the desk. "If we want him to respond to
each of us, we have to set a time limit for every speaker."

This is how Adamovich in his "Table Talk" in *Novy zhurnal* described
one of our meetings:

A meeting at I. I. Fondaminsky-Bunakov's. Poets, writers—"the unnoticed generation." The mood is apprehensive and there is more talk about Hitler and the approaching war than about literature—but someone has to speak—and precisely about literature.

Late as usual, noisily and impetuously, enters Mother Marie Skoptsova (formerly Kuzmina-Karavaeva, author of *Glinyanye cherepki* [Pottery Shards]); flushed, all aglow, with books and bundles under her arms, she wipes her steamed-up glasses and looks with kind, nearsighted eyes at all the guests. In the back of the room, silently, sits V. S. Yanovsky.

"Ah, Yanovsky! Just the one I want to talk to. What kind of garbage and filth did you write for *Krug?* It's nauseating to read! And I almost gave a copy to father Sergei Bulgakov. Luckily I read your piece first. I would have been ashamed to look him in the eye."

Yanovsky turned pale and got up:

"Is that so? Have I written a piece of garbage and filth? And you, you protect the innocence and purity of Father Sergei Bulgakov. And, if I'm not mistaken, you are a Christian, a nun, one might almost say a saint. But if you were a Christian, you wouldn't worry about Father Sergei Bulgakov. You would worry about me, about my lost soul, because I wrote this filth and garbage, as you deigned to call it. If you were a Christian, you would rush to me in the night with Father Bulgakov, you would cry over me, pray for my salvation. But you, it turns out, you are afraid that poor little Father Bulgakov might be defiled! According to you, he must keep his innocence and you with him—as far away as possible from the lepers!"

At first, Mother Marie waved her hands, tried to interrupt Yanovsky, but then she gave up and sat with her head bent low. For Yanovsky's part this was merely a successful polemical move. But basically he was, of course, right; and Mother Marie, who was by no means stupid, understood this—as some years ago the Metropolitan Filaret in the notorious debate with Dr. Gaas[11] (64:1961).

Adamovich reproduced the essence of the argument almost perfectly. He was mistaken only on one point: this was not a pose, not a "polemical move" of mine. At that time we really did think and feel that way.

The meeting over, having missed the last metro, the most reckless nightowls stayed on, and also the inhabitants of the 16th *arrondissement* such as Felsen or Weidlé, and of course the Berlin houseguests of Fondaminsky, perhaps Stepun or Sirin-Nabokov. Again there was tea, a little stronger now; and the gloomy Zenzinov retired into his room, which was also the passage from the dining room to the library and, therefore, rather unprotected.

Regularly present at these meetings were Adamovich, Ivanov, Felsen, Kelberin, Mamchenko, Terapiano, Yury Mandelshtam, Alfyorov, Zurov, Weidlé, Mochulsky, the Fedotovs, Mother Marie, Saveliev, Gershenkron, S. Zhaba, N. Alekseev, Charchoune, Emelianov, Ladinsky . . . I can't remember them all.

There were occasional visitors from groups having nothing in common with us, "activists" whom Fondaminsky tried to help and inject with "the good and the eternal." Also obscure individuals, spies sent from the Soviet Union, or simply wretched emigrés or defectors. All dropped in at Fondaminsky's headquarters. When it became known that his phone was bugged by unknown well-intentioned "patriots," Fondaminsky literally blossomed out. There he was, on the front page of *Paris Soir,* his big smiling face radiant with joy: finally, he had received his long-awaited recognition from the "Elbrus of mankind," Stalin.

I remember one good Russian woman—plump, short, with the thick "sable" eyebrows celebrated in Russian folklore, and pregnant to boot. She had just made her way to Paris from Turkey where her husband, Soviet Ambassador Raskolnikov, had jumped out the embassy window or perhaps been pushed off the roof as persona non grata by his former friends. This was the same Raskolnikov who, in October of 1917, opened fire from the cruiser *Aurora*[12] onto the Winter Palace, thus shattering the last stronghold of the short-lived Russian democratic regime. At that time, Fondaminsky was commissar of the Black Sea Fleet and Kerensky—head of the government and supreme commander-in-chief of the Russian army at the end of World War I.

The pregnant widow attended a few of our meetings and "teas." If I'm not mistaken, Fondaminsky, that saintly soul, for a time even gave her shelter in his apartment. She looked at us attentively with cool, unblinking, colorless eyes, listened to our improvisations and, as I understand now, kept speculating as to whether we were *agents provocateurs* or madmen, or perhaps both. After many years of Soviet experience she probably could not think otherwise.

I confess that a shiver went down my spine the first time I saw her sitting across from a courteous Kerensky in the peaceful dining room. Yet another circle had been closed! It suddenly came to me that history makes sense, often contrary to what we surmise; but to grasp it is difficult while we are in the middle of the process.

How this woman lived through the years of occupation, whether she returned to the "Father of the Nations" and what happened to the child, I do not know.

Here it may be relevant to recount an episode from my personal life, the memory of which evokes in me a similar "sacred shiver."

Many months after my novel *Lyubov vtoraya* (The Other Love) came out, I unexpectedly received a letter from Ivan Nazhivin, a writer who enjoyed quite a reputation in prerevolutionary Russia. He liked my latest book and "cautiously" so informed me. I answered him more or less like this:

Dear friend:

Thank you for your cordial message. I assume that you like *Lyubov vtoraya,* for why else would you have written to me? But to the point:

Once upon a time there lived a boy in Russia. He had failed in French; and in order to be promoted to the second class of the "gymnasium," he had to take a make-up exam in the fall. A university student, Boris Geibiner, was called in to help; he promised to initiate the youth into the mysteries of irregular verbs. The tutor turned out to be a vegetarian and a convinced Tolstoyan. Under his influence I too, immediately became a vegetarian, though not for long. My sisters, out of love or envy, forced me with endless nagging to go back to "nourishing" meat. But this sympathy for Tolstoyans and their books remained with me. I could afford only the cheap "Posrednik" editions and put together a small collection of these pamphlets. Among them was one, entitled, I believe, *O chom govoryat zvyozdy* (Of What Do the Stars Speak), a tale about a Chinese emperor who one night stepped out of his palace and was overwhelmed by the sight of myriads of stars, blinking as if they wanted to tell him something. The emperor immediately called together all the sages and astrologers from his entire realm and ordered them to interpret the message of the stars.

The problem was not an easy one and the elders and magi became depressed. But among them (as always) there was one wiser and more daring than the rest. When finally the council convened in the palace, this wise man stepped forward and, making the proper obeisances, informed the emperor: "The stars, oh greatest of Emperors, speak of love!"

I took a great fancy to this little book and read it several times. The years passed, and the young student had to abandon his library

*

and with, and without, visas crossed many borders, attended the
Sorbonne, learned almost all the irregular verbs, wrote several
books, amongst them *Lyubov vtoraya,* which tells about the heavenly commandment of love on our earth. And now there comes
this letter, like a handshake, like a brotherly blessing from the
author of the cherished tale, *O chom govoryat zvyozdy.*

I do not know, Mr. Nazhivin, how it affects you, but I was
shaken, I felt a sacred shiver when this spiritual delayed-action
bomb exploded in my Paris hotel room and united us through
different earthly times and stages. It convinced me that every step
of ours, even a senseless one, makes sense.
Yours, V. S. Y.

I'm not sure that the reader will approve of this digression, but I
consider it justified and can now return to the Circle and its regular and
occasional guests.

On his own initiative, Saveliev, a short, thickset "Berliner," began to
keep records of our meetings; they turned out to be so interesting that
they were published in *Novy grad.* We were of course dissatisfied with
Saveliev's work, with his style. The result was that Saveliev, a very kind
and honest, but also a very touchy, man, declared: "Write it yourselves.
I'm no longer your secretary." As might have been expected, no one
assumed the task; and no further external traces of our discussions seem
to have been preserved.

However, not all of those present participated actively in the debates. I
believe that Charchoune and Emelianov did not once open their mouths,
yet in their own way they also nourished our talks.

Steiger informed us that he did not speak up much in the Circle because he expressed anything important he had to say in his poems. It
sounded like a pompous lie. We all tried to express in our work what was
most important to us, but the encounters in the Circle served as a testing
ground where we checked out the latest, improved models of thought
and ideas. These meetings undoubtedly charged and infected us with
creative energy. Each of us wanted immediately, the very next day, to sit
down and demonstrate his particular truth!

In *Childhood, Boyhood, and Youth* Tolstoi writes precisely in this connection.

In the metaphysical discussions which formed one of the chief subjects of our conversations, I loved the moment when thoughts

followed each other in ever quicker succession, and, growing ever more abstract, finally attained such a degree of mistiness that you found no means of expressing them, and although you thought you were saying what you meant, you were saying something entirely different. I loved the moment when, soaring higher and higher into the realm of thought, you suddenly grasped all its infiniteness, and confessed the impossibility of proceeding further.

Something similar, I believe, often happened in the Circle. And only wicked, "dead," people did not understand this. However, the parades of the Nuremberg schizophrenics were growing ever more aggressive and disturbing, tinting our get-togethers with their brown color. More and more we were poisoned by vulgar politics.

As a result of these innumerable meetings we began to perceive ourselves as an intellectual or spiritual entity. Our speeches, presumptuous and high-flown though they often were, gave rise to sparks of original thought, testifying to a genuine desire not only to understand life but also to serve it. While next to us, on wide shelves, glorious, familiar volumes stood lined up—like knights with raised visors. Here were our allies, precursors, brothers. As a matter of fact, the Circle was the last emigré attempt, in spite of everything, to justify Russian culture, to confirm it as European, Christian and akin to the West. In this area our Proustians and *Pochvenniki,* Eurasians, and neo-Slavophiles acted in concert.[13]

Before long, Hitler stepped over the Rhine; those who would and could crawled into his *baggage.* Then Stalin entered Europe. And again, whoever had the chance or the wish ran after him; in many cases they had, earlier, sold out to the Germans. The world once more disintegrated into hostile components.

From the start, all of us had rejected the Merezhkovskys as members of the Circle. And Fondaminsky gave in. From Mussolini to Hitler—this actually does not come as a great surprise in D. S. Merezhkovsky's pilgrimage. But a year later, Fondaminsky suddenly put up Zlobin as a candidate for membership. That amazed us. Politically, Zlobin was no better than the Merezhkovskys, and he lacked their charm and talent . . . what did we need him for?

"Exactly," explained Fondaminsky, "Merezhkovsky is a power; to argue with him is difficult and tiring, But Zlobin, who is Zlobin? Are you really afraid of Zlobin? Let him sit here and later report to the Merezhkovskys. Perhaps they'll learn something."

Thus, toward the very end—shortly before the outbreak of the war—
Zlobin appeared at the meetings of the Circle, joining Ivanov on the sofa.

Notwithstanding his democratic attitudes, Fondaminsky knew how to
carry his point against the will of the majority. I remember the regular
election of the officers of the Circle and my naive reproach: "After all,
we should have given 'them' a chance to express their opinion . . ."

"What's the matter with you, Yanovsky?" Fondaminsky interrupted
me. "Don't you understand that the *bona fide* elections took place at noon
last Friday in my apartment? That's when we considered who represents
whom and who would be useful to our cause. Today is a mere formality.
If it turns out that we made a mistake, we can, tomorrow, enroll a new
officer or exclude an old, useless member of the board."

"The *bona fide* elections took place last Friday in my apartment." This
fatal sentence I heard, then, for the first time; only gradually did it dawn
on me what a sin it is: alas, all elections in the emigration were conducted
in this way.

On the one side, the Germans and the communists, waving their
pistols: "Who's against, raise your hand!" they offer. And on the other
side, we democrats: "The elections took place last Friday in my apartment." How many worthy emigré endeavors were ruined by this un-
principled, dastardly, Bolshevik trick (from the era of Ivan the Terrible).

Before elections we exclude unreliable subjects if only for nonpayment
of dues; or, vice versa, we augment the quorum by a dozen or so new,
pleasant, congenial fellows. How can these vile practices of respected
anti-Marxists be explained? Perhaps they do not necessarily stem from
Lenin and Nechaev; perhaps they have deeper, more intimate causes; it is
equally disheartening to read about the election of a Cossack ataman or
the elders of a church.

It's easy to ape Western democratic rules, to import them. But something significant escapes the Russian reformer. Without freedom there
can be no choice. Cheating at the voting place is as absurd as it would be
in the church rites—you cut off the branch on which we are sitting.

After the introductory speech and a short intermission the debate in
which we all unburdened our hearts began. It must be noted that the
degree of freedom we enjoyed in the Paris of those years was seldom
granted to any other generation of Russians: herein lies the explanation
for many of the accomplishments of this particular emigré period.

Religion, sex, politics, Peter the Great and Chernyshevsky, the ideas
of the Right, the Left, and the center, everything could be taken apart
and analyzed to arrive at the truth. Of course, there had been Nietzsche,

the nihilists, and many reviews of values, but those were spawned by Germans and ended uninspiredly in an abstract mirage. While here, for us, the decisive role was played by great, blessed, inwardly and out-wardly free, eternal France—the eldest daughter of the Catholic Church and of the Renaissance.

Our daring speculations in the Circle might have delighted or shocked Anglo-Americans and inspired Germans, but on the "Frenchies from Bordeaux"* they made not the slightest impression. It is interesting that the type of Russian "top of the class" student, transplanted to a French lycée, usually ended up close to the bottom and from there avidly assimi-lated Western culture.

Even the Orthodox priests, renowned in Russia for their backward-ness and ignorance, in France, by the middle of the thirties, had acquired a broadmindedness and an intelligent social insight on a par with the best of the local church leaders; there appeared clerics interested in science, medicine, mathematics, who read Freud and Einstein along with St. Augustine and Kierkegaard.

Thus it is not surprising that Parisian Russian literature also began to sound different, new—arousing the disapproval and even disgust of our epigones of all genres and regimes.

At the second, the "late" tea, we again ate sweet rolls. Whatever Fondaminsky considered "appropriate," he served lavishly.

The combination of largesse and stinginess in our Maecenases never failed to amaze me. I knew people in the emigration who were without doubt pathologically avaricious and who yet considered it their duty to purchase our books and attend our literary evenings. It seemed to me that it might be better to refuse one author and then thoroughly assist another. But no, they gave to everybody according to a fixed rate and thus, paradoxically, earned nicknames such as Yudosheks, Plyushkins,[14] usurers, this while some "generous" souls, who never supported our publications but occasionally treated a poet whom they happened to have run into in a café, were unanimously considered very "Russian" and very noble characters.

When the detailed history of our literature is written, it will become clear that emigré literature survived—together with Bunin and Re-misov—precisely thanks to those dull, grey Plyushkins from the liberal camp. The "right" considered our production, all in all, a curse, a ma-sonic or communist conspiracy, belchings from the elders of Zion. Pro-

---

*Expression coined by Griboedov in his play *Woe from Wit*.

fessional rightists do not need literature. They claim that they adore Dostoevsky, but they are actually fully satisfied with General Krasnov.

When Smolensky's gas was turned off, he went to Sofia Pregel or Mrs. Zetlin for a loan. I asked these ladies: "Why do you help him? When Smolensky is drunk, he calls you 'kikes' to your face." They answered, "How can he manage without gas? He's got children, they have to eat." (Smolensky was not a member of the Circle; his poems, however, appeared in our almanac.)

Since Fondaminsky had no business or career interests, he could remain a dispassionate arbiter in all his emigré activities. Plato's idea of the rule of an elite has to be understood in the light of the fact that philosophers, priests, and political leaders who have already achieved all possible honors and do not seek anything more for themselves are able to administer justice and establish truly objective laws.

I do not know how Fondaminsky behaved in the past, inside his "faction," but here, among us, he was not involved in any intrigues, never stirred up trouble, and did not fight for "power." For that terrible emigré power which, since it is an absolute fiction, remains forever unattainable.

The value and dignity of the Paris emigration lay mainly in the absence of official subsidies. Thanks to this, we preserve the most blissful memories of many figures from that era. Oddly enough, when the United States introduced official subsidies and grants were allocated by American organizations during the cold (and warm) wars, many speculators, smart alecks, and racketeers spontaneously appeared among the new emigrés, pupils of the Soviet educational system, but also among the old, delicate humanists who had suffered under the tsar's regime. To outgrab, to outsmart, to push out—this became the motto of former Komsomols* as well as of fragile members of the intelligentsia. This is especially surprising as far as the latter are concerned, for they all suffered in their youth for their ideals and went to prison because of their love for the people. Apparently, hard labor and other trials were in the spirit of those times; it was the era and not the personal heroic choice of individuals which manifested itself. And now, these same saintly heroes, having shaved their Chekhovian beards, chase from one paragovernmental project to another, from one radio station to another, from one cultural foundation to another, trying to capture for themselves and their groups a bigger piece of the pie.

---

*The Soviet Communist youth organization.

From the above, I believe it can be deduced that the heroism of an entire generation was based on suggestion or fashion and is perhaps nothing but a conditioned reflex, comparable to the secretion of saliva.

An order of the intelligentsia for the purpose of realizing the Russian historical dream was, if not the invention of Fondaminsky, at least his favorite child. And his definition of a member of the Russian intelligentsia embraced any and all outstanding figures. There were Novikov and Lenin, Chernyshevsky, Dostoevsky, and Fyodorov, Chaadaev, and the Archpriest Avvakum. They all technically fitted his definition. According to Fondaminsky, they were united by a sacrificial humanism and suffered for their beliefs. They were an order of knights, unorganizedly acting throughout history, at times openly and at times driven underground by blind, hostile forces. And now again a day was dawning when a secret spiritual order could save the essential treasures of Christian civilization. These, more or less, were the teachings of Fondaminsky.

His religious crisis was a long time coming. It developed slowly and with interruptions, to judge by external signs. Before his imprisonment in the camp at Compiègne, he went to church on Sundays but did not participate in the sacrament. He was apparently baptized in the camp, in 1941 or 1942. Mother Marie and many other friends also passed through Compiègne. Rumor has it that even there Fondaminsky organized lectures, seminars, discussion groups, talks with social implications. An old man, he soon fell ill, so that all the prerequisites for death were at hand (even without gas chambers).

The people of his generation cannot understand why Fondaminsky, who escaped from Paris in the spring of 1940, did not go to the United States like other "public figures." He did not avail himself of his "extraordinary" visa and returned to Paris.

In June of 1940 Fondaminsky lived near Arcachon; my wife stayed in the same house for a while, and several other friends settled there, among them Mochulsky. Fondaminsky had always been famous for his professional optimism; but now, suddenly, in the face of his personal misfortunes—the loss of his comfortable apartment and of his books—he displayed an almost childish confusion.

"What will I do now? How shall I live? People are used to turning to me for help and I cannot do anything!" he would say. These words provoked Mochulsky to make some poisonous remarks. It became known that in Fondaminsky's study there was a secret wall safe where he kept some English pounds. Although it was a relatively negligible sum, everyone was now convinced that Fondaminsky could not forget it and had to drop in at 130 ave. de Versailles, if only for an hour.

And indeed he returned in the fall of 1940, when many of his friends also came back to Paris. Again there were meetings, lectures, but now, to the Orthodox Cause or the Russian theater something else was added—if not overt conspiracy, then at least a foretaste of it: Paris was beginning to organize its first cells of the Résistance. Soon our friend Vildé would start an underground printing press at the Trocadero (Musée de l'Homme). All these barely perceptible vibrations Fondaminsky must have experienced as would a cavalry horse the call of the bugle.

"Well, Fedotov is sitting in a camp near Dakar, and we, here, are still working!" he announced with a trace of sarcasm. "One can still work here!"

He was hypnotized by efficient labor, any kind: he could go into raptures over people hostile to his ideas, only because they knew how to "work." "Oh, what a wonderful worker!" he would say admiringly (about a certified ass or skunk).

He could not fail to appreciate the German know-how and talent for organization during the first months of the occupation. This could explain a certain sympathy he felt for a German colonel who visited him in his study and praised his collection of Russian books: Fondaminsky could fall in love with any Prussian able to quote Schiller or Hegel by heart. After all, Fondaminsky's generation was raised on Heidelberg's yeast.

As I ponder the fate of the revolutionaries of this vintage, I come to the conclusion that their basic historical trait was an utter incapacity for judging people. The vital practical intuition which helps a farmer choose a hired hand or a wife, a ship's captain a suitable crew, this mysterious knowledge was completely lacking in that last generation of Russian rebels. Herein we can probably find an explanation for the legendary Azev affair,[15] a story I believe unique in the diverse annals of "Central Terror." (There were Konrad Wallenrods,* but that is something different.) And this, I'm afraid, explains many fatal mistakes of the so-called February Revolution.

Letters arrived from America, urging Fondaminsky to make use of his special visa; his friends had long since fled from the unoccupied zone. Kerensky crossed over the Spanish border in June 1940; Zenzinov, who had been sent as a correspondent to Finland to report on the infamous slaughter there, made his way via Sweden to New York. The entire SR faction had once more run—and without particular glory.

---

*Hero of Mickiewicz's work of the same name.

Why did Fondaminsky stay on? Does this fact bear witness to the greatness and nobility of his soul? Or, on the contrary, to stupidity or paralysis of the will?

Like all actions people decide on at crucial junctures, it was an alloy of different, often contradictory, tendencies and calculations. Fondaminsky stayed on in Paris because he was again in his comfortable apartment and because he had been reunited with his dear old friends and could continue his beloved work. Fondaminsky did not leave because he had been fed up for years with many of those who did flee; and he decided, once and for all, to be rid of them, physically and spiritually. Of those refugees it can be said that "the likes of them don't drown." They successfully crossed the ocean and, in New York, after their Russian and West European experience, continued their former activities. Quite shamelessly they made fun of Fondaminsky and his new-found faith, explaining "all this" as a senile softening of his brain.

Yet Fondaminsky had for a long time felt the passionate desire of the political fighter at least once in his life not to retreat from the battlefield and, if need be, to die fighting. At least once not to run! And in this act of personal and civic courage he was supported by the kind of Orthodoxy fostered in the Parisian exile, where we counted among the saints "who shone in the Russian land" the priest Avvakum and Lev Tolstoi—both of them rejected by the official Church. All this is no accident, and all is miraculous although absurd.

Chapter 5 · Adamovich, Khodasevich *et al.*

In the early fall of 1928, I found myself one evening in a hotel room on the rue Mazarin (or Bonaparte), where I was supposed to read my first short stories to a group of people; the listeners were Dryakhlov, Mamchenko (in whose room the meeting took place, I believe), Yury Mandelshtam, and Dr. Unkovsky, the same who so frequently figured in Remizov's dreams. Later, Terapiano appeared (already he had to turn his supposedly better ear).

So began my close friendship with Dryakhlov and his partner, Protsenko. When I was particularly hard up, I dyed scarves and ties in their shop, a job that enabled me to survive from one exam to the next. On Saturdays we had hearty suppers in that same shop, drank red wine, and argued to the point of exhaustion. These Russian get-togethers, marked by curses and ridicule, nevertheless proved our genuine thirst for truth and our willingness to make sacrifices in the search for it. Such enthusiasm for fresh thought, such desire to understand and forgive "everything" I have never since encountered. We must all have gradually changed! Those verbal revelations were the more miraculous in that they were mingled with blatant tactlessness and a sadistic or suicidally masochistic frankness.

In that cramped, smoke-filled room, overcrowded with pieces of old furniture and smelling of the Ukrainian borsch that Viktor Mamchenko was preparing for the week ahead (he grew dill and parsley in a box on the window sill)—in that room on the rue Mazarin I stubbornly read my stories for three or four hours, among them "Rasskaz o tryokh raspyatykh i mnogikh ostavshikhsya zhit" ("*The Story of Three Who Were Crucified and Many Who Remained Alive*), published in the Warsaw daily *Za Svobodu* (For Freedom). It centered around Barabbas, whom the good citizens of Jerusalem preferred to Christ. Buried in it there was already the experience which opened to me more clearly at the time of *Lyubov vtoraya*. Some decades later the Swedish writer Lagerkvist received the Nobel Prize for his novel *Barabbas,* a book which I could never bring myself to pick up, out of attachment to my own orphan.

Mamchenko and Dryakhlov liked precisely this story, and they argued about it with the others. As a matter of fact, there never was any affinity between Terapiano, Mandelshtam, and myself.

Mamchenko was a handsome young man with a Cossack's shrewdness, who bore himself with exaggerated dignity; Adamovich had singled out his poems, though they were uneven, unclear and, despite intense *bonne volonté,* lacking an ability to communicate much. Later, the poet became more consistent, learned the craft and the language and affirmed for himself a place of his own.

Mamchenko was born in the south of Russia. He leaned toward philosophy in an obstinate, inarticulate way. He even introduced certain of his convictions into his life, at a slow, yet steady and invincible pace. I believe he was the first among us to espouse vegetarianism. He declared that he did not want to cause animals suffering, and, despite their naïveté, his words sounded convincing. There are such positive people who express generalities in a weighty and even original way. However, he did eat fish, assuming that cold-blooded creatures suffered less or not at all.

In those years, Mamchenko was unable to formulate even the simplest thought in a conventional manner; he twisted his syntax and dialectically obscured any ordinary sentence, accomplishing this tortuous operation with great and mysterious dignity. Some tried to make fun of him (Khodasevich, Poplavsky); but the majority, and especially people with esthetic tendencies (Adamovich, Mochulsky, Gippius), respected him. Apart from everything else, Mamchenko had good common sense, that famous Russian practical intuition. In his hotel room he grew beets and asparagus, pretty flowers and, I believe, even tobacco. There was a time when his borscht was so popular that some people dropped by without invitation, just to partake of it. He worked sporadically and was supported by his wife, a practical nurse. Yet, whatever work he did, whether he painted or plastered, he performed neatly, precisely, to perfection. His practical side was completely opposite to his dialectic nature.

Mamchenko was friendly with such people as Shestov, Mochulsky, Gippius, and at the end of the occupation he was the only decent person left who still visited the Merezhkovskys.

Adamovich, I believe, had long since become disappointed in Mamchenko's poems but never openly said so: ("Compassion, compassion!" the principle of his later years). Khodasevich maliciously ridiculed Mamchenko and his kind, considering them "naked," helpless, and by no means kings.

After the war, Mamchenko began to publish some collections for the

Returning Soviet Patriots, but he himself was smart enough not to go back.

After fifty years in Paris, the poet V. F. Dryakhlov still retained all his national traits. Born on the Volga, he presented a mixture of all the repulsive and attractive characteristics of a "genuine" Russian. In our discussions we always came dangerously close to the "Dostoevskian" limits, where he felt very much at home. Valerian Fyodorovich played a good game of chess, and we obstinately fought over the board, full of hope or despair, sympathy and hatred, vindictively ridiculing each other about personal and literary matters. And when the situation on the board changed, we mellowed, even paying subtle attention to the needs of the half-beaten challenger. Chess is a satanic game.

Dryakhlov was Protsenko's partner in the production of scarves and ties; he squarely declared that Yanovsky should not be permitted to work there, for he was a sheer liability.

"Do like Dovid Knut!" Dryakhlov said with his friendly and poisonous Tartar grin. (Knut, too, managed a workshop of the same kind.) "If a poet from Montparnasse comes to him, he gives him five francs but never a job, because it would hinder production."

Our mutual friend Protsenko, embarrassed yet also amused by this scene, half-tipsy, gesticulating with his fleshy bare arms which smelled of dye, gently calmed him down, reasoned with him and, smiling, led us all to the table and poured us more wine. After a few minutes Dryakhlov, affectionately bending down to me, said: "I know you need a job right now, but couldn't you print the lace a little more accurately? Look, it's full of bare spots."

"Good, I'll try," I agreed mournfully (the next day I had to pass my physiology examination).

"You are my closest friends," meanwhile announced Protsenko. With his disfigured forehead, divided by a deep scarlike crease into two stories, and a tumor on the neck below the ear, he always reminded me of the bust of Socrates; and that's what I called him, the Ukrainian Socrates!

"You are my closest friends," he repeated, gulping down his wine. "You are dearer to me than my own wife." And then began that muddled, chaotic Russian table talk which nourished and inspired us, despite its basic flaws.

Valerian Dryakhlov's poems in the first issues of *Chisla* had their own magic . . . In general, when I leaf through old journals, my attention is often attracted not by the "stars" but by marginal poets such as Zakovich, Dryakhlov, Stavrov.

One spring, Dryakhlov fell seriously ill. I visited him in his attic on the Place de la République. He had a rather banal but very painful herpes zoster. But then the virus caused a sort of meningitis, and he had to be brought to the Hôtel-Dieu, where I worked. Since the examination revealed an old lesion in the lung, we decided that he was coming down with tubercular meningitis, a pathology which at that time was invariably fatal. All this happened so fast, so unexpectedly, that it seemed to make no sense. A week before there was Easter, lilacs bloomed, it seemed that there was enough power to fecundate the entire universe and here, abruptly, the end!

"It doesn't seem to make any sense, but probably there is some sense in it," I said in consolation. And this reassured us all a little. Because we sought "sense" more at that time than a comfortable existence.

Soon, Dryakhlov recovered, but traces of his illness remained: a facial neuralgia, odd behavior, violent headaches. For a long time already he had been interested in mysterious doctrines and esoteric teachings, had read Blavatsky and Kryzhanovsky; now he became deeply involved in the theories of Rudolph Steiner.

There were a variety of Russian anthroposophic groups in Paris which competed with each other, as did Orthodox churches, associations of Russian monarchists, democrats, physicians, engineers, Cossacks. One group was directed by Natalia Turgeneva, the sister of Asya (wife of Andrei Bely); at the head of another group there was Kiselyova, Dr. Steiner's favorite pupil, whom he had allegedly cured of TB.

During one summer I went regularly to Kiselyova's studio, where I performed the eurhythmic alphabet; these light physical exercises undoubtedly had a good effect on tired and unresourceful city dwellers. Apart from the rhythmic movements, it was Kiselyova herself, her modest, feminine nobility, that attracted me. Sometimes I fancied that she was a large, heavy, wounded bird, to everybody's surprise soaring up lightly from the wooden podium.

Natalia Turgeneva belonged to an altogether different race: an intellectual, able to formulate and define the inexpressible, powerful in theoretical debates and not always delicate in the means she chose. However, to her, too, I owe a great deal. And to this day I am grateful for certain books "in limited circulation" which I managed to read thanks to her.

Be that as it may, I could not become a faithful disciple of such a pseudospiritual or pseudoreligious school—but I did benefit from acquaintance with it. Fyodorov and Uspensky, however, never led me toward evil and did not separate me from Christ, though it must be admitted that for some souls there lies a hidden danger in all these teachings.

After his miraculous cure, Dryakhlov retreated into anthroposophy; he immersed himself in the subtle art of meditation, gave up smoking, wine, and meat. In short, the man changed. Possibly he could now distinguish the aura of a flower or of an "elementary spirit," but to us, his friends, he was lost: no more jokes, no swearing, none of the former brilliance, and he stopped writing (or at least publishing) poetry.

Against all this "devilish spirituality" Protsenko stood up, decisively. He himself did not write, but he indirectly influenced a number of us. Original, independent, oblivious to pain and fear, he went almost to the bottom line in his logical edifices. Needless to say, he drank too much, led a disorderly life, and died prematurely. At some point in his philosophizing, Protsenko arrived at the conclusion that it made no sense to exhaust oneself in fighting the rabbit and the dog in man; let the rabbit, and the ape, and the amoeba live inside man as befits them, and man next to them, according to his status, without constantly draining one another.

Two other visitors to the scarf workshop were Konstantin Ivanovich, a kind, decent, gentlemanly bachelor of the old school, a chemical engineer now washing barrels for a chemical factory, and Valerian Aleksandrovich, a judge from Moscow ("Won't you kindly take a seat?"), an enthusiast of Russian church music, young girls, and happy agapes. These agapes, followed by a game of billiards, had a greater and more positive influence on my career as a writer than all German novels put together.

After my reading, that evening on the rue Marazin, Mamchenko decided that I had to meet Adamovich. As Adamovich later laughingly told me, Mamchenko had informed him that a certain Yanovsky who was writing "one hundred percent" prose, had appeared in Montparnasse.

I was supposed to arrive at Adamovich's hotel at noon on a certain weekday. I came exactly as arranged, but Adamovich was still asleep. He had to be awakened, something he slightly resented. He emerged in a robe of an astonishing canary yellow.

Now I understand that our conversation that first morning must have been utterly uninteresting for the unshaven Adamovich, who was constantly pulling the folds of his yellow robe together. In the first five minutes I managed to announce heatedly that I highly valued *Notes from the Underground,* that Aldanov was writing bad novels, and that Tolstoi, as behooves a real writer, had forever sought new forms for his fiction. Of course, such assertions could not but depress the not fully awake poet; I expressed myself in those years very bluntly, without any consideration for the opinions and sympathies of my companions. However, Adamovich was amiable in the Petersburg manner and promised that he would very soon read the stories I was leaving with him. He kept them long enough, though, to lose them. But I must give him credit for his unexpected sense of honor and responsibility. Through Zinaida Gippius he got hold of other copies of the Warsaw *Za Svobodu,* of which Filosofov, Gippius' quondam friend, was editor-in-chief, and thus peace was established between Adamovich and myself. In the spring of 1929, he brought me to the Merezhkovskys'.

I am writing about Adamovich, who was both close and alien to me, whom I loved, criticized, defended, and cursed for several decades. This mixture of different feelings existing simultaneously should not distort the true image of Adamovich; on the contrary, I hope it will help to establish it.

We should be grateful primarily to him for the appearance and development of a special climate of emigré literature. Of course, without him the same writers would have existed, the same poets—or perhaps even better ones—but the "Parisian note" of Russian literature as a particular unified style, recognizable by everybody though only with difficulty defined, I believe would not have existed without him. And for this, I am certain, some time in the future many Muscovites will thank him.

The charm which Adamovich exuded to a greater degree than anyone else around us, this charm and his little weaknesses and sins should not detract from his real achievements. His main sin I consider his "more-or-lessism."

Incidentally, I was one of the Parisian writers who managed, without any preconceived plan, to maintain good (though quite different) relations with both Adamovich and Khodasevich.

Adamovich, formalistic as it may sound, created a school or, rather, an anti-school (which is almost the same) that united the best young writers and poets of the period. Without Adamovich these writers and poets would still have done their work, but the unifying principle would have been missing. As a result, a group consciousness was born: about what is needed and what is superficial in art, what important and what negligible, what eternal and what temporal.

In individual cases, I want to point out, Khodasevich was closer to a limited literary truth: he was more skillful and even more "honest." The term "honest" as applied to an artist is meaningless; it plays the same role as the epithet "brave" applied to generals (as Dostoevsky explained in

Diary of a Writer). Despite his heroic labors, Khodasevich could not create a "school" of emigré writers. More exactly, the "school" that he created was not worth defending.

Adamovich was capricious and sometimes wrongheaded; he eulogized Aldanov's novels, upbraided Sirin-Nabokov, made fun of those who took their own "creativity" too seriously. He staked a villa in the south of France on a card game, lost his own money and that of others, sinned unnaturally, affirmed (after Pushkin) that "literature will pass but friendship will remain," and he often seemed just a skillful manipulator and opportunist. Yet, at the decisive moment we always find him in the ranks and at the most responsible place.

A delicate aesthete, he managed to live off emigré literature and to "lead" its youth without provoking either Bunin or Milyukov or other epigones. Returning from a vacation in Nice, he borrowed money from a Maecenas under the pretext that it was needed for the treatment of his paralyzed aunt, and then lost it all at baccarat. Afterward he trustingly explained to the philanthropist: "You thought I needed the money to pay the doctors while I lost it at the club." All this, despite his unquestionable antipathy for Dostoevsky.

At the beginning of the phony war, Adamovich, aged about fifty, signed up with the Foreign Legion: together with other unfortunates, refugees, and all sorts of criminals—the Legion accepted everybody and washed off everything—he went through basic training in the harsh winter of 1939–1940 in truly dismal conditions.

The captain asked him: "Tell me, why did you join the Legion?"

"Je hais Hitler!"

"Oui, Oui, je comprends, mais avez-vous un casier judiciaire (a criminal record)?" The officer, a professional from St.-Cyr, could not imagine why someone in his right mind and with a valid passport would voluntarily enlist as a private in the Legion.

In these surroundings, Adamovich lasted out the entire *drôle de guerre.* In 1940 he and his fellows were thrown north. I understand that they did not take part in any battles. Indeed it would have been difficult, since those battles were over so quickly.

After the collapse of the front, Adamovich ran back to Nice, wearing the heavy French infantry boots of the previous war. Later, in Nice, he showed me these boots and explained that once, in the fall, he had put them on to go to market and had not been able to make it. "They were like shackles on my feet." In those boots, then, Adamovich and his comrades set out for the Mediterranean! The German soldiers caught up with them and with the multitude of refugees. That was the end! But then the German sergeant yelled to the French crowd: *"Les civils par ici, les militaires f. . .z le camp!"* For a while *les militaires* were on their own. And, with redoubled energy, Adamovich continues south in his clumsy footwear.

When, on another continent, I tried to explain Adamovich's role in our literature to intelligent people unfamiliar with the Paris of that time but who nonetheless occasionally read *Poslednie novosti,* I always felt something like what one feels when trying to describe colors, music, or odors in words.

It is quite clear that his articles, poems, and charming table talk do not exhaust his role. For myself I solved the question somewhat unexpectedly: If we want to define Adamovich's contribution to our literary life in one word, I would say, "Freedom!"

Strangely enough, it was not Berdyaev, not even Fedotov or Fondaminsky, and certainly not Milyukov-Kerensky, Bunin-Shmelyov, or Denikin-Krasnov who helped us to assimilate and grow fond of that special French air of freedom, to feed on it, understand it, and transform it into a new product, life-giving, even if unfamiliar to our Russian lungs.

This special air of Paris I define with the term "Freedom!" The feeling pierces you, takes hold of you, that everything may be thought and said, on the spiritual as well as on the everyday plane, everything may be weighed anew, overhauled and understood in a new way, and with no connection to the violent eruptions of Dostoevsky or Nietzsche, the conflagrations on the Rhine or the Neva, with theories of cognition or fraternization with the people, with churches or mythologies. Freedom in an everyday sense, pragmatic, comfortable, poetical freeedom in an uninterrupted flow. This is France, this is Paris, where Pascal and Descartes still reign, in the slums as well as in the castles, and where ethnic Gauls and *sales métèques* converged not by accident from the entire world, as if invited to a picnic.

With this "elementary" freedom Adamovich was physiologically linked, notwithstanding all his petty, silly, capricious weaknesses. Freedom . . . this all-explaining miracle.

Such is my perception of the "old" Paris and of Adamovich there. To many it may seem the more unexpected as Adamovich very seldom and rather obscurely wrote and spoke about freedom. But his very presence was liberating. That is the gist of the matter!

Alas, he far too often quoted Pushkin's superficial lines about literature that will pass while friendship (assumedly) will remain. Supporting this nonsense, Adamovich often sinned, doing critical favors not only for friends but also "just so" (one of his favorite expressions which proved his independence from cause and effect) for mere acquaintances or sometimes even for enemies.

Of enemies he had many, but also many friends—his charm helped. Most of Adamovich's faults stemmed from his basic quality: he had an almost absolute musical ear and, naturally, was always fearful of false notes. Thus he preferred writers, who were usually silent.

One of his favorite turns of speech was something like this: "Incidentally, somewhere, sometime, I believe, Rozanov said"; and this "I believe" was to save him from any conscious or unconscious error. This is an example of what I call Adamovich's "more-or-lessism." Incidentally, Rozanov and Leontiev had exerted an obvious influence on him, but all in all he did very little serious reading and had finished his education as a *Wunderkind* in St. Petersburg. Yet, all these trifles aside, I always think of Annensky's lines in connection with Adamovich: "You are that messenger who, on New Year's Day, brings us orchids, breathing into your frost-covered *balaclava.*"

The air of Paris is special. Just a look at a landscape by a second-rate French painter convinces you of it. Added to the colors, oxygen, and other matters making up this air, there is one more essential element: a complex molecule of primordial *freedom.* Not Anglo-Saxon legal or political freedom, not the barrack-liberty of Prussian philosophers or the interior freedom of a yogi or of an Athenian hero, all of which are always combined with enslaving living conditions, family, and fate.

In France one still feels a current of pre-freedom (that out of which the universe spontaneously appeared), a freedom which miraculously transfigures all of life, the everyday and the festive, the personal and the social, the temporal and the eternal. This magic air, which we suddenly, undeservedly, began to breathe, recompensed us for many losses and even gave us something more into the bargain. Hence the characteristic feeling of the instability of this happiness and a fear of the future, of what was to come.

These premonitions had begun long ago, when Hitler was perhaps still studying art. In our dreams we had, for inexplicable reasons, to leave Paris, and we would wake up shaking and sobbing. And there was a complementary *cauchemar* which often tormented us: we would find ourselves back in our native country, and mingled with tears of tenderness there was the cold despair of an irreparable, fateful disaster.

The most odious punishment for a foreigner was to be expelled from France: it was expulsion from paradise. We lived a hard life but would

not have exchanged our birthright for the pottage of lentils of America or
Yugoslavia. Some of us had connections or family in other countries,
where we could have lived in relative comfort. But this did not tempt
anyone.

When the poet Alla Golovina had to join her family temporarily in
Switzerland, she perceived it as an "invitation to a beheading." Her
brother, Anatoly Steiger, felt the same way. Lydia Chervinskaya seemed
at a certain moment in her life to have no choice but to return to her
family, which was comfortably established in Turkey. Again, tears and
fits! To lose cold, hungry Paris and an unpaid-for hotel room! ("Who can
forget you? . . .")

Returning from his vacations in Nice and entering a crowded meeting,
Adamovich invariably said: "How good that nothing has changed here.
In the south, I sometimes imagined that I would come back to Paris and
find everything gone."

We lived in a prophetic, subconscious fear, the fear of loss. Not for
nothing did Charchoune, simultaneously rough and unprotected, describe in his wild, delirious fragments how he was being expelled from
France and brought to the borders of the USSR. We *knew* that we had to
expect yet another loss, but we did not realize the extent of it. Nor could
we find a rational basis for our fear.

And it happened. Paris became empty like a robbed hive, like Moscow
in 1812. The Russians floated off ahead of the wave, like wooden chips:
like any minority in any country we were particularly sensitive to the
change in climate.

A year later I saw Adamovich in Nice: he was sweet and lucid, laughed
at my jokes, remembered how once, coming up to the bridge table, I
said, "Today I read *The Possessed*. A poor book." Such whims could
shock Adamovich for the rest of his life. Thus, it seemed, we were
chatting and laughing as usual. But something basic had changed: I was
facing an old man: the bitterness characteristic of defeat and collapse, the
jaundiced face, tiny creases, the extinguished eyes. And yet, he was the
most carefree of men, one of the few in our time who lived his life
precisely the way he wanted to and was, all in all, exceptionally content
with his lot.

Before the summer of 1942 we met several more times, even occasionally in the Casino, right on the waterfront of Nice. It was he who
showed me Felsen's postcard from the occupied zone: "I'm not seeing
the Merezhkovskys any more. They now have completely different visitors." He also, mirthlessly smiling, told me of a letter from a "young"
woman writer to Bunin in Grasse. She had invited the laureate back to

Paris, claiming that "now it has become possible to really unite the entire emigration."

"That bitch is still looking for ideological excuses," we both decided. Actually, Adamovich formulated this thought a little more delicately.

Before leaving for Montpellier, I went to see him one morning. He lived then in a suburb, far from the center of the city. In silence, he handed me a postcard from Stavrov in Paris. "On such and such a date Dikoi died in the hospital after a long illness . . ."

Nausea overcame me. The healthy, aggressive, consistently high-spirited Vildé—in a ditch with a bullet in his chest or swinging from a rope. One wanted to vomit, not to cry.

On the way back to my hotel on the Place Masséna, I noticed a line at a store where wine was dispensed for outdated ration coupons, and I procured two bottles. In the restaurant I was already late, but I did not say a word. Only after having fortified myself with a wartime lunch of turnips and a glass of wine and having received a crust of bread for the dog and thanked the good soul (*"merci pour le personnel"*), only after all this did I tell Irina Grjebine about the heroic death of Boris Vildé, "Vanichka," as his friends called him.

Adamovich's attitude to writers was, as so much in him, entirely capricious. How many times he began to write about me with good intentions but suddenly, as if my image or the subject of my book had aroused a wave of irritation, finished with a heap of adverse remarks. But I forgave the charmer everything, I believe.

At the same time, he possessed an inordinate understanding of human weaknesses and was ready to forgive everybody everything. For himself he had no need of this Dostoevskian trait, for he always behaved with dignity and did not take part in poisonous gossip. And yet, how did this universal, unrestricted forgiveness arise in him, the European, the Petersburger who liked conventions and comfort? He would meet an individual who only yesterday had behaved despicably or had even slandered him personally (e.g., G. Ivanov) and gloss it over with a smile and a jest.

However, Adamovich had real enemies—literary or metaphysical—such as Khodasevich, Nabokov, and some others. For them he had no forgiveness or forgave only most unwillingly.

Technically, his quarrel with Khodasevich was based on petty gossip. Someone started the rumor that Gorky had thrown Khodasevich out of his villa in Sorrento; supposedly he had caught the poet rummaging through the papers in his desk. Khodasevich countered with the announcement that "both Georges" (Adamovich and Ivanov) had murdered and robbed a rich old lady before leaving Petersburg. Such nonsense caused the break between Adamovich and Khodasevich; for an entire decade they did not greet, or in any case did not speak to, each other.

Eventually, Felsen brought all of us, including Adamovich, together with Khodasevich. The years 1935 and 1936 were the time when Montparnasse represented something similar to a New Jerusalem: on the surface it was all harmony, peace, benevolence. The young ones were victorious all along the line; their elders were merely surviving.

Adamovich, by nature a passionate gambler, ready at any moment of the day or night to start a game of cards. *Faute de mieux* he became involved with bridge—at very small stakes. By that time Khodasevich only played so-called commercial games, although a few times in Montparnasse, upon the initiative of the fanatic Ginger, we vied at poker. Once I noticed how Khodasevich, after an additional deal, went quickly through the already-discarded cards. I hurriedly turned away . . . Thus, once, in a New York movie theater, I happened to be sitting behind a Russian thinker with whom I was acquainted and, to my horror, noticed that he was fondling the full bust of the woman next to him. I fled to the balcony, from which I could not see them any more.

But nevertheless, I have always regretted that the controversy over Nekrasov's questionable gambling has not found a more complete exposure in our biographical literature; I believe it insulting to speak about such trifles in hints and whispers. And what was Gogol's secret? (There is not even an allusion to the possibility of a homosexual element.)

Adamovich gambled passionately, in a childish way. He was obviously taken in by the very process of the game; the usually dismal results he accepted stoically, although differently from Ginger, our supreme Stoic. In a club he once lost an enormous sum, I believe his entire inheritance, in a game of baccarat. Adamovich's only short story known to me was published in *Chisla;* it dealt with an Argentinian who lost his fortune and killed himself. The story was naive, but written with genuine passion.

Several times, Adamovich recounted the details of his disastrous experience to me. Rolling his large, dark, childlike eyes with the heavy lashes, he smiled as if reliving an old toothache. "For some reason the croupier raised the cards much too high," he repeated in bewilderment. His tanned yet pale face, thick, raven-black hair, carefully combed and parted in the middle, and his "musical" ears in those minutes made him resemble a little Asian god. "Why did they raise the cards so high? They probably switched them," he added thoughtfully, without expecting an answer.

Khodasevich played bridge seriously, without distracting, abstract chatter, and he valued good partners. "What kind of a game is this? he would say, nervously fidgeting. "It's only slapping the cards around."

It was tiring and painful for him to follow the self-destructive leaps in our talks and arguments. In his presence, the exchange willy-nilly became drier, more prosaic—boring but more honest. We rarely achieved a dialogue with him, and in his presence that triumphant feeling of Freedom could not arise. No, everything in this world is bound and intertwined by a chain of cause and effect, and miracles are permitted only in homeopathic doses.

Khodasevich, the master, the laborer, above all demanded discipline from others; he could be petty, quibbling, even repulsively vindictive. But how he blossomed when he met a writer worthy of praise! He did not believe that literature would pass and friendship remain; in any case the idea did not make him happy.

His collaboration with the newspaper *Vozrozhdenie* only added to his bitterness. In order to establish its *raison d'être* and distinguish itself from *Poslednie novosti*, the other daily, *Vozrozhdenie* had to turn increasingly to the right and began unscrupulously and generously to "give away" pieces of the Russian Far East to the Japanese and of the Ukraine to the Germans. On this basis a band of joyful fellows, who felt at home in the counter-espionage services of many totalitarian (and some democratic) countries, began creeping into the paper. Whether he liked it or not, Khodasevich found himself in this company. Probably, if it had not been for Adamovich, he would have had a place in the respectable *Poslednie novosti*.

Incidentally, when Solonevich, an excellent right-wing journalist and a contributor to the old regime's *Novoe vremya* (New Time), appeared in Paris and offered his description of the communist circus to *Vozrozhdenie*, the editors did not appreciate this outstanding work and returned it to the author. The book was accepted by *Poslednie novosti* and, published in serial form, increased the daily circulation of that democratic paper.

Khodasevich behaved with complete independence at *Vozrozhdenie*, an independence which he probably would not have been able to retain on Milyukov's paper, because of the "*printsipialnost!*" of our liberals. He sent in his Thursday piece on literature without going into anything else, but it was clear that he only remained with *Vozrozhdenie* because there was no other place for him to go.

His earnings of three hundred or four hundred francs a week were just enough to cover basic living expenses. On these terms one couldn't even dream of a summer vacation unless one begged and borrowed and wrote demeaning letters, signed "Respectfully yours . . ."

It is a fact that, during the last years of his life, Vladislav Felitsianovich simply choked under his tedious workload and ceased writing poetry. This is the decisive sign in the biography of a poet, after which there is nothing left but to die.

Thanks to his natural spareness and agility, he always looked younger than his age. In his memoirs, Andrei Bely compares him to a caterpillar. He probably had in mind the unhealthy, greenish color of his face. I would say that, with his small, bony head and heavy glasses, he resembled, if anything, rather an ant. However, quite often, growing youthfully animated, he was not devoid of a special charm.

Already in the twenties, in the Lascaze auditorium at a large literary meeting, my attention was attracted by a bespectacled gentleman with a slightly jutting lower jaw, the picture of the eternal Russian student. It was Khodasevich, the nemesis of young literati who distributed punctuation marks at random (Boris Poplavsky first among them).

As I already mentioned, at this period Khodasevich only rarely attended our meetings. He was not on good terms—indeed in open conflict—with Gippius, Adamovich, Ivanov, and Otsup (the Petersburgers). Living in isolation, proud and offended, his only close contact was, I believe, with Tsvetaeva, a Muscovite like himself.

The young poets respected him: everyone greatly appreciated *Tyazholaya lira* (The Heavy Lyre). But he was not loved, and neither was his poetry as a whole. Those Parisian poets closest to him were not really the most interesting: Terapiano, Smolensky, Yury Mandelshtam.

About the "Parisian note,"[1] which sought to transmit *everything* or, at least, to squeeze what was most important into a page or a stanza— whether it fitted or not—rather than leave it out altogether (for truly important things are always in place and always stick out!), about this particularity of our literature Khodasevich spoke sarcastically. He did not quite understand—or, in any case, disapproved of—our eternal speeches about *the most important,* combined with a general contempt for "literature."

His opinion could perhaps be summarized as follows: if art is a serious matter which, like religion, transfigures life, then one has to treat it with absolute respect, to nurture it and forget once and for all that it supposedly "will pass"; but if art is only a childish game and the main thing, as Adamovich formulated it, is "that French woman who dresses somebody's wounds," then one has to treat it condescendingly: let the literati invent, make jokes, and perform *salti mortali,* and not always demand from it what is "most important." (A very logical but, alas, most unsatisfactory speculation.)

Khodasevich claimed that we all reminded him of an acquaintance with whom he once, in the summer heat, drove to a Moscow *dacha.* The man kept exclaiming about the quiet, the coolness, the fragrance of the forest. "Oh, how peaceful, oh, how beautiful," he repeated over and over, thus destroying the very peacefulness around them. This episode Khodasevich invariably recalled when literary honesty or creative authority was mentioned—and we talked about these matters often in Paris.

Khodasevich suffered from a special kind of eczema which symmetrically afflicted two fingers of each hand. He bandaged them, and with these disfigured, dried-out, greenish, wormlike fingers, skillfully handled playing cards. In the 1930s, bridge was his sole consolation. He played often and seriously, for relatively high stakes, mainly in the basement of the Murat. But he did not disdain to sit in on a game in Montparnasse. By that time he had already separated from Berberova; and his new wife, who later perished in a concentration camp, was also an avid player.

It surprised me that at his age and without means, he had so quickly found another companion (and one who was outside literature). Felsen, considered a specialist on the psychological novel, explained to us that there is a type of man who, when alone with a woman, suddenly becomes utterly charming, and that then appearance, age, status, and money are immaterial. Well, one had to admire this kind of suitor. I, on the other hand, lacking an extra five-franc bill in my pocket, considered it dishonest to return the smile of an ethereal, idealistic young girl in the Luxembourg Gardens.

I am especially grateful to Khodasevich because of one episode in my literary career. It so happened that my story *Dvoinoi Nelson,* which had initially been rejected by *Sovremennye zapiski,* was finally published in the *Russkie zapiski.* The issue was printed in Harbin (or Shanghai). Later, Milyukov became the Paris editor.

One Saturday night, at a meeting of poets in the cafe Méphisto, I was unexpectedly called to the phone: it was Khodasevich. He liked *Dvoinoi Nelson,* but one point was not clear to him. He was preparing his weekly article for *Vozrozhdenie* and needed elucidation. Couldn't I come by the next day and explain? It was urgent and important.

After this telephone conversation my feelings were similar to those of Dostoevsky when he was visited at dawn by Nekrasov and Belinsky, who had just finished reading the manuscript of *Poor Folk*. (Adamovich, of course, could never have acted in this way, for there are much more important things in life.) That Saturday night in the basement of the Méphisto stands out like a classical monument in my bleak past as an emigré writer.

The poet lived in a tiny apartment in Passy; he received me solemnly, with exaggerated respect, as if participating in a special, long-sanctified rite. He, the veteran master who had already overcome all such trials, probably guessed what this meeting meant to me.

I don't remember whether his wife was present; in general she did not concern herself with literary matters or, if at all, always inappropriately. (After Gorky's death, Khodasevich waited an entire evening in Montparnasse for Berberova, so as to divide up between them their memories of Sorrento. Upon his wife's meek observation that, after all, one could do very well without such an adjustment, he only shrugged his shoulders insultingly.)

Having cleared up the point which troubled him, Khodasevich good-humoredly declared that if I had put dots in that place, everything would have been clear: "All those Joyces and Prousts only confuse you," he said, not without bitterness. "There is nothing shameful or *petit-bourgeois* in dots." Khodasevich was not familiar with contemporary Western literature, mainly because—like most of us—he had no gift for foreign languages.

The myth that Russians are natural linguists is, I hope, slowly dying out. There was a time when aristocrats and emigrés of the type of a Herzen or a Sofia Kovalevskaya knew French no worse, and often better, than their native Russian. Thus there arose this myth which has been kept alive up to this day by the French *concierges,* despite the fact that the next waves of emigrés—"Wrangel" and the DPs—stuttered for decades when explaining themselves to the French police.

A year after he won the Nobel Prize, Bunin happened to board a local train in the south of France without having had time to buy a ticket. When the conductor challenged him, he was unable to explain his case and only awkwardly, pointing to his chest, shouted: "Prix Nobel! Prix Nobel!" Of all French literature, he knew only Maupassant thoroughly and him, too, he preferred in Russian translation, thus missing all the idiomatic expressions.

We revere Tolstoi's genius and bow before his vegetarianism, forgetting that, apart from everything else, he was also one of the best educated members of his class, who did not stop learning and perfecting himself up to his last day.

While we were drinking tea, I told Khodasevich that two years previously *Sovremennye zapiski* had rejected *Dvoinoi Nelson*. Khodasevich winced as if in physical pain.

"Why do they meddle with what's not their business?" he asked plaintively, and repeated, "Why, for heaven's sake?"

I had just received my first advance for *Portativnoe bessmertie* (Portable Immortality), still from Fondaminsky who originally edited *Russkie zapiski;* and I was very proud of it.

Khodasevich, disapprovingly shaking his small head, enlightened me: "You labor, create a product, and all you get, once in a decade, is a thousand francs. But Vishnyak (secretary of *Russkie zapiski*), who does not create anything and only gets in everyone's way, receives a monthly salary. A monthly salary!" He gnashed his teeth. (This was the first time in my life as an emigré writer that someone told me that my work was needed and worthy of a greater recompense.)

Suddenly, pacified and mellowed, Khodasevich began to speak about a novella that he had been contemplating for a long time; it was a story that arose from the intimate depth of his soul and, as far as I know, was never written.

Unfortunately, in my state of mind at this meeting, I could not pay much attention to his creation. Besides, he told it in fragments. As far as I can remember, it concerned a type of intellectual, a city dweller familiar to all of us, who suddenly breaks with his former life and settles in a primitive shack somewhere in a wild forest. When, several years later, his friends visit him, they find him in a meadow—an anchorite all covered with hair, with a gigantic, grey bear lying docilely at his feet! It was something along those lines—in any case, completely unexpected coming from Khodasevich.

Next, for no apparent reason, he told me how he had once visited a school friend whose parents kept a little store. From behind the counter there emerged a beauty of a girl, his friend's sister. This was the future Maria Samoilovna Avksentieva Zetlin (Rozanov referred to her in one of his articles as "the Madonna of the SRs." I, unfortunately, only met her in the image of the "Queen of Spades.")

Khodasevich knew many details from the past of the emigré big shots and was not averse to gossip. He was basically a conservative, and "progress" meant nothing to him. About his father, a Pole and a Catholic, I believe, he spoke with great, childlike tenderness.

On the occasion of an anniversary of his poetical activity, Khodasevich's friends organized a subscription dinner. I was not at the meal but came to the restaurant afterward with some other young writers. He was visibly pleased by our appearance; we all went to Montparnasse and settled down to bridge. I don't remember in what connection the theorem that the sum of the angles in a rectangular triangle equals 2d came up. Khodasevich doubted that any adult could still remember the proof. From the pocket of his jacket I fished out the notebook with which Tsvetaeva had presented him, and, on the same page with her inscription urging him to write poetry again, I drew with assurance the simple proof. Underneath, I added an amputated Pushkin line, ". . . it's time, it's time, the heart is seeking peace. . . ."

Having made his four spades, Khodasevich cast a glance at the notebook and angrily said to Adamovich: "The young have no manners. Without asking for permission Yanovsky writes in my notebook, and if geometry has some relation to the previous talk, the rest is completely out of place."

"What did he write?" Adamovich, ever curious and jealous, asked eagerly.

Khodasevich read my line aloud and added, "And he thinks that he is quoting Pushkin!" They both smiled derisively.

Khodasevich suffered from severe attacks of lumbago. I referred him to Dr. Z., who injected something around his sacrum, and the pain immediately ceased.

Later on, the poet, who liked to discourse on medical problems, complained to me. "I asked him to tell me honestly whether what he had injected was a palliative or a real cure. Good God, I know about these things, it's not the first time I've been to a physician. He told me, 'Forget your lumbago forever!' So my wife and I went straight on to visit some friends. Two hours later they carried me downstairs and brought me home. Why such lies? Tell the truth! After all, I know what it's all about . . ."

I believe he really knew a lot about the weaknesses of professionals, of craftsmen, lawyers and artists, and was ready to forgive people who were masters of their trade all their sins.

Khodasevich died somehow quickly, unexpectedly. Shortly before his death his book *Nekropol* (Necropolis) had appeared. At that time I was writing literary criticism for *Illyustrirovannaya Rossiya* (Illustrated Russia). In his book there were some excellent reminiscences of Bryusov, but also many conventional, colorless pages. And this is what I said in my review. (After all, no one knew that Khodasevich was dying.) A couple of days later we buried him; mere gallstones had turned out to be something much more serious.

The service took place in an unattractive, I believe Protestant, church.

When the casket was brought out, I went up to Rudnev, having made up my mind finally to find out about the fate of a lost manuscript of mine. But Rudnev, pale, upset and sad, smiled gently and answered decisively, "Not today, Vassily Semyonovich, not today. Some other time."

And I felt that Khodasevich was again wincing as if in pain and crying out, "Why do they meddle with what's not their business!"

At the cemetery, after the heavy clumps of clay had noisily fallen down, as I was walking to the gates, Sirin-Nabokov, then very slim, dressed in knickerbockers, came briskly up to me. Very excitedly he said: "One cannot write like that about Khodasevich! One cannot write like that about him!"

I mumbled that no one could have predicted his sudden death.

"That makes no difference. One cannot write that way about Khodasevich," he repeated stubbornly.

Felsen, who was walking with me, softly said something pacifying and rational, and we fell silent. But I was very impressed by Sirin's behavior and never forgot it. There was a legend that he was utterly antisocial, took no part in community affairs, and was solely interested in himself and his scribblings. Obviously, it was not quite so. In this case, for instance, he fulfilled what he considered his social duty.

From the cemetery, Felsen, myself, and, I believe, R. N. Grinberg went to the café Murat; there on the terrace, under the awning, we drank cognac and enjoyed the Paris sky, which is especially splendid after a funeral. (At my house I kept the end of a candle which I lit for the first time during the requiem for Poplavsky.) I believe that after a funeral friends should drink together in memory of the departed. The ancient tradition of a feast—to eat bliny, drink vodka, sing and play at the gravesite—seems to me wise and worthy of perpetuation.

I had always loved Khodasevich the poet, but as the years passed it became clear to me that, in his critical essays also, he occupied a special, heroic place. Not once during his lifetime had he ever praised obvious garbage, and he had always been the first to note with joy a new voice which he considered good, even if it issued from an "opposing" camp. And this cannot be said of any other Russian critic.

He was the first, if not the only one, to commend Nabokov unequivocally. He called his *Podvig* (Glory) a heroic work, while *Chisla,* with Ivanov at its head, savaged the author in the most indecent way.

Khodasevich was the only emigré critic (not counting V. Mirny) who criticized the so-called novels of Aldanov. His article in *Vozrozhdenie* about the installments of *Nachalo kontsa* (The Beginning of the End), where he declares that there is no room in Russian literature for *such* a writer, caused a lot of turmoil in the emigré corral. At the next meeting of the Circle, Fondaminsky, pouring tea, asked with animation: "What do you think? Whom does Khodasevich have in mind in his article, the hero of the novel or Aldanov himself?" (The hero of the novel being a French writer.)

To which Zenzinov angrily replied: "You see, you yourself take part in all this nasty gossip."

That same evening, Aldanov had for some reason dropped in on Fondaminsky before the beginning of our meeting, perhaps to say hello to Nabokov, who had arrived from Berlin. Shaking hands with him, Aldanov praised the beginning of *The Gift,* the first installment of which had just been published in *Sovremennye zapiski,* in the same issue as a chapter of his own *The Beginning of the End.*

"Remarkable, truly remarkable, and you read it remarkably well at your evening," he repeated quickly several times, fearfully looking around as if expecting some imminent danger.

My novella *Volno-Amerikanskaya* (Catch-as-Catch-Can) had also appeared in the same issue. At any other time, Aldanov would not have failed to address a lukewarm compliment to me. But after Khodasevich's article, he abandoned his West European delicacy.

This confused, hurt, insecure, plump gentleman, in a bowler hat and suffering from emphysema, during his entire life occupied himself with what was not his business—I have in mind his novels à la *Klyuch* (The Key)—this man reminded me of the scene in *Anna Karenina* in which the noblemen conspire to reject their old regional leader and he, in pants with golden galloons, runs around the hall, resembling a hunted predator, and hopefully looks at Levin, not sure whether he is a friend or a foe.

(Here is the victory of a writer: Proust or Tolstoi can be remembered at any hour, in bed, in the office, in the club: gradually they overlap all of life.)

"Why do you speak so badly of Aldanov?" Fondaminsky once asked me. I explained and then added: "Twenty years after his death no one will seriously remember his novels."

Fondaminsky shook his head in disapproval: "You are mistaken. Not twenty years after, but much sooner!" And he laughed.

All this was, of course, clear to many people. But Khodasevich considered it an act of justice to express it openly, disregarding the subtleties of literary politics. What these politics consisted of I never could understand. People claimed that Aldanov was a Mason and for this reason had to be praised. But that is nonsense. There were many Masons in literature who were chastized, for instance, Osorgin.

When Adamovich complimented Aldanov, he probably thought that it was not a great sin, for in fifty years everything would be forgotten. For Khodasevich there were no important and unimportant, no big or small matters in literature. Everything was significant. As for fun, we shall play bridge at night!

Often, during the game, following the movements of his greenish, wormlike fingers, I involuntarily murmured his lines:

My friends, my friends, perhaps quite soon now
And unexpectedly for all
I'll snap the thread of idle talk
For real—not in a dream—for real!

He would turn his head toward me and angrily let fall: "What kind of a game is this, only slapping the cards around!"

Chapter 6 · Sundays at the Merezhkovskys'

Notwithstanding his moral monstrousness, I considered Georgy Ivanov the most intelligent person in Montparnasse. It is difficult to define the charm of this demonic creature, who resembled a caricature of an old-fashioned ghost. He had the thin, bluish-grey face of a drowned man with dead, wide-open eyes, an aquiline nose, and a drooping, red, lower lip. Lean, tightly pulled together, he was always well-groomed, clean-shaven, with the obligatory cane and bowler hat, and the eternal cigarette holder in his hand. And a cold, crooked, cynical smile, extremely clever, confidential, as if to say: this is exclusively for you!

He understood almost "everything" (he never let himself be drawn into theological discussions), but, above all, he permitted "everything." However, one cannot say that he *forgave* everything. For in his utter selfishness he was completely indifferent to those with whom he came into contact. Besides, to forgive means to admit the reality of guilt, crime, and sin—and those Ivanov could no more perceive than a blind man colors. But poetry he loved and, I daresay, he sacrificed a lot for it (indirectly).

Among artists one comes across such monsters quite frequently; Ivanov was by no means an exception in the Paris of those days. He became unique thanks to the high standard of his poems. (Smolensky and Zlobin belonged to the same family of "amoralists.")

Georgy Ivanov—a man without principles and devoid of those organs with which we distinguish good and evil—was a member of the Circle and even exerted a certain influence there. How he achieved this it is difficult to say. In those years, many (e.g., Khodasevich) thought that his poetry originated from two or three stanzas of Fet's which he dexterously kept juggling around. But the younger poets feared, obeyed, and loved him.

Despite their external slovenliness, the Montparnassians nevertheless valued "morals" (in contrast to the poets of the notorious Russian Silver Age[1]). We sought to unite mysticism with common sense, Tolstoi with

St. John of the Cross. This, perhaps, defined *our* squaring of the circle. For each remarkable epoch travails over its own squaring of the circle, and this determines its style and spirit.

Thus, Merezhkovsky became embarrassed when I once suddenly told him that the acts of a person bear witness to his spiritual condition, as a rash on the skin betrays an internal disease.

"Well, it's difficult to put it so simply," he mumbled in confusion.

Ivanov's influence on young poets could not be explained only by his poetry. His charm and skill in literary "kitchen matters" also played a role. He was smart, if one can call a man smart who gambles on a defective horse. Through flattery and threats he got his way. Thus Varshavsky, who had the reputation of an "honest" writer, published, upon Georgy Ivanov's demand, an abusive article about Sirin-Nabokov in *Chisla*. ("Why did I do it?" he naively lamented twenty years later in conversation with me. "I can't understand it.")

Ivanov made the round of wealthy Jews and borrowed money from them. Later, he was to do almost the same with the German occupiers. Nevertheless, people shook hands with him. Ivanov went to the National Union of the Working Generation (or was it the Young Generation?),[2] in those years a patently pro-Nazi organization. Later, in Montparnasse, he amiably reported that in this Union they call Dostoevsky the Dia*mont* of Russian literature. Whenever he went there, he would explain, "Tonight I'm busy, I'm going to the Dia*monts*." There, at an open meeting he had organized, these dia*monts* compared Adamovich to Smerdyakov.* But Ivanov still managed to remain on friendly terms with "George." (The latter alone probably had plumbed the entire depth of Ivanov's spiritual infirmity.) And once again Ivanov got off with a pun, only to spread, the next day, the most malicious gossip about Adamovich and then come back to make peace with him.

In the life of every writer, scholar, thinker, comes a moment when he seeks ultimate recognition: followers, an audience, even a monument in a public square of his native town. This is not merely the voice of vanity and pride but a normal expression of inner growth.

Such recognition Ivanov finally desired—general, imperial recognition. At some time or other we all want a thousand students, who applaud us, unhitch the horses from the carriage, bring orchids to the podium. "I won't be an emigrant for the second time," he warned us,

---

*Repulsive character in *The Brothers Karamazov*,

"and as for Moscow, I'm ready to return even with Hitler's wagon train."

Finally the Germans arrived in France. At a time when many of his friends were destitute, Ivanov sought merely to exploit his new, uniformed acquaintances according to his old recipe. When they were beaten (yes, he *had* bet on a defective horse) and were running from Paris, Ivanov immediately wanted to join the Union of Soviet Patriots.[3] The writer B. dissuaded him. And he became once more the leading poet, almost an ideologist, this time of the DPs. Ivanov was a charmer; despite his moral and physical ugliness, people fell under his spell.

"I see where you have written in a story about someone with the blue face of a drowned man," he said to me confidentially, in a half-voice. "So you really did notice and describe something like it, did you?" And on another occasion: "You are a writer of imperial scope, not like all this small fry."

At the time, for some reason, he considered it advantageous to flatter me. And such compliments did captivate and help to forgive him a lot. As a matter of fact, Ivanov claimed that flattery always acted positively, even if it was a flagrant lie. ("Flatter them, flatter!" according to Dostoevsky).

In connection with the Ivanov-Burov incident I was involved in a dirty plot. I frequently met Burov and knew where he took his lonely morning walks. When Burov, in response to Ivanov's demands for money, sent out a circular letter about the commercial operations of Ivanov and his wife, the poet decided to meet up with him and punch him in the nose. But I refused to divulge the secret of Burov's daily route. This very much surprised my honest young colleagues; only Adamovich declared that I was absolutely right.

I report these details to show how easy it actually was to maintain good relations with Ivanov while not compromising one's own conscience. But Poplavsky's affliction—"to over-insult or over-bow"— remained widespread.

Ivanov did not play at cards, nor at games of chance or so-called commercial games, and his sexual life was rather dreary. In the Circle, which was frankly hostile to his moral-political image, the poet was nevertheless respected and heeded. Ironically, Khodasevich was not invited into the Circle (although we published him in the magazine).

Whenever I leaf through Fet, I remember Georgy Ivanov. Up to this day I cannot understand why the latter was so much admired by the starved young emigration. Of course he was a real poet, but did we not also have Khodasevich, Tsvetaeva—certainly of no lesser scope? I think the attraction lay not only in his poetic art; reading Georgy Ivanov, one involuntarily feels that nothing matters: one can step from one counter-espionage into the opposing one; cheat a *bourgeois* father; blackmail a Jew, then a German colonel; join the National Labor Union, then run over to the Soviet Patriots. Everything is permissible.

> In this world there is only
> The shade of the drowsing maples;
> In this world there are only
> your shining, maidenly-thoughtful eyes . . .

This is Fet—Ivanov was inspired by such lines.

His prose, though, is exceptionally graceless, three-dimensional. I am referring to his novels: *Peterburgskie zimy* (Petersburg Winters) is something apart, and *Raspad atoma* (The Disintegration of the Atom) is interesting from the autobiographical point of view.

Ivanov always leaned toward the "reactionary" sector, although he had hardly any convictions or principles. Unconsciously he liked and respected only a powerful regime and a great empire; he demanded order and, above all, a hierarchy, on condition that he, Ivanov, would be included in the elite.

After the victorious end of the war, I received a letter from Ivanov, who was in the south of France. At that time my novel *Amerikansky opyt* (American Experience), was being serialized in *Novy zhurnal*. Ivanov praised it—"exactly such writers we need . . ."—hinted at the possibility of arranging a French translation on the strength of his connections and, in conclusion, asked me to send him a length of material for a grey suit; all this was very typical. One just had to keep in mind that, if I had sent him the parcel, he would immediately have paid me back with some intrigue.

"A grey suit is out of the question," I answered him, in reference to our Odessian poet Stavrov's favorite story: "Calling for help, a citizen hangs out from a window of a building that is on fire. From below they shout to him: 'Jump!', to which he yells back: 'Jumping is out of the question!' " This was one of the most highly appreciated jokes in our Montparnasse.

Here I seem to be trying honestly to tell about a man whom I knew, yet I feel that the essential, the secret of his soul escapes me. It isn't true that only Pushkin (Lensky*) carried the mystery of his personality with

---

*Character in Pushkin's *Eugene Onegin*.

him to the grave. We all, and especially such distorted figures as Georgy Ivanov, guard and nurse a hidden wound (an ulcer) about which others can only guess by the diligence with which we push outsiders—friends as well as foes—onto a wrong track.

I called Ivanov completely amoral, but this was not so where his work was concerned. For his poems he probably made sacrifices and must have accepted some rules and laws, albeit of his own making. It is possible that he considered the rest of life rubbish, mitigated only by the measure of comfort it could provide, and therefore to lie, to blackmail, to betray were of no consequence. The only reality was his poems! And there he did not spare himself.

Toward the end of the thirties, when Hitler cast his shadow across the Rhine and over the French landscape, our nerves slowly began to give in. The air smelled of blood, perhaps the blood of our kin, and Ivanov's jokes were becoming dangerous; besides, the police also suddenly seemed to be waking up. At that point Ivanov waxed more cautious— not as at the time of the Front populaire: what a body of poisonous prophecies did he not spew forth then!

During the last year of the Circle, he sat in silence, with a stony face, sporadically goading our sole (platonic) Hitlerite, Lazar Kelberin, into impetuous attacks. The latter saw himself as a temporary mixture of Pascal and Rozanov. Having stimulated Kelberin's outcries, Ivanov might gently and patronizingly join in.

Once, arriving at a meeting of the board of the Circle, I found out that we were to discuss the candidacy of a new member, V. A. Zlobin. How Ivanov convinced Fondaminsky to accept him and who else took part in this plot, I don't remember. But I was the only one to object. Even Fedotov kept squeamishly silent.

"What's going on!" I was outraged. "We didn't invite the Merezhkov-skys, from whom we could perhaps have learned something. And now you advance a candidate with all their faults and none of their merits."

"Are you afraid of Zlobin?" Fondaminsky asked triumphantly (know-ing the answer in advance). "Well! So let him sit here and listen. Perhaps we'll even influence him a little. But the Merezhkovskys are powerful adversaries. Who wants to waste time now, arguing about elementary principles? Only Kelberin could be seduced by their speeches, maybe one or two others. No, the Merezhkovskys I don't want here. But Zlobin is not dangerous."

His persistence and, above all, the preciseness with which he took up the dispute anew at exactly the place where it had been interrupted the last time, paralyzed us, and we gave in.

Thus, in 1939, Zlobin, an agent of the Merezhkovskys, joined our group: a man who was probably more than anyone else responsible for the ugly behavior of the Merezhkovskys in their last years. Quiet, pointedly the guest, he sat on the couch next to Ivanov, where they formed a sort of dark faction. However, from time to time he would pose a provocative question, as for instance after an address by Kerensky:

"Don't you think, Aleksandr Fyodorovich, that, apart from selfish designs on the Ukraine, Hitler honestly hates communism and wants to annihilate it at the roots?"

To which Kerensky, flirting with impartiality, replied:

"I admit such a possibility."

Kerensky was the hostage of the Russian historical miracle. For several months he had led and defended a truly democratic Russia, the same Russia which for a thousand years had been sweating in the vise of despotic pranksters. This fact can never be erased. (Sakharov seems to be trying to continue these ideals.)

"The Supreme Commander!" Ivanov said, ironically, yet with Petersburgian trepidation. "Did you notice how he grabbed my buttonhole and wouldn't let go? Only think, the Supreme Commander of a superpower in time of war!"

When someone, as often happened, quoted Khodasevich's famous blank verse, "I have shaken hands with beauties, poets, leaders of nations . . ." Georgy Ivanov invariably pointed out, "By the latter he has in mind Kerensky. He knew no other leader of nations."

Once, a right-wing lady, a chance visitor at the Merezhkovskys' table, told us that she had come upon Kerensky in a Russian grocery store where he was choosing pears. "Can you imagine, Kerensky, and he dares to buy pears!" she screeched, convinced of her righteousness.

That day we were debating the subject for the next meeting of the Green Lamp. Merezhkovsky, with his usual brilliance, formulated it this way: "A dirty trick played on the 'Nation of Godbearers.' " To our surprise the ultra-patriotic lady who forbade Kerensky to buy pears was outraged. "We'll come and throw rotten tomatoes," she announced. "Perhaps we'll even shoot!"

However, the liberals, the Social Revolutionaries, and the Populists also protested when they got wind of the topic, and we yielded cravenly to "public opinion."

The Merezhkovskys walked to the end of their ideological path quite shamefully. More than anyone else Zlobin was responsible for their downfall; he was the evil spirit of their house, who decided all practical matters and who served as their link with the outside world. I assume that he, the majordomo, told them: "That's what you have to do: write, speak, talk on the radio. Otherwise we won't be able to make ends meet, we simply won't survive." The octagenarian, the immortal sorcerer, and his red-headed witch were too terrified to stick their noses out into the occupied streets. Yet, after so many years of exile, they very much wanted to taste the sweetness of life and fame. "What's the matter?" Zlobin insisted. "You always maintained that Marx is the anti-Christ. Well, Hitler is fighting him. Which makes him anti-Satan."

In the twenties and the beginning of the thirties, Merezhkovsky's salon was the meeting place for the entire emigré literary world. And young writers were even more welcome than established ones. There were many reasons for this: snobbishness, the desire to discover new talent, the hankering after something fresh, the need to attract disciples.

The receptions at the Merezhkovskys resembled old-fashioned, private theatricals. There were all kinds of talents in abundance, but there was no chastity, no honor, no integrity. (These values were not even to be mentioned.)

Merezhkovsky was primarily neither a writer nor an original thinker: he asserted himself mainly as an actor, perhaps an actor of genius . . . Someone had only to strike a new note for Merezhkovsky immediately to take it up. Bending down toward the floor, as if planning to stand on all fours, shaking his little fist in the air above the table, he would begin to expatiate on someone else's thought, rolling his defective r's, using his voice to its full extent, convinced and convincing, like a leading man on the stage. His best part, of course, was that of priest or prophet. Anything could serve as the pretext for such a performance: an editorial by Milyukov, a murder in the Halles, a quotation from Rozanov-Gogol, or an innocent remark by Gershenkron. To Merezhkovsky it was all the same. He feared no authorities: methodically he corrected the texts of new and ancient saints and even of the Apostles. He would discern from the distance an acute, vital, hemorrhaging topic and fall upon it like a shark attracted by the scent and the convulsions of the wounded victim. From that fresh thought Merezhkovsky would squeeze out everything possible (and even impossible), then gnaw at the bones, suck out the marrow, and triumphantly arrive at a sophisticated conclusion. A master vampire! (As a matter of fact he looked like a bat that feeds at night on infants' blood.)

After a long life spent entirely at his desk, Merezhkovsky was singularly lacking in independence of thought. Was he a popularizer? A plagiarist? A journalist with a caustic pen? Perhaps. But above all he was an actor of genius, inspired by other peoples' texts—and by applause. How he produced his monologues! "Emoting" in the style of the old school, not always letter-perfect, improvising, but what moving, tear-provoking improvisations!

The paradox of that house, where everything proceeded under Zlobin's black shadow, was Zinaida Gippius, the only original, independent creature amongst them, although limited in her potential. She seemed more intelligent than her husband, if by intelligence we mean something that can be controlled and accounted for, while Merezhkovsky was borne along by "mysterious" forces. He resembled a reckless horseman, though at times it was not clear who was responsible for his daring stunts: was it the rider or the wild mustang?

Someone at the table mentioned Violette Nozier, the heroine of a criminal affair (she had killed her father, by whom she had been forced to entertain an unnatural relationship). "Here you have it!" Merezhkovsky burst out, his little fist pounding the air above the table. "Here you have it: from Jeanne d'Arc to Violette Nozier. That is contemporary France!"

"What a splendid journalist he would have made," Aldanov, with whom I had left their place, marveled not without envy. "What a journalist! Just the mere headline: From Jeanne d'Arc to Violette Nozier."

These were the kind of brainstorms—on the metaphysical plane as well—with which Merezhkovsky shone. But a special depth and even freshness, true originality, seemed to be lacking. And there was no truth, or not the full truth. (From Jeanne d'Arc to Charles de Gaulle would be more just and meaningful.) There are and were Violette Noziers everywhere, and at all times. But Merezhkovsky's main aim was to produce an effect, to collect his applause before the curtain fell.

Demonism means that a man's soul does not belong to itself: it is in the power not of passions in general but of one overriding, often secret passion. I believe that Merezhkovsky was utterly demonical, although it is not clear to me who and what possessed him.

On Sunday afternoon people gathered at the Merezhkovskys' long table in the narrow dining room. Zlobin served the tea. When the bell rang, Zlobin answered the door.

The guests usually talked among themselves. But all of a sudden Merezhkovsky would hear someone mentioning Christ, Andrei Bely, or Proust's moonstruck heroes, and he would pounce on it like a predatory bird on carrion: would begin to claw apart the newly mentioned name or theme, swaying back and forth, beating the air with his small fist, warming up, waxing more and more inspired, improvising, hypnotizing himself, and finishing with a brilliant paradox, in time for the curtain, festively rolling his r's.

Those of the older generation, such as Zetlin, Kerensky, Aldanov, listened respectfully, sometimes disagreeing or posing a complicated question. Some youthful desperado might impetuously cry out: "I think Christ would never have said about homosexuals what St. Paul permitted himself . . ."

"Will you be in Montparnasse tonight?" someone whispers.

"No, tonight I'm at the Murat."

Merezhkovsky started out in literature as an extreme decadent. He was friendly with the outstanding revolutionaries of his time, e.g., Savinkov. He supposedly fought against bolshevism and Marxism, although in the NEP period he conducted negotiations for the Moscow publication of his collected works. Next he traveled to pay his respects to Mussolini and received an advance for a biography of Dante. This is how he reports his meeting with il Duce.

"As soon as I caught sight of him at his desk in his gigantic office, I loudly addressed him in the words of Goethe's Faust: 'Who art thou then? *Wer bist Du denn?* . . .' And he in answer: '*Piano, piano, piano.*' "

One can only imagine how, turned inside out by his slavish enthusiasm, Merezhkovsky howled, so that the Duce had to rebuff him: "Quiet, quiet, quiet!"

Merezhkovsky received several advances on this contract. His *Dante* was translated by Rinaldo Kuefferle, a well-known, Russian-born, Italian writer and poet who also translated two books of mine: *Altro amore* and *Esperienza americana.* From him I gathered certain details about Merezhkovsky's transactions.

Merezhkovsky himself was not the least bit embarrassed to describe his relationship with Mussolini: "One writes—they don't answer! One explains—they don't understand! One appeals—they don't give!" This became a standing joke in Montparnasse with regard to our own affairs.

Merezhkovsky compared Dante and Mussolini, giving the edge to the latter. It would be amusing to read this esoteric work now, in the Italian translation. However, soon Hitler ripened, and our vipers openly began to stir, crawling out from their dark crevices into the bright sun. Merezhkovsky fluttered toward the Nuremberg light with the fervor of a young butterfly. The idea was crystal-clear, long since thought through: in Russia, the regime of Stalin had triumphed, as prophesied by Gogol and Dostoevsky. Hitler was fighting communism; whosoever faced the dragon must be an archangel or, at least, an angel. Marxism was the anti-Christ; anti-Marxism was anti-anti-Christ: *quod erat demonstrandum!*

About Mussolini he inquired, "Who art thou?" but with the Germans there was no need to ask; everything was clear and comforting.

By that time most of us had stopped visiting the Merezhkovskys. In their tiny apartment embellished with images of Gippius' beloved Little Theresa, the blood of the innocents was already oozing from under the rugs. Now "completely different people" (as Felsen would later say) began to make their appearance on the rue Colonel Bonnet. Georgy Ivanov of course joined the victorious wagon train and prepared to become at last a national poet, the idol of Russian youth. But I think that only Zlobin felt completely at ease in those days.

Zlobin, a Petersburg dropout, friend of Ivanov, a "lefthander" with mystical inclinations, had replaced Filosofov in the Merezhkovskys' household. I was bewildered by this set-up and asked Felsen about it. He explained with an air of the utmost good humor: "Well-informed people tell me that Zinaida Nikolaevna has some sort of anatomical defect," and chuckling condescendingly he added, "they say that Dmitry Sergeevich likes to look through the keyhole."

Whatever it was, Zlobin gradually acquired a ruinous influence over this decrepit and ever more senile couple. Probably he frightened Gippius with the approach of winter—the cold, hunger, and disease. Yet, on the other hand, there was the fight against the Satan of communism, there were extra rations, the mirage of a special Berlin-Moscow train, the epoch of the Third Testament,[4] the new universal church and (last but not least) the *de luxe* complete edition of Merezhkovsky's works. Influence, admiration, disciples!

Guesses all, but how else to explain the stupidity of this professional sage who so blindly followed the German blockhead? What became of Merezhkovsky's famous intuition, his knowledge of esoteric paths and underwater kingdoms, of Atlantis and Celestial Jerusalem? The tottering old man always seemed to me an illustration for Gogol's story "*Terrible Vengeance.*"

And indeed, at a big, unifying meeting of the French-Russian intellectuals, where Merezhkovsky appeared next to André Gide, the young French students gaily, in unison, chanted at the sight of him:

"*Cadavre! Cadavre! Cadavre!*"

Gippius offered the guest her dry bony hand and with an amiable smile uttered some compliment: "I read your story today," or "That was a good poem of yours." Toward some, however, she shoved her paw wordlessly, almost fiercely. In the general confusion of mixed-up hands,

Zakovich, so the saying goes, before leaving, once kissed Merezhkovsky's wrist, which by no means surprised the latter.

In conversation, Gippius dropped the names of Theresa of Lisieux or
St. John of the Cross as if they were cousins of hers; the Third Testament
and Original Sin fell with the same familiarity from her lips. If Merezhkovsky instead of metaphysics had occupied himself with Marxism or
physiology, she would probably have been flirting with Engels or quoting Pavlov. Notwithstanding her interest in theology and her poetic
independence, I regard this basically malevolent creature along the lines
of Chekhov's "Darling." In her youth she was supposed to have been of
an "angelic" beauty; this is probably true—although I have noticed that
this same myth is attributed to many temperamental, literary old crones.
In my time she was already dried-up, stooped, wilted, half-blind, half-
deaf, on brittle, unbending little legs, a witch out of a German fairy tale
(but there was still something Botnian in her coloring). It was scary to
remember her lines, "And I, who am so good, when I'm in love I'll suck
your blood, and like a gentle cobra, caressingly, will wrap myself around
you . . ."

She liked the young and made protégés of several poets; I think that
there are many who should be grateful to her. Among the prose writers
the poor dear singled out only one, Felsen (this, of course, before the
arrival of the Germans).

And then, later, the Germans began their retreat, and the Merezhkovskys were left alone. Even kindred souls, such as Georgy Ivanov, vanished and tried in one way or another to save themselves. The proud
Gippius wrote of this period: "There remained only one consolation:
Mamchenko."

Not much of a consolation!

I believe that a great many of Gippius' poems will survive: more than
of Merezhkovsky's orations. But all in all, there was something unnatural, spiritually corrupting about this couple.

Once, at a large meeting of either the Green Lamp or *Chisla* (*Chisla*
replaced the Green Lamp in our lives, just as later the Circle ousted
Chisla; but at a certain period they overlapped) Ivanovich-Talin blasted
our emigré literature, contending that there were only two good writers,
but that one was directed exclusively toward the past and the other saw
only evil in life. Merezhkovsky, who presided, grew animated and
wanted to know whether "this writer, in facing the past, is not perhaps
seeking an answer to our contemporary problems?" and so on, obviously assuming that Ivanovich-Talin was referring to the author of *At-*

lantis and *Leonardo da Vinci*—his works! Upon which Talin called out from his seat: "I'm being forced to name three authors, while I had only two in mind: Bunin and Aldanov." In response the entire audience, in rare happy unanimity, applauded, howled, and whistled. Aldanov, squeezed next to me into an armchair too small for his bulk, began to fidget; he sighed and looked anxiously around.

"You see, and you thought he meant you . . ." Gippius, who was also on the dais, said with wistful irony.

For a minute or so the greyish-green, stooped Merezhkovsky confusedly mumbled something, trying to save face in an embarrassing situation. It was painful to watch him, and disgusting to behold the triumphant crowd. Whence stemmed this elementary joy? Why such general approval of a blow below the belt?

I once happened to see Merezhkovsky, on a weekday, in the church on the rue Daru. An empty cathedral, a dessicated, tiny body in a Russian fur-lined coat with beaver collar, he resembled a dried-out insect or a paralyzed rodent . . . For a long time he lay prostrate on the floor, reminiscent of the final scene in Leskov's *Chertogon* (Exorcism).

Merezhkovsky's visitors of the older generation included Kerensky, Zetlin, sometimes Aldanov, Bunin, and chance pilgrims from the provinces. Kerensky's presence always made for a festive atmosphere. At times I could have sworn that I discerned a laurel wreath on his famous crewcut. There are certain lucky people—or call them failures—who soar like brilliant comets across the horizon, leaving behind them an unaccountable, often undeserved imprint in our hearts. I experienced such a feeling at the sight of Kerensky, Lindbergh, Auden, Sirin-Nabokov, John Kennedy, Poplavsky, Vildé. This is the mystery of the "shooting stars."

But Aleksandr Fyodorovich Kerensky had only to open his mouth for me to blush for him. He was possessed by an elementary force that swept him along—at no great depth and in no definite direction. He belonged to the race of the "unsuspecting" (as Tolstoi called them). In my opinion he was simply not very intelligent. How it happened that he was sent forth to "persuade" the soldiers and muzhiks of Russia to fight remains a secret to me. Quite possibly it can be explained by the lack of intelligence of an entire "unsuspecting" generation.

In personal exchange, however, Kerensky sometimes came up with some striking observations. In answer to a critical remark of mine he once said: "Everything that is happening in Europe, and has been going on and digested for decades, began in Russia. Like in a pantomime, in the prologue to a classical tragedy, which becomes clear only at the end of the spectacle. If we had had the experience of what was later to happen in Italy and Germany, we should have been able to behave quite differently." I report his words from memory but I guarantee their general meaning.

In New York he often came to the meetings of the Third Hour, in Helene Iswolsky's cramped apartment. By then he was ailing, had undergone several operations, was losing his sight, and in general steadily going downhill. His former ideological and party friends had gradually given him up, because his "convictions" had radically changed. If I'm not mistaken, someone went so far as to accuse him of anti-Semitism

At the corner of 79th Street and Third Avenue there stands a nursing home for the aged. That's where Kerensky was put after he returned from a trip to England. One day, when I happened to be in the neighborhood, I decided to pay him a visit (actually to say good-bye). I was told the floor and room number and was permitted to go up. There was no one in the wide, empty corridor. I knocked at the door and, in answer to a hoarse voice, entered.

"Who is it?" bewildered or frightened. He was sitting in an armchair, his legs wrapped in an old-fashioned traveling rug, staring in the direction of the door, although I was already in the center of the fairly large, bright room.

"It's Yanovsky," I quickly called out. "I've come to visit you."

"Oh no, I'm busy right now."

"I understand, I'll only stay a minute. Do they often leave you alone in the room?" (From a professional point of view this was almost a crime.)

"No, not often. She went out to buy something for herself."

In connection with the Third Hour I was supposed to find out about a certain emigré who wanted to become a collaborator, an individual whom Kerensky, as I suddenly remembered, had known in Munich. I asked him about this person, and Kerensky became very animated.

"He is an awful man. He does not understand that we cannot let the Americans talk to the Russians that way. He told me quite frankly: 'I don't give a damn about anything. I'm saving up to buy a villa in Italy. Nothing else concerns me; I do as I am told.' That's the type of man he is!"

"How is your health, Aleksandr Fyodorovich?"

"Oh, much better. It was a mistake to have gone to England. They almost finished me off."

"May I call you if ever I have some other questions?"

"Yes, yes, call me." He was openly relieved. "But now I am busy."

He turned his cropped head toward the phone, which he could not possibly have reached and obviously did not intend to. These last words of his reminded me of the writer Saltykov-Shchedrin, who died a slow, agonizing death. People who came to visit him would hear him yell to his servant: "He is busy, tell them, dying!"

In the hall I met his nurse, a Japanese woman who had been taking care of him for many years. I tried to explain to her that there were many misfits of the Gorgulov type for whom it would be a direct route to the hall of fame to take a shot at Kerensky. But the Japanese did not believe, or did not understand, me.

The mere mention of Bunin was apt to evoke a smile at the Merezhkovsky's tea table, where we discussed such things as the Third Testament, Proust, or the doctrine of the Troubadours. We have to remember that Bunin and Merezhkovsky were competitors for the Nobel Prize in literature. Since this could not generate good feelings, Bunin dropped in less and less often.

It was very easy to pick on the intellectually helpless Bunin. As soon as abstract themes were broached, he, without noticing it, lost his footing. He was most successful with oral improvisations, reminiscences not about Gorky or Blok but about restaurants, about sturgeon, or about the *wagon-lits* on the Petersburg-Warsaw express.

"He is a well-shaved horse!" he might declare of a respected political figure. And immediately the fog would clear: indeed, a horse, and it shaves.

Bunin's power and brilliance lay in such concrete images. Also, of course, in his personal charm. When he would lightly lay his hard, cool, white hand on you and with the utmost attention and respect pass on his latest *bon mot,* it seemed that he spoke so sincerely and intimately only with you. Yes, the magic of the eyes, the intonation, touch, gestures . . . how rich was old Russia in charm, and where has it all gone?

Among the new fugitives there is everything in abundance: talent, erudition, sometimes conviction, ideals. But grace and charm are, alas, absent.

If in Aldanov's presence one invariably thought of Anderson's *Naked King,* then fate had played an entirely different trick on Bunin, wounding him for his entire life. From his youth, elegantly and suitably attired, he strode through the palace of literature but was consistently proclaimed a half-naked imposter. That was still in Russia, during the fireworks of Andreev, Blok, Gorky, Bryusov. It is evident that it was precisely the Russian catastrophe, the emigration, which promoted him to the leading place. Among the epigones in exile he was truly the most accomplished. And now, in Soviet Russia, they write about him that "he absolutely has to be included in the high school anthologies," not realizing that the place of a great writer is by no means in textbooks.

Thus Bunin easily occupied the first place in the old-fashioned Russian prose writing; the new prose, inspired by the European experience, defined itself only in the mid-thirties and had to educate a readership. Bunin's poetry, however, elicited ironic smiles even among the editors of *Sovremennye zapiski*. As a matter of fact, he no longer offered it for publication and perhaps did not even write any more poems until the war, when the historic circle closed once more and there arose a demand for the native landscape with mooing cows and the smell of wormwood or fresh steaming milk. I understand that the masters of social realism now hugely enjoy Bunin's verses and admire their monolithic character. Still and all, the initial rejection was a bitter experience which left deep wounds; merely to touch them would elicit a violent reaction. The mention of Gorky, Andreev, Blok, or Bryusov brought forth a stream of abuse. One could see how much and for how long he had suffered in the shadow of the fortunate ones of that era.

Bunin passed over all of Russian symbolism[5] without the slightest interest, stubbornly pursuing his dialogue with oak copses, birches and skylarks. A ridiculed but independent outsider, he could finally take revenge on his tormentors. Undoubtedly, for the present politburo Bunin's poems are still more understandable and famliar than those of Andrei Bely or Annensky.

To Bunin's credit it must be said that he never put on airs, never aped anyone, never wanted to be "in fashion" but remained always himself: a proud dinosaur condemned to extinction.

His writing seems familiar to us on the basis of other, earlier authors. But he, I daresay, "makes" it better than even the greatest of his precursors. This is the law of the epigones. Bunin describes willows bordering a swamp, or a peasant woman's calves perhaps more successfully than did Turgenev or Tolstoi; his people drink wine from goblets . . . But Tolstoi's and Turgenev's merits are not in such descriptions—or not only in them.

To perform a neat acrobatic trick over a solidly spread net in a big circus, this is the fate of epigones. But what about the first acrobats who flew from one trapeze to the other without a safety net below?

It is characteristic that Zurov, a follower of Bunin, in other words the epigone of an epigone, describes even more artfully the kiss of a peasant girl or the crusty winter snow. Here we see some law at work.

In a drawing room or at meetings Bunin was elegant and courteous. Close-shaven, pale, greyhaired, pointedly erect and dry—a nobleman, a European.

"He assumed this posture after they removed his hemorrhoids," Ivanov declared, sticking out his protruding lip even more.

At night, in Montparnasse, sitting down with us at the Select or at Dominique, Bunin was simple, and graceful in a masculine way. One could not, and should not, speak to him about abstract matters. God forbid any mention of the gnostics or Kafka or even great Russian poetry. He had an inordinate liking for Maupassant, whom the French do not acknowledge as a great writer (just as the Americans underestimate Edgar Allen Poe!). Which did not prevent Russia from going crazy over both these writers.

God forbid that one should mention Bunin's personal acquaintances to him: Gorky, Andreev, Bely, even Gumilyov. For all his contemporaries he had bitter, biting words, like a former servant avenging himself on his hateful old masters. He claimed that he had always despised Gorky and his works. However, his best, if conventional poem ("The Forest like a Colorful Castle") was originally dedicated to Maksim Gorky. Later, in the emigration, he reprinted it without the dedication.

"Leave Father N. alone!" he might suddenly cry out in an impulse of magnanimity, though we had no intention of saying anything against Father N. "Leave him alone, he is my Mitya!"

Here we can discern an interesting contradiction, which casts a light on the process of Bunin's creativity and on the limitations of his horizon. In his novel *Mitina lyubov* (*Mitya's Love*), the protagonist ends up as a rather banal suicide, while the real young man entered a monastery and soon became an outstanding member of the hierarchy.

Having been neglected in his youth, Bunin's natural inclination was to ridicule, curse, debase. When a wealthy businessman treated him to a fine dinner, he behaved capriciously to show his independence, criticized the wine, ordered the waiters around, yelled, "If they offered me such sturgeon in Moscow I would . . ."

Watching him, one could easily believe that, in Russia, people who were not necessarily bad smeared mustard on the nose of the waiter or smashed heavy mirrors only to show their independence. And the owner of the restaurant understood it no less than Freud or Adler would have done.

Bunin was interested in the sexual life of the Montparnassians; in this respect he was completely a Westerner—without shudders, sermons, or repentance. However, he felt that women should not be granted the same freedom as men. For some reason that angered the poet Stavrov.

Bunin's family life proceeded in rather a complicated manner. Vera Nikolaevna, his wife, who described the bleak early youth of "Yan," as she called Ivan, in detail, does not touch upon his later adventures, or in any case she did not publish them.

Besides Galina Kuznetsova—at that time a healthy, red-cheeked young woman with a little snub nose—Zurov, too, lived with the Bunins. Ivan Alexeevich had singled out Zurov as a "congenial" author and invited him to leave his native Baltic and join their household. Gradually, however, Zurov, instead of gratitude, began to feel something akin to hatred for his benefactor. On top of it all, despite Madame Bunin's solicitous care, or perhaps because of it, Zurov suddenly became mentally ill, periodically succumbing to attacks of madness. He had for a long time been writing a gigantic epic, *The Winter Palace,* which for many reasons he could not or did not want to publish in the emigré press.

In his later years, Bunin, with a sarcastic wink at Zurov's room, would inform his guests: "He is still writing *War and Peace,* ha-ha-ha!"

Telling me about it in New York, Aldanov concluded: "I respect that, I respect it very much, but personally I couldn't work for ten years on the same book."

When Aldanov was writing his play for Fondaminsky's theater, he methodically went through the most famous dramas, contemporary as well as classical. "There are no good plays!" he informed me with some sadness. We were sitting upstairs at the Murat. Bunin had just returned from Italy and happily repeated Mussolini's declaration that he would not permit Spain to be divided into two parts! One ought, of course, to have explained to Aldanov why he had not noticed any good plays. But Bunin interrupted to tell us that he, too, had once upon a time attempted to write a tragedy but had failed and destroyed the manuscript.

"Now that I don't understand," Aldanov reproached him in the tone of a careful housekeeper. "Why not put it aside, save it? At a later date it will come in handy."

"That would bother me," Bunin reluctantly explained to his friend. "The fireplace puts an end to it."

I believe Galina Kuznetsova was Bunin's last prize, romantically speaking. When she eloped with Margarita Stepun, a whole part of Bunin's life was over.

In the south, in Grasse, Kuznetsova, flaunting her perhaps somewhat banal prettiness, would emerge from Bunin's room and in her slight stutter say to Vera Nikolaevna, "Ivan Alekseevich received a very interesting letter from Paris." (This in the presence of others.)

"Well, if it's interesting, he will tell me about it himself," Madame Bunin replied with great dignity.

Khodasevich called Kuznetsova-Zurov "Bunin's feudal theater."

In Montparnasse, Bunin visited our different poetesses, trying to investigate the local mysteries. Later he said: "My darlings, you haven't invented anything new. In Moscow there was a certain Inna Vasilievna . . ."

The typical trick of an inveterate provincial: at the sight of the Louvre to remember a native museum; while reading Proust to eulogize some Siberian genius who drank himself to death fifty years ago. Now Zaitsev was a man of much greater culture: he knew several languages and appreciated the West—in any case, the art of the West.

As I think of those late evenings spent in the company of Bunin, I am unable to recall anything said that was the least bit meaningful in the abstract sense. Not a single thought of a general character, not a single association worth serious attention. Nothing but colorful little pictures, idiomatic expressions, sarcastic jokes, and criticism—criticism of everybody and everything! Incidentally, Tolstoi also criticized many people, but he resented not a Gorky or a Blok, but Shakespeare and Napoleon.

"How are you making out, Ivan Alekseevich, sexually speaking?" I usually asked when meeting him by chance after midnight in Montparnasse.

"I'll hit you between the eyes and you'll find out," came the answer. And this old-fashioned expression, "between the eyes," sounded like the waltz "On the Dunes of Manchuria" . . .

The one thing he ever said that made an impact on me and which I remember often, as I do quotes from Proust or Dostoevsky, were his words regarding reviews, criticisms, and articles about him. "Up to this day—and there has been so much of it," I heard him once say at Dominique, "up to this day, whenever I see my name in print, I immediately feel here, in my heart" (he scratched his chest on the left side); "I feel something here akin to an orgasm."

Such revelations of the sensual world were characteristic of him. And this I also remember: during the occupation, Adamovich, in Nice, once showed me a postcard from Bunin. He wrote that a certain gentleman had come for a visit and that to get rid of him in such times was impossible. "He probably has nowhere to go." These last words I remember exactly; they sounded to me like Pushkin's ". . . and for compassion for the fallen he called." It was unexpected and splendid.

When Bunin was awarded the Nobel Prize, all the correspondents, and the Russian press in particular, noted how elegantly, in what a courtly manner the laureate bowed to the King of Sweden. Bunin's tails, his shirt, everything was impeccable! But one thing they forgot to mention, or mentioned only in passing: the contents of his speech. Translated by someone for Bunin, perhaps with the help of Andrei Sedykh, and delivered in his bad accent, the speech was flat and colorless.

This seemed his chance to stand up to his full height, to cry out some truths about the Bolsheviks, about the war, about the heroism of the emigration, about freedom, real and conventional. Within one hour, the entire world would hear him, read him, repeat his words. But no, Bunin had nothing to add to his works. He was a local, Russian, phenomenon. He could only impress Europe and America with his elegant tails and courtly bow.

Despite our frequent encounters there was almost no personal relationship between Bunin and myself. Once we sat for an entire evening alone in a corridor, waiting for the end of a meeting where Adamovich, Gippius, Weidlé, and even Khodasevich were praising Felsen's prose (and where the latter on the spot read a couple of fragments from his work). Bunin suffered from the "social contract" of our critics as much as I did. So we talked and gossiped in whispers for about two hours. He was an intelligent, sarcastic, nasty interlocutor, redeeming ignorance with charm. Everything that I wrote was utterly alien to him; his "psychological" novels seemed to me repetitious, in the Russian manner, of the Maupassant or Schnitzler era—that is, replete with delicious hors d'oeuvres, skylarks, and sunsets.

Whenever a new book of mine came out, I sent the laureate a politely inscribed copy. At our next meeting he would thank me, sometimes paying me an ambiguous compliment. Thus he said (approximately) about *The Other Love:* "The religious transfiguration is well done. But your heroine mentions her menstruation. You don't know women. They never speak about that."

I could only sigh deeply and smile; I wouldn't argue with him about such matters. Finally I told him: "Ivan Alekseevich, you only know Russian women of the old regime. Admit it, you never had a romance with a European woman!"

"I'll hit you between the eyes, then you'll know," was his unsophisticated answer.

Madame Bunin often argued with her husband about the details of one or another occurence he described: where, when, with whom . . . She was a "saintly" Russian woman, created to unconditionally, sacrificially

follow her hero to Siberia, into the mines, or to Monte Carlo and Stockholm, no matter. It so happened that she did not have to follow him into
forced labor, but she would not have been afraid to share the fate of the
wives of Volkonsky and Trubetskoi,[6] perhaps would have even preferred
it to Grasse and 1, rue Jacques Offenbach.*

For the yearly ball of the Union of Young Writers and Poets,** or for
large group or individual readings Vera Nikolaevna untiringly collected
donations, sold tickets, thanked, and bowed with dignity. She made the
rounds of the Russian delicatessens, carrying away donations of sprats
from Riga and Polish kilbasi for the buffets. She took an interest in the
fate of any poet or journalist, indeed of any acquaintance who was in
trouble; and she ran out into the cold, the wet, the dark—to help.

There was a certain Roshchin, a contributor to *Vozrozhdenie* (he later
went back to Moscow). It was he who recounted with pride how he had
treated Kuprin to a fine dinner where he seized the opportunity of reading aloud to him his own new novel. Kuprin, asking for more brandy,
benevolently cried out: "You should write and write and write!" (Incidentally, it was assumed that it was in fact Kuprin who had composed a
less than flattering epigram about Roshchin: "The little one has found a
simple solution: he sits down, shits, and signs it Roshchin.")

This Roshchin suddenly seduced the legal wife of a Russian taxi driver
(with a child) and then could not manage to feed his family with his
creative work. Vera Nikolaevna took care of this problem, about which
Zurov or Kuznetsova will probably some day tell us in detail.

After having finished medical school, in order to get my diploma of
Docteur de l'Université de Paris, I was obliged to *publish* my dissertation. And that cost money.

Vera Nikolaevna shuttled from one well-nourished philanthropist to
another with a list of donations for my Thèse de Paris. I felt bad about it:
after all, a diploma in medicine has nothing to do with literature. Why
should she put herself out? But she, with a cool smile on her pale, matte,
oval face—somehow reminiscent of the Gioconda—explained: "I enjoy
doing it. Usually I address myself to these practical people to ask support
for poetry which they don't know and won't ever read. But now, for the
first time, I can approach them about something tangible that will give
them pleasure: a man needs to publish his dissertation, then he will settle
down and begin to help others. That they understand!"

In Bunin's presence, Zurov conducted himself strangely, to say the

---

*The Bunin's address in Paris.
**Writers' organization, established in Paris in 1925.

least: always silent, rarely addressing him directly and, when Bunin told one of his stories, listening with a smile which I called Gorgulovian—as if he knew some truth about Bunin which contradicted all appearances. Later, when Zurov fell ill, he threatened many times to cut Bunin's throat, and it became Vera Nikolaevna's lot not only to take care of the sick man but also to prevent sharp razors from falling into his hands. When a guest wanted to hang his coat on the first available hook in their entrance hall, she warned in a whisper: "No, this is Leonid Fyodoro-vich's hook. It will upset him. Hang your coat on the next one."

Bunin did not like any contemporary prose, whether emigré or Euro-pean. He praised (lukewarmly) only Aldanov. When *Russkie zapiski* be-gan to appear, Aldanov, as with his novels in *Sovremennye zapiski*, took up fifty pages in each issue. In Montparnasse we joked that after Alda-nov's death there would be lots of room in the emigré press; alas, we did not realize that others would also leave, and first of all educated readers. In connection with Aldanov's new creation, *Punshevaya vodka* (The Vodka Punch), I even managed to embarrass Bunin, pressing him to explain what was so good about it. Giving a few feeble reasons, he quite unconvincingly concluded, "But how well it is written!" "Badly writ-ten, Ivan Alekseevich," I retorted. "Aleksei Tolstoi writes divinely in comparison with such imitation."

Bunin, of course, cursed Aleksei Tolstoi but rated his vigorous talent highly. I believe that Bunin's taste was utterly provincial, even if he did genuinely and seriously like Lev Tolstoi.

By character, upbringing, and general inclinations, Bunin could have tended toward fascism. But he did not fall for it. His true hatred of the Bolsheviks did not lead him toward sympathy for Hitler. He was re-pelled by both regimes, and above all by their vulgarity.

On his visit to Kuznetsova in Germany, he was searched by the S.S. at the border. (They stuck a finger in his anus, looking for jewels or what-ever.) I remember with what fury he spoke about this experience. I believe that episodes of this kind played a greater role in the life of the biologically integrated Bunin than all kinds of theories and programs.

In all those years, Bunin wrote me only two or three times, always short, matter-of-fact notes. But there was to be one exception. In the summer of 1942, before leaving for the United States, I wrote to him from Montpellier, asking for addresses, Aldanov's and others, in Amer-ica. Bunin answered by return mail from Grasse, and he wrote most thoroughly. He gave me the necessary addresses, adding one or two on his own. "Are you writing, I mean literary writing? . . ." he asked, and continued: "One must write, especially in such times. It is the only worthy answer still within our means!" (I am quoting from memory.) This letter was the more touching and supportive in that for him my writing had no meaning—and I knew it. This mixture of natural elegance, tact, and compassion with the coarseness of an uneducated nobleman was especially moving in Bunin.

At the Ball of the Russian Press, on 13 January, I once found myself next to the gracefully stooping Bunin in tails: around us, half-nude women moved in un-Russian dances to sinfully promising music.

"Ivan Alekseevich," I said to him, "don't you think that we have screwed up our lives?"

He was not surprised by this strange question nor offended by my familiar "we"; thinking for a moment, he replied very soberly without, however, taking his eyes from the circling couples:

"Yes—but *what* we tried for!"

In those years, Aldanov invariably paid Merezhkovsky compliments: "Dmitry Sergeevich, in Germany they consider you the foremost Russian writer, although a reactionary. As the *Berliner Tageblatt* says, "*Ein eingefleischter Reaktionaer.*"

Flattered, Merezhkovsky grinned, but repeated with bitterness: "*Eingefleischter Reaktionaer!*" He did not consider himself as such.

When Aldanov's interminable trilogy, *Klyuch,* started to appear, he frequently showed up at the Merezhkovskys. Once the following conversation took place in the corner of their drawing-room.

"Mark Aleksandrovich, I intend to give *Klyuch* a bad review. Will you be very disappointed?"

"Very much so, Zinaida Nikolaevna, you cannot even imagine how that would hurt me."

So, Gippius did not write about *Klyuch.*

"What really is your new novel? Is it a mystery story?" she asked on another occasion, moving her lorgnette in all directions, not daring to look straight at Aldanov, an important editor of *Poslednie novosti.*

"It's a psychological novel," Aldanov explained ingratiatingly, looking around warily, as if afraid of being overheard by outsiders.

"Mark Aleksandrovich," Merezhkovsky called over, interrupting a discussion about Marcion. "We have decided that Zina should begin to contribute to *Poslednie novosti.* What do you think?"

"Many people won't understand such a literary divorce," Aldanov replied gently.

It is the miracle of Aldanov's career that he was never abused in print (except by Khodasevich). In bewilderment, I often asked experienced literati: "Please, explain! Why does the entire press, including the extreme right, eulogize him?"

Later, the DPs also skillfully inserted compliments to Aldanov into their articles: a little vignette, something they had used earlier, in Russia, with regard to Stalin, the Father of the People. They arrived at this ploy instinctively, claiming that thanks to such pronouncements, their articles were sure to be accepted without large cuts and would even be met with approval by influential critics.

What was the mystery of Aldanov? Was he such a good writer, did he always write in such an excellent style that there was never a reason for our patriots to sling mud at him, as was done to all other Russian literary martyrs?

Tolstoi was caught in grammatical errors, as Dostoevsky, Pushkin, Lermontov, Dershavin, Gogol, and Pasternak. Who in Russian literature was not crucified for his grammar or syntax? But not Aldanov. He was never reproached for anything. Whatever he produced was met with uniform praise. What happened to the professional emigré critics?

In Montparnasse, Ivanov quoted lines from Aldanov's latest installment, in which his heroine, Musya, tries to behave "like a woman." Alas, Aldanov was outside all sexual contexts. Like many of our humanists, he married once and thus solved all his intimate problems, never betraying his wife and never engendering a child. Vishnyak, Zenzinov, Rudnev, Fondaminsky, Fedotov, Berdyaev, and many Marxists, all of them were people with no offspring. Astonishing, how many eunuchs there were in that generation!

Thus the lines in which poor Musya is flirting or occupied with her toilet, coming from the somber Georgy Ivanov, acquired a commically sinister aspect. We all laughed mirthlessly: Aldanov took up half the space available for prose in the magazines and probably half of the critical reviews.

He was considered a paragon of kindness and amiability: he never refused anyone anything. But there was no great profit to be derived from his favors either. I was repulsed by his constant over-readiness to be helpful.

A highly talented, highly cultivated essayist and journalist, he for some reason decided to write endless novels. And that was a fatal mistake. Whenever I reread *Dead Souls,* I quite involuntarily, however, always at the same pages, think of Aldanov: "The newly arrived guest also argued, but somehow exceptionally skillfully, so that everyone saw that he was arguing, but arguing pleasantly. He never said: 'You led . . .' but would say: 'You were so good as to lead,' 'I had the honor of covering your deuce,' and so on."

In her charming *Grassky zhurnal* (Grasse Diary), in which she does not say a harsh word about anyone, Galina Kuznetsova, a writer of great delicacy, nevertheless remarks about Aldanov: "During the entire trip, there and back, he plied me with questions. That is his manner. He tirelessly asks, and one feels that everything he is told is being put in the enormous storage room of his memory, whence it will be pulled out at the opportune moment. He posed questions about absolutely everything: how we have arranged our life here, whether there was hunting, horseback riding, why Ivan Alekseevich did not hunt, did not ride, why he did not fish—and so on and so on."

How can we not remember the famous chest in which Chichikov* "had the habit of putting anything that he could lay his hands on." And in another passage from *Dead Souls:* "After that, of course, the letter was folded and put into the chest next to some posters and a wedding invitation which had been resting there in the same place, in the same position for seven years."

When a writer sent Aldanov his new book, he would by return mail receive a postcard with thanks and best wishes for success. Bunin, if he wrote at all, would not do so unless he had read, or at least leafed through, the book.

"May I enquire what you are working on?" Aldanov would ask, and the young writer looked around bewildered, not sure that the words were addressed to him. And when he got his answer, Aldanov would continue politely: "And where do you plan to publish?" This question, perhaps appropriate in Moscow, made no sense under our conditions.

I once happened to observe Aldanov at a semipolitical meeting, and thus I came to understand a great deal. The meeting had been called at the demand of Milyukov, president of the Union of Writers and Journalists, to exclude Alekseev, one of the members, on the suspicion of collaboration with Soviet counter-espionage. It was a stormy meeting. His colleagues from *Vozrozhdenie* stood up for Alekseev, most vociferously of all the infamous Surguchov, author of the play *Osennie skripki* (Autumn Violins), whose violins began to sound as sweet as spring in 1940. They all kept insisting that there was no proof to support the accusation.

"Shame! Shame!" yelled Surguchov.

---

*The main character in Gogol's *Dead Souls*.

"Shame, shame!" took up Meyer, another journalist, from the front row. And the tiny auditorium of the Russian Musical Society vibrated very unmusically.

For some reason many young writers, who had their own Union of Writers and Poets, were present at the meeting. I guess that all the "avant-garde" forces had been mobilized.

The chairman was Zeeler, general secretary of the Union, a man whom I also considered an escapee from *Dead Souls* (Sobakevich). Several weird, troublesome persons took the floor, to Zeeler's confusion and irritation. Our attitude toward a possible member of the Cheka[9] was unequivocal, and we calmly waited for the vote. It has to be noted that, over the years, several dozen writers had gathered in Paris, who during the entire emigration never flirted with the embassy on the rue de Grenelle,* who later did not don the green German uniform and did not collaborate in the "new order" German press. The historian of Russian literature will some day have to note this fact with approval. (What happened to Maklakov, Kerensky's ambassador to France, was a special phenomenon after the armistice—a spontaneous reaction to the miraculous salvation of Russia.)

During the intermission I asked Aldanov: "And you, Mark Aleksandrovich, what do you think of this business?"

"It's all very sad," he answered reluctantly, "what is there to think?" (Almost the same answer he gave me later, in New York, in relation to the quarrel between Bunin and Zaitsev-Zeeler.)

When it came time to vote, I by chance, at the most intense moment, looked back and saw the plump Aldanov—reminiscent of a walrus with flipperlike hands—slip with great agility out of the door and disappear, avoiding the open vote.

Much in Aldanov seemed to me—and was—sham, his wish to be taken for a native of St. Petersburg or of Western Europe, for example. There was a legend that he drank a lot and wrote his novels in a café, exactly like the *poètes maudits*. Even his benevolence, his helpfulness, his decency seemed tainted; there was the tinge of a lie, so hated by Lev Tolstoi, whom Aldanov venerated.

"The key to *War and Peace* is lost, it cannot be found!" he complained in a confessional mood. It was assumed that each literary work had its "key," and if Mark Aldanov could not find it, no one ever would.

Aldanov understood that one *had to* praise Proust; I don't think that he

---

*The location of the Soviet embassy.

read him. Mentioning him with respect, he immediately quoted some other writer whom one could not possibly name in the same breath—for instance, Marquand. Moreover, there is not a trace of Proust in Aldanov's work. But he often reiterated that he could not forgive himself two fatal mistakes: that he had never traveled to Yasnaya Polyana and that he had not seen Proust while he was still alive, although both these possibilities had been open to him. That was characteristic of Aldanov: to read Proust was not a must, but to have cast a glance at him from a corner of a café was *de rigueur*.

Incidentally, what a nightmarish literary anecdote is that of the sole meeting between Proust and Joyce in this life! Introduced in a crowded, fashionable salon, they stood for a while next to each other, exchanged conventional greetings and phrases and parted: they had absolutely nothing to talk about. Here it is appropriate to recall an episode from my personal life; on a different level it also bears witness to the tragic shortsightedness of the human race . . .

In June 1942 we sailed from Casablanca to the United States on the Portuguese ship the *Serpa Pinta*. After boring stops at the Azores and Bermuda, we cast anchor in New Jersey at the end of the month (and not in July, as has been erroneously reported by some). During the trip my attention had been attracted by a dishevelled, badly groomed young woman, always in the same brownish dress that smelled of sweat. To add to this, she seemed to talk incessantly, and, although her French was impeccable, on the level of Descartes and Pascal, the tone of her speech, droning on without pause, rapping stubbornly, insistently, hysterically, frightened me. I avoided her like the plague and seeing her at the stern fled to the bow (or vice versa). I did not even once attempt to speak to her. The young woman's name was Simone Weil.

Chapter 7 · Our Philosophers

For a time I lived in Vanves, on the rue de l'Avenir (see *Portativnoe bessmertie* [Portable Immortality]); from my window I could observe the railroad tracks leading to Meudon. When I went through a miniature tunnel to the other side of the road, I was in Clamart. There one could meet Berdyaev, a majestic, handsome old man with silver-grey hair, in a blue beret, spastically clenching a stubby empty cigar holder between his teeth, thus suppressing his nervous tic. He descended the stone stoop of his small villa (a present from an American lady) and carefully picked his way down the street to the Clamart station or to the streetcar which ran as far as Châtelet, in the center of Paris. In the opposite direction this streetcar ran to the very edge of the forest of Meudon.

Berdyaev was one of the few emigrés in Paris who had preserved aristocratic dignity and lordly independence. Ordinary "refugees" were mercilessly thrown hither and yon, like the Jewish tribes in the diaspora . . . Minor French officials, fashionable deputies, and chauvinistic tabloids in one voice accused the late Tsar's officers, lawyers, academicians, chauffeurs, and their wives of all seven cardinal sins. There could be no two ways about it: the *sales métèques*★ were responsible for all French calamities.

And indeed, looking at them, one was surprised by the lack of solidity, the dishonesty and the particular flimsiness of their existence, by their clumsy enterprises and grandiose fly-by-night projects. And, to boot, an utter misunderstanding of the local laws: fear of the police, uncertainty about their own rights, lapsed papers, efforts to win the right of asylum and an *avis favorable* (working papers), and an abundance of defeatist anecdotes.

This fostered a rapproachement of the different generations, strata, and waves of the Russian emigration, strengthening the creative traits,

---

★Dirty foreigners.

gathering all in one living cluster. Of course, a specific role was played by the French air, the landscape, the juice of the grape—and the law (*lex*). A particular characteristic of French culture is the purely Roman definition of nationality: the place where you legally belong, your passport, as the definitive criterion; Anglo-Saxons (America included) and Russians continue to be guided by racial or religious considerations. Herein lies the advantage of the Latin countries in the inevitable collaboration with the peoples of Asia and Africa.

Two colossuses, the USSR and the USA, both primitive and almost equally materialistic, are preparing for mutual extinction in the name of freedom and progress. And both these empires have yet to solve their own basic tribal and racial contradictions.

France, like the Roman Empire, is guided exclusively by legal distinctions. And our self-styled philosophers who decided that *Marianne* is bankrupt are perhaps a little hasty: the primacy of legal and cultural values over ancient genetic attributes is undeniably a cornerstone of the Christian world.

Thus, in France, one could observe the Judification of the Russian emigration, an overall process, except for lucky archdukes and plain dukes who had tsarist gold in the bank and comfortable villas in Menton and lived independently. Anyway, until the arrival of Hitler, they expressed themselves less and less on matters concerning culture.

Right-wing emigrés did not purchase tickets for our meetings and did not support our literature. They were indifferent and also apprehensive. "You are all Masons," these smart alecks said, winking meaningfully. Anyone except General Krasnov they considered superfluous and even suspect; some of them, it's true, occasionally referred to Dostoevsky, but they hardly ever read him.

The employees of *Poslednie novosti* invented a funny sort of game. One or the other would suddenly announce: "Listen! The door opens and Chekhov enters, stooped and alive, carrying his latest manuscript. He wants to know whether the editors will accept it." And we have to improvise a suitable reaction. To general laughter one of us would say: "There's that old devil again with his stories!"

The truth of such a joke lay in the fact that, because of the tight emigré market and the enormous competition—excessive supply, limited demand—Chekhov, like Remizov, would have had to humble himself to place his work and make a living. Yes, just one decade of hopeless poverty had radically reduced the Russian intelligentsia to beggars.

However, there were people of yet another type. The famous game played in *Poslednie novosti* would come to a halt when the door opened and an imaginary Lev Nikolaevich Tolstoi entered . . . everyone stepped aside to let him pass immediately into Demidov's office: in this case a condescending or familiar tone would clearly be out of place.

Berdyaev, in emigration, behaved like someone who belonged, by right, to that race of "lions." He was supposed to be a descendant of the Bourbons and carried himself accordingly, as the first among equals or an equal among the chosen.

I first saw him at a Russian meeting. All the chairs in the overcrowded, uncomfortable room had long since been taken, and I sat down on a narrow table against the wall in the back, looking over the motley emigré heads toward the dais from whence the impressive philosopher hurled forth his brief sentences. Suddenly I became aware that, with his head and wrist, the speaker was making abrupt, spastic motions in my direction, apparently wishing me to relinquish my comfortable seat. Reluctantly I got down. "A radical thinker, but he doesn't permit his audience the slightest breach of etiquette," I said to myself.

After the meeting I complained—to the laughter of my friends. It turned out that I had mistaken his famous tic for a gesture directed at me. This persistent tic, aimed simultaneously at every person in the auditorium, was of course not an accidental phenomenon. It bore witness to an old injury which had left him with a festering wound. Here we have the difference between a sage and a philosopher: there were many of the former in the ancient (agrarian) world; the latter have multiplied since the invention of the printing press.

The wise man lives by his ideas and teachings. All that is demanded of a "philosopher" is knowledge and the talent for analytical or generalizing thought. I believe that Socrates, Diogenes, Tolstoi, and Skovoroda could have rid themselves of such a Berdyaevan tic, but not Freud or Solovyov.

Another of our professors, Fyodor Stepun, had to stop smoking on doctor's orders. He sucked, in a humiliating way, on dead cigarette butts, watched the clock, figuring out how many minutes there were left until the next cigarette, and complained bitterly about his fate: just when he was doing his most important work he had to give up tobacco! His wife, a straightforward, intelligent woman, said angrily: "What kind of philosopher are you? If you can't overcome even one of your weaknesses, then you are simply a jerk!" (I quote the words of Margarita Stepun, his sister.)

I believe that every sage—that is, someone who lives in accordance with his teachings—becomes a teacher of life as well and can be enormously useful even if his system is outwardly primitive. A philosopher, on the other hand, unfortunately teaches only philosophy. We have somehow forgotten all this, while in the "backward" countries there are still many wise men left, people who integrate thought and action.

From Berdyaev I inherited only one valuable idea, and it was of social import. From him I heard for the first time that one cannot speak to a hungry man about the Holy Ghost: that would indeed be a sin against the Holy Ghost.

This simple truth led me to an inner reform. I understood that it is possible to participate in the liturgy by working for the improvement of the public welfare, that, while fighting Marxism, we can be brothers to the exploited.

For this modest inheritance I forgive Berdyaev his "new middle ages," his messianism, his elaborations on the Russian "national soul," and other dangerous ravings.

The time has come to remember that the "national idea" is an invention of pagan German romanticism. Yet some thinkers, even those who fight the Prussian spirit and defend the Christian church, nevertheless refer to that notorious "national soul" as if it were a reality of the Christian experience.

The doctors of the church, the saints, and the early Christians did not advance the concept of a national soul. They did not embrace this nebulous concept. They stressed that which is personal, individually chosen, and purified in the fire of the Holy Spirit.

A national soul exists in a natural, pre-Christian, herdlike way of life. "The Jews require a sign . . ." This is a national idea, before the second birth. "The Greeks seek after wisdom. . . . but we preach Christ crucified. . . ." All are Christians: Greeks and Jews, Japanese and Romans henceforth have only one name by which they are saved, one door, one way. To use the national idea within the framework of Christianity is as absurd as to lie down on the Freud-Jung couch or, with rolled-up pants, to run after Darwin.

In 1931, my novel *Mir* was published. I sent Berdyaev a copy and was honored with several letters from him. He claimed that I was under the influence of Céline's recently published *Voyage au bout de la nuit*. In answer I explained that being, like Céline, a French doctor, I was of course prey to the same temptations of topics and mannerisms.

Berdyaev was attentive to the younger generation and quite frequently turned up in the Circle, though leaving early, to get home to Clamart. For his lectures he usually prepared a brief outline which he would consult, now and then, as he continued his lucid speech, which consisted of simple and terse sentences. He would patiently listen to our objections and argue seriously, without resentment.

There is a widespread opinion that during the Paris era, Berdyaev, Fedotov, and Adamovich influenced the emigration. This is, of course, true; but it does not exhaust the subject. For, on the other hand, there was also *our* influence. So that it is difficult to judge *who* influenced *whom* and *how*. I happen to believe that certain talks and readings by Poplavsky (and other young writers) affected Berdyaev and Fedotov and other "intellectual leaders" and evoked a creative echo in them.

In the Paris of the thirties, a team of master craftsmen laid out a complicated, wonderful mosaic; one might say that we all—or most of us—gathered honey with equal zeal. Therein lies the value of that era; and only thanks to the participation of an entire team was it possible—up to a point—to arrive at a unity of style, taste, color, and tone. To assume that emigré culture blossomed only while Kuprin, Bunin, Khodasevich, and Merezhkovsky were alive and that with their end everything decayed, betrays ignorance of the basic miracle of an emigration.

It so happened that my wife, Paulina, whom I put on the train leaving Paris on 10 June 1940, after twenty-four hours landed at Berdyaev's house in the south of France. They did not know her personally there; but after a short, fully justified moment of suspense, she was invited in and put up for several days, until she was able to travel on to Fondaminsky's place in Arcachon. There were many temptations in this situation, but Berdyaev behaved like a sage and a teacher of life.

I read my *Plan Sviftsona* (Swiftson's Plan), which was later published in *Novy grad,* to the Circle. Milyukov, who had accepted *Portativnoe bessmertie* for *Russkie zapiski,* omitted that chapter under the pretext that he did not share the opinions expressed in it.

In my plan for all possible reforms I suggested, among other things, that we choose the leaders of our cells from the worst, and not from the best, brethren. Thus there could be no power struggle and no jealousy. I proposed the same for the ecumenical liturgy, namely, to recognize one of the weaker churches and accept its rites. Fondaminsky, who naively believed in an "elite" (the intelligentsia), hastened, before Berdyaev's departure, to clear up precisely this point, which had astonished him greatly. With a smile, Berdyaev supported me.

He was backed up by the aura of a blessed authenticity: no one could imagine bribing this nobleman (whereas with Merezhkovsky one immediately sensed a potential metaphysical sellout). Berdyaev spent the years of occupation in heroic and dignified isolation. After the victory, in which the Russian "*katyushas*"* played such a decisive role, his recogni-

---

*Nickname of the mobile multibarrelled gun.

tion of Stalin's empire was psychologically just as inevitable as Maklakov's visit to the Rue de Grenelle.

In the New York magazine *The Third Hour* (Iswolsky, Manziarli,
Lourié, Yanovsky) we continued long afterward, to Fedotov's outrage,
to publish Berdyaev's patriotic articles at the front of the magazine. Now
it is, of course, clear that Fedotov was right.

We sent Berdyaev parcels of dark buckwheat, which our European
philosopher of Bourbon descent simply adored. At requiem services for
Berdyaev, in the Russian Cathedral on Second Avenue, Fedotov came up
to me and, with the hysterical precipitation of the Russian intellectual,
forgave Berdyaev everything for which the latter had not asked forgiveness, declaring: "He died at his desk! Like a soldier at his post! Like a
soldier!"

I said nothing in reply: it was a difficult and shameful moment. For all.
For Fedotov, because of his unconvincing tone and gestures; for myself
and my own, inept, judgments. For the deceased, even if he did die at his
post. We were all confused by terrible Russia, "patriotism" and "mo-
therland." What is true in Paris ought to be true in the Kremlin as well;
an Englishman's light cannot be a shadow for a Russian—and vice versa.
"Our fatherland is where our heavenly Father is."

Decades later, when Cardinal Spellman visited Vietnam and told the
American recruits, "My country, right or wrong, . . ." we wanted to
hold our noses to escape the stench of a newly rising paganism. Let Anna
Akhmatova be right for herself personally, when, catlike, she would not
leave her native home; but three times as right is the sacred emigration
which in prophetic wrath attempted to repulse, tie up Russia, the beloved, violent maniac, and put her into a straitjacket.

Berdyaev did indeed sit daily at his post, his writing desk! All his life
he wrote every morning. After lunch he slept three hours or so—a Russian landowner's sleep. Then tea, and back to his basic occupation. Merezhkovsky also wrote regularly, four hours in the morning, for sixty-
five years. So did Remizov. There were no other diversions for these
martyrs. Neither sports nor women, neither wine nor cards. How many
tomes can one write in this way? And what does it prove? A man's
endurance? His talent? Or his unfitness for any other reality?

I had occasion to be present at the meetings of two sages and friends,
Berdyaev and Shestov. It was a most touching sight: the two old men
used the familiar "thou," and something boyish peeped through when
they addressed each other in that way. Timid, chaste, and tentative
sounded this, their probably last living "thou."

"Why don't you send it to *Sovremennye zapiski*?" Berdyaev inquired solicitously.

"They've already published me once," Shestov answered, justifying the journal. In his frock coat, tall, thin, round-shouldered, with a grey goatee, he resembled a country doctor's aide whom "old-timers" trust more than the doctor.

"And why don't *you* send something to *Sovremennye zapiski*?" I asked Berdyaev.

"I don't need to," he answered condescendingly, "and sometimes I do give them a piece."

Berdyaev was readily published by foreigners, for some reason very frequently in South America. He also had admirers in France and Spain.

Getting into the mood, the two venerables began to banter; Shestov told an old joke, and Berdyaev smiled distractedly and radiantly. I vaguely recall that it was something comical about their readers. Remizov had supposedly said to Shestov: "Lev Isaakovich, yesterday I saw your reader on Nevsky Prospect. He very cautiously crossed the road and stopped in front of a shop window." (Something along these lines, but much funnier.)

At that time I was not yet troubled by the absence of readers; I assumed that it was a passing, temporary phenomenon. Two or three hundred people bought our books, came to our meetings, participated vicariously in the literary kitchen. This seemed sufficient for the time being. The main thing was to write and to promulgate: to throw a bottle with the latest manuscript into the ocean—the ocean of time.

Georgy Ivanov defined a writer as someone who has found his publisher. Without a publisher you are perhaps a genius, but you are not a professional writer!

Only much later, in other decades and on other hemispheres, did I understand: the word must be spoken, and it must be heard by two or three; otherwise it is not a word but only a sound. All fauna—and even flora—produce sounds.

Alas, our readers have died out sooner than their writers! The new DPs could not become genuine interlocutors. They turned the emigration back to the twenties, to provincialism, to tsarist "denunciatory" literature in reverse. The overwhelming majority of these refugees are indifferent to religious questions and devoid of theological intuition. Not for nothing did Belinsky and Turgenev assert that "the Russian *muzhik* will devour God. . . ." To think that there was a time when we were supposed to believe that the Russians were the nation of "Godbearers," of the most orthodox Christianity, unselfish martyrs as well as magnificent rebels seeking Verity and Truth (for there is a subtle difference between the two).

But it turned out that the Russian peasant community (even the Soviet) is a biologically conservative entity, accepting everything when sober but each dreaming of owning a calf and a private garden plot. If worse comes to worst, we'll get drunk, burn someone's homestead, smash up a piano, and end the night in the police station or the drying-out ward.

As for theological intuition, no one needs it; the populace is obviously content with socialist realism and has been so for a long time.[1] If only they had permission to raise a piglet behind the stove or in a drawer. The new escapees joyfully visit a church and, after the service, feast on pork with horseradish. But in the old Russian-emigré dialogue about God-Love and God-Omnipotence, about Free Will and Predestination, about Reality, obvious or factual, about the bankruptcy of entropy and the resurrection of the body, in these superfluous discussions, "ex-gulag-denizens" cannot participate.

Mysticism is alien, hostile, not only to the Komsomol but also to the neutral Soviet citizen. And the notion of honor does not exist. It never existed! That Western feudal honor, which Dostoevsky mocked, describing little Polacks and Frenchies. (Tolstoi did not approve of it either.)

Deprived of the concept of knightly honor and of theological culture, the downtrodden orthodox people were supposed to develop a sensitive "conscience," instinctively tending toward Justice and Truth. But this, too, turned out to be another illusion in Soviet reality.

In Russian history, women play an extraordinary role. It was they who shook off foreign and domestic foes, built barracks and metros, fed piglets in the bathtub, dug in the garden between two overtime shifts, taught the children Lenin's wisdom and interrogated (tortured) White officers during the Civil War. For these females there was no sick leave!

In general, the participation of women in history is a characteristic distinction of every country. The specific weight of the roles of husband and wife is different in different cultures. Here is a great field for the unbiased researcher!

It is obvious that the Russian woman's participation in history is considerably greater than that of her German sister. The Fritzes have no one remotely resembling Marfa Posadnitsa (or Zoya Kosmodemianskaya). Joan of Arc, of course, is a completely different, unique phenomenon. For Prussian history (whatever that is) the German soldier is above all responsible. His woman helped him in the sense that, receiving from the eastern front bacon or blood-stained diapers, she gratefully accepted and used the goods (cited from a letter found on a German soldier killed in Russia and published in a French newspaper). But apparently the dreams of Gretchen or Margarete did not end with these offerings, else why did they become so readily intimate with *Untermenschen*?

The Russian woman is an autonomous quantity: if the male had left her alone, she would long since have built a strong, functioning household-state, fending off invading hordes no less effectively than in former times. Without theology, but with church hymns, fruit brandy, smoked fish, dance and choral games—a solid, ideal household-state. The Russian woman harbors elements of hermaphroditism, unobserved by such bards of female locks and shoulders as Turgenev and Tolstoi. (Pushkin and Dostoevsky descended to a woman's legs.)

In peacetime, Marfa Posadnitsa and Zoya Kosmodemianskaya build subways. And Joan of Arc, between two wars, becomes the hostess of a political or literary salon where Monet, Clémenceau, and Proust can find patrons. How many Russian women took shots at governor-generals or the tsar (in the spirit of Charlotte Corday); but isn't it remarkable that, among all the saints who "shone over the Russian land," there is not one of the universal significance of the two Teresas and Catherine of Siena? This matter deserves reflection.

In the thirties, Russian Paris was in an especially messianic mood. Berdyaev was not a little responsible for this postrevolutionary trend. We were ready to defend all the "achievements" of the October Revolution on the condition that "the primacy of the Spirit" (our official formula in those days) be recognized. This resulted in a mad crossbreeding, a hybrid of Slavophiles,[2] Eurasians and Westernizers, a synthesis of Marxism and Christianity. "The Tsar and the Soviets!", the program of the Mladoross, is another example of such an alloy.

Shestov did not take part in this wild farrago. Leaving his place after my first visit with him, I noticed on his desk three tomes displayed there with a certain dramatic insistence: Aristotle, Hegel, and still one other authoritative voice.

"You see, I'm carrying on my struggle with them," said Shestov, embracing in a good-humored gesture the three volumes and himself.

He had been struggling quite successfully against the Obvious and against Linear Logic; so much so that, in the beginning, Hitler's theoreticians even referred to Shestov in their myth making—until they came to understand him better.

I had sent him my novel *Mir* with an ingenious dedication, something like "To the lion Lev★ Shestov." In answer I received an invitation to tea. He lived in Passy, not far from the place to which Remizov later moved.

We had tea together in the kitchen. He spoke about my book in the time-honored way, making several detailed references to the text. *Mir* contained diverse iconoclastic religious discussions in the vein of our classic literature, something he decidedly liked. Several times he repeated someone's, perhaps Dostoevsky's, pronouncement: "If you want the reader to shed tears, you must experience pain yourself. . . ."

A tall, dry, stooped old man with a grey goatee, in a frock coat, almost childishly naive. And yet, his litigation with the Obvious was serious and dangerous.

Shestov lived a long, chaste life and probably never uttered a falsehood or a malicious word. And, in an "iron age," he never committed an evil act. What a strange misunderstanding! A naive philosopher, cherishing brilliant trinkets such as Regine Olsen, Kierkegaard's lost fiancée, or Abraham's sacrifices as interpreted by Kierkegaard, while he did not notice the true golden sand in his own garden. Verily, his *life* was Lev Shestov's most profound creation.

In those years I was supposedly moved deeply by the tragic figure of Spinoza (who called God a "substance"). I even contemplated writing a biography of the stubborn lens grinder. Shestov supported me in this plan but immediately pointed out the difficulties. He thought that for such a work one had to familiarize oneself with the entire canon of the philosopher.

"Spinoza is encased in the armor of his geometrical method. Unless you gnaw through that protective shell, you won't get to the core."

I loved Spinoza's poetic metaphors: "They have as much in common as the constellation of the Dog (canis) and a dog, the barking animal . . ." and: "If a falling stone could think, it would think that it is falling by its own volition."

Here was a Proustian method of comparing subjects or situations from completely different fields, opening up a new dimension and throwing an unexpected light on the reality under study. It is quite possible that these two poet-thinkers are descended from the same ancient literary school. The comparisons are to such an extent perfect and creatively infectious that they acquire an autonomous value; we forget the reason for which they were initially introduced.

★Russian Lev = Leo (lion).

Indeed, why would a falling stone *think* that it is falling by its personal will? Where and when did such an event occur? On the contrary, we are aware of circumstances in which free geniuses imagined that they were neutral executors of an alien, objective will. And fallen angels justify themselves at every step, claiming that exterior, social conditions caused them to fall.

In the official biography of Spinoza I came across the name of a young girl he used to see. Then the relationship ceased abruptly. From that episode I thought it possible to develop an entire psychological novel. Shestov did not like this conceit at all: nevertheless he provided me with several of Spinoza's works. As for myself, I soon cooled off to the project.

Shestov "discovered" Kierkegaard for the Russians—and perhaps for the French. I think he enlarged the Dane's personal drama (impotence) into a cosmic catastrophe. It was slightly comical to listen to this old man, with his naive, chaste beard, talk about the love drama of the young Danish couple, accusing God the Father, the Creator of the universe and God of Love, of this latest injustice (reminiscent of the tortures of the boy in *The Brothers Karamazov*).

In a long article on one of Shestov's books, Berdyaev wrote didactically, "Perhaps the marriage of Kierkegaard and Regine Olsen did not fit into God's plan." Something ironical along these lines.

Shestov's was a rare case of plagiarism in reverse. Writers will sometimes appropriate another's ideas or achievements. Shestov, however, attributed his most brilliant thoughts to other philosophers. To read his book on Brandes and then to go through Brandes himself is a disappointing experience.

Shestov's wife, a medical doctor by profession, became in Paris a practical nurse (on a miserable income).

"It's very easy," he explained guilelessly to me. "I simply never open the purse on my own initiative. I buy only what's on the list my wife hands me."

Shestov, just like Remizov—and later all of us—suffered from the absence of readers. He valued the interest of the younger generation; I'm afraid that toward the end he felt like a fossil, a mammoth.

Mamchenko frequently came to see him and, because of his inarticulateness, would strike Shestov as strangely profound. A very shrewd boy, this Mamchenko, a "gentle calf" which, according to the Russian proverb, "suckles *two* mothers," But he seems to have been genuinely fond of Shestov.

Stimulated by our exhibit of emigré literature and the subscriptions for

new publications, we thought of creating something like a Russian Prix
Goncourt to lure readers and booksellers. For the jury, Felsen and I
envisaged Shestov, Gippius, and a third, about whom we remained un-
decided. As an example of our mood in those days, I must mention that
we seriously considered Boris Pregel.

Felsen was supposed to negotiate with Gippius, I with Shestov. But I
happened to seek out this good man at a most inappropriate time and
place. He was reluctant to take part in any kind of literary intrigues, but
on the other hand he was tempted by the promise of genuine activity
and the company of young people to step out from his honorable
loneliness—of course, without any compromises. Thus he procrasti-
nated, unable to say yes and unwilling to say no.

I had looked him up at a school (probably the Institute of Eastern
Languages) where he was on the staff. There, in a room filled with
students' desks, he lectured on Kierkegaard. Before him on the benches
sat sad-faced old crones who, it seemed, would all precipitately leave the
classroom if given free tickets to a movie theater. I told Shestov: "You
shouldn't be reading from the manuscript; it sounds monotonous." He
answered: "I do it so as not to see the faces of my listeners."

In the emigration, Shestov "discovered" Tolstoi's *Notes of a Madman*
and also his "Master and Man"; he presented these stories with such keen
insight that we began to speak of the "Arzamasky terror"[3] (from the
Notes) as of a reality familiar to all of us.

Shestov was a pure-hearted creature and probably never did anyone
any harm. I think he was never seduced by temptations of that kind. I
don't know whether he succeeded in refuting the Obvious—he avoided
the modern theories of physics—or whether he forced Aristotle to the
wrestling mat, but about Tolstoi he was truly revealing.

"You think that Lev Nikolaevich read Nietzsche?" he said, smiling.
"Of course not! What for? He just heard 'Beyond Good and Evil,' and
that was enough."

Our proposition to be on the jury he finally refused.

For his seventieth anniversary friends organized a solemn celebration.
It was like a funeral; a few dozen of the older generation showed up, but
there were hardly any young people.

And, in due course, Lev Isaakovich Shestov began losing weight. He
went to see Dr. Z., who treated him with scraped apples and nuts and
confided to me that it probably was a cancer, and too far gone to operate.
"His entire belly is covered with wrinkles," which, according to Dr. Z.,
was proof of the patient's general debility. Shestov's wife took him to a
specialist who placed him in a private clinic in Passy.

Several days later (like Einstein) he peacefully gave up the ghost, without complicated medical tests and operations, undoubtedly testimony to his innate wisdom!

There were other Russian philosophers in Paris, but they were more interested in literary topics than in the theory of knowledge. Over and over again Alyosha Karamazov and Platon Karataev—those *ochi chornye* (dark eyes) of Russian religious thought.[4]

Konstantin Mochulsky was grounded in literature. In the twenties, Adamovich introduced me to him, assuming that religious interests would unite us. Mochulsky liked my short story "Sluzhitel kulta" (A Servant of the Cult), in which a priest, at the time of military communism, commits suicide, basing his action on the Gospel's "Come unto me, all ye that labor and are heavy laden, and I will give you rest." But a genuine closeness did not develop between us. Later, in the thirties, we often met in the Circle.

Mochulsky's was the difficult path of the homosexual. Difficult, because he resisted. After a religious crisis he "straightened out" and overcame temptation. He was close to Mother Marie's Orthodox Cause and spent his free time at her place on the rue Lourmelle. He befriended her young son, Yury; and they would retreat into a corner of the huge, dusky dining room, which smelled of cabbage and scrubbed boards, and happily play chess. Both played badly but did not allow anyone to give them pointers.

I remember a meeting, the Congress of the Orthodox Cause, which took place at Mother Marie's suburban house in Nogent. I rode there on my bicycle; Fondaminsky and Fedotov traveled the same route by bus, sometimes passing me, sometimes falling behind.

At night, the men all slept in one room, I on the floor. Yury, shirtless in Western fashion, lay on a narrow bunk, only partly covered by an army blanket. His bare torso would probably have been attractive to young girls. Head to head with him, in a straight angle, lay Mochulsky on a more comfortable bed, giggling confusedly in return to Yury's banter. It suddenly occurred to me that, for Mochulsky, Yury was as tempting as a half-naked young girl would be for me. I pitied him with all my heart, even said a prayer.

After midnight it grew cold; there was a draft from the cracks in doors and windows. Groping around in the dark, I pulled someone's coat down from a nail, wrapped myself in it, and fell into a sweet slumber until the triumphal crowing of a Gallic cock. It turned out that I had wrapped myself in a cassock belonging to G., a student at the Orthodox

Academy who dreamed of becoming a monk. (Soon he married an English girl and ended up as an Anglican priest.)

"You'll be a monk," G. joked in the morning, picking up his cassock from the floor. "Or *you*'ll become a sinner," I replied without thinking.

In those days, Mochulsky still looked like a balding, fortyish but enterprising bachelor, one of those who don't smoke and don't drink but have a fondness for the weaker sex. He reminded me somewhat of Vasily Borisovich in Melnikov-Pechersky's novel *In the Woods*.

In Russian philosophical thought he danced, as had become the established custom, to the tune of Dostoevsky and Solovyov. Soviet theoreticians dance to Marx's and Engel's tune and do it with apparent delight. Russians, even more than Germans, like order, rank, the hierarchy of bowing and scraping, in church as well as at banquets and in science. This, too, it seems, our classicists have not noticed.

Vladimir Weidlé was of another order. Also a literary scholar and also concerned with ecumenism, he, however, clung less to the usual Tolstoevskian melodies. He loved and was thoroughly familiar with Western European art. I think he was less knowledgeable about literature. Thus, wishing to impress us, he would all of a sudden announce that there existed a new, phenomenal American literature. In discussions he cited many second-rate names and overwhelmed us with his thoroughness. Very likely he knew everything, but he did not understand everything.

Weidlé started his career modestly with a little article on Khodasevich's poetry, or on the mosaics of the early Renaissance. In appearance he resembled a Baltic assistant professor; when he irritated me, I called him General Pfuhl (from *War and Peace*). Such irritation was evoked only by certain abstract ideas, for neither the content nor the form of his talks ever gave ground for offense or hostility.

Weidlé's influence grew slowly but unswervingly. Whatever field he looked into, be it religion, literature, painting, or politics, he always perceived the priority of European civilization over all others in history. This sometimes aroused anger, particularly if the argument concerned the India of the time of Gandhi. But all in all, he was of course right.

He grew unexpectedly and inordinately animated by the topic of love. Once upon a time he had been mortally wounded by Tyutchev's lyrics, with their eternal, transient remembrance of the past. In moments of excitement he stuttered; and then the honorable, bald, lymphatic, sallow-complexioned, freckled professor, swaying and stuttering as he spoke about Tyutchev's last love, cut a tragicomic figure.

Despite his European rationalism and his praiseworthy thoughts on religion and art, something in him bore witness to a deep personal injury. I always felt that Weidlé, perhaps unconsciously, stopped short of expressing what was most important to him.

Officially he collaborated with Fondaminsky, Fedotov, and Stepun on *Novy grad,* but he was a man of an entirely different mold. He recognized the "madness of the Cross" only in works of art. Fedotov, who partially rebelled against this "madness," nevertheless accepted it without reservation when the chips were down.

In a discussion I once referred to Hindu monks and early Christians who were basically illiterate yet fulfilled their role. With a crooked smile Weidlé replied: "You bring your big guns to bear on trifles." It was precisely talk about "trifles" (architecture, mosaics, musical notes), without reference to more important things, that seemed to me at the time puzzling, comical, and even harmful. And yet, the secret of culture lies in this very self-limitation, discipline, and classification.

It is painful that even Herzen, who spent all his mature years in the West, berated the Europeans for their *petit-bourgeois* stinginess, their methodical, calculated narrowness and moderation. In Herzen himself there was a lot of Russian derring-do, as there was also in the gendarmes who carried him off in troikas into exile to Perm and Vyatka. The main thing which these great Europeans, with the exception of Turgenev, could not forgive the West was its pettiness, its consistent and conscious stinginess, achieved (like any virtue) only through continuous effort.

When I heard an English gentleman who was buying tobacco say, "No, that's too expensive, I can't afford it," I flinched and blushed in shame. How can he, in the presence of a lady, admit his inadequacy? From childhood on we were taught that a real gentleman can permit himself anything. Money mustn't stand in the way; if need be he'll steal or kill!

As long as the old East of the sultans does not realize that "pettiness"—that is, taking into consideration real possibilities and means—is essential for a healthy spiritual as well as material household, no five-year-plan will cut through the knot of its inherent historical handicaps.

It is a fact that the best Russian "Westerners," with Herzen in the lead, were unanimously repelled by the so-called stinginess of Europeans. This proves that there was much that they did not understand in the lands where they lived as distinguished foreigners. The "largesse and munificence" of agrarian, poverty-stricken, feudalistic Russia filled the hearts of the exiles with joy: even opponents of slavophilism asserted that the Orthodox East would yet tell those "shopkeepers" the last, the saving, Christian word and that it would sound convincing despite the whistle of Russian whips and flails.

Europe, too, had its period of feudal largesse, when Vikings and knights presented one another with villages, castles, and wives—generously, without hesitation or calculation. Europe's thriftiness is of a later, Christian, origin, the recognition of a new order.

In old Russia, a simple man would consider it a sin to throw away a piece of a cracker. And many messianistic compatriots were enraptured by this trait of the simple folk of "God-bearers," just as they were by the bread put out on the windowsill "for the Unhappy Ones" (escaped prisoners). The same goes on in Western Europe; only here—oh wonder!—the upper classes participate in the tradition. And thriftiness concerns not only a scrap of bread or a piece of string or wrapping paper—it is a sin to discard anything created by God or man. Whatever exists has to fulfill its purpose in some way.

Money, like any other gift, one is permitted to spend—but sensibly, with moderation. If the capital was amassed by your ancestors, it does not belong entirely to you and must be passed on to the rightful heirs.

Aleksei Tolstoi, a truly "prodigal" man, when visiting England, was outraged by the stinginess of his writer colleagues: he was treated to a meager dinner, "not at all like in our Moscow."

Herzen, a noble, daring, intelligent *boyar,* and Aleksei Tolstoi, almost his opposite, both similarly criticized English thriftiness. There is something strangely superficial in this approach.

Incidentally, in the old days, Swiss peasants left a supply of crackers and firewood in their mountain huts for lonely wanderers, and Bretons put bread and fish at night on the windowsill for the unfortunates who were fleeing from justice.

Of all our philosophers it was Professor Stepun who *looked* most like one. A native of the Volga region, of German or Swedish descent, he was a representative of an especially Russian, traditional type (like Boris Pilnyak).

A restless spirit, he was torn apart by subconscious contradictions. Despite his solid grounding in classic philosophy, complex, poisonous vapors of decadence floated around him. A contemporary of the Russian "Silver Age," a guest in Vyacheslav Ivanov's "Tower," an admirer of Hegel's dialectic pendulum, a liberal, esthete, former army officer (like the poet Fet), and a scholar, Stepun was for us, in Paris, to which he periodically came from gloomy Germany, a picturesque mixture of brilliance, erudition, depth, and a rather frightening innate touch of metaphysical rottenness.

In the emigration, Fedor Stepun stuck strictly to the accepted Christian principles. Together with Fondaminsky and Fedotov, he took part in the building of *Novy grad* and also helped the editors of *Sovremennye zapiski* in their painstaking labors. It was he who would stand up for a new author or for an article by a slightly conservative religious thinker whom Vishnyak and Rudnev vituperated.

Stepun was not only a professional teacher of philosophy but also a talented novelist. At *Sovremennye zapiski* his opinion was highly respected. M. Zetlin devoted his attention almost exclusively to poetry; prose was not his element. The poetry department of *Sovremennye zapiski* was exceptionally rich; most of our poets were represented.

All in all, the emigré periodical press treated poetry tenderly. From Riga's *Segodnya* (Today) to New York's *Novoe Russkoe Slovo,* everywhere the poems of Knorring, Chervinskaya, Steiger were faithfully reprinted.

The fate of prose writing was completely different. SRs, SDs, KDs,★ and other intellectuals of the right or left were perfectly at home in prose and did not need anyone's advice. Here, strange as it may seem, the same principle was at work as with the gendarmes: "Hold on and don't let them through!" Poems, of course, are portable; they take up little space and can be inserted as vignettes between two surveys of failed five-year plans or an article on the dissolution of the legendary Constituent Assembly. Besides, it is not shameful for an old liberal to acknowledge that he does not understand modern poetry. "If Adamovich approves, we print it!"

In prose, however, I beg your pardon, Rudnev Vishnyak understood everything; no one could fool them. As a consequence of such, mainly psychological particularities, emigré prose carried, and still carries, a double burden.

Fondaminsky and those close to him helped us as much as they could, and, indeed, gradually, by the end of the thirties, had brought the entire young generation into the *Sovremennye zapiski*. (By that time, Slonim's *Volya Rossie* published nothing but translations of Panait Istrati.)

I had sent Fondaminsky the first part of *Portativnoe bessmertie* for the *Russkie zapiski.* Zenzinov read it without definitive conclusions. Luckily Stepun turned up; Fondaminsky passed on the manuscript to him—and there I was, with a thousand francs in my hand. My first, and probably last, Russian advance!

★SDs = Social Democrats; KDs = Kadet party members.

Soon after, Fondaminsky left the *Russkie zapiski*. Milyukov took over, with Vishnyak as secretary general. The latter complained disgustedly: "Who arranged that? How can one hand out such advances!" He criticized Fondaminsky both for his "Christianism" and for his friendship with "fascists." About himself Vishnyak once proudly told me that he had not changed by one iota since 1917. I considered this a monstrous waste of life and time. Meanwhile, thanks to Stepun, I received one thousand francs, which made possible a summer vacation in Alsace.

At night we sat again at Fondaminsky's tea table. Zenzinov angrily walked through, from the toilet to his room. Stepun, shifting his weight from one heavy leg to the other like a restrained shaft horse, stood behind his chair at the head of the table and, gesticulating heavily, tried to prove to us in an already hoarse voice that "inaction in emigration is also an action."

"Open the parentheses, change the signs in the equation to their opposites, drill one more hole in the metaphysical vacuum."

My involvement with "memory" attracted his attention and, perhaps remembering our nightly vigils, he wrote, twenty years later, about my *Chelyust emigranta* (Emigrant's Jaw): "A basic favorite thought of Yanovsky seems to me the difference he makes between two forms of memory: the linear, which preserves only what happened to the exterior world, and the vertical memory which, as during an explosion of lightning, retains the silhouettes of objects belonging to another world" (*Novy zhurnal*, 1958).

Stepun impersonated with great gusto his contemporaries, such as Aleksei Tolstoi or Vyacheslav Ivanov. I imagine he could have made a successful career as an actor (a characteristic typical of some Russian writers). In the course of one evening, Stepun might begin with Vishnyak as the secretary general of the Constituent Assembly and arrive at Andrei Bely and his fights with Rudolph Steiner, which did not amuse all those present.

In 1958, recalling our meetings in Paris, F. Stepun wrote me a long letter which I still have and from which I quote: "In connection with the basic religious themes, I became interested in your theory of double memory. Of course, life flows in irreversible progression of time, but it is impossible to represent it *in depth* using the chronological order. You are right: linear memory is no help in solving this problem, because the past is vertically reconstructed in our souls. That is why, as you say, it is necessary to apply vertical memory. . . ." And he continues: "Very clearly and distinctly you define love as a tiny, oblique window into eschatology. Very good and new is your phenomenological description of the short moment when, waking up, a person does not orient himself in his room, as a mystery of the separation of soul and memory. These words directly open up the platonic problem of memory and Christian immortality. With the mystery of the separation of soul and memory is also linked the thought that, apart from other properties, death does not have a past. Not to have a past means not to have memory. . . ."

Yes, such conversations and letters rewarded us for many deprivations.

Fedor Stepun personally met Dr. Steiner and liked to tell how Andrei Bely once, before witnesses, interrupted Steiner, calling out to him: "*Herr Doktor, Sie sind ein alter Affe!*" This I also heard from Khodasevich.

When Hitler came to power, Professor Stepun immediately retired, thus decisively refusing any direct or indirect participation in the German myths.

Other philosophers touched us rather less. From time to time, Frank showed up at Fondaminsky's. A large, what one calls "dignified" man, he looked like an American executive, an administrator or director of a big corporation. Kartashov also conveyed the impression of a clever administrator.

Frank lectured on Pushkin at the Circle, dissecting him according to his own taste. He claimed that we must distinguish two kinds of religious experience, the prophet-thunderer and the mild, saintly mystic. According to Frank's classification, Pushkin was not a prophet but a mystic, much higher than crusaders or fighters for the truth. We argued that the *Gavriliada* and the "goblets to be poured over the simmering fat of the cutlets" could not possibly fit in with such deep spirituality.

I always, and decisively, disliked Vysheslavtsev, even though he was very popular at the YMCA among middle-aged and elderly ladies. A big, well-built, long-legged man with graying, shiny whiskers, a classical forehead, heavy Scandinavian skull, and, I believe, blue eyes. God had rewarded him with especially flexible and attractive hips. Standing at the podium, eloquently and coldly declaiming on the Holy Trinity or Sophia, God's wisdom, he coquettishly displayed those attractive hips, laying one or the other huge hand on his elastic waist. Smolensky also flaunted his waistline—but not so successfully.

During the occupation, Vysheslavtsev collaborated with the Germans, traveling to countries of the Russian diaspora to preach about "the new order." This "knight without fear and reproach" as the elderly ladies used to call him, died in Switzerland after the war, never having dared to return to Paris and face French justice.

The Russian painters lived in a separate group and did not meet often with us, except sometimes at the Brasserie des Lilas for a poker game or at big general meetings. (Incidentally, Larionov stands next to me in the group photo of *Chisla*.)

Yury Annenkov was no exception either. Only very shortly before the war he appeared at Fondaminsky's and proposed staging Dostoevsky's "A Bad Joke" in Fondaminsky's theater. But something interfered and the production never materialized.

Annenkov was a secretive, very Russian person—shrewd, coarse, talented, a man of all trades.

Once, at the end of the twenties, I visited Osorgin in connection with *Koleso* (The Wheel), and he complained to me: "Here is a novel the author sent me. I would like to help him publish it. It's a good book. But I don't know how to contact him. There's no return address."

The novel, I don't remember its title, was signed "Temiryazev" and had been brought to Osorgin by an unknown lady who promised to return for an answer but never came back.

"I have a hunch," Osorgin continued, "that the author still lives on a Soviet passport and is afraid of compromising himself. Temiryazev is of course a pseudonym."

Indeed, the novel turned out to have been written by the painter Annenkov. Osorgin recommended it warmly to *Sovremennye zapiski,* where it was published, I believe with cuts, as is the tradition in the free press.

I read it, more or less: a realistic story, without an original, personal, real theme, written in what specialists call modern, experimental prose.

In his paintings, graphics, and theater designs, Annenkov also "fabricated" in constructivist, cubist, surrealist styles, enchanting one after the other—Blok, Trotsky, and Jean Cocteau.

When, for the celebration of the first anniversary of the October Revolution, the new government needed a responsible artist to decorate the Soviet capital, Annenkov was for some reason appointed president of the "Flag Commission."

"In 1921, the Soviet Government commissioned me to paint a portrait of Lenin," recalled Annenkov. And he traveled for the sittings to the Kremlin to "Ilich." When Lenin died, the Superior Military Editorial Council charged Annenkov with illustrating the volume dedicated to him.

At the Lenin Institute, Annenkov was "primarily struck by a glass jar containing Lenin's brain in alcohol." He surreptitiously made a sketch of it and "just as surreptitiously copied some short notes hastily jotted down by Lenin."

In 1923, Annenkov was asked to make the portraits of the main leaders of the Revolutionary Military Council and "first of all of Trotsky." And Annenkov, drew, painted, sketched illustrated them all. Five times, "if not more," he visited headquarters. Military and civilian dignitaries liked him, conversed with him about art, carried on civilized discussions. Zinoviev, Lunacharsky, Tukhachevsky, Radek, Voroshilov, Enukidze,* and so on and so forth.

In Paris he corresponded with Rakovsky, the Soviet ambassador, who invited him "to drop in, simply for a chat" (11 October 1926). At the same time he painted a portrait of Krasin, the Soviet ambassador to England.

Eventually, he was forced to occupy himself seriously with his career as a Parisian stage designer, in which he was also successful. He befriended the best "local" artists, from Picasso to Foujita, collected their sketches and drawings.

When Aleksei Tolstoi came to Paris, Annenkov drank cognac with him and chatted, although he was perfectly aware of "Alyoshka" Tolstoi's character and morals. For some reason he drove the "count" in his car to V. Krymov. The same thing happened with Ehrenburg, that scoundrel who for decades cheated and seduced French intellectuals with his descriptions of Stalin's paradise, although he himself rolled on the floor in hysterics each time he was called back for a visit to Moscow.

When *checkist* Efron, husband of Marina Tsvetaeva and president of the Union of Soviet Repatriates[6] (or an organization of that order by another name), organized a gala ball, and another agent and murderer, Eisner, a Russian poet from Prague, wrote a farce to be performed at the gala (something about a young girl—that is, emigré literature—seeking a husband), Yury Annenkov painted the decor for the play. Not one decent person went, but Georgy Ivanov was, of course, present.

During the German occupation, Annenkov behaved quietly and, as far as I know, correctly. (Not like Serge Lifar.) He continued to work as a stage designer, not being responsible for the content of the plays that were performed; successfully married a youngish actress and wrote the *Dnevnik moikh vstrech* (Diary of My Encounters). Soon after the victory he joined the respectable *Pensée Russe,* where he ran the department of art exhibits.

He easily sold his archives to an American university and placed his two-volume memoirs with a good publishing house, feats which few of us have managed to accomplish up to now.

---

*All prominent Soviet leaders purged in the 1930s.

Tolstoi writes with admiration of the 1812 general, Dokhturov, who, as if by accident, without pushing ahead, always turned up at the most dangerous and responsible spot. Whenever I come upon that page in *War and Peace,* I think by a strange association, of Annenkov:

> Again Dokhturov was sent to Fominskoe and from there to Maly Yaroslavets, the place where the last battle was fought with the French and where it is plain the final destruction of the French army really began. And again many heroes and men of genius are described to us in accounts of this period of the campaign. But of Dokhturov nothing is said, or but a few words of dubious praise. This silence in regard to Dokhturov is the plainest testimony to his merits. (Translation by Constance Garnett.)

This is how I see Yury Annenkov, only in reverse (*au rebours*). I speak about him in some detail here, because such ambiguous figures are not accidental in any emigration.

Chapter 8 · Mother Marie

At the beginning of the thirties, the readers of *Poslednie novosti* became interested in a series of articles, signed with initials only. A certain Mother M. was traveling across France and writing about Russian life in the provinces; the fate of isolated colonies was in many respects sadder than ours. Poverty, injustice, suppression, prejudice, drunkenness, and denunciations reigned supreme. Particularly disturbing was the installment devoted to Boris Butkevich (in Marseilles), whom the author presented as a typical, prematurely doomed, Russian derelict: he labored as a dockhand, drank more and more heavily, and died (exactly as in a Gorky story). If memory serves, the correspondent went to the morgue in person, with friends of the deceased who identified his body (already marinated for the dissecting room).

"And yet," I quote from memory, "people claim that Butkevich was an educated man, that he wrote short stories which appeared even in *Chisla* and that he was praised by our most important critics." Alas, all this was absolutely true.

Before *Chisla,* Butkevich had also published in a "little magazine," edited by Adamovich and, if I'm not mistaken, Vinaver. There I read his short story about a former officer of the Imperial Guard, drinking himself to death in Marseilles; this story is one of the best emigré works of that period.

I knew that Butkevich had disappeared, "melted away," in Marseilles; but such a monstrous, "Volga boatsman's," end shocked me. The whole tone of the article was affecting. It combined genuine love and solicitude for a human being, a compatriot, student, officer, and poet, with a complete lack of sentimentality.

I tried to find out from my acquaintances who the author of the article was. And finally, Evgenia Ivanovna Shirinsky-Shikhmatov, an eternal schoolgirl, enthusiastically informed me: "It is Mother Marie, a former socialist revolutionary, terrorist and poet who has become a nun of a special kind, a 'nun in the world!' She has furnished a house, where she will feed and shelter the needy. She'll even give them a decent burial. That's the kind of person she is!"

From her I also learned that Mother Marie, in order to support her family, exterminated bedbugs in the apartments of emigrés. She advertised in *Poslednie novosti*: Cleaning, washing, disinfection of walls, mattresses and floors, extermination of cockroaches and other parasites . . .

In general, one could observe among our emigrés this noble national trait: rather than appeal to various foundations (in one way or another connected with "idealistic, freedom-loving" counterintelligence agencies), they would accept any honest labor that turned up. When Helene Iswolsky arrived in New York, she became a maid-of-all-work at Aleksandra Tolstoi's farm; Galina Kuznetsova cleaned refugee apartments on an hourly basis; my sister worked for twenty years as a sewing-machine operator in a Puerto Rican sweatshop. And Mother Marie exterminated generations of bedbugs, claiming that this was a creative act!

"Yes, that's the kind of person she is!" rejoiced Evgenia Ivanovna, whom we had nicknamed Princess Savinkova. An active revolutionary, the sister of an SR terrorist who rescued her future husband, Boris Savinkov, from the prison Fortress and later himself perished on the gallows, Evgenia Ivanovna was a typical representative of her era. The peculiarity of those people was that they quite often performed heroic deeds but never in their lives sweated on a job forty hours a week, fifty weeks a year. Evgenia Ivanovna personally carried dynamite from Finland to St. Petersburg, was a close friend of Sazonov's fiancée, could not abide the smell of herring, and represented a mixture of *bon ton,* underground, conspiracy and exhausting chatter.

For a time we lived near each other, at the junction of Clamart-Vanves and Issy-les-Moulineaux, met frequently and kept discussing the founding of yet another literary journal. Occasionally I contributed to Shirinsky's post-revolutionary publications . . .and in the evening I listened to his tales about riding to the hounds, about horses, and about the Cross of St. George, which it was harder for an officer of the infantry to obtain than for an officer of the artillery.

There were two photographs on the wall in the prince's study: a portrait of his first wife and one of his favorite bitch, an often decorated showdog (a cocker spaniel, I believe). His philosophy of breeding consisted in mating an ideal bitch with her brothers and repeating the procedure with her pups. Yury Alekseevich asserted that in the seventh generation the ideal bitch, a copy of the original ancestor, would appear.

As an officer of the Imperial Guard, he had fought in the Great War, where knightly duels still occurred, and had taken part in deep reconnaissance and cavalry raids. He spoke very convincingly about the feeling he experienced when, as a young officer, he dismounted with his patrol and, hiding in a Polish hut, suddenly through the window saw heavy, fair, helmeted Germans whom it was permitted to kill. "As if we had been shown a group of young women and been told, 'Rape them!' " Thus, more or less, he defined his military experience.

These vigils in his company were a delight for me; I often forced myself to go to the Post-Revolutionary Club and sit through an entire lecture about the future ethnic organization of the nationalities of the Russian state, so as, later, to hold a tête-à-tête conversation with him.

The way of life with which the prince was by tradition connected was reminiscent of the period directly overlapping that described in *Anna Karenina*. The Shirinsky-Shikhmatovs had participated in the life of the court. Yury Alekseevich's father had been procurator of the Holy Synod. He was the one who, as a member of the Council of Ministers, liked to repeat that to the right of him "there was the wall." During the first years of the emigration, Yury Alekseevich himself belonged to several reactionary groups. However, under the influence of the miraculous émigré magnetic field—whose components included the Eurasian movement, Berdyaev, French influence, Evgenia Ivanovna, and an unshakable regard for the historical borders of Russia—he gradually evolved, until finally he, a prince, a descendant of Genghis Khan and the Ryuriks, found death in a German concentration camp.

In August 1940, my wife gave birth, at the Port-Royal Hospital, to a daughter, Marie. Yury Alekseevich visited her in the ward. (Mrs. Shirinsky-Shikhmatov had been terminally ill since the spring.) In the conversation with my wife he let fall that he was waiting for an opportunity to put on the yellow (Jewish) armband. Even if he never actually did so, such words were characteristic of Prince Yury Shirinsky-Shikhmatov, as well as of all our "rotting" emigration, and of the Paris of that time— shattered, doomed, but still shining and eternal.

The prince worked as a taxi driver; at the stand, waiting for a fare, he read avidly in the dim light. Besides the Slavophiles, Berdyaev had a great influence on him. (Berdyaev's emanations were stronger, purer, more important and indicative than the man himself. That's why I accept him in his entirety.)

In his post-revolutionary ideas, Shirinsky-Shikhmatov probably went too far, especially when the matter even remotely touched the "Third Rome."[1] Very soon quarrels arose in the prince's club. Such quarrels were typical of the political life of the emigration, where a soup was cooked up from one and the same bone in different kettles (let's say:

Berdyaev, Milyukov or General Krasnov). Some "informed" persons began to claim that in such and such a year the prince had quite casually turned into the Rue Grenelle (where the Soviet Embassy was located). Curiously enough, the majority of those witnesses later became involved in the so-called Oboroncheskoe movement[2] and, in the company of M. Slonim, were put into the internment camp which the French police had organized for Communists and fellow-travelers.

Yury Alekseevich and I thought up a game which we called "Quizzes for the Guard."

"What was the name of Vronsky's* horse?"

"Frou-frou."

"Who overtook her?"

Answer: "Gladiator, a chestnut stallion."

"In which work does Dostoevsky describe a dog? What is the dog's name?"

"Of what fabric was the shawl which Marmeladov's** wife cherished?"

The game presented the familiar literary domain at a new angle. And it was fun to think up questions.

Incidentally, Prince Yuri Alekseevich claimed that Tolstoi's description of the Royal Cavalry Guard attack at Austerlitz was historically incorrect. According to him, the color of the horses of the first squadron was wrong.

Sometimes his stepson, the very young Lev Borisovich Savinkov, listened to these conversations. I say "very young" because, when I saw him for the first time, he was a tender adolescent; but not long after he grew into a young man who sported a South American mustache and more and more frequently expressed opinions of his own. We were friends—I would often intone for him a frivolous refrain: "Fate plays with man . . ." and he would pick up, "It's fickle, very fickle." In the fall of 1936 he took off for Spain, where he fought honestly for a year and a half, was injured, and returned beaten and disillusioned. He told me that "over there" he would sometimes, in difficult moments, hum the familiar refrain: "Fate plays with man . . ."

In the summer of 1940, Lev's mother, Evgenia Ivanovna, was dying of cancer. To lie in bed, doomed, during those oppressive nights in a half-empty Paris where the Germans were masters—this must have been doubly painful! In those days one had to possess an extraordinary clair-voyance to distinguish the liberated Stalingrad in the far distance.

---

*Of *Anna Karenina*.
**Of *Crime and Punishment*.

I still have photographs of Evgenia Ivanovna, full face and profile, taken by the tsarist police. A young girl with long tresses—out of Turgenev. How beautiful they all were, those rebellious women! And there were her tales . . . Her first marriage, a marriage of convenience for a passport; then Boris Savinkov, Finland, Nice, Paris . . . Where did all this vanish? The feeling grew in me that it was still there, beyond a thick pane of glass, entirely visible. Yet to touch it, to draw closer was impossible.

Later on, Yury Alekseevich Shirinsky-Shikhmatov was denounced by his former post- or prerevolutionary comrades, arrested, and deported to a German concentration camp. It was said that, there, he interfered on behalf of a fellow-inmate and was summarily shot. Of course, there are not, and cannot be, definite witnesses to acts of this kind. This also goes for the heroic sacrifice of Mother Marie, who allegedly changed places with another inmate and went to the ovens in her stead. Isn't it wondrous how rumor creates these blissful myths? Our soul thirsts for saintly deeds, believes in the presence of spiritual hosts and seeks their earthly incarnation. And this in itself already represents a miraculous reality.

Thus, the Shirinskys introduced me to Mother Marie and from then on, in the course of the years, I met her in many different places. She was large, red-cheeked, very Russian, with a nearsighted smile and equable demeanor, as if she were outside our conflicts, our noise and agitation. Yet she herself moved quite a bit, made noise with her heavy boots and long dark skirts, slurped tea and argued.

Monumental, flushed, in a black robe and men's shoes—the face of a Russian peasant under a nun's black veil! Well-intentioned people often pitied her precisely on account of those clumsy boots, her unclean nails, the whole aroma of voluntary poverty—cabbage, bedbugs, rotten floorboards—which pervaded her house of hospitality. Apple-cheeked (because of a net of scarlet capillaries) she always looked healthy and joyful. During meetings and lectures at her place, Mother Marie never remained idle: she knitted, or mended rough, dark garments, biting off the thread with apparently healthy strong teeth.

In France *une brave femme* is the national ideal of womanhood. By day a housewife, at night a mate, intelligently and readily fulfilling all of God's ordained duties! These *braves femmes,* mothers of families, lovers of invalids, sit in the métro booths selling tickets but all the while knitting a sweater or folding a dress pattern. They are not averse to committing a sin and having some fun if it entails no loss for their households—on the contrary, perhaps even increases the family income. But they won't betray their men! To go to bed with someone extraneous without giving away anything is no crime; she'll even permit her husband some moderate diversions. If she's lucky, she'll become the hostess of a literary or political salon.

I often imagine the *braves femmes* of other nations; after all, they are the basis for the way of life, the family and even the form of government of their countries. Of course, Mother Marie was also a *brave femme,* but a Russian one: with bombs, poems, the "eternal questions," symbolism, and church choirs. A comparative study of the *braves femmes* of different nations could solve many historical puzzles and even cast a light on the future of, let's say, the Republic of China.

The French idea of the *brave femme* includes hard, conscientious work on the job, housework, the family, her man, and a meticulous *toilette intime* (for an active, joyful sex life goes without saying).

In the quiet, pragmatic, courageous, always good-natured, red-cheeked Mother Marie, with her past as an anarchist and poet, and her present as the practical builder and abbess of a monastery, I saw an ideal of Russian womanhood—of the immortal Marfa Posadnitsa, capable, if need be, of marinating mushrooms, milking cows, and digging a subway. Among the Western saints she reminded me most of Teresa of Ávila (a Jeanne d'Arc does not fit into the Russian reality). Now I see that she was the counterpart of our own Dorothy Day.

Everything one heard about Mother Marie's work filled the heart with gratitude. To feed her charges, she set out at night for the Halles, where she was already known among the "Frenchies from Bordeaux." At no cost they heaped her two-wheeled cart with the remains of their fresh root vegetables and greens, an occasional cheese or enormous bone with some meat still clinging to it. (The square around the Halles had to be cleaned up before sunrise.)

Loaded with all these aromatic wonders, Mother Marie solemnly returned from her campaign, giving her kitchen assistant, the so-called chef, a former mental and tubercular patient, a hand with unloading the cart.

As a rule, her boarders—retired alcoholics and widows of army captains—did not like their protectress and often, querulously, taught her lessons in Orthodoxy, genuine humility, and even in good housekeeping. Some went to church officials or the police to complain about her; some wrote perfect Russian specimens of denunciation. I believe that her saintliness manifested itself in peacetime in her house no less than, later, in the German prisons.

In the Orthodox Cause she was assisted by F. I. Pianov, also a very colorful personality, somewhat like an American Quaker. Indeed, the

USA resembles Russia in many respects. In its ingenuousness, the experiment in Prohibition was reminiscent of Lenin's dialectics. However, the American *brave femme* stands apart, gradually superseding her male counterpart, she who with the Bible and a rifle went to the Far West, singing democratic hymns and delivering babies.

Mother Marie personally made the stained-glass windows in her church on the rue de Lourmel after having studied the secrets of that medieval art. Her church looked like a decoration for *Boris Godunov;* this probably pleased many Russians (just as do the church themes in the opera). I could not appreciate either these or the poems which Mother Marie continued to write. Even her prose did not have the necessary effect on me. One might have expected a person with her spiritual experience to write more lucidly and convincingly about "Mistika chelovekoobshcheniya" (The Mystique of Human Relations) in an article thus entitled which she contributed to our first issue of *Krug*. On the one hand, it gave proof of an undeniable religious experience; on the other, there was little clarification and true nourishment. Naturally, the question of whether to publish Mother Marie's work was never raised. We gratefully accepted everything she offered! But . . . Many members of the editorial board expressed misgivings. Fondaminsky, however, put an end to our idle deliberations: "What is there to talk about! It's her personal experience, what more do you want?"

The fact that Fondaminsky could defend a contribution to our magazine with such an argument proves how far he had already succeeded in separating himself from his former comrades such as Rudnev-Vishnyak.

The article "The Mystique of Human Relations" appeared in *Krug;* and I have not read it to the end up to this day, probably because of my own inadequacy.

At the start of yet another five-year-plan, a severe famine broke out in Russia. Prince Shirinsky-Shikhmatov—a man of brilliant ideas and even some talent for intrigue but, I daresay, rather an inefficient organizer—decided to "mobilize public opinion in the West," collect the needed money, hire a freighter, load it up with cereals and fats, and send it off as a present to Leningrad!

The meeting to discuss this plan took place at Mother Marie's house, on a spring night, when all of dirty Paris smelled sweetly and vibrated amorously, as only that city can. It must have been in May, for the trees on the crowded boulevards were in bloom.

In the large dining hall, which smelled of wet floorboards, twenty-five or so emigrés of indeterminate age and past sat at the long, frequently scrubbed deal table. (Fondaminsky's wife was already ailing, and he did not join us.) Mother Marie, a large, calm figure in black, had settled to one side, somewhat aloof, silently knitting. Only toward the end of the meeting did she say a few words, indicating that she approved of the undertaking but could tell us whether she would take part in it only after consulting with a certain person (I understood: with Father Bulgakov).

From time to time three young girls in white spring blouses, giggling mysteriously, would come running into the room. True Turgenev types, but lighter, more fragile, they chirped over what seemed to be some happy secret, ran out into the street again but soon rushed back into the grey, dark place where we sat. One of these laughing girls was Mother Marie's daughter, Gayana. She left not long after for Moscow as a protégée of Aleksei Tolstoi; there she soon perished under obscure circumstances. Ehrenburg, who in his memoirs gives a secondhand account of Mother Marie's work in France, would have been more honest if he had informed us in detail about the death of her daughter in Moscow.

In the meantime, the meeting "for the mobilization of public opinion in the West" grew visibly animated. Shirinsky, to my naive surprise, became the target of bitter reproaches and of the most unexpected insinuations. Some claimed that the appearance of a ship in the Leningrad roadstead carrying food in time of hunger might cause a revolt that Shirinsky could use to establish his dictatorship. Passions ran high; a little more and the cherished epithet "scoundrel" or "saboteur" would have been thundering beneath the vault. Alas, this is the fate of emigré get-togethers.

Sometimes, Mother Marie spoke at the Circle. Once, I remember, she recounted her personal memories of Blok. And again it was puzzling: Remizov, Adamovich, Mochulsky could have told us about this poet— why should she choose such a topic? (In the background, Ivanov made snide remarks concerning Marie Skobtsova's looks at the time of her meetings with Blok.)

I often argued with Mother Marie or, in her disputes with others, took their side. I confess this with sadness. I would have liked to share her opinions, but in practice it did not work out.

The first issue of Krug carried my short story "Rozovye deti" (Rosy Children), in which the mating of two dogs plays a crucial part. At the meeting of the Circle for the discussion of the first issue, Mother Marie excitedly announced that the editors had put her in a difficult position. She had personally given a copy of the magazine, which also contained her "Mystique of Human Relations," to Father Bulgakov; and he had come upon that story by Yanovsky.

"If the editors had warned me, I wouldn't have given the magazine to Father Bulgakov," she declared.

To this I replied that if the very Christian Mother considered my work an incarnation of evil, all the more reason for her to inform Father Bulgakov so that, together, they could deliberate on means for the salvation of my soul, crooked as it might be, yet still worthy of salvation.

"The two of you ought to have come to my house at night and not left me until I saw the light." So, approximately, I told Mother Marie.

Around this incident there sprang up something akin to a legend, traces of which still remain. Even now, when I meet an old member of the Circle, we inevitably return to this debate with Mother Marie, a nun who, I hope, will in due time be canonized as a "Saint of the Russian Church who shone in exile."

I vividly remember a conversation which took place over tea at Fondaminsky's. It was after Munich, when we were all aware of the approach of the end. Heretofore, Mother Marie had usually been with us, the younger generation, *against* Munich. But when it actually happened, she suddenly began to speak about the previous war in skeptical tones, obviously disapproving of all epic enterprises. I remember her telling us about her brother, a student who volunteered when he was a cadet in an artillery school. Unwilling to sit and wait until he was called up, he joined the infantry and went to the front. Yet at home he was for quite some time considered a deserter from the military school . . . Later, Mother Marie saw him off, on his way to join General Denikin in the south.

"And what remained of all that inspiration and heroism?" she asked. Steam from the hot tea befogged her steel-rimmed spectacles; she repeatedly took them off to wipe them, peering at us nearsightedly with her big, protruding, dark eyes. "What is left of all the ardor and sacrificial enthusiasm? Absolutely nothing," she continued slowly and convincingly. "Perhaps just one more small grave at Perikop.[3] His death was utterly unnecessary and didn't change anything. He could still be alive and work here with us."

"One more small grave" and "absolutely nothing"—these words she pronounced with such feeling that I consider it my duty to perpetuate them.

Later, we celebrated New Year's Eve of 1940 together, for the last time in free Paris. We made an effort to be gay, but the shadows of the approaching European night were already hovering over our old emigré world.

We'll never find out exactly how they died: Mother Marie, Fondaminsky, Felsen, and the others. Anyhow, it is quite unnecessary: There is something sinful in curiosity about factual details. Undoubtedly, they had all for a long time been moving—steadfast and unwavering—toward their martyrdom. And they died, each of them, an active, creative death.

With complete indifference I passed over some acknowledged writers of the emigration (now, actually, of Soviet Russia). Kuprin, Shmelyov, Zaitsev. I got nothing from them, and I owe them nothing. However, I sometimes met up with Boris Zaitsev and was repelled by his indifference—although he allegedly wrote on Christian themes. His "transparent" style struck me as lukewarm and sterile. Somewhat acquainted with his family life and his energetic wife, I think that in some basic way he was under her influence.

In 1929 I was twenty-three years old; for a couple of years I had been keeping the manuscript of a completed novella in my briefcase, because there was no place to publish it. Suddenly a notice appeared in *Poslednie novosti* about a new publishing venture for the fostering of young talents: manuscripts to be sent to M. A. Osorgin, 11 bis Square de Port-Royal.

Within a couple of days I was sitting in Osorgin's office facing the Santé prison, deliberating the fate of my book. He liked *Koleso* (referring to the wheel of the Revolution) but asked me to "clean it up."

Osorgin looked very youthful, although he was probably over fifty at the time, fair, with the straight blond hair of Sweden or the Russian arctic coast. He was one of the few true gentlemen among the Russians in Paris. How to explain that there were so few decent people among us? Of intelligent and talented ones there were plenty. The old Russia, the new Soviet Union, the emigration abounded in outstanding personalities. Yet, decent, well-brought-up people were scarce.

I often played chess with Osorgin. In the time-honored Russian tradition he sang while pondering his moves; his theme song was Lensky's "Kuda, kuda vy udalilis." He played with enthusiasm. Although by European standards he was above average height, Osorgin had to stretch to reach the chess set on the top shelf. Then his young wife, Bakunina, invariably exclaimed: "No, Mikhail Andreevich, I don't want you to do that. Tell me and I'll get it for you." And I noticed to my surprise that after any abrupt movement the breathing of this youthful, blue-eyed "Viking" became labored, and his face paled.

He worked hard and without respite. Like Aldanov, Osorgin made a point of the fact that he had never accepted subsidies or charities from any public organization. He wrote two weekly articles for *Poslednie novosti,* and even these features and travelogues gave evidence of his mastery of the Russian language. (His book, *Povest o sestre* [The Story of My Sister], I consider the best novel of that time).

Yes, the Russian language—this chronic sore of our writers! All constantly accused one another of illiteracy. Some day I'll collect an anthology of the opinions of famous writers concerning one anothers' grammar, syntax and, even, spelling. Verily, it would be a sad and instructive book.

Beginning with Pushkin, who asserted that Derzhavin wrote in the Tartar tongue, up to Remizov, who, with a sharp pencil, underlined the latest trespasses of Bunin and Nabokov—throughout Russian literature an ugly, internecine war has been waged, reminiscent of the most troubled times in Russian history. Men of letters of the Western world rarely permit themselves to accuse great, even classic, writers of not knowing their mother tongue. There exists a general level of the French language which all young people reach who finish the lycée and acquire their *bachot*. Writers of super-class such as Gide or Proust write better—here enters the mystery of style. The same apparently happens in English culture: youths who graduate from Cambridge or Oxford may have different sympathies and beliefs, temperaments and styles; but their language-culture will remain the same. And, what's more, they do not have to go and learn from their "*muzhiks*," to improve or freshen their speech.

When James Joyce, a stylist of genius, performs *salti mortali* on a tight-rope, the critics take note of it: He is an acrobat! However, if a "failure" has not passed through the accepted school, it is so obvious that no one ever mentions it: Gentlemen don't notice when someone burps at the table . . .

As a general rule, if Western writers voice an opinion about a colleague, they do it with underscored politeness and caution, like challengers at a duel. For it is clear to anybody that contemporaries are competitors; no one but a hypocrite and liar can deny that. Only in Russian literature, where pretensions to a "mighty, rich, great language" exceed all other national boastings, do writers constantly carry on fights among themselves, often using the most vulgar idioms of the street. And their quarrels have nothing whatsoever to do with whether Dostoevsky was a mystic and Saltykov-Shchedrin a liberal, or vice versa.

Envy is a very real and universal human trait. After the Fall, envy, jealousy, vanity eroded not only the Russian "all-embracing" soul. But to the west and south of the Rhine, and especially in the Anglo-American world, everyone knows that if one well-known writer begins to list the errors of another, he does not do it out of noble disinterestedness. (Even the altercation between the young Tolstoi and Turgenev is an example of jealousy.) Instinctively aware of all this, as educated people, Anglo-American writers refrain altogether from critical pronouncements about their competitors.

However, besides a low cultural level and bad Russian habits, one more circumstance ought to be noted, namely that, according to the testimony of highly knowledgeable, if interested, people, no one writes perfect Russian. It appears that, for the time being, it is impossible to express oneself correctly in Russian. In other words, we are dealing with a language which is still in a state of evolution.

A great, a powerful, a perfect language I call one that is known in its entirety to academicians and not to the *muzhiks*. It must possess a complete academic dictionary which is republished with additions every ten or fifteen years. (The old edition can then be bought on the market for less.) Alas, all this goes only for the English, the French, and the Americans. Incidentally, the archaic Dahl[4] was worth its weight in gold at that time in Paris.

Koleso arrived from Berlin, where it was printed, and Osorgin took me to the Moskva bookstore. He probably guessed what Yanovsky was feeling—I didn't understand that I was happy.

A damp Parisian winter, wet streets next to the School of Medicine, and at my side a recognized writer, slender—I would say "lithe"—in his foreign (Italian?), wide-brimmed hat, strongly resembling Verkhovensky Senior from *The Possessed*. At Rue Monsieur le Prince we entered a bistro and had a cognac, touchingly clinking glasses. Now I understand that everything we did was part of an ancient ritual.

At the bookstore we were received by a worried and not a bit romantic-looking man, a tight beret over his shaved scalp. A tall stack of *Koleso*—alive, still smelling of printer's ink—was brought out. The title on the cover had been composed with Latin letters: The Russian capital L was made of a Latin V turned upside down. This had been Osorgin's idea, and he prided himself on it. As for me, at that time I considered all questions concerning cover, color, and type ridiculously unimportant, as having nothing to do with the essence.

Osorgin pulled a list out of his pocket with the names of people to whom, according to him, I ought to send my book; and I began scribbling right and left "with best wishes . . . yours." Ironically, we did not send a copy to Khodasevich, with whom Osorgin had quarrelled.

Before my *Koleso*, Boldyrev's novel *Malchiki i devochki* (Boys and Girls) had appeared in the New Writers series. Gazdanov's *Vecher u Kler* (Evening at Claire) had also been slated for publication, but Chertok got there first and captured it for his own publishing house, Parabola. Gazda-nov, a stocky fellow with broad shoulders and a short neck, resembling a hornless buffalo, and pockmarks on his large, ugly face, was nevertheless quite a success with the ladies. In literature, his major weapon, besides stylistic brilliance, was a nagging, permanent irony: an empty and empti-fying skepticism.

I never could credit humor and satire as having an autonomous value. I remember how I rejoiced when I first heard from Shestov, "Since when is laughter an argument?"

Soon after the publication of his book, Boldyrev committed suicide. (His real name was, I believe, Scott—he was part Scottish.)

With a mild, basically Russian face, blue-eyed, slow in speech and movement, Boldyrev began to develop his writing under the influence of Remizov. He was considered an excellent mathematician and made his living tutoring private pupils. Occasionally I met him in Montparnasse in the company of a young woman whom I did not know. Once I told him that we were planning a new magazine and asked whether he would like to participate. Boldyrev looked at me in painful surprise; (in 1941, in Montpellier, I recognized this same look in Vildé, when I asked him to remember me to our friends at the Select.)

"No, this is not for me right now," Boldyrev slowly replied, "no, this isn't for me."

We stood in silence for a minute and separated—forever. A few days later he killed himself. As I subsequently learned, he had been sick for a long time and had been told by his doctors that he was in danger of completely losing his hearing. Deaf, how would he live? This was the end! Having cultivated in himself English rationalism and Scottish com-mon sense, he decided that a merciless conclusion had to be drawn. And he took an adequate quantity of the appropriate pills.

How many people, particularly writers, I remember, who perished because they got entangled in the thickets of a false philosophy of life or art. I even think that the Russian Silver Age could have been a complete success if its heroes—Blok, Vyacheslav Ivanov, Balmont, Bryusov, Sologub, Andreev, and several others—had not stubbornly pursued an illusory, false school of thought. And what about those nineteenth-century enthusiasts of the "simple folk" and the bards singing of patched sheepskin coats? From Gogol to Gorky—they were all victims of their own, *voluntary* social contract.

"I don't blame him," said Osorgin. He spoke agitatedly, lighting yet another of his Russian-type cigarettes. "What would he do, deaf, at his age? Beg for help from the Writers' Union?"

After church I found myself in the company of two strange poets, Kobyakov and Mikhail Struve. They were united by an odd practice: both had tried to commit suicide but had been found in time and taken care of. An obituary of M. Struve by Andrei Sedykh had even appeared in *Poslednie novosti*.

"Boldyrev made a little mistake!" said, or rather quacked, Kobyakov, his enormous Adam's apple moving convulsively like a bird's beak on his scrawny neck. "Boldyrev misjudged it by five minutes!"

"Yes," Struve agreed distractedly, "I see it the same way."

I did not wish to argue with these specialists: something in Boldyrev's decisive act frightened and offended them.

Thus, the entire series of New Writers in fact came to an end with Yanovsky, and Osorgin preserved a sort of fatherly affection for me. He passed on all the addresses of his translators to me and as a result *Koleso* was translated; it appeared in French under the title *Sashka, l'enfant qui a faim*. Only in the course of the years, after having been given many "dead" addresses by other writers, could I truly appreciate Osorgin's generous help. On his advice I sent *Koleso* to Gorky and received two letters, which quite turned my head.

In Montpellier, A. A. Polyakov, whom I was initiating into the mysteries of belote, gave me a package of black olives which Osorgin had sent him. Polyakov himself could not eat them, or was afraid to, because they were stale. Soaking them in wine, I made good use of them and sent Osorgin a few words of thanks. I received a long answer. That was our last "meeting."

In New York I learned of his death. I am glad that he died in his beloved Europe, to the south of the Loire, under the blessed Gallic sky. Osorgin liked to describe the charms of his native Kama, but he did not spend more than ten years on its shores. And I daresay that in Moscow he would have died of boredom. (Like other genuine emigrés: Herzen, Turgenev, Gogol—all differing from each other, yet in some respect similar.)

It seems to me that a good deal of the ugliness in Russia's history can be explained by her vile climate. Poets cheat the average man when they sing hymns to the snow, to Father Frost, dashing troikas with bells, and a lark (high, high up!) in the blue sky. Actually, dear friends, it's pretty nasty to live in Russia—meteorologically speaking.

Incidentally, the periodic famines which have beset Russia (as well as China) from the times of the Ivans up to and including that of Nikita Khrushchev: this ice-age starvation is in large measure due to the climate.

Only think, there are countries where they reap two or three harvests a
year. (And where the birch is not revered as a sacred tree!)

At Easter, I received a letter from Aleksei Mikhailovich Remizov in
response to *Koleso*. In his idiosyncratic Cyrillic script, so very difficult to
decipher, he attested; "There is lyricism in your book. Without it one
would not know how to live on this earth." Included was an invitation
for a certain hour on a certain day.

All reminiscences about Remizov begin with the description of a
hunchbacked gnome, wrapped in a woman's shawl or cloak, with a soft,
clear voice and probing intelligent eyes . . . This creature seemed to be
moving on all fours around the apartment, which was decorated with
handmade monsters and fairy-tale puppets. Some such gnome answered
the door—his apartment was still on the Boulevard de Port-Royal—and
let me in.

But alas, a feeling of uneasiness sprang up in me right away and only
increased with the years. Very often I simply could not look Remizov in
the eye, as happens when one suspects one's neighbor of a flagrant superfluous falsehood. At first unconsciously, but gradually ever more clearly,
I began to realize what exactly irritated me about Remizov and his household. It was the chronic, incurable, all-embracing hypocrisy. Actually,
his literature too was not devoid of mannerism and clownery, notwithstanding the penetrating, sincere outcries of pain.

In this house pretentiousness reigned. There were constant allusions to
nonexistent grievances and persecutions. All the familiar "tricks" of
Remizov, those flamboyant dreams and nightmarish monsters missed
their mark, as does any unjustified invention. He soon became aware of
my feelings and stopped boring me with his tiresome sketches, dreams,
and vague hints. He became much more sincere, simple, and likable.

It's interesting that many of our writers, after having fallen in love
with him at the beginning, passed through more or less the same kind of
disenchantment; some even ended up with genuine loathing, unable to
stand the pseudoclassical atmosphere around him.

From the late twenties to the early thirties, Remizov was the idol of the
young Paris writers. But after a few years, he was always mentioned
with a derisive smile, and people rarely came to see him. Strangely
enough, they often said; "Just wait, some day I'll tell the whole truth
about Remizov!" However, there really was no special "truth" except
the truth that Remizov constantly asked for sincerity while he himself
playacted and exaggerated incessantly.

It was said that Serafima Pavlovna Remizova-Dovgello, a woman who suffered from a generalized transformation of all tissues into fat, exercised a beneficial influence on her husband. She taught Russian paleography, and his Cyrillic script as well as many other "tricks" of his originated with (or in) her!

I have had occasion to convince myself that the so-called salutary influence of women is more often than not an attempt to strangle their mates under some commendable pretext. This goes for Dante and Beatrice as well as for Otsup, the editor of *Chisla* and his "Beauty" (Dante, of course, had other, more serious guides).

I think that Serafima Pavlovna was to a considerable extent responsible for her husband's pharisaism, hypocrisy, and chronic mendacity. No one in their house, it seems, ever gave up anything for the good of a neighbor; but for himself Remizov demanded evangelical love.

They lived, of course, poorly; but I have met poor, even homeless people who sometimes managed to help others. The Remizovs, on the other hand, sought to put every visitor to instant use. ("Every little bit helps.") A translator? Let him translate for free. A collaborator on *Poslednie novosti*? Let him explain to Milyukov that Remizov is not being published enough. A well-to-do businessman? Perhaps he'll buy a book, a manuscript, a drawing! An energetic young man? Let him sell tickets for a Remizov reading. Young poets? They'll find a new apartment and lend a hand with the moving. Dr. Unkovsky? He can fix the old rotten tube of the enema bag: just the job for a doctor, ha-ha-ha! Kelberin? Let him tell Otsup that Aleksei Mikhailovich has seen him in a dream (and give him all the details).

For Remizov had worked out an unpleasant practice bordering on blackmail: He saw important persons in his dreams. And, to boot, he was able to direct these visions of his. Some people appeared to him under favorable and others under humiliating circumstances, And he published his dreams with commentaries. So that Khodasevich was once obliged to write Remizov, "Henceforth I forbid you to see me in your dreams!" And this, if I'm not mistaken, helped.

From childhood on, due to various social and psychological causes, Remizov had felt isolated, helpless, perhaps even worthless, and had realized the value of an organization. But to join an outside association as an equal or perhaps even as an inferior did not suit him. He invented his own "Lodge of the Apes," of which he appointed himself master and delivered corresponding certificates to pleasant people. That, of course, was a game, but, like everything in this house, an ambiguous game.

The visitor who sat down at the Remizovs' tea table immediately fell prey to a strange depression. Aleksei Mikhailovich in his Moscow-Suzdal manner of speech, soft yet as distinct and clear as if he were stamping out coins, would tell a complicated story from which one could deduct that he had been harmed, cheated, shortchanged. It went without saying that all noble-hearted and intelligent people were only waiting for an occasion to come to Remizov's defense. It was assumed that the entire outside world was in conspiracy against our host and that we, assembled under his roof, were now deliberating measures to counteract the forces of darkness and evil. Everyone began, willy-nilly, to feel like a conspirator and precisely that created the asphyxiating atmosphere of a pseudoclassical drama.

Remizov did not live any worse than other writers of his generation. He was able to dedicate himself exclusively to his chosen work and inhabited an apartment with kitchen and bathroom, even if the rent may have been sometimes overdue.

Since he rarely stepped out of the house and, because of a deficiency of sight, read less and less, he wrote a lot, perhaps too much. I think that he must have left behind more than a hundred volumes; old sagas retold, dreams, memoirs, and novellas. But he also published sufficiently, in any case no less than Zaitsev, Tsvetaeva, and Shmelyov. So that his lamentations were simply typical of the general emigré misery.

Sometimes it happened in my presence that he would copy a page for the last time, nearsightedly, meticulously outlining each separate letter. It influenced a casual witness, infected him with creative energy! A half-blind, massive dwarf, his bulging chest pressed against the desk, writes: a scribe of the Muscovy chancellery, scribbling away, molding the separate syllables with his lips.

Leaving him after such a lesson, one had the urge to sit down to one's own manuscript and write with great gusto in the same way, sculpting every letter with one's mouth, artistically filtering the text.

He taught us to pay attention not only to the words but also to the syllables and letters, to take into account the ratio of vowels versus consonants and to avoid the terrible, hissing Russian participles.

"I looked at your handwriting," Remizov let drop to me, gaily, on the run, occupied with more important guests, at my first visit. "You must write out every letter separately, that is the secret of a good hand."

People often voiced outrage about Bunin's *Memoirs*. Indeed, Bunin did not express the slightest sympathy for any contemporary (the only exception, I believe, was Ertel). But Remizov did exactly the same; he criticized, reviled, and demolished everybody—the difference being that he was a typical "failure," without the Nobel Prize, and therefore must be forgiven a certain amount of jealousy and bitterness.

According to him, all his contemporaries were, of course, ignorant of the Russian language and had no business writing. He aimed particularly at those who had attained a measure of success—Bunin, Nabokov. Remizov would grab the latest issue of *Sovremennye zapiski,* where Sirin-Nabokov was at that time continuously published, and read aloud the carefully underlined sentence: "In poems she looked for the genre of driver-don't-whip-the-horses." "What does he do?" Remizov complained in outrage. "He replaces an overused gypsy romance image with a line from a vulgar song and he thinks that he has created something new! All this, because he should not be writing at all!" In his malicious attitude toward Bunin there was something of class hatred. And when Osorgin, who venerated Remizov, was lucky enough to pick up a substantial sum from the Book-of-the-Month Club in America, he considered it a personal affront.

In these raids against his enemies he had Serafima Pavlovna's silent support. She sat there, gelatinous, overflowing with fat; she had no neck, but her face, with its tiny childish nose, had preserved traces of its former prettiness. Despite her affliction, or perhaps because of it, she was forever chewing something. She spent several hours a day at a grocery store owned by friends, where she allegedly helped out at the cash register and systematically devoured mountains of raisins, chocolates, and nuts.

His popularity with the young writers flattered Remizov; this was the trump with which he beat Bunin in one area. There was a time when twenty to thirty young writers would converge around his Sunday afternoon tea table. But that animation did not last long, and the departure of the young people left one more wound in his heart.

I met Zamyatin at Remizov's after his arrival in Paris. The impression I gained was of a solid, purposeful craftsman. Having left the USSR, Zamyatin, however, behaved with the utmost caution, unwilling or unable to cut all ties with the regime. We expected fiery words from him, daring disclosures, a *J'accuse* à la Zola or Victor Hugo. But at his public readings he gave us *Blokha* (The Flea) (after Leskov), and composed scenarios for Russian films made in France, such as "Les Batelliers de la Volga." He talked about the Moscow writers: he said that Sholokhov had apparently made use of someone's diary in the second volume of *Quiet Flows the Don.* I distinctly remember that it concerned only the second volume, not the entire work.

At that time, many writers later to be martyred by Stalin, were still alive: Mandelshtam, Babel, Zoshchenko, Pilnyak . . . Zamyatin was aware of the fate that awaited them, but he did not touch on this subject.

I know that he was proud of the success of *Blokha* in Moscow and still received royalties from there. Above his desk in Passy hung a huge Soviet poster for *Blokha,* and he never uttered his *J'accuse* or damnation.

It would be wrong to stigmatize him for it. Other Soviet authors who spent some time in Paris behaved in the same way: Babel, Kirshon. Pasternak, Fedin, Vsevolod Ivanov, A. Tolstoi (not to mention the infamous Ehrenburg).

In classic Russian literature there are various examples of saintly persons: Father Zosima,* Platon Karataev, Alyosha Karamazov . . . These personages lead saintly lives, but of *honor* there is no mention.

Our masters of the old school considered it obligatory to scoff at the Western Catholic concept of honor, *honneur,* just as they mocked the "Frenchies" and the "Pollacks." Consider how many exemplary noblemen—not only *muzhiks*—there are in *War and Peace* and not a single worthy Frenchman. Napoleon and his marshals, and all other foreigners, indulge in sheer nonsense and theatrical bathos . . . And this in Tolstoi! As for Dostoevsky, there is an almost indecent pasquinade of all Westerners (except Englishmen).

Open contempt for such bourgeois conventions as honor and personal dignity was fostered in Russia long before the Bolsheviks. Russians did not all arrive at genuine Christianity or Gogolian Orthodoxy, but on "honor" they agreed, and missed out completely—not only in practice but, what is worse, ideally, metaphysically.

The Russian *muzhik* as well as his boyar believed in adages such as "Your head won't fall off if you bow," "A submissive head won't be cut off," and other such nuggets of wisdom. Khrushchev danced the hopak around Stalin's table, thinking (as in Chekhov's story): "I'll get the promotion!" while other candidates looked on with envy and approval.

After Zamyatin's sudden death, Remizov told me: "Last night I saw Evgeny Ivanovich in my dream. His nose was squashed in, and blood was dripping down from it. I realized that this was his soul, the cartilage smashed and thick dark blood pouring out. I understand: He suffers greatly, but there is no help. It's too late. He ruined himself with *Blokha* and similar successes."

I report from memory, certain that among Remizov's papers the corresponding notation has been preserved. He did not forget such dreams and did not burn his notebooks.

I once failed to attend his traditional spring reading. Afterward he

---

*Of *The Brothers Karamazov.*

violently berated me: "And what did you do with the ticket I sent you, wipe yourself with it in the toilet?!" And he repeated, smarting from the offense: "Wipe yourself with it!" as if I had committed that sacrilege. (He worked all winter long on those tickets of his: painted them and made collages with scraps of Christmas paper.)

After publication of my novel *Mir,* chapters of which he had read in galleys, Remizov praised only one passage, an indecent incident. "It's good that the cat ate it up," he said, smiling blissfully through his thick lenses. "Yesterday I showed this description to Mochulsky. He was simply appalled, and yet, he himself is quite a rascal. I sometimes look at my visitors and think: How do you, darling, do it at home?" Again he grinned mysteriously.

His different poses—gnome, sorcerer, confessor of the swamps, will-o'-the-wisp—were a game, an obligatory tribute to his era. There is in it something of Blok, Leskov, Sologub's *Petty Demon,* Melnikov-Pechersky with all the ancient slavic folklore.

"Read my *Posolon,*" he advised his admirers. "There's my theme."

I argued that Flaubert, with his method of hard labor and eternal "brushing up" had probably also influenced him.

Remizov smiled. "That's true, of course, but that was later. I came into my *own* through Melnikov-Pechersky." ("Remizov is almost a genius, yet he learned from a second-rate writer," I thought with surprise.)

Having undergone the experience of great need, he became most indignant when a modest demand of his was countered with, "These days everyone suffers." This he considered the limit of egotism and hypocrisy.

On my flight from Paris I had to carry with me a puppy which had been abandoned at our doorstep in Toulouse. The refugees around us were outraged and sometimes even started fights under the pretext that "This is no time to think of dogs while children are perishing." Then I remembered and fully appreciated Remizov's hatred for the Philistines' "everyone suffers."

During one summer, when everyone was away on vacation, Felsen started to visit Remizov on Sunday evenings. And one of his ladyloves also turned up. After a short stay they would walk out together.

In the winter, when I asked him why he was no longer going to the Remizovs, Felsen answered: "My foot won't step across the threshold of that sanctimonious hypocrite. Imagine: I ring, Aleksei Mikhailovich opens the door and says right away: "You know, Nikolai Berngardovich, my house is not a trysting place."   .

"Really!" I exclaimed. "And what did you do?"

"Nothing at all, I did not say anything," Felsen continued with great self-assurance (and I understood: yes, that's the way to behave!). "I went into the living room where N. N. was already waiting, shook hands all around, chatted for five minutes and left. I won't ever cross his threshold again."

Remizov also recounted this episode to me with a mixture of pride and fear. "Now *you* will understand," he said several times, in such a tone that I felt obliged to affirm:

"Of course, you were right, Aleksei Mikhailovich!"

Chapter 9 · The Union of Writers and Poets

THERE IS A MUSEUM OF ETHNOGRAPHY IN THIS CITY. . . .
—N. GUMILYOV

In those heroic years the organization of the young, the Union of Writers and Poets, flourished in Paris. The Union of Writers and Journalists consisted by then of elderly, inactive people.

We often elected Yury Sofiev as president of our Union. A lieutenant of the artillery (in the Civil War), he belonged to a family of professional artillerymen, graduates of the Mikhailov Academy, I believe. His grandfather, Colonel Bek-Sofiev, was still a Moslem.

Sofiev's poems had a touch of Gumilyov. He was a good comrade, despite a natural inclination for intrigue and trouble making. With reddish-blond hair, somewhat resembling an ancient Gaul, he rose at dawn in the winter to wash the windows of department stores and office buildings; the skin of his hands testified to this. Having suffered the indignities of such painful work, he had become thoroughly class-conscious and at all our meetings (even in the Inner Circle) defended the interests of the working class.

Religious questions did not interest him; he loved a song, a glass of wine in a circle of friends, and frequently fell in love in a simple Hussar way. He spent his summer vacations on a bicycle; his wife, the poet Irina Knorring, was too ill with diabetes to accompany him. He returned to Paris with memories of the vineyards and castles of the Loire and accounts of some quite innocent, romantic episodes. He was an admirer of Western Gothic, of churches, masons, and all the magic of the "closed" medieval society. He and his wife had a small son who in my presence once said: "I'm sick and tired of sleeping!"

Sofiev is in Central Asia (if he is still alive); Irina Knorring died long ago; and their little boy is by now a provider, the head of a family, and so forth. (Life, as they say, goes on.)

After the victory, the Parisian emigrés (not all, though) went to pay their respects at the Soviet Embassy; Sofiev, of course, was one of them. He, like Ladinsky, who was also a wartime officer, not only took a Soviet passport but also conscientiously left for the USSR. There, despite the fact that he was fifty or so, he "volunteered" for an expedition beyond the Urals. (Ladinsky, however, stayed behind and died in Moscow. Lyubimov and Roshchin, contributors to *Vozrozhdenie,* stayed there also; but they were of an entirely different ilk.)

Many interesting documents were preserved in the archives of our Union. When I was elected secretary for a certain year, I immediately asked Sofiev about this "historical material" (for instance, Gorgulov-Bred's application to join our Union; I remember his final sentence: "Period! A fat, round period!").

"I keep them separate; I don't want them to get lost," Sofiev reassured me. I don't know what happened to those rare documents.

After his frequent quarrels, Sofiev usually suffered pangs of conscience and, in this repentant mood, sought friendship, love and trust. He tried hard to love those of us from the Inner Circle. It was in his character to "betray" a friend with a pun or a facile word. But how he repented afterward, how sorry he felt! And we believed him . . . not that henceforth he would be "a faithful husband, good father, loyal friend" (as he says in one of his poems), but that this was what he truly desired.

As our president, Sofiev *watched* over the unity of young emigré literature. Like Ivan Kalita he sought to "assemble and organize" all Russian writers and poets outside of Russia under the cultural leadership of Paris. His imperial, political bathos made us laugh, but it sometimes gave rise to bloody internecine battles which threatened the monolithic ideal.

Thus, Terapiano and Raevsky started a new poetry circle and magazine, *Perekrestok* (Crossing). (The poet Dovid Knut had suggested the name. "We met at a crossing!" he said.) The idea was to lean toward Khodasevich's ("formal") method. Obviously, neither Poplavsky nor Chervinskaya joined them.

Perekrestok consisted of five or six members, the most flamboyant of whom was Smolensky. (Raevsky, Otsup's brother, at that time would often let fall, "I and my group . . .")

Sofiev took up arms against this group, accusing it of trying to destroy "organizational unity." Anyway, it very soon broke up without any special efforts on the part of Sofiev. The best that remained of *Perekrestok,* I believe, was the "Diary," in which the members playfully entered their collective poems. I remember an epigram about me (the author, I believe, was Smolensky) with witty puns about my novels *Mir* and *Koleso.*

Prose writing in the group was represented solely by Anatoly Alfyorov, who appeared in Montparnasse with a single short story, "Durachie" (Fools), to his name and seems never to have published anything else. Ivanov nicknamed him "the rising star of the art of painting," for Alfyorov made his living as a house painter (at a time when another "artist"—beyond the Rhine—had already gained full recognition).

Alfyorov was also lucky: he soon met a nice Russian girl from a well-to-do, right-wing family and, as a promising contributor to *Chisla,* had no difficulty in marrying her. He settled down to the complicated life of a prosperous businessman, probably remembering with horror his Montparnassian past.

However, many writers continued to visit him in his bookstore. In the beginning he readily helped his former colleagues out with small donations but gradually tired of this practice. (At the first hint he once handed me several hundred francs for my quarterly rent, and did so unquestioningly, simply, and without any sermonizing.)

There was something old-Russian or rather Slavonic in him, something soft, sincere, naturally talented, so that his success with young women was completely understandable. But his "literature" did not work out! Art as a profession is something unnatural.

To have a talk with him was pleasant but not interesting. Prose, like paper money, calls for the existence of a solid gold reserve; poetry (according to Pushkin) is permitted to be slightly stupid.

Finally, Alfyorov refused a donation to N., who had been bugging him persistently. The latter reacted as if it were a disappointment of a cosmic order. He claimed that he visited Alfyorov so often solely to protect him from being besieged by unceremonious, impertinent intruders. (In other words, N. was afraid that without his help and advice Alfyorov would squander all his capital . . . This anecdote is very characteristic of the Russian Paris of the thirties.)

Vladimir Varshavsky's fate was exceptional for Paris: everybody loved and even respected him. And not only as a man and citizen, an intelligent companion and convinced democrat, but specifically as a writer of fiction. Yet, during the entire prewar period, he published only two short stories. His book he wrote after the war.

Thanks to Adamovich—who especially valued anything that would put in doubt the whole future of literature—Varshavsky was called an "honest writer." By "honest" at that time was understood a serious writer, without inventions, truthful in the manner of Tolstoi. Yet Tolstoi himself, aside from honesty and genius, was endowed with a wild imagination: he constantly sought not only God but also new artistic forms, from "Kholstomer" (Strider) to "The Story of the False Coupon." The meeting of Nekhludov and Katya at the trial (*Resurrection*) can also be considered "invented." The use of the epithet "honest" with regard to a writer reminded me of a chapter in Dostoevsky's *Diary of a Writer* wherein he makes fun of the French for unanimously declaring that Mac-Mahon is "a brave general."

"When one can only say about a general that he is brave, it means that this general is not particularly bright." (I quote from memory.) I always felt something similar when I heard the attribute "honest" (and nothing else) applied to a writer of fiction.

"Big deal! He wrote one little story and now will be considered a writer his entire life!" grumbled Poplavsky, who had had a falling-out with Varshavsky.

Varshavsky inspired confidence, thanks to his "modesty," emphatic conscientiousness, not quite genuine disconcertedness, and a mixture of *printsipialnost,* and submission. His thoughts, although they were not always original, came from the best sources: Bergson, Tolstoi . . . and he expressed them with such sincere excitement that one could not but feel sympathy for this nice young man. Once, after a lecture by him, someone called out from the auditorium, "Horses eat oats!" and Adamovich had a hard time convincing the audience that even such a simple truth was not devoid of value.

And no one suspected that Varshavsky was a sick young man, that he was a born left-hander who had been retrained, that he was organically unable to finish a piece of work, whether one of his own short stories or someone else's philosophical treatise. Having lived for many years in one room with his mother after his parents separated, he was forever seeking a "hero" and much too readily put himself under the protection of Adamovich, Fondaminsky, Vildé, Father Schmemann, Denike, and many others. He could be simultaneously "in love" with several of them and loyally heed their words, a fact which they almost always appreciated. Varshavsky honestly took part in the *drôle de guerre* and, after his return from captivity, was awarded a French military medal. In the years after the war he matured and published two valuable books.

Besides Alfyorov's successful marriage, I can think of one other bourgeois union in Montparnesse. With precisely this in mind, Adamovich brought Stravinsky's daughter to us, and Yury Mandelshtam married her. The young bride had tuberculosis, just as in a nineteenth-century novel; after a short time she died, leaving behind a baby girl.

In 1937, I believe, I cycled through Alsace; near Colmar, on a mountain called Schlutz (or something phonetically similar), I met Yury and held the bundle with his tiny daughter in my arms while speaking with him about Grunewald, whom I had just "discovered."

Mandelshtam was deeply devoted to literature and wrote indifferent poems with great enthusiasm; with the same enthusiasm, and also poorly, he played chess and bridge.

After a decade of Yury Mandelshtam's creative activity, Adamovich, who surely was a gentle, tactful ("musical") critic, wrote in his Thursday column: "Incidentally, it is not too late for Mandelshtam to begin signing his poetry with a *nom de plume.*" (I quote from memory.)

But Mandelshtam had no plan to give up his name. His parents, old Muscovites, adored their son and daughter (the poet Tatiana Stillman). Yury was the only one in the family to convert to Russian Orthodoxy, after having undergone the appropriate religious experience; he was also the only one to perish in a German camp. Strangely enough, it happened in connection with bridge. Yury adored the game, although he had no great talent for it. One night he walked up from his apartment to the next floor, to the apartment of a colleague from *Vozrozhdenie.* There, four of them sat down to a game of bridge. Yet Mandelshtam, as a non-Aryan, had to stay home after 8:00 P.M. The police happened to stop by and arrested him. He was taken to Compiègne, where he met Mother Marie and Fondaminsky. Then they all vanished. What a collection of absurd coincidences!

Mandelshtam belonged to Terapiano's group. Many beginning poets, among them Smolensky, put themselves under Terapiano's aegis. But, as soon as they were able to spread their own wings, they threw off that superfluous ballast and often repaid Terapiano with ingratitude. But Mandelshtam remained to the end true to his godfather.

Sofiev dreamed of uniting all emigré literary groups into one organization, while Terapiano wanted to teach the art of poetry according to his own taste. The shadow of the masters of versification, Gumilyov and Bryusov, haunted Terapiano. This was a pity, for, aside from his poetic talent, he certainly lacked their magic and charm. His poems were rather pallid, but he loved and knew a great deal about poetry. For prose he had no ear.

Terapiano helped those young poets who acknowledged his authority. Smolensky began under his auspices (in Khodasevich's camp). There was something in Smolensky which was akin to Ivanov and Zlobin, some moral rottenness. But he did not possess Ivanov's talent or intelligence. Smolensky could talk well and with gusto about his own death; the subject seemed tragic and meaningful to him. But, in contrast to Ivanov and Merezhkovsky, who also liked to expatiate on the subject, Smolensky died young—which, in hindsight, explains a great deal about him.

As a student he fell in love with and married a rosy-cheeked, full-breasted girl; wrote verses about a "white-breasted swallow." Gradually he took up vodka and separated from his wife. A good-looking, naturally tanned boy in a tailcoat, coquettishly swaying his hips, he declaimed from the podium about "a poet and his drunken muse," and that "every night is an eternity." When introduced to a lady, he immediately and rather crudely began to flirt with her. At night he sat perched on a barstool at Dominique, clinked glasses and smiled wickedly. All of a sudden he might start a quarrel with the pretty, tubercular, diminutive poetess A.

"You're a new Anna Karenina," he said mockingly.

A. grew even paler and bit her tiny red lips.

"I'll beat you up," I once yelled. "Let's step outside!"

Smolensky was perhaps a *poète maudit,* but he was a cowardly *poète maudit.* His face grew contorted, and he did not answer. A few days later, "Anna Karenina" quite unexpectedly told me: "I consider you a man of principle!"

All in all, our literary ladies were not adapted to the rough and tumble of life. Difficult living conditions, lack of sleep, poor nutrition, tobacco and, last but not least, incessant, soul-searching talks paralyzed many normal physiological propensities. With respect to sex they became simultaneously victims and vampires. As Maria Ivanovna, the wife of the poet Stavrov, muttered: "They say there are orgies going on in Montparnasse. Big deal, they go to bed together! Orgies!"

Nevertheless, Khodasevich found it possible to treat the topic in his famous four-liner about women making their career in literature.

Once, at the Select, two ordinary-looking young women advanced toward the table next to us, with the hips, calves, and other attributes of normal girls. Adamovich, with a truly dispassionate smile remarked: "My God, if two such normal females were suddenly to appear in our midst, what a miraculous metamorphosis our poets would undergo!"

Before the war, an attractive, thin, blonde girl began to show up in Montparnasse, Smolensky's new fiancée and later wife. She was said to have religious leanings and to be planning to "save" the poet. Perhaps she did indeed save him. But during the occupation, he, like Merezhkovsky, Ivanov, and Zlobin, blossomed ideologically. After the victory, the Russian poets in Paris boycotted them for a while. Thus, in their first postwar anthology, *Fourteen* (or *Thirteen*) Smolensky, Ivanov,

Odoevtseva, Gippius, and Zlobin were not included; as former collaborators they *could* not be included. The same goes for the collection *Estafet* (Relay).

The Rudnevs lived at Metro Convention, almost directly across the street from the offices of *Chisla*. I was fond of this childless, quiet, amiable couple of Russian intellectuals, populists (*narodniki*), liberals, and so forth. However, Vadim Rudnev's role in the *Sovremennye zapiski* seemed to me harmful.

He made no secret of the fact that he did not "understand" poetry and never meddled in that department. But, with regard to prose, he and other editors, alas, expressed definite opinions.

"Take Rudnev, a practicing Russian Orthodox believer," Vishnyak explained to me with obvious relief. "And he completely agrees with me that such metaphysics don't belong in the journal."

The truth was that Rudnev, a lifelong member of the Russian church, thought that religious questions should not be the subject of discussions and arguments; faith was a personal matter, and to express an opinion about it in the presence of outsiders was unseemly.

Over a glass of red wine and a simple snack we would try to have a quiet talk without irritating each other unduly. I respected his honesty, dependability, integrity, and that special, long-vanished, old-time, disinterested decency. We had medicine in common as well; he had been a Moscow district physician and considered the profession of a doctor to be one of dedicated service. I believe he was also touched by the inordinate deprivations which my generation had to suffer.

His wife, a short, stocky, typically Russian woman with clear, honest eyes, would listen peacefully to our conversation. Thanks to medicine, I immediately landed, wherever fate brought me, at the center of real, basic life and saw the underlining usually hidden from the eyes of foreign observers. My medical experiences could, at times, have interested him.

I well remember Rudnev's handshake: he had some defect of the right hand; I believe that part of his little finger was missing. They had no children, as was the rule in that milieu. I don't know how to explain it, but the fact that Vishnyak, Nikolaevsky, Zenzinov, Aldanov, Fondaminsky, and many, many others left no descendants seems to me astonishing and worth exploring.

After their flight from Paris, Vladimir Rudnev lay for a long time ailing in Pau, in the Basses Pyrénées. They operated on him, but unsuccessfully, and he died caring for others, as behooves a Russian revolutionary in exile (he tried to help me, too). Helene Iswolsky, who lived in Pau at the time, has given a good account of his last days.

Having buried her husband in the Pyrénées, the widow came to New York, where I sometimes met her in the early days. She asked me to Sunday luncheons with her old friends, such as Vishnyak and Zenzinov, but nothing constructive grew out of those meetings. In passing, I criticized Aldanov's new novel and was almost thrown out of the room. In their close circle it was perhaps permitted to criticize Aldanov, but never, God forbid, in the presence of outsiders.

On the occasion of a lecture by a well-known Gaullist I went to Horizon, the Russian club in New York. During the intermission, walking back to my seat, I came face to face with Mrs. Rudnev, who was moving in another human stream.

"How are you?" I just managed to ask cheerfully and, without waiting for an answer, continued, carried on by the flow of people. And suddenly I heard her voice: "Bad, very bad," before we were divided by the crowd.

This angered me. Why did she have to say such a thing? She was no worse off than the rest of us. "These days everyone suffers." However, I decided to call her soon, perhaps to drop in.

A few months later she died. Suddenly, on the street. She worked as a sewing-machine operator (as did my sister), sometimes went to the theater or a concert. Returning at night from Carnegie Hall, she collapsed on West 72nd Street. She was picked up, and the address of Mrs. M. Zetlin, who lived at that very corner of 72nd Street, was found in her handbag. The police called her up, but Mrs. Zetlin, deaf and old and ailing, was already in bed. She gave them Zenzinov's address.

Among the last of the SRs, Zenzinov was considered a man of decision, action, and even armed intervention! It was he, however, who had let the double agent Azev slip out of Paris and who, during her first escape, let the NKVD* abduct Kasiankina from Aleksandra Tolstoi's farm near Nyack, whence they delivered her to the Soviet consulate; there she jumped out of a window, making good her escape.

Whenever the aging SRs needed "a man" they turned to Zenzinov, whom, incidentally, they had nicknamed "the old maid." So, in this case too, Maria Zetlin gave the police his telephone number. And Zenzinov, the most honest, modest, and principled of men, dressed in a hurry and, in the dark of the night, went to identify the body of Mrs. Rudnev, whom he probably had known half a century ago, when she was a blonde student at the Bestuzhev Institute.[1] ("Oh bard, nightingale of yore, how you would sing the glory of those warriors!")

---

*The NKVD are the Soviet secret police.

From the Rudnevs or from *Chisla* I walked to the *Porte de Versailles,* where I took the streetcar home to Vanves (bordering Clamart).

The large and solid family of Viktor Chernov, who was the leader of the SRs, had settled in Clamart. His three daughters had married Reznikov, Sosinsky, and Vadim Andreev, the son of Leonidas, respectively. The Chernov "colony" lived amicably though poorly; before they took Soviet passports, Sosinsky and Andreev were considered as sharing our convictions and were members of the Circle.

The "Chernovs" worked in a printing house, wrote in their spare time and were ardent tennis players. They had managed to rent a private court for a pittance; the padlock at the entrance carried the acronymic code CRTC, standing for Christ Resurrected Tennis Clamart. I wonder whether now, in the Soviet Union, the NKVD is aware of this secret code.

Konstantin Balmont, the poet, lived close by with his daughter, Mirra, who had tried marriage several times. By then it had become very difficult to communicate with the aged poet.

Balmont's birthday. Summer, August perhaps: the paths of the Chernovs' little garden were strewn with pale rose petals. To honor this fading personification of "the gracefulness of slow-motion Russian speech" (a line from one of his poems), the Chernovs had arranged an afternoon tea party (one could no longer serve wine in Balmont's presence).

The poet, his still leonine mane dishevelled, was installed near a flowerbed; the dying French flowers smelled intoxicating. Decrepit, grey, with a short pointed beard, Balmont nevertheless resembled an ancient god, Svarog or Dazhebog*—in any case something old-Slavonic, pagan. The drifts of rose petals around him inspired Sosinsky to collect a pailfull of this summer snow and present it to the drowsing former thunderer. Balmont, an alien stone idol, smiled sleepily and thanked him. When the talk turned to technical progress, the poet, suddenly wide awake, declared excitedly that rather than engaging in all sorts of stupidities, it would be better to send an expedition to the Azores, for clearly that was where Atlantis was buried.

On a tree, some feathered creature uttered its song or whistle. And we, the young ones, began to argue about what kind of a bird it was. Later on, when we had turned to other subjects, Balmont suddenly, as if waking up, reproachfully let fall: "A chiff-chaff!" And again I saw on

---

*Slavic gods.

that small stump in the garden, surrounded by drifts of rose petals, a dishevelled dying Slavonic god.

I once met another "dethroned" celebrity, the poet Igor Severyanin, at Remizov's. How banal was everything he wrote and said! Yet, how mysteriously majestic he looked! Well-built, tall, powerful, a man who liked cognac and skiing, he carried himself with complete dignity. And his forehead was one I had seen before: the forehead with the invisible and yet discernible laurel wreath of a victor (if only for one hour). I have seen such foreheads on Lindbergh, Kerensky, Sirin, Auden, Kennedy.

What is the secret of success? Suddenly, a thousand students acknowledge someone as a king, a spiritual leader—a hairdresser, a novelist, a Fuehrer . . . and in twenty-five years it may be a riddle how it all came about, and one is ashamed to remember this mass hypnosis. The king, obviously, was outrageously naked. Who was right? Impressionable soldiers who went into attack stirred by Kerensky's orations or pragmatists who transferred Russian rubles into German marks and lost everything?

The Union of Writers and Poets held regular, large gala readings. But the main attractions were the readings in café basements, first at La Bollet, later at Méphisto. There, something similar to the "Hamburg rating of circus performers" took place, and even if the criticism was at times delivered with a bludgeon, it nevertheless charged us up creatively. Outsiders also flocked to such intimate gatherings, wild people who often read ludicrous verses. Thus one young boy declared with bathos that "one hand kissed the other."

There was a middle-aged poet who chose "Bulkin" for a pen name. When asked why Bulkin, he explained: "Pushkin, Bulkin, what's the difference?" He treated us to such lines as, "I run at once in different directions," and, "How often will the treacherous Delilah clip Samson to the scalp!" A bald man with a straggly goatee, he looked like a lawyer or a doctor from the turn of the century. He did, however, deal quite successfully in gasoline. And at the height of the war performed feats of amazing bravery, marching as a volunteer with the battalions of General Leclerc from Lake Chad in Africa to the Arc de Triomphe in Paris.

Freshly arrived from Berlin, Boris Vildé presented his awkward prose for the first time at the Méphisto. Long prose pieces were seldom read in those basements. At that time Vildé called himself a writer and poet—he even had a pen name: Dikoi. He spoke Russian with stress on the wrong syllables. All I remember of the long story is the lyrical refrain at the end of each brief chapter: "The artist has talent, the artist has TB."

Chervinskaya had mentioned some time before that a new writer had appeared, "who very much resembles you." From her smile I understood that no flattery was intended. (In general, such statements evoke only bitter feelings.) It was then that I heard Boris Vildé's name for the first time. A native of a Baltic state, he came to Paris from Berlin and found his way to *Chisla*. He was somehow connected with André Gide and delivered regards from the latter to Otsup—or, vice versa, undertook to deliver a note from Otsup to the Maître.

A few days later, at our first meeting, we looked each other over closely, hiding the hostility so usual under such circumstances. Vildé had probably heard from the same Chervinskaya about our alleged resemblance, and it did not sit well with him either. Alas, people strive to be "unique," "incomparable."

Soon after, we met one evening in Montparnasse. He was accompanied by a pale French girl, his future wife; and I did not feel like sitting at a table, paying for my drink and speaking French. Besides, from our previous exchange we had already decided that we had little in common.

After he acquired French citizenship, Vildé began to express himself in simple but fluent French. His Russian also improved in Paris.

"So I'll tell Gide," he yelled, leaving the tiny office of *Chisla*. We smiled, embarrassed for him. (Otsup, believing in his supposed friendship with André Gide, had wanted to convey some message to the latter.)

When Vildé arrived in Paris, he lived for a time in the attic maid's room of André Gide's apartment. This undoubtedly entitled him to give his address as c/o André Gide. How he happened to become acquainted with the French writer, known for his stinginess and reserve, has remained a mystery to me, as have many other things of that period. Before coming to Paris, Vildé had lived in Germany, and he expressed radical convictions. André Gide had been there, too, traveling in the circles of avant-garde blonde boys, before making a trip to Russia. At that time he may have offered Boris shelter in Paris, should he ever need it.

This, the address of André Gide, was almost all the capital with which Vildé arrived at the Gare du Nord—and he squeezed the maximum out of it.

Primarily a man of action, energetic, aggressive, and not at all of a contemplative nature, he could have been a success in America. He liked his comforts: good wine, French *cuisine,* pleasant girls. All this, however, did not interfere with his true ideals; it even helped him to steadfastly continue the fight for them! Incidentally, he was in many ways not Russian.

So, Vildé put a note on the bulletin board at the Sorbonne: Young
student, emigré, offers Russian lessons in exchange for French. Address: . . . . c/o André Gide. He received an answer from a young girl
with a long corn-yellow braid, whose mother was Russian and whose
father was a professor at the Sorbonne. And Vildé put down roots in
Paris, found there his second, or perhaps his first, home. He married the
girl, acquired French citizenship, a process which we old-timers could
not and did not even want to go through with. He studied archaeology at
the Sorbonne and, I believe, was even sent on a dig. A strong, intelligent
worker, he aimed at a professorship and, in the meantime, held a job at
the Musée de L'Homme (Trocadéro) in which he also advanced.

Then he did the obligatory year's military service. On his furloughs he
always showed up at our meetings: tanned, tired, thinner, but physically
and mentally alert. He would order a "sergeant's drink," a combination
of different liqueurs which did not mix in the tall glass but floated in
thick rings, the colors of a rainbow, one above the other. Laughing,
twirling the French *képi* in his hands, he announced: "You see, I always
knew that I would be a marshal!" (He was *Maréchal des logis*.)

In the very beginning, before his marriage, he had been in a car accident; his collarbone was broken, and he collected some money for the
injury. While lying in ace bandages in his room, he was visited by some
writers who became his friends. Being an aggressive type, Vildé liked
pliable, even weak people and stood up for them.

I played chess with him, and he sometimes managed to win; but he
was much better at bridge. Though flushed with the excitement of the
game, he could calmly and methodically deal the cards. Instead of holding the deck upright, he held and dealt the cards crosswise. I have never
since seen it done this way and don't know how he came to adopt this
method. Kelberin happened to sit next to us, chattering away; *he* held his
cigarette not between his index and middle fingers but between the
middle and ring fingers (for some reason, an irritating mannerism).

Emigrés from all the eastern limitrophes poured into Paris after Munich. Among them was a young man from Tallin to whom Vildé on and
off, unobtrusively, slipped five francs. That young man assured me that
Boris Vildé was a wonderful human being.

For a time Poplavsky and Vildé were courting a certain Russian girl. It
was then that, over a purely abstract issue, both "candidates" began to
wave their fists threateningly; Poplavsky panted, scowled, grew angry
(probably more at himself than at the challenger), but Vildé's eyes suddenly became joyful and icy clear. He was obviously relishing the fight.

There was something un-Russian in this; and even Pechorin, of whom he reminded me at this moment, came to seem un-Russian to me.

Yury Ivask (who lived on an Estonian passport) told me in New York that he had known Vildé in high school in Tallinn. Boris, he told me, liked to walk up to a couple, comfortably installed on a park bench at night, and, slowly pulling out just the muzzle of a revolver, say: "Would you care to buy an excellent gun?" When the man stutteringly refused, Vildé would ask him for a "contribution."

I do not know how often he performed that trick, but the story seems in character. There was something of the noble adventurer in him, combined with genuine ideals and spiritual richness. If I had to look for the fictional character psychologically closest to Vildé, I would name Julien Sorel, of Stendhal's *Le Rouge et le noir.*

All the above must not detract from the significance of Boris Vildé's sacrifice or throw a shadow over his historical act. I am not painting icons, I am writing a report, an account for future generations; I want to show a living, passionate and enormously self-controlled man, to trace along a dotted line the road traveled by a hero from a park in Tallinn to the polygon of the Mont Valéry prison, from teenage adventurism to the mature, calculated heroism of a conspirator.

On a certain Saturday in the spring—with the sun overhead and a wind from the Channel—Otsup had arranged for a group photograph of the contributors to *Chisla.* Vildé, also considered a contributor, came with his wife to the hall of the hotel where the picture was to be taken. She sat facing the group as we were being assembled and assigned our places. She looked at us, and we had to look at her.

The "generals" took up the first row: Merezhkovsky, Gippius, Adamovich. Chervinskaya tried to solve the ancient problem of how to be in two places simultaneously. At the decisive moment Larionov contrived to light a cigarette, which irritated Poplavsky, who hated fakes and envied them.

That morning I had acquired, at the *marché aux puces,* a bluish-green almost new suit and was tinkering with the overly long sleeves.

I do not know what Vildé's wife was thinking about while we were being twice photographed. But she did not smile. And now, looking at that picture from *Chisla,* I wince with pain: clearly, we were all condemned, each in his own way. Incidentally, Vildé often went to see the dentist and displayed an abundance of dully gleaming gold crowns, which brought to mind a skull, a skeleton, the framework of *anthropos.*

He was among the first to be targeted by general mobilization. A sergeant, having undergone regular military training, he was immediately called up. For the entire "*drôle de guerre*" he remained stationed in Alsace.

In Irina Grjebine's ballet studio there was a young Dutch girl to whom Vildé had taken a fancy. When war was declared and the citizens of neutral countries had to leave Paris, the girl nevertheless kept in touch with Boris; she managed to get a permit to return to Paris in the winter of 1940 (no small feat!) when he had his furlough. They met in Grjebine's studio and vanished for twenty-four hours. At his wife's place he showed up a full day later. He had probably left his company in Alsace a day ahead of the officially stamped date; Vildé knew how to arrange such matters.

I cannot force myself to cross out the above, despite the urging of my friends. It seems to me that any unexpected message which might now reach Mme. Vildé, like one more light wave from a long-extinguished star, would, apart from everything else, give her joy.

When we were discussing whether to admit Vildé into the Inner Circle, there were objections. Some said that he was reserved, secretive, "too lucky." Not everyone trusted him.

Thus Varshavsky and I were assigned to sound him out. I mention this to emphasize once more how difficult it is to evaluate one's neighbor justly, even if he be a hero, a saint, or a genius. After all, didn't André Gide reject the manuscript of Marcel Proust?

The three of us met in a café on the Boulevard St. Michel. I would have preferred to stay on the terrace, but Vildé, looking around, led us inside. I explained this conspiratorial behavior by the peculiarities of his family life. When he smiled, he exposed his lower jaw with the dully gleaming gold crowns, which made the bones seem heavier, more skeletal. Apparently I always experienced this feeling of the skeleton, of the skull, in his presence.

We reported the result of our "interview" to Fondaminsky, and Vildé was accepted into the Inner Circle. That was what he wanted.

After the *débâcle* and the fall of Paris, I landed in Montpellier. In the winter of 1941 Irina Grjebine told me about a letter she had received from Vildé: he was coming to the free zone, officially for demobilization, and would be in Montpellier. We knew already that he had escaped from a prisoner-of-war camp.

I met him, after dinner, in a café on the Esplanade. He was wearing a new grey suit (I was in patched clothes), a good shirt—with cuffs and cufflinks—and was smoking *gitanes jaunes;* at dinner with Grjebine, he had ordered game and a vintage wine.

Re-reading Savinkov's *Memoirs of a Terrorist,* I am struck by that same, special, underground mixture of sacrificial heroism and champagne.

We had coffee with cognac and talked gingerly. He hinted that there was still a lot to be done and asked whether it was true that I had decided to go to the United States.

At that time I was outraged by France, by the easiness with which she put herself at the mercy of the enemy. From the palaces of the *nouveaus riches* to the shacks of the have-nots, all wanted undisturbed work and to be left in peace (*"qu'on me fiche la paix"*). I dreamed of joining a regular army; this war could not be won by guerillas. And there was one other hope: Russia! Monstrous, totalitarian, savage, Tartar, Muscovite, Byzantine, Avvakumian Russia! Every time a real danger threatened humanism, Russia joined the enlightened side and, sustaining the heaviest losses, together with them crashed the latest enemy of mankind. So it was with Genghis Khan, Charles XII, Napoleon, Wilhelm's Germany, and so it would be with the Germany of the Third Myth. In limited wars Russia made mistakes, serious mistakes: from Poland to Finland, from the Caucasus to Hungary and Turkey. But in universal conflicts, Moscow has always miraculously chosen the historically "right" way. Perhaps her guardian angel pushed her toward it.

Vildé argued: Russia was an ally of Germany now, and our enemy. America would help us. That the United States would enter the war, he foresaw; but he missed out on Russia's epic contribution.

Upon this, more or less, our talk ended; there seemed to be no reason for future intercourse. He did, however, give me the address of someone influential in the local *préfecture,* in case I needed "administrative" aid. When I asked about our mutual friends in Paris, he said that he did not see them anymore.

He told me about his escape from captivity: apparently it had been easily accomplished, since an army of a million men was fenced in without an adequate number of guards. (In fact, if he had not escaped, he would probably still be alive today.)

Vildé returned to Paris by a roundabout way, stopping in several cities in the South, organizing underground cells, I imagine. Despite his involvement in the underground, he sometimes met with Fondaminsky in Paris and provided him with permits for legal travel into the free zone. Thus the Fedotovs got to Marseilles with documents produced by Vildé.

I can imagine Fondaminsky's bliss when he received Vildé, who was living under an assumed identity in Paris. The third generation of valliant, heroic, illegal members of the intelligentsia! It was cause for pride; the historical experience of the Russian humanists had not been wasted. The torch of the fight for freedom, equality, and fraternity, taken up once upon a time by the *narodniki* had now passed unsullied into the hands of the younger generation . . . Fondaminsky could rightfully think so, he whose apartment at 130 avenue de Versailles was changing from an emigré headquarters into a museum of Russian culture.

Vildé was walking out of a café when several heavily built thugs in civilian clothes jumped him, twisted his arms and threw him into a car. I see—oh how well I do see!—his clear cool look and the bared jaw with the dully gleaming gold crowns. (This was probably the source for my *Chelyust emigranta* [Emigrant's Jaw].)

In the spring of 1942, passing through Nice, I visited Adamovich. In silence he handed me a postcard from Stavrov, who had returned to Paris: "Yesterday, after a long illness, Boris Dikoi died in the hospital." How is it that we instantly guessed that "hospital" stood for prison and that death meant execution? That too is a historical tradition: Radishchev, Pushkin, Belinsky, Dostoevsky, Saltykov-Shchedrin—they all used this Aesopian language. When in communist Petrograd the news made the rounds that "the Tent was taken," everyone connected with literature understood that the poet Gumilyov (author of *The Tent*) had been arrested.

On the bend of a river there is a quiet village near Paris, next to a famous racetrack. There, my wife worked as a nurse in a hospital, named for Marchal Foch, I believe. I visited on Sundays. On the calm waters fishing and pleasure boats floated; the restaurant served fish in every imaginable form and, of course, wine. Everything was fresh, sweet-smelling, and very boring. On the way to the railroad station, I saw with disgust the military fort of Mont-Valéry, with a high, whitewashed wall enclosing an empty, almost square area. I believe that it was at this particular spot that I always began feeling sick to my stomach; I attributed the nausea to the double portion of fish. It was there, an eternity later, that the first seven men of the Résistance (apparently transferred from Fresnes), with Boris Vildé at their head, were led out to be executed.

In his diary, fragments of which were published posthumously, Vildé writes that he preferred to die then, at the height of his strength and energy, and not "later," when force and courage might fail him. These lines directly echo the words of Stendhal's hero when he was offered a chance to escape from prison.

One of our poets was a certain S. Rogalya-Levitsky. In the days of Poplavsky, the three of us, for no obvious reason, roamed the streets of the city at night, whispering poems or arguing about Tibetan sages. After Poplavsky's death Levitsky and I, walking from the Panthéon to the Seine,

invariably repeated, ". . . and a wave of heat made them quiver . . ."
(from Poplavsky's *Flagi* [Flags]).

"Do you understand how good that is?" I would insist. And Levitsky,
long-sufferingly, replied: "I understand."

He was not included in *Yakor* (The Anchor), an anthology of emigré
poetry, although he had claimed that "if Bulkin is in, I also belong," and
I had discussed his case with Adamovich. From the postwar collection of
Parisian poets, *Fourteen*, Ivanov, Gippius, Smolensky, and Zlobin were
excluded, since they had collaborated with the Germans. But Rogalya-
Levitsky's poems are there, with the epigraph, "And a wave of heat
made them quiver."

When Melgunov, the editor of the new postwar magazine *Vozrozhdenie,* commissioned him to write an article annihilating all emigré literature
with the exception of the contributors to his own magazine, Rogalya-Levitsky enthusiastically undertook the task, choosing as his main target
those very lines of Poplavsky, obviously making fun of Melgunov.

I mention S. Rogalya-Levitsky, the poet, because I must say a word
about his brother, Anatoly Levitsky, who was executed together with
Vildé and his group. In his hotel room, S. Levitsky once introduced me
to a radiant young couple, newlyweds or about to be. Everything in
them was asmile and evoked smiles—despite Western European reti-
cence and reserve. The young man was Anatoly, the brother of our
Rogalya-Levitsky; the girl, if I'm not mistaken, spoke only French. He
was a scientist, preparing his doctorate and working at the Musée de
l'Homme.

Now there is a plaque at the museum, with the names of àll those
cheerful and gallant young Russians who were among the first to fight
for the liberation of France.

("There is a museum of ethnography in this city. . . .")

Chapter 10 · Meetings

There are in literature certain, accidental, people. For a time they distinguish themselves, are respected or appreciated, and then, suddenly, vanish, as if swallowed up by the earth; they disappear, seduced by family happiness or business enterprises. You may even hear of them again—for they makes noises in an office or on the stock exchange.

Such a one was Lazar Kelberin. As far as I remember, he did not create anything of note, although he wrote poems and talked incessantly. However, a number of influential poets—Ivanov, Zlobin, Otsup—paid attention to him. In the years preceding the war he cried out against democracy (the democracies) and even somewhat praised the Germans, a thing that could seem only ridiculous. To his poetry, I believe, he did not attach great importance. About one of his essays in Gippius' *Smotr* (Parade) Adamovich wrote in *Poslednie novosti:* "If Khlestakov (Gogol's Inspector General) had wanted to compete with Pascal, he would probably have written this way." (I quote from memory.) To Kelberin's credit it must be said that he did not resent such criticism.

A man of mystical inclinations, Kelberin had several times entered into (legal) wedlock. One of his first wives was Lydia Chervinskaya. Chervinskaya . . . sleepless nights, talks until dawn, and tears whether sober or drunk. And, at times, good poems.

During the days of *Krug* I saw her almost every evening. She could be impossible, with all the faults of a snob (always keeping an eye out for the chefs of the literary kitchen). But once she accepted a person, she became, if not a loyal comrade, then a warm and amusing drinking companion.

Chervinskaya lived in an artificial world, led an artificial life full of artificial relationships and as a result of this set of artificial inventions, her artful and authentic poetry came into being. In her imagination she created tragedies of love and jealousy which could not be simply shrugged off, since our true existence is often based on such unmaterialized realities.

"She needs another kind of help—religion, God, Christ! Why don't you explain that to her?" I said to Adamovich, who had just gotten rid of Chervinskaya and was about to settle down at the bridge table.

"You can't tell someone who comes to you for support such things," Adamovich replied and, assuming a pointedly distracted mien, rolling his eyes, announced: "Two spades!"

At that time Chervinskaya was living alone. Tall, stooped, bony, with a pretty face and hairdo à la Greta Garbo, she did not work, was starving and could be turned inside out, literally and figuratively, by a modest little glass of vodka. At our parties it was, for some reason, my duty to take care of the "cadavers." There were New Year's celebrations when I incessantly stuck my finger into one larynx after another and distributed weak coffee.

In the apartment of Andrei Bakst (son of the famous painter) Chervinskaya vomited all night. Both of us leaned up to our waists out of the window, she spitting sour coffee onto the glass roof of the concierge's *loge*. I watched with horror how, down below, lights were switched on and off ever more rapidly and convulsively. Finally the outraged concierge came up and, in a language as pure as Descartes's, explained to Bakst why she did not like the *sales métèques*.

At one of the yearly balls of the Russian press, always held at the eve of 14 January, in the Salle Hoche (near the Arc de Triomphe), I once knowingly sacrificed my well-being for the sake of Chervinskaya and since then have remained fondly attached to her.

That year Smolensky and I acted as helpers to Maria Samoilovna Tsetlin, who supervised the organizing of the Ball. In Paris, at least in Russian Paris, the telephone was still a rarity. To hire an orchestra or secure a team of waiters, one needed messengers. Taxicabs being out of reach, we literati, for a small remuneration, ran across Paris helping the lady organizers. In the evening we converged at Mrs. Tsetlin's apartment to report on our accomplishments and, after a light snack, to receive instructions for the next day.

"Have you noticed," Teffi said to me at one of these committee meetings, her intelligent lively old-woman's eyes sparkling, "have you noticed how people's voices change when they go up to the buffet table?"

Indeed, only moments before complete boredom had reigned, as Zaitsev, lukewarm, tanned, with red blotches in his cheeks, mumbled on. Then, all of a sudden, there was noise, animation, movement: the loud laughter of a former dragoon from Nizhny Novgorod who had downed a full glass of vodka; even Boris Zaitsev began to express himself more clearly and to the point.

My assignment was to hire people for the buffet; I engaged several professionals and slipped in my friend Sh., who, unfortunately, was a universal dilettante. A Moscow judge, he now sang in church choirs or worked as a kitchen helper but mainly subsisted on unemployment benefits (*chômage*) which had led him to change his mind about Léon Blum. He was a former teacher of Protsenko, in whose workshop we became acquainted. I loved Sh.'s stories about old Moscow's civil servants or the life of the "gilded youth." He colorfully impersonated the different figures, intermingling his talk with the cries of street vendors ("cherries and roots!"), the lamentations of a blind beggar, or the thundering introit of a deacon. There were also risqué stories; but they were always naive, unsophisticated, and more humorous than those of the following generations.

If one dropped in on him in his hotel room on the rue Mazarin (next to the entrance, an *invalide* made and sold *pommes frites*) Sh. invariably greeted one with, "won't you have the kindness to take a seat!"

Sh. shared the room with a former actor who was a future monk of the Monastery of St. Sergius, also a very colorful personage. Both slept on the same, narrow cot, for which they had constructed a cardboard divider.

Sh. once suffered a light stroke—the first bell!—in the daytime, walking on the street. He sat on a bench on the Place du Châtelet, having strange, nebulous, and fantastic visions. The memory of that lonely pilgrim, on a bench in the center of the city, struggling with a fatal seizure, later helped me to find the epilogue for my *Chelyust emigranta*.

Thus, I hired Sh. for the night of 13–14 January (1937, I believe), to help out at the bar. The attraction of the job lay not in the negligible pay but in the opportunity to enjoy free drinks and snacks, in a word "to shake oneself up," as Sh. put it.

Even on the thirteenth, we were still carrying out complicated assignments in different parts of the city. A bluish, deathlike Paris day, one of those which no French painter ever puts on canvas. Smolensky and I are racing from one Russian food shop to another, collecting, half-gratis, items for the buffet. And in each of the shops Smolensky announces: "What's the matter? Let's have a drink, after all!"

"It's not right," I answer, frowning. "We'll have to account for it." And we clink glasses, Smolensky assuring me that it is all part of travel expenses. After all, he is a bookkeeper by profession and must know about such matters.

In the evening we separated to get dressed for the ball. When we arrived there around ten o'clock, Smolensky, in flapping dress coat, was definitely "under the influence"; I looked "sick," according to Zeeler. Immediately there was trouble about the account; Mrs. Tsetlin could not understand why we had spent so much. It was not an auspicious beginning.

The ball, however, seemed, as always, to be proceeding successfully. Bunin took delicate bites, contemplating the bared shoulders of former and future ladies; the orchestra, Askoldov's, I believe, sang of things irreversible.

"Ivan Alekseevich," I asked emotionally, "don't you think that we have screwed up our lives?"

"Yes," Bunin answered, "but *what* we wanted to achieve!"

Ivanov pointed to a clean-shaven man in a tuxedo and whispered: "There goes the least talented of all emigrés." I broke into laughter; it was Alekhin.

Serge Lifar, star of the Parisian opera, and his brother generously treated a group of Pushkin scholars to champagne. All in all it was boring.

Suddenly I bumped into Chervinskaya. "Come, I'll stand you a drink," I offered in a rush of inspiration and led her to the bar, where Sh., already quite crumpled up, was presiding in a white jacket and chef's hat. "Valerian," I said firmly and a little too loudly, enjoying my mastery of speech, "Two, Valerian, you understand!" indicating the number of drinks with my fingers, so there would be no mistake. Sh. understood and filled two "*bocks*" (for beer) with vodka.

Chervinskaya and I clinked glasses. However, at this point, I noticed bewilderment in the poetess's intelligent eyes. Hastily I drained my "*bock*" and, realizing that she would be killed by such a dose of vodka, snatched hers away from her—she had only taken one sip—and, in knightly fashion, emptied it myself. I remember that I had had in mind immediately to eat something substantial in order to counteract the alcohol and that I grabbed a fried chicken leg. But at this point darkness set in.

As I later heard from many friends and protectors, they prevented me from falling down and, holding on to my elbow, half led and half carried me through the ballrooms, while I, spasmodically clutching the chicken leg, spat and groaned.

In the very center of the magnificent Salle Hoche there is a platform, intended perhaps for a large orchestra. That is where they put me down, in full view of everybody. And there I lay for about three hours as an ominous warning to the celebrants on the floor below.

From time to time, Chervinskaya, Adamovich, Zurov, and some

others stopped by and gave practical advice. For weeks afterward, some dozen well-wishers assured me that they had saved, supported, taken care of me that night.

Present was an SR, a big bore, a failure, a public figure and unsuccessful publisher (*éditeur ruiné*, as we joked about his *Éditeurs Réunis*), Ilya Nikolaevich Kovarsky, an intellectual with a Chekhovian beard, who occupied himself all his life with what was none of his business. Only later, in New York, when he returned to the practice of medicine, did he find himself again and became a useful member of society. The same could be said of Soloveichik, Kerensky's secretary, who turned into a highly competent professor of geography at an American college.

This Dr. Kovarsky, with a bald patch and a nasty, malicious chuckle, told me later that he had taken care of the tea table at the ball. Since it was a "cheap" table, it had been set up in the corridor. But next to him, a well-known, old, and sick Maecenas installed himself. "I said to him," Kovarsky explained to me, chuckling with pleasure, "I said, 'Why are you sitting here, in the draft? Go inside, where they are dancing.' 'No, no,' he answered firmly, 'I came to the ball with one aim only: to see our contemporary Russian writers, and from here I'll see them all.' Hardly had he finished, when you were being led or carried past in that condition, ha ha ha! Indeed, he did see our contemporary writers!"

Be that as it may—to characterize how we felt in those days I want to stress that in the years to come I remained convinced that I had sacrificed myself for my neighbor, and I was proud of it. Of course, one could pour out the drink or not touch it at all, but that's a different approach. Of my protégé, Sh., I shall only say that he did not fulfill my expectations and also vanished soon in some closet or basement.

It was around that time, I believe, that Lydia Chervinskaya decided to fall in love with N.—the sensitive, delicate, and easily upset father of a large family, whom she tormented with her endless, sophisticated "heart-to-heart" talks. N., a well-known, middle-aged aesthete, needed a completely different relationship: this was probably the first time that he had been unfaithful to his wife. But Chervinskaya did not understand . . . I remember how N. once ran up to our table and, addressing Felsen, loudly and desperately repeated: "I can't take it any longer! I can't take it any more!" (It is curious that this same expression, "I can't take it any more!", was often used by those whom Chervinskaya victimized.

In the years before the war, after meetings of the Circle or in Montparnasse, I often sat out the night with Chervinskaya—until the first Metro. She was highly conscious of the established hierarchy: if N., this very intelligent man, had not also been well received in the Green Lamp, she would perhaps not have started an affair with him. Her snobbery seemed naive and vulnerable, combined as it was with a genuine inner honesty. On her "bad" days, she showed up in Montparnasse in worn shoes on bare feet, with a trail of ether behind her.

After the exodus from Paris, Chervinskaya lived for a while with Kelberin's family in the south of France. When I met the truly magnanimous Saveliev, who worked for the Jewish Teitelev Committee in Montpellier, I was able to arrange a monthly stipend for several writers, all of whom were of the Christian faith. A few days later I received an affectionate letter from Lydia, thanking me for the two or three hundred Teitel-francs and recalling how I had saved her from a "bock" of vodka.

There was a talented prose writer by the name of Ageev, who lived in Constantinople on a Uruguayan passport. He sent his manuscripts to Paris, and we all tried to help him. Felsen and I published his *Roman s kokainom* (Novel with Cocaine) as a separate book in our Writers and Poets series.

When Ageev needed to renew his lapsed passport, he sent it to Paris; why he did not see to it himself, in Turkey, I can only guess. Otsup passed on the document to Chervinskaya. But alas, she did nothing about it and when, about six months later, Ageev asked for the return of the passport, it transpired that Lydia had lost it. How characteristic of her: that she, as a good comrade, should have been entrusted with the task and that, catching sight of Adamovich or N. on the other side of the street, she should run after them, leaving behind her pocketbook, money, and documents.

I always remember the Ageev affair when Chervinskaya's role in the French Résistance and her trial (after the war) are mentioned. She had been let in on a secret upon which the lives of several dozen Jewish children depended. This secret she revealed to an untrustworthy lover. Here, the fault was not hers; it lies with the leaders, the organizers! In such times, to charge Chervinskaya with a responsible, practical task was sheer madness!

Before the Union of Writers and Poets there were other literary circles. At those prehistoric gatherings, stars of the earlier period made noises: Evangulov, Bozhnev, Ginger, Zdanevich, Charchoune. In the basement of a cafe, Evangulov would stand on a table, drawn up to his full height, and exuberantly (in the manner of Mayakovsky) howl his poetry. When a befurred lady descended into the basement, he interrupted his recitation to invite her most respectfully, "Over here, Countess, please, over here!"

Of all those poets, Ginger seems to be the only one whose work has survived. In 1941, I met Bozhnev in Marseilles; he reminded me, then, a little of Felsen, not in coloring but in manners: courteous, correct, and, to all outward appearances, limited.

Charchoune was an old Parisian: at the time of World War I he was already studying art in Paris. His paintings were not simply abstract but esoteric. I believe he considered himself an anthroposophist, although he never managed to speak coherently on this topic. He was the only Russian involved in the Dada movement. It was Charchoune from whom I heard, at the end of the twenties, about Kafka for the first time, and for that alone I am grateful to him.

For a long time he wrote early "surrealistic" prose but was only published in *Chisla* and *Krug*. Thanks to *Chisla* he became, for a time, a fashionable writer, a development which, I'm afraid, ruined him. His paintings have but recently become appreciated (thanks to Malraux). Charchoune belonged to the class of what I call graphomaniacs, that is, writers who, while endowed with indisputable original talent, are completely deprived of selectivity! There were, of course, great artists with graphomaniac tendencies: Joyce, Thomas Wolfe, Andrei Bely, Remizov . . . Sirin-Nabokov.

After an excerpt from his *Dolgolikov* had been accepted by *Chisla,* Charchoune lugged everything he had accumulated over the years to the editorial office. It turned out to be childish babble. A thin-skinned creature, he reacted fast and intensely to any brush with life; the result was a stream of words which he carried to the editor with the trustful look of a greying deer.

He was a vegetarian and a bachelor. Most probably he prayed and perfected himself in loneliness and poverty; in his presence I felt that a pure small spring was shooting up from the depths. The dinners he prepared for himself consisted of thirty to forty vegetables and raw roots; the basic ingredients were ground peas and scraped carrots. And in the evening, when he came close up to whisper, "So, tomorrow, I'll bring it in," or, "So I'll give it to him tomorrow," people shrank away from the pungent smell of garlic and onions which he exuded.

Once, at our exhibit of emigré literature, Charchoune told Felsen and myself that a Swedish woman translator, whom we had all met at the Merezhkovskys and promised to introduce to Remizov, had later, in a letter to him called Charchoune a "cowardly pimp." We roared with laughter: it was such an unexpected and utterly unsuitable definition.

"No, don't laugh," he said worriedly, shaking his huge, staglike head with the dark horn-rimmed glasses. "No, no, here she caught on to something real."

Poplavsky admired those heavy glasses in "esoteric" frames: "They make him look like a *sous-secrétaire d'état!*" he claimed.

Why undersecretary and not a full secretary? This Boris did not wish to explain and started cursing.

On the other hand, Slonim wore a pince-nez, or something very similar, something light and delicate, which looked merely ridiculous. At the end of the twenties and the very beginning of the thirties, Slonim's *Kochevie* (Nomads) flourished. Most of literary Paris converged on Thursdays in a café facing the Gare Montparnasse. It was the time when the fame of Babel, Olesha, the early Zoshchenko, Leonov, Kataev resounded in Russia. One could still take Soviet literature seriously. And that was precisely Slonim's occuption. But when, at the beginning of the first five-year-plan, the screws were finally tightened, there was no more reason to speak about Soviet literature. All of us realized it right away— all, except Slonim, a conceited, self-assured man. And *Kochevie* languished and died.

Everything about Slonim was provincial, second-class. For any difficult question he immediately had an answer. He expressed his opinions, never suspecting that they might be wrong or stupid. (He belonged to the breed of Russian "star pupils.")

From his example I understood for the first time that Eastern "second class" is inferior to West European. It is senseless to compare representatives of a super or first class. Who is best—Tolstoi, Shakespeare, Proust; *Don Quixote, David Copperfield, Anna Karenina, Madame Bovary;* Pushkin, Mickiewicz, Shevchenko; Chekhov or Kafka? They are all "best," for the Spirit is absolute and infinite.

But among the second class one may and must compare, in order to size up the cultures of different nations. How superior is this class west of the Rhine to the same class in Russia? Is and was and will remain so for a long time, cosmonauts notwithstanding.

Slonim's main field was politics. But he also found time to occupy himself with art and apparently liked that occupation. And he did not confine himself to one culture. He was aware of French literary schools, Italian novels, American movies; for a Russian intellectual who successfully fought the tsar's regime (Slonim was an SR) there could be no vulgar, *petit-bourgeois* limitations.

Tsvetaeva used to come to *Kochevie* in its heyday. Of course, we all acknowledged her enormous talent. There were even those who patiently endured her tiresome, harsh prose readings. With the years her talent and poetical mastery grew, but our attitude toward her changed for the worse. Unexpectedly, the reader, the listener, the admirer would wake up in the morning with the sorry conviction that, after all, Tsvetaeva was not a genius, that she lacked something essential.

I gradually became convinced that, in some way, she was simply stupid, an opinion that explained a lot. When one is young, one easily and nonchalantly forms such opinions.

"Full of mannerisms (*poserka*)," fearfully looking over his glasses, whispered Remizov, who particularly disliked her prose writings and her manner of declamation.

The consensus was that Remizov was a "marvelous reader"; he read, not like an author following an interior rhythm but like an actor who used his exemplary diction to best advantage. I do not like "performances" and therefore distrust the testimony of witnesses who rave about the readings of Gogol, Dostoevsky, and Turgenev. There are no such legends about Tolstoi.

In conversation Tsvetaeva could be impossible, even rude, yet easy to take offense at the slightest lack of attention. Despite her phonetic brilliance, she conveyed little that was new or interesting. Even what could be perceived as valuable—the mysteries of the poetical workshop—got lost, because it was offered as a special discovery, with intense pressure on all pedals!

Nearsightedly proud, she was inordinately lonely, even for a poet in emigration. True, from Homer to Thomas Wolfe and Joyce most artists have felt hideously rejected. (All pioneers!) Marina Tsvetaeva suffered also from her intense poverty, but again, that condition is familiar to many, many artists. In old Moscow, she was one against all. Even took pride in it. The same repeated itself in emigration; and in the USSR she hanged herself. Her suicide, I believe, was of a different order than Mayakovsky's or Esenin's. These bards, under different circumstances would have continued to live happily and pleasantly. Tsvetaeva killed in herself what had tortured her during her entire life and what would not let her find communion with the world: perhaps a luciferian pride? Guesses, guesses, guesses. . .

"Simply stupid" I called her because of her utter inability to listen to anyone else. In her own speeches, which were stubborn, stilted, and wordy, she sped along like an inexperienced bicyclist on a perfectly straight line or made desperate figure eights, without any control over steering and brakes. To talk, that is, to exchange ideas with her, was almost impossible.

She was very nearsighted and often would not respond to a bow; people took offense and stopped greeting her. This surprised and angered her. "Among them there may be other nearsighted people who don't notice *you*," I explained brutally. This she simply could not take in.

I met Marina Ivanovna privately at the home of the Shirinskys; there I also became acquainted with her "dear family," as Pasternak called them in his memoirs. They lived close by, in Meudon. Tsvetaeva also read at our literary meetings at the Post-Revolutionary Club and dropped in at the Circle.

By the "dear family" I have in mind her children. I saw her husband, Efron, a Chekist and for many years the permanent president of the Union of Students from the Soviet Union[1] (I don't remember the exact title), only from a distance at those meetings of the Union where such guests as Babel, Tikhonov, and so on, came to read.

Her daughter Alya, a sweet, frightened girl of eighteen, kind and modest and, in her way, attractive, was the complete opposite of her mother. Tsvetaeva consistently mistreated her. Why, I do not know, and, without Freud, there is probably no explanation. Objectively speaking this also was an expression of Tsvetaeva's lack of understanding, especially if compared to the unbounded adoration with which she listened to every hiccup of her son, an obese, unpleasant *Wunderkind* of fifteen or so. He behaved with the presumption of an established genius, interrupted the discussions of the adults and impudently expressed his opinions on any subject, considering himself an authority on early Renaissance painting and the philosophy of Solovyov. Whatever absurdity he uttered, his mother listened with tender approval, which probably definitively ruined him. Alya conscientiously took care of this lymphatic lump. Meanwhile Tsvetaeva offended and exploited her daughter.

At the beginning of the thirties, having drawn closer to Yury Shirinsky-Shikhmatov, I suggested that we establish a literary department in his magazine *Utverzhdeniya* (Affirmation). We seemed to have all the ingredients for it; we lacked only money.

At that very moment a writer-moneylender, V. P. Krymov, had moved from Berlin to Paris. The story on him was that he had become rich once more in Berlin, discounting huge Soviet promissory notes for which a broker received 33 percent, since in the early twenties very few were ready to lend the Bolsheviks cash—out of economic rather than moral considerations.

Rumors began to circulate to the effect that Krymov, a childless millionaire, sought to become useful to emigré literature; that, being a writer himself, he understood the misery of his brethren and sympathized with them. I used to believe that these stories were propagated by

Krymov himself, in accordance with the old Russian saying: Whether you intend to buy or not, there's nothing wrong with bargaining.

But soon we began to hear about ominous *rejections!* For, naturally, everyone who had the slightest relation to literature (from former friends of Kamenev to "future" heads of state) were irresistibly drawn to Krymov's villa in Chatou-sur-Seine. Curiously, these unfortunates were also the same who most vigorously slandered the hoped-for Maecenas, using epithets such as "usurer and Bolshevik," "Old Believer and atheist," and, above all, "graphomaniac." Yet, his first novel, *Khorosho zhili v Peterburge* (We Lived Well in St. Petersburg), was an excellent book.

Vladimir Krymov, dressed English-fashion in a dark blue, velvet smoking jacket, half-blind, with thick "Joycean" lenses, treated each guest to a goblet of Mumm and refused to give any handouts. He used to say that champagne had a magic effect, softening the blow and creating a nostalgic, prerevolutionary atmosphere. One eminent critic went to Chatou for a loan. Later, when our relationship had become unambiguously settled, Krymov told me about him in this way.

" 'Have a heart,' I said to him, 'some day you may want to write an article or a critical review about me. How can I possibly give you money!' "

The critic left, declining the champagne.

Another time, Polyakov-Litovtsev rushed there for a loan. Felsen most amusingly described that occasion. Krymov supposedly pleaded with his guest: "Let me at least sleep on it!" And in the morning refused.

His genuine love of literature and desire for fame notwithstanding, Krymov's attachment to money, his pathological, demonic avarice, was stronger than anything else and, as I see it, brought him, as a writer, to a complete dead end. His pseudoscientific background also played a certain part in it: Krymov had taken a degree in the physical sciences at the end of the nineteenth century and still suffered from a naive rationalism.

He was being published in England, paying for the translation himself. He claimed that the English compared his *Sidorovo uchenie* (Sidorov's Education) to the best works of Dickens. Krymov was undoubtedly a talented writer with a great mastery of the Russian language; the trouble was that he turned out to be a businessman of genius, a fact which influenced all of us and distorted his image.

Burov, also a businessman-graphomaniac, who became famous thanks to his fight with Georgy Ivanov, asserted that, directly after his arrival from Berlin, Krymov had really dreamed of establishing on his property a kind of colony "for the most gifted poets." He had imagined noble visitors arriving on weekends to eat noodles and write saleable poems under shady trees. In the evening, over a bottle of Mumm, they would declaim their works and eventually dedicate them to the generous V. P. Krymov.

Perhaps he did imagine something in this idyllic vein in the beginning. But when it became clear that the Parisian literati were all hooligans whose only aim was to "rip him off and run," having befouled the teahouse to boot, then he could justly feel offended. For, strange as it may seem, such cruel, indeed merciless types as he have exceptionally sensitive, demanding and resentful souls. However, I heard that, toward the end of his life, he mellowed and became truly kind.

When we were sure that we had everything needed to start a literary-philosophical supplement to the magazine—everything except money—it seemed natural to appeal to the honorable Krymov for support . . . And so, on a cold, snowless winter day—I believe it was a Sunday, but I clearly remember that it was exceptionally cold—Prince Shirinsky-Shikhmatov, his wife, Marina Tsvetaeva, and I set out in the prince's little old Renault to pay our respects at Chatou. With difficulties, including roadside repairs, we reached our goal at around two in the afternoon. Krymov, his "young" wife, and her father seemed glad to see us. The day was such (December or January) that dusk was already setting in.

We sat in the book-lined library and heard (once again) that our host was being successfully published in England and that the critics were comparing him to Dickens! Krymov read me a page from his diary—an extremely pessimistic excerpt in which he likened man to a fly caught on sticky paper. I pitied him sincerely and advised him to pray from time to time. But Krymov was proud of his nineteenth-century atheism. Soon dinner was served. At the table we were joined by one more couple; the husband was a former publisher or editor from St. Petersburg. Krymov had taken them under his roof and cared for them, an act of genuine compassion which ought to be remembered.

We ate veal and there was Mumm with the dessert, Mumm *Cordon Rouge,* which had been fashionable in the last years of the Russian Empire. Krymov spoke at length about grand-dukes who were besieging him with demands for help. Shirinsky's slanted eyes contracted and became more predatory and ironical. Right away the father-in-law reacted with a mysterious sign, as if starting an old-fashioned engine; the prince and I went out to the car and got it going to warm up the motor. The wind blowing from the Seine was as cold as if it had been from the Neva.

The same kindly father-in-law had descended several times to the cellar and brought up, one at a time, bottles of Mumm. After the third or fourth glass, Tsvetaeva suddenly pulled out, perhaps from her bosom, a manuscript and began to exhort our host to publish her fairy tale in verse with Goncharova's illustrations. Shirinsky and I were horrified, absolutely outraged. Instead of joining a united front on behalf of *Utverzhdeniya*, she was pushing her personal interests. Fortunately, Krymov immediately answered that he had read the fairy tale and did not like it . . .

Now I decided that the time for "action" had come and proceeded to unfold our splendid plan for a new postrevolutionary literary-philosophical publication with Vladimir Pimenovich Krymov as collaborator. But Krymov tried to shake me off; he said that after a good meal with perfect wine it was difficult to discuss serious matters.

"Do you really think that we came here to eat veal?" I asked rather loudly, so that the host became embarrassed. "Next time, there may be chicken," he answered conciliatingly.

I guess that when they had discussed the menu, Krymov had insisted that veal was cheaper; there would have to be champagne, and that would make up for everything . . . Something in his figure and tone of voice reminded me of Yudushka Golovlyov (from the novel *The Golovlyov Family* by Saltykov-Shchedrin)—and up to this day I cannot rid myself of that image.

Alas, we did not have a chance to pursue our business; again Tsvetaeva came to Krymov's aid: all of a sudden, after a few glasses of champagne, she felt sick to her stomach and had to beat a hasty retreat to the bathroom.

The host's thick lenses glistened demonically. I don't know what prompted me to talk about love, God, Christ and the Devil. Smiling happily, Krymov argued with me: a man of higher education who had traveled three times around the world could not possibly believe in the resurrection of the dead. Thus did an exuberant Gagarin, later, assert that he had orbited the earth three times and had nowhere noticed God in the cosmos.

On this we parted, duly presenting each other with our politely inscribed books.

Later, in the days of our exhibit of émigré literature, Felsen and I went to see Krymov and persuaded him to contribute several hundred francs for publicity and other initial expenses. When I met Sofia Pregel in New York, she told me that Krymov had right away "forced" her to give him back a few hundred francs—presumably half of what he had handed us! I fully believe Pregel's story.

When a mediocre novel of Krymov's came out, Yury Mandelshtam gave it a thoroughly bad review in *Vozrozhdenie*, whereupon Krymov rushed to us at the exhibit with a complaint: "I support the Writers' Union with money, and its members throw mud at me!" In his sickly mind he imagined that he had once and for all, and quite cheaply at that, bought off the entire young literary generation.

After the Krymov episode we were all depressed for a whole week. I berated Tsvetaeva in the presence of witnesses, and Shirinsky said of our mood that it was "as if we had all bathed together in one filthy bathtub." True enough.

In 1938, the papers reported that agents of Stalin had killed Reiss, a former member of the Cheka, at the Swiss border. Following this news, several Russian emigrés fled Paris: S. Efron, Tsveteva's husband, the poet A. Eisner, and the Klepinin couple. The fact that they all disappeared into the Soviet Union can be considered proof of their participation in the crime.

Soon Tsvetaeva also decided to move to the kingdom of the victorious proletariat, of course together with her son. Alya had left before them. Here everything seems madness or stupidity: Stalin's crimes, socialist realism, her husband, a Chekist, a murderer—how did Tsvetaeva fit into all this? Could there be any doubt as to how it would finish for her? And quite soon.

Shortly before her departure I went to her hotel room, somewhere in the vicinity of Metro Pasteur. I was an avid collector of secondhand leather jackets, and the poet Anna Prismanova had told me that Tsvetaeva would like to sell an English jacket of her son's. The boy was obese, overfed, and there was hope that the jacket would fit me.

Prismanova and I walked up to Tsvetaeva's room. She was already completely packed and could not, or did not want to, open up closed suitcases. We separated without a smile or conventional good wishes: the words froze in my throat. The bleak, charred image of that haunted or possessed, proud creature presaged an imminent and terrible end. I think that she was, then, simply very sick. If there had been an intelligent hero among us, sufficiently concerned about her, he could by force have restrained this wretched, stubborn, remarkable woman from her unconscious act of hara-kiri.

Prismanova, her face asymmetrical, as if one cheek were perenially swollen (one sees such dried-up, yellowish women in Flemish paintings), remained with the poet in tête-à-tête and caught up with me in the street. Dutifully, she praised Tsvetaeva's poetry. As if poetry could exhaust all of a life.

The rest was simple and clear. The outcome was foreseeable. I do not know the details, but for some reason I imagine: rope reins, a noose, a Russian stable.

Whenever I read Turgenev's *Clara Milich,* I think of Marina Tsvetaeva.

Big, gala evenings—parades of Russian literature in Paris—took place on the premises of the Geographical Society (Metro Solferino). Emigrés of Herzen's and Mickiewicz's times had assembled there, and that was where Adamovich organized his yearly literary benefit meeting. In order to attract the public, he would invite Kerensky or Merezhkovsky to take part in the debate. I remember a Franco-Russian symposium with André Gide after his visit to the Soviet Union, when outraged young Frenchmen greeted Merezhkovsky with cries of "*Cadavre! Cadavre!*"

The lectures of *Sovremennye zapiski* also took place there; and Fondaminsky habitually rented the auditorium for large assemblies, for instance, when Sirin-Nabokov read in Paris.

Most of us caught sight of the latter for the first time precisely there, on the podium. I arrived feeling belligerent. Sirin, who wrote shallow reviews for a Berlin Russian paper, had run down my *Mir*. Many in the overcrowded hall felt similarly envious and vengeful. The older generation—Bunin and company—could not forgive Sirin his brilliance and "easy" success. The young thought that he was writing "too much."

I must remind the reader that the Paris school was educated on "honest" literature; this is, of course, laudable if the writer has other undeniable qualities besides. But for a time we subscribed to a very primitive interpretation of "honesty." It excluded any inventions, fantasies, flights of fancy. We should not make Adamovich alone responsible; he gave the first push—the others pushed it *ad absurdum* on their own. They based themselves mainly on Tolstoi, forgetting that he has a gelding tell the colts his life story at night and also the complicated adventures of his owner . . . Actually, not a very successful conceit.

Sirin-Nabokov's "inventions" derived mainly from foreign, not Russian literature. He often exaggerated, naively assuming that in every novel there must be a trick, a charade which has to be deciphered.

On that evening he read a chapter from *Despair* in which the protagonist—completely by chance!—runs into his double. An old but still topical theme; from Dostoevsky's *Double* to Sirin's *Soglyadatai* (The Eye) serious writers have always been attracted by the mystery of personality. But his listeners, the professionals, resisted malevolently.

For me there was something festive, heroically triumphant in the lean young man in a tuxedo, with a (seemingly) sunken chest and the heavy nose of a boxer, inspiredly swallowing his "r's" as he confided his innermost secrets to those belligerent strangers. I was ready to go over to his side. A pale young sportsman in a black suit was appealing to the blind demos. I wished him success, notwithstanding the fact that in him the culture of writers of the level of a Kafka and Joyce is linked with the vulgarity (*poshlost*) of a Vicky Baum.

Alas, only very few were converted that evening. There was no way of bringing the oldsters to their senses. After all, Bunin had missed out on Bely and Blok! As for our poets, they generally despised prose and opposed Nabokov on account of his poems, which they considered on a level with Bunin's outdated creations.

The public figures declared in one voice, "Wonderful, wonderful, but who needs it . . ."

This same attitude was expressed on quite a different occasion, at a meeting of Soviet students in the Salle Lascaze, where several writers from Moscow made an appearance. Fedin, cool, polite, in manner slightly reminiscent of Felsen; Vsevolod Ivanov, a shrewd, wary peasant, speaking a juicy Russian; Tikhonov, a soldier, like the heroes of his ballads; Kirshon, with a thick, ruddy bull's neck, deeply worried about the party line and soon to be shot by the NKVD; the infamous Ehrenburg; Babel, in coloring and diction resembling Remizov or Zhabotinsky. Their readings and speeches done with, questions were permitted; and I, as usual, posed my one and only question: "What do you think of our émigré literature?"

Babel answered quite honestly: "Some among you write exceptionally well, skillfully and even brilliantly." (Everybody knew that he was referring to Nabokov, whose *Ivitation to a Beheading* was at that time being serialized in *Sovremennye zapiski*.) "But to what purpose? In the Soviet Union such literature is completely superfluous."

That was their perfidious criterion. Very soon Babel himself—with his saturated sunsets—turned out to be completely superfluous and ended up with a bullet in the neck.

When Nabokov settled in France, Fondaminsky, who liked to exaggerate, darkly informed us: "You must realize, he lives with his wife and child in one room. In order to create, he locks himself in a tiny toilet, sits there like an eagle and types."

This could not impress us; in Paris, many did not even have their own toilet. It reminded me of the Europeans who raved about Gandhi because he drank only goat's milk and lemon juice . . . Indian colleagues told me that, in India, milk and lemon juice were great luxuries, that millions of natives chewed only a dozen grains of rice daily. Incidentally, one Tibetan elder reproached the Mahatma for submitting to an appendectomy, considering surgery a snobbish caprice.

After reading *Invitation to a Beheading,* which I liked very much, I said to Nabokov at Fondaminsky's tea table, "yet it is strongly influenced by Kafka."

"I've never read Kafka," Nabokov asserted, and wanted to add something. (But at that moment, in a light Mackintosh and sneakers, Sirin, his alter-ego, showed up and Nabokov turned away.)

When I told Khodasevich what Nabokov had said, he smiled cynically. "I doubt that there's anything he hasn't read." (Legends were already springing up about Sirin-Nabokov's strength and gifts.)

In Paris he was always on his guard, as if in the enemy camp; courteous but reserved, yet not without charm. In conversation, the thoughts and feelings of the other person rebounded from him as from a mirror. He seemed lonely; and his life, I surmise, was generally dull, between stretches of creative ecstasies (if such existed). He probably never cheated on his wife, and he did not drink vodka; he knew only his craft, and no longer did he enjoy solving chess problems. Reading about the sad, maniacal life of Thomas Wolfe, I often think of Nabokov. However, the latter had a family.

The maximum of ill will toward Nabokov surfaced when Fondaminsky was staging his plays. Nabokov was then living in the south of France; and poor Fondaminsky, almost in tears, lamented: "It's to laugh . . . the prosecutors sit in the first row and are only waiting to pick his work to pieces!"

I mention this episode because, up to this day, academics consider the failure of Chekhov's *Seagull* at its first performance a shameful injustice and the sufferings of Soviet writers unbearable. Quite correctly so. But the humiliations and insults an emigré writer has to endure are painful too. And we must remember that some quite poor plays were written in Yalta and that novels just as good as *Doctor Zhivago* were created in the emigration.

As Poplavsky said bitterly: "I know, they also ran out of funds. Andrei Bely or Blok wired to St. Petersburg from Venice, 'Send money for tickets. We are stranded.' Now you just try to go to Italy and wire for money!"

Yes, we lay like moss-covered stones, not moving but manifesting an enormous strength in our inertia. Not only without means but without a passport, visas, clothes—lacking the entire psychological basis necessary for travel. Only people who carried proper papers traveled to foreign countries, not we.

The poet Anatoly Steiger had a Swiss passport and constantly moved around. Czechoslovakia, Yugoslavia, Rumania and, of course, Paris-

Nice. In Berne there are still some barons of the Steiger family. When the Russian Steigers fled back to Switzerland (not all of them did), they found that they could lay claim to a cantonal pension. To Anatoly fell a very small sum (by Swiss standards), but it was a fixed income that allowed him to organize a life in Prague or Paris; and when he was hard up in a foreign country, he could always seek refuge in his half-native Switzerland, at times even in a sanatarium, to take care of his lungs—for Anatoly Steiger had tuberculosis.

In our life in Montparnasse it was assumed that we were all equals. And this was of course true: the differences depended on talent. But nevertheless, his Swiss privileges gave Steiger a constant edge. He arrived in Paris, looking cheerful, tanned, and rested, from Belgrade or Budapest where he had been feted by his Mladoross party friends. After reading his poems in Montparnasse, reestablishing contact with Adamovich, Tsvetaeva, and Gippius, and visiting Fondaminsky and some editors, he was off to Nice for tea with the "tsar."

Although his perception of politics was mainly emotional and aesthetic, Steiger, a highly educated, civilized, pleasant, and intelligent man, was a member of the Mladoross party. As a Mladoross he found friends, room, and board in all the centers of the Russian diaspora, so that his travel expenses amounted solely to the railroad ticket. Everywhere there were comrades: in their cells, hospices, community houses, he was received as if into his "own" family. I put *own* in quotes, for I suspect that the poet, an aesthete, ill with tuberculosis, and a homosexual, must have sometimes wrinkled up his nose at the company of these noble but often primitive legitimists who had sworn allegiance to their *head,* Kasem-Bek.

Thanks to an innate *savoir-faire,* Steiger was accepted not only by monarchists but also by SRs, postrevolutionaries and, of course, in Montparnasse. Fondaminsky, tenderly crinkling his thick eyebrows, declared: "Yesterday, the little Baron (that was what he called Steiger) came to see me. You should have heard him! It warmed my heart. The boy is growing, growing."

When in Paris, Steiger never failed to visit the Circle. But he sat there quietly, assuring us that he had already expressed everything of importance in his poems, a statement which once threw the socially committed poet Sofiev into a rage. Steiger sometimes stayed with the Shirinskys (Metro Muette): he was friendly with Lev, the young Savinkov, but he never criticized his friend's poetry. There I would run into him during the years before the war: twisting and turning in front of the mirror in the entrance hall, as he put the last thick layers of cream on his matte elongated face with suspiciously red lips.

"I must stop by at Fondaminsky's! He's selling tickets for my reading, and after that at Tsvetaeva's," he explained, licking his scarlet lips.

"The entire Circle is selling tickets for your evening," I corrected him pedantically.

Steiger did not reply, only gave me an ironic look.

In connection with this task we had had battles with Fondaminsky, who demanded that all members of the Circle take part in this "common cause," that is, sell tickets for Steiger's reading. In the end it amounted to Fondaminsky taking a dozen tickets, and two or three members, Felsen for example, buying a ticket each. Why present such a to-do as a collective action of the Circle, I argued. Besides, Steiger could not be fooled; he knew perfectly well to whom to be grateful.

He managed his poetical household—a miniature one in fact, but leading into depths—in a masterly fashion, squeezing the maximum out of it, thanks to his intelligence, taste, and tact. Only toward the end did Ivanov begin to object: "To compare Steiger to Annensky!" he stage-whispered, making his lower lip protrude even more in disgust and casting a sidelong glance in Adamovich's direction. The latter had pricked up his huge ears to catch the words, "Steiger to Annensky!"

(Such grievances came up again and again. Thus Otsup did not mind the fact that Poplavsky was called the best poet among the young . . . But only among the *young!*)

Steiger was most amusing, in my opinion, when he occupied himself with the "literary kitchen, resembling Ivanov in this respect. And also when he told about his romantic adventures, like an excited young girl out of Turgenev. "At the Opéra . . . passing . . . with just a glance! I look back . . . he was following me . . ." Steiger described the scene with such naive exuberance that the listener's heart began to beat faster.

He died at the height of Hitler's victories, in a hospital bed with a view of the Alps. He died in civilized surroundings, with a nurse, thermometers, and aspirin, at a time when many of his friends were perishing at the front, in the underground, or in concentration camps. It might be said that in many respects, he was even lucky. I really don't know. But I believe that he would have preferred to finish his life actively fighting a hated enemy (even, as we then perceived it, without any chance of winning). However, we must remember that this excellent poet always considered his poems the full expression of his essence and did not plan to add anything more to them.

They say that an empty vial of sleeping pills was found at his bedside. It happened at the high point of the humiliating retreat of the Allies, when many good people fell into despair. And some did commit suicide.

On the other hand, next to chronic patients, there always collects a battery of empty vials and bottles.

Our few "tourists" also included Dovid Knut, who boasted a Rumanian passport. There came a moment when he suddenly took off and began to roam the countries around the Mediterranean.

Knut's was a rather strange family. His parents opened a small restaurant in Paris, where the father strictly exhorted the younger son, Dovid's brother: "Simkha, serve the cutlets!" Soon the parents fell ill and died; the restaurant closed.

About Knut's mother, who was dying in a university hospital, a French professor said: "Why are all nations reconciled to dying, and only one does not accept death?" And he sounded offended. We mentioned this episode to Berdyaev. Frowning, as if trying to decipher an illegible inscription, he said: "That's precisely why Christ was born into this nation."

When, out of politeness, I sometimes inquired about his brother, Knut always gave me the same answer: "He hasn't much of a choice; it's either prison or the hospital."

And indeed, Simkha became a professional thief, who specialized in picking pockets. He did not work *solo* but with a group and belonged to an influential "union." Once, at an accidental meeting, Simkha proudly informed me that he was being sent "on tour" to London. I don't know what became of him during the war. The entire family was decaying, its only hope Dovid Knut, an outstanding poet!

Small, swarthy, with a heavy nose, he possessed an extraordinary temperament and enjoyed an enviable success with the ladies. Once, in the Luxembourg Gardens, he read me a whole lecture, his thesis being that people of small stature were stronger, healthier, more vital, and enduring than tall ones, who died earlier and among whom there were hardly any geniuses. He told me this with conviction, although with a certain embarrassment; in Europe I was considered above average height.

Sadly, Knut died young, in Switzerland, shortly after the war. Both his parents had died of cancer, as did his first, extremely kind and modest wife. By that time they had already been divorced; she left behind two or three children. After trying several temporary unions, Knut finally married Ariadna, the daughter of the composer Scriabin, a colorful and passionate woman.

Out of the blue he obtained a subsidy to publish a Franco-Zionist paper. They settled in a luxurious private house. Ariadna converted to

Judaism, with such chauvinistic fervor that the captain of Israel's sole school-ship, the *Sarah II*, stopped up his ears when she began to preach and proselytize among Montparnassian believers in other values.

The story of this Russian woman would not be complete without its characteristic epilogue: According to witnesses, she died in 1944, in the south of France, fighting a German patrol.

Chapter 11 · Newspapers and Journals

The role which the Circle assumed in the latter part of the thirties had previously been played by *Chisla* and still earlier by the Green Lamp. All these, of course, overlapped as the changes occurred.

Chisla had come into being as a result of many accidental and objective causes. However, one thing is certain—without N. Otsup there would not have been any *Chisla,* at least not the *Chisla* as we know it.

At the end of the twenties, in the heyday of *Kochevie,* which was under the direction of Marc Slonim, R., a young apple-cheeked, well-fed bachelor, obviously attracted by the "sweeter" things of life yet not without "ideas," used to come to these literary meetings. He worked at Hachette, fearlessly chattered in French and, at one time, was enrolled at the Sorbonne.

I do not know how it came about that he made the acquaintance of Irma Vladimirovna de Manziarli, an eccentric woman who associated with Tibetan wise men and fed exclusively on rice and certain outlandish vegetation. In any case, it turned out that she was disposed to support the founding of a Russian journal.

I became friendly with Irma de Manziarli in New York, at the height of the Second World War, when, together with Helene Izwolsky and Arthur Lourié, we published *The Third Hour,* an ecumenical magazine in three languages. It was then that she said to me about *Chisla:* "I thought they would write the way Russian students used to—something honest, elevating and pleasant. Instead they promoted a sort of canine copulation, so indecent that one couldn't even show it to one's friends."

It took a lot of effort on my part, here in New York, eons later, to explain to her that *Chisla* was the best journal of the emigration.

"Why only of the emigration?" Nikolai Avdeevich Otsup used to protest. "It probably is the best Russian journal ever."

R. initiated negotiations with important persons in Montparnasse. Eventually, Adamovich and Ivanov supported the candidacy of Otsup, a member of their Petersburg group, as editor of *Chisla*—a most successful choice! In 1951, in New York, Aldanov proposed Vera Aleksandrova as editor-in-chief of the Chekhov Publishing House, the only subsidized Russian publishing house abroad—a miserable choice!

In the announcements and even, if I'm not mistaken, on the masthead of the first issue of *Chisla*, R. still figured as editor of the philosophy section. Later he vanished completely from the pages of the journal. To finish up with him I may say that, at Hachette, some most absurd accounting errors were discovered. Illustrated *de luxe* editions were missing. In Montparnasse, R., sometimes, after midnight, offered these costly books to his friends: "Would you like to have it? Take it, please!" And he presented these gorgeous volumes to drinking companions with whom he was barely acquainted. He all but forced Felsen to take home a colorful encyclopedia on parrots.

The lively bachelor, then, was brought to court. Independently of the outcome of the affair, he, a foreigner and an undesirable one to boot, was bound to be expelled from France. And indeed, despite all his resourcefulness and the help of influential friends, he had to leave blissful France. I don't remember for what purpose, but in the offices of *Chisla* (Métro Convention) a collection was taken up to meet his dire needs. Later in New York, having changed his image and even his temperament, R., owner of mines and moving-picture enterprises, rewarded me a hundredfold for the five francs which I had contributed; it turned out to have been the best investment of my life.

Thus Otsup became sole editor of *Chisla* and set out resolutely, independently, heeding only the advice of such authorities as Adamovich and Ivanov.

Adamovich was indispensable to the journal. A strong protector was needed against the stream of abuse and jealous slander that followed the first few issues of *Chisla*. Adamovich's reviews in *Poslednie novosti*, his participation in the journal's open meetings and, most of all, his *Commentaries*, which appeared regularly in every issue, fended off the attacks. As a matter of fact, the *Commentaries*, along with Poplavsky's and perhaps Charchoune's prose, constituted the most original and valuable material to appear in *Chisla*. Although, as Merezhkovsky claimed, Rozanov's shadow stood behind those *Commentaries*.

However, I cannot understand why Otsup respected and feared Ivanov's opinions so much. Just as I was unable, at the time, to explain Ivanov's influence—by no means of a literary character alone—on so many young poets.

A novel by Odoevtseva, his wife, had been published in English translation and seemed to be a success in London. The couple collected quotes from the English reviews in a very intelligent fashion and forced Otsup to publish several pages of vulgar self-promotion in *Chisla*. The word "genial" (which we took to mean "genius") they modestly translated as "talented," with the original word in parenthesis. Otsup tried to resist but for some reason yielded in the end.

The same thing happened in connection with Ivanov's hounding of Sirin-Nabokov. *Chisla* could have avoided polemics on such a low level. But in this Ivanov was supported by many honest and not so honest, reliable and not so reliable literati and non-literati. It is worth noting that Adamovich, who flatly rejected Sirin's prose (from the position of Tolstoi), did not take part in this slander, which included even unflattering references to Sirin's mother.

Besides the prose writing mentioned above, the best things in *Chisla,* which endure to this day, are the poems! Among the poets, some outsiders of the type of Zakovich or Dryakhlov will perhaps survive many celebrities of emigré literature.

Chisla was also a center where, on Thursday afternoons, many new, promising writers would converge, seeking abstract truths and concrete gossip. In the small square room on the ground floor (which on other days served as the office of some obscure businessmen, Berlin friends of Otsup) former or future contributors to the magazine squeezed in and talked to whoever was close by. Poplavsky tried to "conquer" some accidental guest such as Nikolai Nabokov or Gershenkron; a frightening gentleman with a provocative beard read aloud his pornographic diary while Otsup attentively studied the expression on the faces of the listeners, debating in his mind the difficult question of whether the work was worth publishing or not. I suddenly began to argue that for Tolstoi it was no accident that Stiva Oblonsky, Anna Karenina's brother, was a gourmand and womanizer! A Polish visitor, I believe Count Chapsky, a painter and essayist, who had to stoop as he entered, arrived with a letter of recommendation from Filosofov. As he shook hands all around, giving everyone the same attention, he said: "You are all Russian writers here, aren't you?"

For a private talk with Otsup one had to go out into the hall, near the stairway and the elevator which, with its surrealistic accumulation of iron bars, gates, and apertures might perhaps give inspiration.

Otsup spoke in a particular basso: an emphatic, senatorial, sonorous voice. His overly dignified way of speaking reminded me, for some reason, of stories about card sharps who, in order to be let into a club, had to show off with fine Swiss linen shirts and genuine diamond studs. This is of course a completely inappropriate comparison; yet his manners and intonation, his pseudo-majestic air, evoked in me just such depressing thoughts. Ivanov and Poplavsky liked to tell an old story of how Blok once asked, "What does Otsup mean?" and someone allegedly explained, "It's an acronym for Organization for Taste and Savor in the Usage of Potatoes."

"Yanovsky," patronizing and pompous, Otsup droned next to the elevator, "you must understand that *Chisla* cannot pay a regular honorarium. But, if ever you should be very, *very* much in need of money, come to me and I'll try to help you out."

Some people, i.e., Adamovich, Ivanov, and himself, he recompensed adequately. According to Felsen, Otsup once told Adamovich: "You know, Georges, I have come to the conclusion that it's much more difficult to write articles than fiction. Which means that they have to be better paid!"

The people who came to the Thursday meetings were often unknown or uninteresting, but Otsup knew how to attract them and use them for the common cause. The ladies carried away leaflets describing the aims of *Chisla* and collected contributions. Otsup made me sign a list of contributors, but illegibly, ". . . so that it can be taken for Yakovlev," (a famous artist of the time) . . . It's no easy undertaking to publish the best journal in the emigration!

Of course Otsup was aggressive, a go-getter, but that is why *Chisla* survived. Who knows how Diaghilev would have proceeded if he had not had the backing of the old Russian nobility and business world. Literature was Otsup's element, and his taste was probably no worse than Diaghilev's.

For a while Otsup "lived off" *Chisla,* something Montparnasse could not forgive him. But what, actually, was shameful about it, since he dedicated all his talent and strength to the enterprise? Nevertheless, Khodasevich expressed the opinion of the majority, when he referred to Otsup in an article as a "wheeler-dealer."

Otsup, who had only recently returned from a trip to Italy and was ignorant of all the changes that had occurred during his absence—namely, the blossoming of the Circle and the fact that Khodasevich was now playing bridge with Adamovich—ran to the Café Murat, planning to punish the defamer. But his own friends stopped him, and Felsen led him away.

At this point he should have understood that the power structure had changed and that he would have to start over from scratch. Instead, he was offended and proudly turned away. Thus he faded out in loneliness and together with him *Chisla,* which apparently had played out its role.

Otsup spent the war years in Italy, as is evidenced by his *Dnevnik v stikhakh* (Diary in Verse), a book which is in some ways quite extraordinary but is weakened by the introduction of the theme of Beatrice. As I have already said, I do not believe that Beatrice "saved" Dante; in general, I don't believe that women "save"; Christ is the Saviour. I know that many men have been "ruined" by women—and perhaps this kind of "ruin" is often very welcome. Otsup, too, was probably crippled by his "Beatrice," a "beauty," a former actress from the silent movies, in Otsup's imagination an angel and the ideal of wisdom and goodness. I met her once, fleetingly, and the pronouncements of this tyrannical, middle-aged woman seemed to me only boring.

Otsup saw much more clearly the character of Boris Yulevich Pregel, a prominent banker and Maecenas with huge, puffy, bloodthirsty hands. When the two of them carried on "business" deliberations (and the editor of *Chisla* basically had nothing to sell!) I felt like the accidental witness to a battle of giant tyrannosaurs . . . Pregel, rising, addressed Zelyuk, who was sitting quietly in his chair: "I contribute one thousand francs to this marvelous journal. Now what do you say?"

By God, there was something epic in such speeches!

Zelyuk, the owner of a big Russian printing firm, a cruel and sentimental man, suddenly softened and expressed the intention of "doing his best." Only the genius of Nikolai Avdeevich Otsup could have united all these awesome and, for the journal, indispensable people.

One night, in 1933 or 1934, I visited Sofiev in connection with the Writers' Union and met there Sofia Pregel, a poet from Berlin and the sister of Boris, a plump, kindly, energetic lady, who with her smile and dignity slightly resembled England's Queen Mother. Remaining alone with Yury Sofiev and his wife, Irina Knorring, I learned that Sofia Pregel was "extremely rich" (she had arrived in a chauffeur-driven limousine); Knorring got to know her in Constantinople, the first stage of their emigration.

Pregel came to read her poems to our group and published her own little collections. In her verse there were kind old men and women (her grandparents?) who were always eating or drinking something. So that, when Smolensky angrily declared that this was "culinary poetry," we all involuntarily smiled.

Sofia Pregel was a good human being; she helped many poets, and very soon her social activities, if not her writings, were accepted without reservation. Felsen and I often met with her in connection with our exhibit of emigré books and, later, our book publication. She always received us graciously and hospitably.

At the beginning of the war Pregel came to New York and started publishing the journal *Novoselie* (The New Abode). She turned out to be a most sensible editor: she knew exactly what she wanted and was ready to pay for it. (This latter quality Otsup did not possess.)

In her personal life, Sofia Yulievna was not lucky. She had studied music and singing professionally, but nothing serious had come of it. After the war she returned to Paris, where she introduced Irina Yasen, who, in her turn, helped several poets to get published.

Sofia's brother, Boris Yulievich Pregel, businessman, scientist, and even composer (how easy it is, with money, to excel in many fields!) once came to our benefit evening for young writers at the Tsetlins' apartment. There he met Mrs. Tsetlin's daughter and fell in love. For his subsequent happy family life he was, one might say, indebted to the Paris Union of Writers and Poets.

When we were "putting together" the Inner Circle, some among us dreamed of "realistic Power" and to this end proposed wealthy, influential people for membership. First of all Boris Pregel was mentioned. But, after some hesitation, Fondaminsky rejected his candidacy. "I had occasion to speak with him about other business, and I looked at his hands," he explained not quite coherently. "Did you ever notice his hands? With such hands one could strangle a man. No, he doesn't suit us!"

It always seemed to me that Fondaminsky, like Kerensky and most of the SRs, was primarily an artist and not a politician or strategist.

The morbid desire for pseudo-power and pseudo-influence compromised the best emigré aspirations. How many good and noble associations collapsed because of this naive opportunism!

Chisla naturally invaded the neighboring artistic fields; given a little more time, Otsup would have even reached out to the ballet. All in all, the art exhibit, organized by *Chisla,* was successful. Otsup later sold some of the oils at auction in Vichy, with the help of enthusiastic doctors, bankers, and speculators. Of course, a few little errors also crept in: several paintings which had only been lent to *Chisla* were also sold. Thus I once was witness to a rather unpleasant exchange between Otsup and one of the better painters, Lazar Volovik, whose beautiful landscape had been sold without his knowledge or permission.

"In such a great enterprise one can't avoid errors," Otsup explained to me after the painter had left. (He was inconspicuously swallowing air, probably feeling heart palpitations.) As a man accustomed to the excitements of games of chance, he got hold of himself after a moment and, with a pseudo-lordly rolling of his "r's" finished condescendingly: "What did I need that Volovik for, anyway?"

At that time, the *Chisla soirée* was the high point of the season (as formerly that of the Green Lamp) with the "Tout Paris-russe" attending. The dignified hall, where usually musicians performed, was overcrowded, so that once even Mikhail Tsetlin, the editor of *Sovremennye zapiski,* could not get in and was obliged to go home. This was gossipped about with glee.

At the meeting for issue 2–3 of *Chisla,* in which my "indecent" story "Trinadsatye" (The Thirteenth) was published, the air was charged with scandal. Milyukov spoke—for a change—about the "crisis" in contemporary art. From the audience there came invectives and abusive language, and Otsup and Merezhkovsky, who were seated on the dais, excitedly argued with each other, Otsup claiming that the advantage of the West over Russia was that it professed the principle of *"chacun pour soi, Dieu pour tous,"* while Merezhkovsky countered that this was the wisdom of a *concièrge.* He was right, of course.

Then Poplavsky announced that the Russians were a mean, vile people: one had only to remember the native saying, "One alone in the field cannot fight." At that moment there came from the last row the sadly howling voice of Mrs. Sazonov, reporting about four Russian escapees who had perished while heroically swimming across the Danube (*Poslednie novosti* had recently written up their story). The "Young Russians" (Mladorossy) had long since been whistling and stamping patriotically. Things were heating up.

Milyukov, accustomed to "obstructions" from his youth on, waited calmly, but Otsup, rather daringly, hissed at them and, having quieted them down, announced an intermission.

On such occasions, all who took part in the discussion and their friends usually assembled in the small "artists' " backroom. They split up into different groups, listening to established authorities or to editors of journals. Individuals who had no opportunity or cause to join such a group remained standing in proud isolation.

The time of intermission was of course the most welcome moment for an emigré writer . . . He could put a witty *mot* into circulation, repeat some gossip, make a date, enquire about the fate of his manuscript, gather valuable information and, last but not least, shake hands with a pleasant lady or a star of the magnitude of Chaliapin, Alekhin, or Kerensky.

Some speeches might have seemed dull or boring, others exciting, but the intermissions were almost always equally interesting, though not devoid of a certain bitterness. Thus, for the first time, during such an intermission at a *Chisla* meeting, I underwent a cruel "social experience."

I was standing proudly by myself, listening distractedly to various voices around Milyukov and Gippius, when I suddenly saw N. N. alone in the opposite corner of the room; it quite naturally occurred to me that rather than remaining detached, we would both enjoy the wait for the bell if we were in company. I went up to him but immediately noticed that he was looking askance at me in quite a hostile way. I was not welcome. Quickly, I retreated to my corner, where I was joined by a familiarly chattering M. M. Now it was my turn to look displeased and to barely answer his questions. The company of M. M. completely demeaned me, as apparently mine would have "compromised" N. N. These complex "social" mechanics opened up to me in all their significance: the same laws were equally at work in court circles and in the emigré caravansery.

Alas, nowhere is snobbism, reverence for rank, the pecking order, developed in its ugliest pathological form than in the vacuum of an uprooted milieu, which is forever deprived of its share of a "government" pie. Fights, intrigues, backbiting are terrible sins, familiar even to the old Adam (in any case to his sons), but they are most disgusting when there is no rational cause for any competition whatsoever . . . Thus it is that the most terrible battles take place in the world of dreams—battles of Chinese shadows on the wall.

In the life of emigre letters, *Poslednie novosti* played an outstanding role. Not the least because we all contributed to it. As for Adamovich's Thursday articles, they created a genuinely literary atmosphere.

Poslednie novosti, under the leadership of P. N. Milyukov, was of course a political, democratic organ; fiction and poetry were viewed only as a sort of bait to lure the pedestrian reader, a syrup to sweeten the bitter quinine of social truths. And so it was for a while: Bunin, a symbol of what was best in the past—then Aldanov, Sasha Chorny, Don-Aminado, the translation of a mystery novel, everything that is expected of a major daily publication.

But the pressure of the incessantly growing, young, Western-Russian literature was so great that conventional barriers were finally swept away . . . Poetry entered first: from Poplavsky to Terapiano, from Chervinskaya to Knorring. But little by little almost all our prose writers found a place there. Even in the articles religious names and themes began to crop up. Milyukov simply changed everywhere "the doctors of the Church" to "ancient sages," which seemed to him more appropriate. However, such terms as "grace" or "original sin" he simply crossed out.

Adjusting to this neo-Aesopian language, even moderate obscurantists could contribute to the paper. But Milyukov never let Merezhkovsky or others like him close, sniffing with his broad Tolstoyan nose not only the smell of apocalyptic sulphur but of the furnaces of Krupp as well.

For the longest time Gippius attempted to penetrate by herself, without her husband, the pages of *Poslednie novosti*. Aldanov, not exactly refusing his help, said only: "Such a literary divorce would seem very strange to everyone." "She would write only small things, like the pieces Teffi gives to *Vozrozhdenie*," Merezhkovsky insisted.

As a matter of fact, Berdyaev, too, did not contribute to the paper. At a large meeting he had very reasonably dwelled at length on the role of the devil in connection with the activities of the Bolsheviks, and Milyukov had noted ironically that Berdyaev must be very familiar with the nature of the prince of this world if he could speak about him with such authority. This, for some reason, offended the philosopher.

"I really don't need these people," he explained with dignity. "Other publications accept me gladly."

But he never did have a newspaper "of his own." And Fedotov also had no place there. In short, professional Christian thinkers, with the exception of Mochulsky, had no access to Milyukov. All this applies to the old guard; the young, from the mid-thirties on, if they obeyed certain rules, could publish their most characteristic work in *Poslednie novosti,* at least in small doses.

Poslednie novosti reached every corner of the Russian diaspora. Milyukov's authority was recognized not only by liberal emigrés but also by influential foreigners. His editorials were read on the Quai d'Orsay; and the paper influenced, in some measure, even *Real Politik*. A regular contributor could attain some anemic glory on five continents. The poets were reprinted, gratis, in the Riga *Segodnya* and in the New York *Novoe Russkoe Slovo*. As far as prose was concerned, the provinces, as I already mentioned, had their own opinions and did not need our creative efforts.

Besides honor and glory there was one more reason why we all sent everything in the least bit suitable to *Poslednie novosti:* the honorarium! Notwithstanding the European economic crisis, Milyukov, a practical, even stingy man, had so organized his paper that it was bringing in an enviable profit. The main source of income, as always in the press, was the advertisements, those advertisements of which Don-Aminado doggerelled:

For the right to use the bath,
I instruct in advanced math.

The main collaborators participated in a profit-sharing plan. There was also an excellent health insurance policy. As for occasional contributors, a minimum wage was established for us which even native literati might envy.

I believe I began at seventy-five centimes per line but soon advanced to a franc or more. And for one franc, even a Blum franc, one could still buy a pound of bread or a liter of wine; a flacon of perfume or a bottle of champagne was twenty-five francs. Having a free or a somehow, miraculously, paid-for room, one short story in *Poslednie novosti* assured survival for an entire month. Nothing to equal that has ever been offered by any Russian paper, not even in America. Willy-nilly one misses, if not his editorials, then Milyukov's ability to conduct a commercial enterprise profitably and honorably.

In the thirties, the offices of the paper were situated on the second floor, near Métro Arts et Métiers. You entered a windowless anteroom, illuminated by an eternally lit, naked bulb and with a switchboard against the wall. On duty was Ladinsky who, between chatting with the visitors and working on his own article, laconically but efficiently answered the phone and connected callers with the business office, printers, editorial room, etc.

Thus, in this closet, and by night at home, Ladinsky managed to write, besides his poems, two novels on Roman and Byzantine life respectively.

Antonin Petrovich Ladinsky had been an officer in the Great War; after the civil war he was evacuated from the south and went to Cairo, where he acquired some knowledge of English; thus he was able, when need arose, to translate a chapter of a serialized detective story for the paper.

He wrote lyrical sketches, saturated with nostalgia for his childhood and his native Pskov; however, he was inspired as well by "the copper of Latin," as he put it. Like many officers and civil servants he was intimately bound to the "Empire," the great country, the Dardanelles, the historical Russian frontiers—ever further extended—and to all the other elements of a sensual patriotism. He stood, of course, for freedom of the press, legal rights, limitation of government powers—in a word for the program of P. N. Milyukov. But all this later—when the borders of the empire would be 100 percent secured and the national interests of Russia fully protected.

In the Circle, at the time of the Soviet-Finnish slaughter, Ladinsky, who wrote exalted, neoromantic poems, vigorously defended and justified the strategy of General Shaposhnikov, pleading that "in such times" one could not possibly leave Leningrad open to the Finnish guns in

Vyborg. Could one wonder that these loyal sons of Great Russia, after the hard-won victory of the Red Army, applied for Soviet passports? Ladinsky, like Sofiev, honestly returned to the Soviet Union where, some years ago, he gave up the ghost. In human history, imperialism has seduced more men than cards, women, and alcohol put together. Yet, in the Bible it is not listed as a mortal sin.

Ladinsky survives in two or three exquisite poems, but one could never have an interesting conversation with him. Tall, lean, of somewhat Nordic (Swedish) appearance, but with a Russian officer's red nose, he reminded one at that time of the Soviet writer Tikhonov, also a romantic poet and a soldier. Ladinsky lived exclusively off his literary activities (if the duties at the switchboard can also be considered as connected with literature). I was depressed by that windowless anteroom with its eternally shining bulb. Out of boredom we gossiped. About one noisy literary figure he several times expressed himself in this way: "If I had his energy I wouldn't be sitting here," (at this point he always cast a glance around him and lowered his voice), "but there, in the office of the chief."

Whatever Ladinsky did, whether it was his duty at the switchboard, the translation of a mystery novel, a sketch, or verses, everywhere he expressed one and the same "organic" conscientiousness, characteristic of the Russian artisan, craftsman, laborer, tiller of the soil or soldier. There exists a firmly established legend about a national dissoluteness, about the Russian "perhaps," "if," "somehow," "for the time being," about laxity, backwardness, anarchism, indifference, grossness, even dishonesty, about a combination of rebellion, a search for God and a thirst for "absolute truth." Perhaps that is so for a certain class, for students, businessmen, *lumpenproletariat;* I don't know. But there is another national trait: to stand fast to the end, regardless of the circumstances, even in Nicholas's Sebastopol, to deliver only perfect products, finished in every detail, regardless of the pay. That is the trait of a craftsman, an artist, Leskov's character, Levsha,* a doctor, a teacher, an essayist, equally characteristic of a Rozanov, a Chernyshevsky, or Captain Timokhin of *War and Peace.* This striving, by intelligentsia and peasants alike, to deliver a perfect product, has up to now not found due recognition. In the classic works we mainly find descriptions of the legendary sloth, dissoluteness, ignorance, vodka, rebellion, and thirst for immediate, church-given justice. There is some sort of contradiction in this.

---

*From the story "The Steel Flea."

Foreigners, listening to the stories about Bolsheviks, about Ivan the Terrible and Nicholas I, may well ask in wonderment, "How is it that Russia still exists, continues to grow and become stronger?" To this there is only one logical answer: "Russia is saved by the conscientious work of the craftsman, the laborer, the scientist, the infantryman: in the field, in the factories and laboratories and, alas, even in the Siberian labor camps.

After half an hour of waiting, I was finally admitted into Demidov's office, where I heaved a sigh of relief. A huge room with two windows and a door to a balcony which looked out onto a miniature triangular *place,* where cool houses had been standing, unrenovated, since the time of Louis XVI or the Jacobins.

Igor Platonovich Demidov was considered "my editor." I had dealings only with him, and he apparently supported me. I do not know what writers Milyukov himself "read," although he was often mentioned in connection with rejections: "*Papa* did not let it through! *Papa* didn't want it!" *Papa* referred of course to the infallible Pope in Rome. This is a ploy used by all editors and executives, and it was used particularly often by emigré politicians. In *Sovremennye zapiski* Fondaminsky served as such a bugbear before he began meeting with us.

Demidov, with sideburns reminiscent of the Decembrist epoch, beetle-brows, and muddy-greenish (like a stagnant pond), intelligent eyes in an emaciated, almost ascetic face, was thin and carried himself in an exaggeratedly erect way ("he's swallowed a ruler," as we say in Russian). He reminded me simultaneously of a Napoleonic senator and of a Russian Byzantine icon. He was interested in esoteric schools, Freemasonry, theosophy, spoke eloquently about the God of love, and apparently did not wish anybody harm. In the old times, such Russian dignitaries engaged in spiritualistic séances and were attracted by fashionable Jesuits or Quietists.

He must have liked my short stories; otherwise they would not have been published, for I had no other protector on the paper. But it was difficult to fathom my editor: I thought that a certain piece would suit him and he rejected it; but another, weaker one (proposed in despair) he praised and accepted.

Demidov was slightly deaf and cleaned his ears twice a day. From his drawer he would extract a wad of cotton, scissors, and matches, arranging all this neatly, precisely, seriously. (In the beginning I even thought that this ritual had some relationship to my manuscripts.) Then he would roll some cotton around the end of a match with his long white fingers, skillfully and energetically. And without hesitation would begin to dig into his ears.

Our favorite story about this precise, somewhat pedantic man concerned a conversation he had with Dr. Manukhin (the one who treated everybody, including Gorky and Katherine Mansfield, with irradiation of the spleen). Around Easter time, Manukhin called up Demidov, and Demidov shouted into the mouthpiece: "Christ is risen, Ivan Ivanich!" But Manukhin, perhaps also a little hard of hearing, did not understand him and Demidov began to spell it out: "*Ch* like Christopher, *R* like Rachmaninov, *I* like Igor . . . Yes, exactly Christ is risen! What? Can we meet? Sorry, I'm terribly busy. Oh, for lunch, did you say? That can be arranged . . ."

Great influence was wielded by A. A. Polyakov, the page-setter. Although he was by no means an editor, the important, permanent contributors delivered their pieces directly into his hands and thus made a living. The people whom he befriended found it easier to subsist in Paris. Polyakov used his power not capriciously but only according to professional considerations: everything that was good for *Poslednie novosti* could, and had to, be printed! Anything that would not improve circulation was detrimental, even stupid.

The composing room (which they called the "fire-room") was noisy, smoke-filled and, in its own way, gay. Polyakov, with his shaven, half-bald scalp, pale-yellowish, serious, businesslike face, stretched out his hand, not taking his eyes off the papers, smiled in the wrong direction and, pushing his pack of cigarettes toward the visitor, concentrated again on the local Russian news.

He smoked rather rare, very strong cigarettes, Gauloises rouges, which hit you like a bullet from a long-range gun. A friend of mine, a police doctor, every night read *Paris Minuit,* published especially for "night people." This tabloid journal of midnight activities and the "red" cigarettes are coupled in my memory as peculiarities of Parisian life, inaccessible to the average tourist. Always, when visiting the "fire-room," I made it my business to smoke one or two of Polyakov's cigarettes, in the strange conviction that it gave him pleasure.

Aleksandr Polyakov was one of those gentlemen who under all circumstances observe the basic rules, the rules of the game; he treated me, as he treated everyone, correctly and even with sympathy. In all fairness, my contributions could not always be considered "advantageous" for the paper; besides, I was under Demidov's jurisdiction, which meant I involuntarily belonged to a semi-hostile camp. As in every remunerative job, there, too, a struggle for influence, with the usual intrigues and infights, was taking place.

Often a short story accepted by Demidov was put on hold by Polyakov and had allegedly been sent to "Pavel Nikolaevich Milyukov." I even naively dreamed of passing under the jurisdiction of Polyakov, who was highly regarded by Osorgin and Adamovich, but such a passage was, alas, impossible.

In every enterprise there exists an invisible axis around which the entire business rotates. Tolstoi wrote that in every household there is such a person, a nanny or a grandmother . . . These "saintly" people find their *raison d'être* only in work; they cannot sit idle, never count the working hours or ask for overtime pay.

It is possible that it was worth sacrificing one's life for such an excellent paper as *Poslednie novosti*. But, arriving in New York in 1941, Polyakov settled into a similar role on *Novoe Russkoe Slovo*, as a watchdog of morals and spelling. People of such a nature simply break down when deprived of their customary occupation, and, sure enough, during summer vacations, Aleksandr Abramovich would almost always fall ill and, with redoubled effort, visit doctors' offices. In his eighties, he still hoped to catch a disease at its inception.

Polyakov exposed his excessive hypochondria for the first time after the funeral of Shumsky, a former colonel on the Russian general staff. The right-wing *Vozrozhdenie* called this collaborator of *Poslednie novosti* an impostor because Shumsky was his pen name; he had finished the military academy under a different appelation.

So Colonel Shumsky suddenly expired, one might say on the run, and his colleagues attended the cremation in the chapel of the Père Lachaise cemetery. I saw Polyakov immediately after this ceremony and barely recognized the old gentleman: he seemed faded, weakened, resigned. But a week later he was again himself: a dry, serious, self-assured professional, playing an interesting and responsible game according to once-and-for-all established rules. (If only it could go on forever!)

Another employee of *Poslednie novosti* was Slovtsov, who went quickly to his grave and who did not leave any trace. He was plump, had a childish voice and suffered from dispnea. Besides technical work in the offices of the paper, he punctually delivered, every week, two pieces dedicated to French books of "general cultural" interest. He followed the new publications of this kind, recapitulating their contents logically and intelligently, only sporadically adding a personal opinion of a humanistic nature. I considered such workers miracles of diligence. *"Ce sont des as!"* we joked mirthlessly in Montparnasse.

It should be remembered that if for some reason a place on the paper became temporarily vacant, those same miracle workers undertook additional duties so as not to let any outsiders in. Slovtsov always replaced Polyakov in the summer.

Poplavsky told me with horror that, when he went on leave—before the reforms of Blum and paid vacations—Slovtsov prepared eight or nine articles ahead of time for an entire month. Thus he did not lose his honorarium during his time of rest. That meant that, besides his regular contributions and everyday work in the composing room, he had had to read eight or nine additional volumes and write the corresponding articles. Yes, this man was indeed fully engaged in useful activities. And after he died, not one of his colleagues ever mentioned him again. As if a cow had licked off a fly with her tongue (Russian expression, worth reproducing).

The paper kept a fund which regular employees could turn to for loans. In my presence the accountant, Mogilevsky, once counted out 10,000 francs to Aldanov for a trip to Italy. Aldanov, confused by the presence of an unexpected witness, quickly distributed the heaps of bank notes in his diverse pockets with his little hands that resembled a seal's flippers and disappeared. That night, in Montparnasse, Adamovich informed me that Aldanov had asked him to explain to me that he had taken out this sum as a loan to be worked off in the winter.

The reporters for *Poslednie novosti* were A. Sedykh-Zwibak and N. Vakar, both energetic, active people who were very valuable to the paper. Sedykh reported on the Chambre des Députés, on crime and refugee problems. Vakar wrote about intrigues in the extremist political parties, about the election of a Cossack ataman (even then a complicated and elusive affair) and about differences within the church. During the absence of one of them, the other stood in for him. So the gossip was that Sedykh, in one of his replacement reports, had written that "the general was presented with a *portrait* of the Virgin."

Nicholas P. Vakar stood head and shoulders above his colleagues. After coming to the United States in 1941, he taught at a New England college but, what is more important, wrote an extraordinary book, *The Taproot of Soviet Society* (Harper & Brothers, N.Y.: 1961).

It is now fashionable among our contemporary Tolstoevskys in exile to eulogize P. A. Stolypin, the tsar's premier and minister of the interior, whose program was to help the better-off, strong peasantry to get stronger and richer, assigning additional land to them and thus creating a reliable class of *kulaks* who would naturally support the tsar and his order. At the same time, Stolypin also hanged thousands of rebellious *muzhiks* who had burned down mansions of the nobles. The liberal press was horrified by these gallows, which they named "Stolypin's neckties." Among others, the famous writer Korolenko published an alarming essay entitled "Bytovya yavleniya" (Everyday Occurrences) in 1910 in the journal *Russkoe Bogatstvo* (Russian Wealth) and Tolstoi wrote his famous *Ne mogu molchat'* (I Cannot Be Silent). Not long after, in 1911, Stolypin was shot by a double agent in the Kiev theater at a great gala attended by the tsar.

Our Tolstoevskys now see Stolypin's program as the salvation of the future Russia, while Vakar's thesis is that Stolypin's *kulaks* were virtually transformed into members of the Communist Party—ten million of whom suck the blood of the rest of the population, belong to the "*nomenclatura*" and support by all available means the regime that gave them their privileges. (Of course, they executed millions to Stolypin's thousands, but that is perhaps the result of progress, a development about which Hegel wrote long ago.) This is how Vakar presents his case:

The Communist war against the "kulak" had generally the ironic consequence of raising the most successful of the breed to positions of command in the nation. Through constant redefinition of peasant classes, in order to segregate those on whom the Party could rely, the Soviet state has selected both for subjugation and for preferment not economic classes but appropriate *human types*. The type which advanced under the brutalizing and immoral terms of the struggle could not help being just that kulak whose shrewd, hard, cruel, grasping nature earned him the fear and hate and envy of the villages he ruled. Counting only his own interests, paying lip-service here to God, and there to Marx, never handicapped by any sort of idealism, he was perfectly suited to the dog-eat-dog times of purge and liquidation. With a sure sign of which way the battle went and a dark corner in which to change his uniform, he could be counted on as a vigorous supporter of the winning side.

In the Soviet dispensation, the kulak type found he could do rather more easily and effectively what he had always done—make his fortune at the expense of his fellows. Under the developing capitalism effected by Stolypin's reforms, it had been necessary to get money first in order to acquire power over people, then to squeeze out of them significant wealth. Under Communism, the road was political and more direct. One joined the party and acquired at once the necessary power over people to build and feather one's own nest. This to the wise man was the sense of the Bolshevik revolution. He would thank his luck that he had been too young or too poor to have made the fatal mistake of becoming a kulak too soon, and so was saved to become a commissar in good season. (*The Taproot of Soviet Society*, p. 59)

Sedykh blossomed when Bunin received the Nobel Prize. I saw him at the offices of *Poslednie novosti* on the occasion of their celebration for the laureate. In a dress-coat, with flying tails, he gave the impression that it was he, Sedykh, who was the object of the celebration. Later he accompanied Bunin to Sweden in the capacity of secretary, interpreter, and even nanny. The laureate knew no foreign languages: in French he could only put together a couple of rudimentary sentences. It is perhaps worth mentioning that in the first edition of his memoirs Bunin does not mention that Sedykh went with him to Stockholm.

Up to his last hours, P. N. Milyukov remained true to himself—a rock! (Why Paul and not rather Peter?) Trying to move him from his position was a vain undertaking. Several things he understood, and understood much better than some friends from his own camp. And I have in mind more than politics or history. Nevertheless, there were subjects, even entire areas of human activity, in which he proved to be organically deaf, blind and, perhaps, dead.

With a brick-red face, more so after he underwent a vasectomy, thickset and massive, moving gingerly, cautiously in his old age, thus I often met him in our new "exile," in Montpellier, where we lived in the same neighborhood. Side by side we rummaged in the university book stores. It turned out that he was an admirer of Marcus Aurelius and could quote him by heart. The great school of Montpellier is one of the oldest in France, and the presence of antiquities, culture and Arab-Roman scholasticism, created a special, propitious atmosphere for conversations in which Milyukov, forgetting about the constitutional democrats and the Dardanelles, presented himself in a new light.

He was somewhat acquainted with the young emigré literature. In general, he had "heard" about everything. During the book exhibit organized by Felsen and myself, I had visited his home—at Metro Convention—and had come away with the impression that, if this was indeed our metaphysical enemy, he was a noble enemy whom one had to treat with respect. Anyhow, at that time he was very amiable and granted my requests regarding advertisements and manifestos in the paper. His desire for popularity with the young turned out to be an unexpected trump in our hands, an advantage we imperceptibly lost with the years.

Milyukov, as head of a "thick" journal, *Russkie zapiski,* had read many young prose writers and had formed a definite opinion of them. This was the cardinal flaw of his spiritual and intellectual life: once and for all established and hardened beliefs and convictions.

To my surprise he advised me, once, in Paris: "Subdue your devil!" Since this came from an apparently completely unreligious man, I did not quite see what he had in mind.

At the time of our meetings in Montpellier, Stalin was gathering the crumbs from Hitler's table: The Baltic countries, Lithuania, and Eastern Poland fell into the jaws of the Father of the Peoples; then Bessarabia, Chernovice. There were rumors about the Dardanelles, and Milyukov very calmly told me, "They are doing what I would do if I were sitting in the Kremlin."

This testimony horrified me: not the "Dardanelles" in particular, but the cold-bloodedness with which Milyukov, if on only one point, could identify with Stalin.

In New York, after Milyukov's death, I happened to mention this conversation to Professor M. Karpovich, editor of *Russkie zapiski.* After a minute's thought he shocked me with the reaction: "Well, there is nothing extraordinary in that. Basically, Milyukov had spoken and written in that vein for a long time."

The American Consulate in Marseilles required a "moral recommendation" before issuing a visa. For this purpose Milyukov composed a rather flattering recommendation, which I still preserve together with my Nansen passport (God bless Nansen!). Milyukov, incidentally, was fluent in French and English.

It happened that Mark Vishnyak, a Russian socialist who was already in the USA by that time, was applying for a position as a professor of history somewhere in Illinois; and he asked Milyukov to support his application. Since Vishnyak did not get an answer to this request, he wrote to me, asking me to find out from Milyukov how matters stood.

Upon my questioning him, Milyukov firmly declared that he could not recommend Vishnyak for the post, an answer I immediately passed on to the latter. During our conversation, Milyukov expressed opinions about certain social and political collaborators. It was sad (but fun) to listen to him. Alas, he had no illusions concerning people . . . He mentioned only Zenzinov with approval.

The Milyukovs lived at that time in one spacious room; food, of course, was all *ersatz*. Somehow, a supply of smoked eels turned up on the market, and I presented him with a pound. However, the employees of *Poslednie novosti* who had also been evacuated to Montpellier had already, each in his turn, brought him packages of the famous eel (for which they were reimbursed). I felt embarrassed, but Milyukov's youngish wife imperiously reassured me: "It's all right. Pavel Nikolae-vich likes eel, and he will eat it all."

Soon after, they moved to Aix-en-Provence, where he died. With him I always felt as if I were in the presence of a mammoth: I was bewildered by the traits and capacities of a mighty and mysterious antediluvian creature.

In July 1942 in Marseilles, I made the acquaintance of the former Russian consul, who continued to supply emigrés with the references needed for immigration to the United States. I don't remember his name—something Ukrainian; he was a mild, intelligent, greying southerner, who was confined to his bed with a chronic ailment.

Since his daughter, who usually served as his secretary, happened to be absent for a few days, I had to type my own references under the dictation of that very kind and very shrewd man. Neatly arranged on his bed table were all the paraphernalia: medicines, cigarettes, rubber stamps, stationery. Something had happened to his legs, so that he was completely unable to move about. We became friendly and as a result he sold me, at no profit, a pack of black market cigarettes and shared the local gossip. "Although I live outside Marseilles, all the important people come to me, even primadonnas," he said with a grain of irony.

Winter and summer he lay on his bed in a room overcrowded with furniture like a pawnshop. Beyond the large window Provençal sunsets were burning. Out of paradisiac exhaustion birds stopped singing and couples embracing. An intoxicating fragrance saturated the very tissue of existence, of sky and earth, of sea and mists. All this, despite the southern dust, hungry insects, and the proximity of numerous outhouses.

All our "old" (pre-Bolshevik) consuls were of a special breed, cultured, talkative, and obviously not overworked. I remember Kondaurov from Paris, an obese, important Freemason, who usually met me with the same friendly-sarcastic remark: "Hello, young poet, I understand that you believe in three gods."

Famous for his charm and *savoir-faire* was Maklakov, the Kerensky-appointed ambassador. But he belonged to the caste of ambassadors, which was something altogether different. His Petersburg "r" could persuade and charm even Chiappe, the prefect of police. However, Maklakov was a bureaucrat, with all the attributes of an administrator, a civil servant—unexpected traits which no one has hitherto mentioned.

As our conversation continued, the consul told me about a famous Marxist Menshevik[1] who came to him for his birth certificate and objected to the official Western European text. He asked for the phrase "son of a parish priest" to be added after his name.

"By God, I felt ashamed," the consul confessed. "It's true, he is the son of an orthodox priest, but all his comrades are Jews, and he was going to the United States on a 'Jewish, exceptional' visa. It's disgraceful to set oneself apart under such circumstances." And he finished with the familiar refrain, "In the past, the Russian intelligentsia . . . now, it's everyone for himself!" (Later this same learned fellow, this son of an Orthodox priest, became *persona grata* at the Hoover Institute in California.)

Here it is appropriate to bring up a more famous personality among the exiles, Vladimir Sirin-Nabokov. In *The Nabokov-Wilson Letters, 1940–1971* (edited by Simon Karlinsky for Harper & Row: 1979), Edmund Wilson, the great critic, and a gentleman, writes to Nabokov on 7 July 1943: "A man named V. S. Yanovsky has written me asking for literary advice. He enclosed a little story from *Novoselie* which seems to me not bad, and a preposterous scenario for a novel, which sounds as if it had been written as a joke. Do you know anything about him? He tells me that 'he enjoyed a certain popularity in the Russian milieu in France.' "

I had sent Wilson my story "Zadanie-vypolnenie" (*Task and Realization*) and a short outline of Portativnoe bessmertie.

It seems that, under the circumstances, nothing could have been simpler for a Russian gentleman and writer than to support a newly arrived emigré and, regardless of personal preferences, to tell the influential American, "If you like his story, why not help him get it published?" But that would have been too "*poshlo*"[2] for Nabokov. Here is his answer: "July 1943 . . . Re Yanovsky. I have often met him in Paris and it is true that his work was appreciated by a certain coterie. He is a he-man (. . .), if you know what I mean." (The editor was obliged to put dots, indicating a deletion.) "He cannot write. I happened to tell Aldanov that you were responsible for the facility I have in publishing my things here, and I suppose the story is going around, and you will get many more letters from my poor brethren."

Poor Nabokov! Here I can't help but mention that he never gave anyone any professional help. He spoke with the same derision about all our writers, perhaps with the exception of Khodasevich. To him Dosto-evsky is "third-rate," and *War and Peace*—as I heard from him in Paris—is in need of "finishing touches." Nabokov belonged to the rather nu-merous type of artist who feels a need to stamp out everything alive around him in order to assert his own genius. Such people are basically very insecure.

In the thirties, Felsen and I went to see Gabriel Marcel at the publishing house where he was editor, to find out about the fate of the books we had proposed. In Marcel's office, we encountered Sirin-Nabokov, who was just about to leave.

"Here is Mr. Sirin," said the philosopher (at that time he was not yet an existentialist). "He is offering us his novel, already translated into French." And he pointed to *Despair*, which was lying on his desk.

We could not possibly appreciate *Despair*; in those days we did not care for "inventions." We thought that literature was too serious a business to let entertainers and acrobats meddle with it. When Sirin, at his evening in the Salle Lascaze, read the first chapters of *Despair*, in which the hero, out on a walk, accidentally runs into his double (or something like it), we could hardly refrain from laughing.

However, Felsen, the pure soul, quickly and decisively responded: "I know the book. It's a very good novel." Upon which Sirin, slender in those years, bowed deeply to his poor brethren and said, "*Merci beau-coup*."

But this is already a chapter from a new book, on another continent, even another hemisphere. While that extraordinary Parisian decade is finished and belongs to history.

Brothers, sisters of future slaughters and uprisings, will you hear our living voice?

Life with its anguished breath we shan't regret.
What's life and death? But we'll regret that fire
Which shone over the entire universe
And retreats, weeping, into the night.[3]

Notes

Chapter 1

1. The Green Lamp, a literary and philosophical discussion group founded by Zinaida Gippius and Dmitry Merezhkovsky in Paris in 1927, took its name from a well-known literary circle of Pushkin's day.

2. Yasnaya polyana, Lev Tolstoi's family estate, served, for most of his life, as the writer's permanent residence.

3. The museum was named after Nikolai Konstantinovich Roerich (1874–1947), the painter, stage designer, and archaeologist. Roerich worked as a stage designer for Diaghilev before the Revolution. He emigrated from Russia in 1920 and lived for many years in Tibet. There are Roerich museums in New York and other major cities.

4. The Socialist Revolutionary (SR) Party was a Russian agrarian socialist party which came into being in the 1890s. In the years preceding the 1917 Revolution, the Terrorist Organization of the Socialist Revolutionary Party was responsible for the assassinations of a number of high officials in the tsarist government. After the February Revolution, Socialist Revolutionaries participated in the Provisional Government; and, after the October Revolution, many Socialist Revolutionaries fought against the Bolsheviks during the Civil War.

5. The "thick" journal is a form of publication that has dominated Russian journalism since the early nineteenth century. Thick journals are distinguished by the diversity of their content, ranging from works of literature and reviews to serious articles on topics of scientific, social, cultural, historical, and philosophical interest. Most nineteenth-century thick journals carried more or less direct political overtones, which were usually expressed very forcefully in the literary critical section of the journal.

6. The Constituent Assembly was elected and convened to draft a constitution for Russia. Elections to the Assembly were held in November 1917, with the Bolsheviks receiving only about 25 percent of the vote. The Constituent Assembly met for only one day, 18 January 1918, before being disbanded by the Bolsheviks.

7. The Zemgor (Zemsko-gorodskoi Soyuz) was an organization established on 10 July 1915 to assist in the Russian war effort on the home front. The Zemgor cared for the sick and wounded, supplied the army, and mobilized

national defense industries. After the Revolution, the Zemgor, operating in France, Yugoslavia, and Czechoslovakia, continued its relief efforts among refugees.

8. The Battle of Borodino was fought on 7 September (26 August, old style), 1812, during Napoleon's invasion of Russia. The Napoleonic troops narrowly defeated the Russian forces under General M. I. Kutuzov, and a week later Napoleon occupied Moscow.

Chapter 2

1. NEP (acronym for "New Economic Policy"). This policy was instituted by Lenin in 1921 to revive the Soviet economy, which had been ravaged by war and revolution. Under NEP a limited degree of private free enterprise was permitted in various spheres of the economy. The NEP period ended in 1928 with collectivization and the first five-year plan.

2. The Post-Revolutionary Club was organized by Prince Yu. A. Shirinsky-Shikhmatov as a synthesis of the political "Right" and "Left" of the emigration. Some of the members called themselves National-Maximalists.

3. The Front populaire was a coalition of left-wing parties in France in the thirties under the leadership of Léon Blum.

4. The "phony" war (la drôle de guerre), so called because of the tacit truce observed between French and German forces during these months, occurred during the period between the fall of Poland on 28 September 1939 and 10 May 1940.

5. In this sacrilegious narrative of 1821, Pushkin, under the influence of Voltaire, retells the events of the conception of Christ in scabrous terms.

6. The National Workers Union (Natsionalny Trudovoi Soyuz), a Russian fascist emigré organization sympathetic to the Nazis at the time, was originally called the National Union of the New Generation. Established by M. A. Georgievsky in 1932, the group drew most of its members from emigrés living in Yugoslavia and Bulgaria.

Chapter 3

1. Kryuchkov the Cossack, a character from a World War I cartoon series, singlehandedly fought and conquered entire German regiments.

2. The Maginot Line, the defensive fortification built in northeast France in the 1930s, was outflanked by German troops who invaded through Belgium in 1940.

3. The battle of Kulikovo, fought on Kulikovo Field on 8 September 1380 between the Russians, led by Prince Dmitry Donskoi, and Tartar forces under Mamay, was the first major Russian military victory over the forces of the Golden Horde.

4. The term *"Slanderers"* refers to those Western European countries who protested against the tsar's policies with regard to Poland. The reference comes from an 1831 patriotic poem by Pushkin entitled "To the Slanderers of Russia."

Chapter 4

1. The Orthodox Cause (*Pravoslavnoe delo*) was a religious-philanthropic movement begun in Paris by Mother Marie to help people in need.

2. The *Mladorossy* belonged to a monarchist emigré political party active in the 1930s (similar to the "young Turks" in the nineteenth century). The group drew its members from the "younger" generation, who had come of age in Europe after the Revolution. They went under the slogan Tsar and Soviets.

3. The "going to the people" movement, a populist crusade (ca. 1872–1874), sent large numbers of young intellectuals and radicals into the Russian countryside to educate and politicize the peasantry. It soon ended in dismal failure. Fondaminsky was willing to use the method, however, when it appeared necessary.

4. The Land and Freedom Party (Zemlya i Volya) was a secret society founded by the Populists in 1876 to promote peasant uprisings. It took its name from an earlier group (1861–1864).

5. The Decembrists were a group of young officers and intellectuals who wanted to see far-reaching changes in the imperial regime. The Decembrists' ideas were heavily influenced by Western liberal thought. On 26 December 1825, the day of Nicholas I's ascension to the throne, they staged a rebellion in St. Petersburg and the Ukraine, which was swiftly quashed. Five leaders were executed, and 121 were exiled to Siberia.

6. The Brest-Litovsk Treaty was a peace treaty signed by the Bolshevik Government on 3 March 1918 with the Central Powers (Germany, Austria-Hungary, Bulgaria, and Turkey); thus abandoning Russia's allies, France and England.

7. The Holy Synod (1721–1917), the governing body of the Russian Orthodox Church, was instituted by Peter the Great to replace the office of Patriarch of Moscow, in effect, turning the Church into a government department.

8. The Maximalists, a faction which split off from the Socialist Revolutionary Party, were widely involved in terrorist activities in the years following the 1905 Revolution, including the bombing of Stolypin's country house in 1906.

9. Kalyaev and Sazonov, together with Savinkov, organized the terrorist act against Grand Duke Sergei, Governor General of Petersburg.

10. The Petrashevsky Circle were a group of young Russian intellectuals who, from 1848 to 1849, met in the Petersburg apartment of M. Butashevich-Petrashevsky to discuss literature, philosophy, and French Utopian Socialism. In 1849, the majority of the members of the Petrashevsky Circle were arrested, imprisoned in the Peter and Paul Fortress, and tried. While some were soon released, others, Dostoevsky among them, were subjected to a mock execution and then exiled to Siberia.

11. Dr. Gaas, a saintly man, had a famous discussion with the notorious nineteenth-century Metropolitan Filaret, who defended the flogging of soldiers for misbehavior.

12. On 7 November 1917, the cruiser *Aurora* fired on the Winter Palace in Petrograd, leading to the surrender of the palace to the Bolsheviks.

13. The *pochvenniki* (Men of the Soil)—prominent among them Dostoevsky and his brother Mikhail, Nikolai Strakhov, and Apollon Grigoriev—believed that the Russian educated classes had cut themselves off from the soil and had to rediscover their roots in the peasantry. However, unlike the Slavophiles, who were in a sense their predecessors, the *pochvenniki* advocated a synthesis of Russian and Western culture.

The Eurasian movement, an emigré intellectual and political movement in the 1920s and 1930s, focused on Russia's unique geographical and cultural position straddling Europe and Asia. The Eurasians stressed the unavoidable nature of the Revolution and argued for a special Russian mission in contributing a spiritual dimension to Western technological culture.

14. Yudushka (Little Judas) is one of the protagonists of Saltykov-Shchedrin's novel *The Golovlyov Family*. Plyushkin is the miser in Gogol's *Dead Souls*.

15. Azev was a double agent, the chief of the SR terrorist organization at the time when he also worked for the tsar's secret police.

Chapter 5

1. Parisian note was a term used to characterize a trend in emigré literature among writers of the younger generation in Paris in the early 1930s. The expression is said to have originated with Boris Poplavsky; it was popularized in the literary criticism of Georgy Adamovich. The poets whose works best exemplified the style were Lydia Chervinskaya and Anatoly Steiger. The distinguishing features of the Parisian note were formal simplicity, an intimate tone, and a preoccupation with themes of evil, suffering, loneliness, and death.

Chapter 6

1. The Silver Age is an epithet applied to the artistic and intellectual renaissance of the early years of the twentieth century when Russian literature was dominated by the Symbolist poets. The term was derived by analogy from the "Golden (Pushkinian) Age" of Russian poetry.

2. The National Union of the Working Generation (Natsionalny soyuz trudovogo pokoleniya) was an emigré political party which for a time sympathized with Hitler.

3. The Union of Soviet Patriots was an organization founded in Paris after World War II among pro-Soviet emigrés. It published the newspaper *Sovetsky patriot*. The Union was shut down by the French government, and many of its members were deported.

4. The Third Testament was a central tenet of Merezhkovsky's idiosyncratic vision of Christianity. The first (Old) Testament of the Bible was that of the Father, the second (New) Testament was that of the Son, and the third and true Testament would herald the Second Coming and the Kingdom of the Holy Ghost.

5. The symbolism that flourished in Russia in the last decade of the nineteenth century and the first decade of the twentieth, although influenced by the French movement of the same name, differed from its French counterpart in its attraction to religious mysticism, especially to the philosophy of Vladimir Solovyov. The first generation of Russian symbolists included Gippius, Merezhkovsky, Balmont, Bryusov, and Sologub; the main representatives of the second generation were Bely, Blok, and Vyacheslav Ivanov.

8. Mesdames Volkonsky and Trubetskoy were wives of Decembrists who gained reknown for their steadfastness and loyalty when they left behind the comfortable life of the capital to follow their husbands into exile in Siberia.

9. Cheka is the acronym for the First Soviet secret police, of whom Dzerzhinsky was the head.

Chapter 7

1. The literary doctrine of socialist realism orginated in 1932 as the sole acceptable approach to literature in the Soviet Union and dominates official Soviet literature. In socialist realism, literary form is subordinated to the propagandistic portrayal in an optimistic vein of the historical victory of communism as embodied in the "Positive Hero."

2. Slavophiles were adherents of a movement among Russian intellectuals in the 1830s and 1840s. In opposition to the Westernizers, the Slavophiles argued that solutions to Russia's problems and the path of Russia's future development should be sought in traditional, religious pre-Petrine Russian values and institutions (such as the village commune). The primary exponents of Slavophilism were Ivan Kireevsky, Aleksei Khomyakov, Konstantin Aksakov, Ivan Aksakov, and Yury Samarin. The Slavophile-Westernizer debate has resurfaced persistently in Russian thought up to the present day.

The Westernizers were proponents of a line of thought prominent in Russia during the same decades. The Westernizers admired the reforms of Peter the Great and believed that Russia's future development should proceed along Western lines. The Westernizers embraced a broad political spectrum, ranging from the liberal Professor Timothy Granovsky to the more radical Herzen and Mikhail Bakunin, though with their individual deviations.

4. Alyosha Karamazov and Platon Karataev were characters from *The Brothers Karamazov* and *War and Peace,* respectively.

5. The Tower was the famous literary salon hosted by the poet Vyacheslav Ivanov in Petersburg before the Revolution.

6. The Union of Soviet Repatriates was a collection of organizations founded

among emigrés in France and other countries by Soviet representatives in the years preceding the Second World War, their purpose to lure emigrés back to the Soviet Union.

Chapter 8

1. Third Rome, the doctrine of Russian messianism, was reportedly conceived by the monk Philotheus of Pskov during the reign of Ivan III. The doctrine held that the first two "Romes" (Rome and Byzantium) had fallen away from the true faith, a belief ostensibly encouraged by the capture of Constantinople by the Turks in 1453, and that the spiritual center of Orthodox Christianity had moved to Moscow. "Two Romes have fallen, a third stands, a fourth there shall not be. . . ."

2. The Oboroncheskoe movement was active in the mid-1930s as a means of defending the Russian territories. The members of the movement looked at Germany and Japan as potential aggressors.

3. Perekop, the isthmus connecting the Crimea to the mainland, was the site of Wrangel's last-ditch defense.

4. The four-volume *Sensible Dictionary of the Living Russian Language*, compiled in 1863–1866 by Vladimir Dahl is the much-sought commodity.

Chapter 9

1. The Bestuzhev Institute, founded in 1878 in Petersburg, was one of the first institutes of higher learning for women.

Chapter 10

1. The Union of Students from the Soviet Union was a pro-Soviet association allegedly made up of students from the Soviet Union living in Paris.

Chapter 11

1. *Mensheviks*—At the Second Congress of the Russian Social Democratic Party, held in Brussels and London in 1903, the Party split into two factions. The majority were called the Bolsheviks and the minority, Mensheviks. The latter were less dogmatic and democratic Marxists.

2. *Poshlo* was a favorite expression of Nabokov, meaning "trivial." Triviality was worse than any sin as far as Nabokov was concerned.

3. The quotation is from A. Fet.

Persons Mentioned in the Text

GEORGY VIKTOROVICH ADAMOVICH (1894–1972). Important emigré critic and Acmeist poet, emigrated in 1922. He was one of the most influential emigré critics of his generation, serving as chief critic on *Poslednie novosti* (1928–1939). In his criticism he promoted the so-called Parisian note in emigré poetry.

M. AGEEV (real name: Marc Levi). Emigré prose writer. First gained recognition on the emigré literary scene with the publication of an excerpt from his *Novel with Cocaine (Roman s kokainom)* in the last issue of *Chisla* (1934). In 1936 the novel was published in its entirety in a separate edition by the editorial board of the Paris Union of Writers, which consisted of V. S. Yanovsky and Yury Felsen. After the publication of his novel, Ageev, publishing nothing further of importance, faded from prominence. Recently "scholars" have promoted the groundless claim that Ageev was a pseudonym for Nabokov.

ANNA ANDREEVNA AKHMATOVA (née Anna Gorenko) (1889–1966). Major Acmeist poet. Wife of Nikolai Gumilyov. Akhmatova remained in Russia after the October Revolution, but after 1922 her poetry was not published there. In 1946, Akhmatova, along with Zoshchenko, came under personal attack by Zhdanov and was expelled from the Writers' Union. During the "Thaw" period after Stalin's death, Akhmatova was once again able to publish in her home country, although some of her works—notably the long poem *Requiem* (1935–1940)—have yet to appear in the Soviet Union.

MARK ALEKSANDROVICH ALDANOV (pseud. M. Landau) (1886–1957). Prolific emigré prose writer. Aldanov emigrated from Russia in 1919 and came to Paris to live in 1924. Although closer in age to the "older" generation of emigré writers who had made their reputations in Russia before coming to the West, Aldanov became known as a writer only in emigration. His reputation was launched with the publication (1921–1927) of a tetralogy of historical novels. He was probably the most successful writer of his generation with non-Russian readers, and his works were widely translated. In 1940, Aldanov moved to New York, and, in 1947, he settled in Nice, where he lived until his death.

A. A. ALYOKHIN (1892–1946). Chess player. Alyokhin emigrated from Russia in 1921 and was world chess champion from 1927–1935 and 1937–1946.

VERA ALEKSANDROVNA ALEKSANDROVA (real name: Shvarts; née Mordvinova) (1895–1966). Emigré critic, a member of the Menshevik party. Aleksandrova emigrated from Russia in 1921 and took up residence first in Germany and later in France. She published extensively in the Menshevik journal *Sotsialistichesky vestnik*. After the fall of France in 1940, Aleksandrova moved to the United States. From 1951 to 1956, she served as editor-in-chief of the Chekhov Publishing House in New York.

NIKOLAI NIKOLAEVICH ALEKSEEV (1879–1964). Professor of history. Alekseev emigrated from Russia in 1920 and settled for a time in Yugoslavia.

ANATOLY ALFYOROV. Emigré prose writer. Alfyorov contributed a few short stories to *Chisla* and published an excerpt from a novel in *Krug*.

DON AMINADO (real name: Aminad Petrovich Shpolyansky) (1888–1957). Satirical poet. Emigrated from Russia in 1920. Don Aminado was a permanent contributor to *Poslednie novosti* of humorous verse and stories poking fun at emigré life and politics. He also collaborated on *Satirikon* when an attempt was made to revive the former Petersburg satirical journal in Paris in 1931. After the Second World War, Don Aminado published a volume of memoirs entitled *The Train on the Third Track* (Poezd na tretiem puti).

LEONID NIKOLAEVICH ANDREEV (1871–1919). Prose writer and playwright who enjoyed great popularity in Russia during the early years of the twentieth century. Among Andreev's best-known works are the stories "The Red Laugh" (1905) and "The Story of Seven Who Were Hanged" (1908) and the play *He Who Gets Slapped* (1915). He left Russia in 1917 in opposition to the Bolshevik Revolution and died in Finland.

VADIM LEONIDOVICH ANDREEV (1902–1976). Writer of fiction, poetry, and memoirs. Son of Leonid Andreev. The Andreevs left Russia in 1917. Vadim Andreev participated in the French Résistance during World War II and, in 1946, took Soviet citizenship and returned to the Soviet Union.

YURY PAVLOVICH ANNENKOV (pseud. Boris Temiryazev) (1889–1974). Painter, prose writer, and set designer. Annenkov emigrated from Russia in 1924. Although an artist by vocation, primarily known as a portrait painter, in emigration he proved himself to be a talented writer as well. Annenkov's literary works include the story "The House at 5 Rozhdestvensky Street" ("Domik na 5-oi Rozhdestvenskoi," 1928) and the novel *A Tale of Trifles* (Povest o pustyakakh, 1934).

INNOKENTY FYODOROVICH ANNENSKY (1856–1909). Outstanding poet, critic, dramatist, teacher and translator of Classical Greek. He published his first collection of verse in 1904. Although his poetry was clearly influenced by the French Symbolists, Annensky played no role in the growth of the Russian symbolist movement, but he was greatly admired by the Acmeists. He was the main influence on the Parisian note in emigré poetry.

ASKOLDOV. Orchestra leader.

W. H. (WYSTAN HUGH) AUDEN (1907–1973). Influential poet and man of letters.

ARKADY TIMOFEEVICH AVERCHENKO (1881–1925). Popular pre-Revolutionary writer of humorous stories and one-act plays. Averchenko served as editor of the satirical journals *Satirikon* (1908–1914) and *Novy Satirikon* (1913–1918). The writer left Russia in 1920 and settled first in Constantinople and later in Prague.

NIKOLAI DMITRIEVICH AVKSENTIEV (1878–1943). Leading Socialist revolutionary. Avksentiev served as minister of the interior in the Provisional Government and, during the Civil War, was involved in the anti-Bolshevik government at Ufa. He emigrated to France, where he became a member of the editorial board of *Sovremennye zapiski*. Avksentiev emigrated to the United States in 1940.

ARCHPRIEST AVVAKUM (1620–1682). Leading apologist for the Old Believers who broke away from the official Church in the mid-seventeenth century in reaction to the reforms of Patriarch Nikon. Avvakum's *Life Written by Himself* (1669–1676), in which the author describes in graphic detail and in vivid colloquial language the persecutions he suffered for his beliefs, is among the most striking works of old Russian literature. Avvakum was burned at the stake in 1682.

EVNO-MEYER AZEF (Evgeny Filipovich Azev) (1869–1918). Notorious double agent. Acting as an informant for the Russian police, Azef rose to a high position in the terrorist apparatus of the Socialist Revolutionary party. He became head of the party's terrorist organization in 1903 and, in 1905, became a member of the SR Central Committee. He was responsible for arranging the assassinations of Plehve and the Grand Duke Sergei Aleksandrovich. Azef's ties with the police were exposed in 1908, causing a major scandal.

ISAAK EMMANUILOVICH BABEL (1894–1941). One of the most important Soviet prose writers of the 1920s. Babel's reputation rests primarily on his short stories on Jewish life in Odessa and on his most famous work, *Red Cavalry* (1926), a cycle of stories based on his own experiences as a war correspondent with Semyon Budyonny's First Cavalry during the Civil War. Babel was arrested in 1939 and disappeared in the camps. According to official reports, he died there in 1941.

FATHER BAKST. Russian priest. Originally a Protestant minister in Latvia, Bakst converted to Russian Orthodoxy in Paris and ended up in Marseilles.

TATIANA BAKUNINA OSORGINA. Literary scholar. Wife of M. A. Osorgin.

KONSTANTIN DMITRIEVICH BALMONT (1867–1942). Major symbolist poet. Balmont was extremely popular before the Revolution and had already established his place in Russian literature when he emigrated to France in 1920, and, by that time, he was generally felt to be well past his prime. In emigration he published a number of collections of verse (most notably, *V razdvinutoi dali* [1930]), a novel entitled *Pod novym serpom,* and short stories.

VISSARION GRIGORIEVICH BELINSKY (1811–1848). One of the most influential literary critics of the nineteenth century. Belinsky originated the enduring Russian tradition of using literary criticism as a forum for social and political commentary.

ANDREI BELY (real name: Boris Nikolaevich Bugaev, 1880–1934). Major symbolist poet and novelist. Influenced by the philosophy of Vladimir Solovyov and by the anthroposophy of Rudolph Steiner. Bely's novels include *The Silver Dove* (1910) and his masterpiece, *Petersburg* (1916, 1922). Bely lived in Europe from 1921 to 1923, when he returned to Russia and remained there until his death.

NINA NIKOLAEVNA BERBEROVA (1901–). Emigré poet, prose writer, and critic, Khodasevich's second wife. Berberova left Russia in 1922 and took up residence in Europe. She moved to the United States in 1950 and later taught Russian literature at Princeton University.

NIKOLAI ALEKSANDROVICH BERDYAEV (1874–1948). Philosopher. Berdyaev was exiled from the Soviet Union in 1922 for his religious views and took up residence in France. His philosophy traces its roots back to Dostoevsky and Vladimir Solovyov, and its main tenets are Christian personalism and existentialism.

HELENA PETROVNA BLAVATSKY (née Hahn) (1831–1891). Russian spiritualist. Traveled extensively in Europe, the United States, Asia, India, and Tibet. A founder of the Theosophical Society in New York, she served as editor of the society's journal, the *Theosophist,* from 1879–1888. Her most important work on theosophy is *The Secret Doctrine* (1888).

ALEKSANDR ALEKSANDROVICH BLOK (1880–1921). Leading symbolist poet and playwright. Initially greeting the October Revolution with enthusiasm, as expressed in his 1918 poem *The Twelve,* he died disillusioned. For later Russian intellectuals, Blok came to symbolize the spirit of the Russian intelligentsia, with its dreams of a "liberating" revolution dashed by the authoritarian reality of the Soviet State.

LÉON BLUM (1872–1950). First Socialist Premier of France. Presided over the Popular Front coalition government in 1936–1937.

IVAN BOLDYREV (real name: Ivan Andreevich Shkott) (1903–1933). Emigré prose writer. Boldyrev's novel *Boys and Girls* (Malchiki i devochki) was the first work to be published in the short-lived New Writers Series under the editorship of M. A. Osorgin. He committed suicide in 1933.

BORIS BOZHNEV. Emigré poet of the "younger" generation. Bozhnev's three books of poetry—*Struggle for Nonexistence* (*Borba za nesushchestvovanie*, 1925), *Fountain* (*Fontan*, 1927), and *Silentium sociologicum* (1936)—earned him a respectable reputation in the Parisian emigré community.

VALERY YAKOVLEVICH BRYUSOV (1873–1924). Symbolist poet, prose writer, editor, and critic. Bryusov was the self-proclaimed founder and, for a time, the acknowledged leader of the Russian symbolist movement as well as one of its chief poets. His most successful collections of poetry were *Tertia Vigilia* (1900) and *Wreath* (1906). Bryusov broke with the symbolists toward the end of the first decade of the twentieth century and turned his energies to translation and scholarly studies. Before his death, Bryusov served in a number of official posts in the new Soviet literary administration, and, in 1920, he joined the Communist party.

NIKOLAI IVANOVICH BUKHARIN (1887–1938). Leading Bolshevik theorist. His works include the *ABC of Communism* (1920) and the *Theory of Historical Materialism* (1921). He was tried at a show trial in 1937, condemned to death for high treason, and executed.

SERGEI NIKOLAEVICH BULGAKOV (Father Sergei) (1871–1944). Religious philosopher. Bulgakov was exiled from Russia by the Soviet government in 1922 and took up residence first in Prague and then in Paris, where he taught at the Russian Orthodox Theological Institute.

A. BULKIN (real name, Aleksandr Yakovlevich Braslavsky). Emigré poet.

BUNAKOV. *See* Ilya Isidorovich Fondaminsky.

IVAN ALEKSEEVICH BUNIN (1870–1953). Prose writer in the realist tradition, first published in 1888. Bunin emigrated to Paris after the Bolshevik Revolution, and, in 1933, became the first Russian writer to be awarded the Nobel Prize for literature.

VERA NIKOLAEVNA BUNINA (née Muromtseva) (1881–1961). Wife of Bunin. While still in Russia, Bunina translated Flaubert into Russian. In 1959, in emigration, she published her book *Zhizn Bunina* (The Life of Bunin). Her reminiscences appeared in *Novy zhurnal* and *Grani*.

ALEKSANDR BUROV. Businessman and writer. Burov published in *Chisla,* and his early books of short stories were received favorably by emigré critics.

BORIS BUTKEVICH. Prose writer. Author of some very good short stories published in several emigré journals, including *Novy korabl* and *Chisla.* The young writer's career was cut short when he died in Marseilles, where he had been working on the waterfront as a stevedore.

LOUIS-FERDINAND CÉLINE (pseud. Louis-Ferdinand Destouches) (1894–1961). Major French writer. Collaborated with the Nazis.

PYOTR YAKOVLEVICH CHAADAEV (1794–1856). Philosopher. His most famous work, the *Philosophical Letters* (1829, originally written in French), is a harsh critique of Russia and the Russian Orthodox tradition that has had a lasting influence on the development of Russian thought. The publication of the *Philosophical Letters* in Russian in 1836 brought Chaadaev into disfavor with the authorities. He was declared insane and placed under house arrest for over a year by Nicholas I.

FYODOR IVANOVICH CHALIAPIN (1873–1938). World-famous Russian basso. Chaliapin was discovered in 1896 by the producer Savva Mamontov. He sang with Mamontov's Private Opera Company and the Bolshoi Company in Moscow and at the Mariinsky Theater in Petersburg. From 1901 on, Chaliapin toured widely in the West, and, beginning in 1909, he appeared in Diaghilev productions. Chaliapin emigrated permanently from Russia in 1921.

COUNT CHAPSKY (Czapski). Painter and essayist, editor of *Kultura* after World War II.

SERGEI IVANOVICH CHARCHOUNE (Sharshun) (1889–1975). Painter and writer. Charchoune settled in Paris in 1912 and became the only Russian painter involved in the dadaist movement. Although primarily known as a painter, he earned a reputation as a writer as well, based on excerpts from his novels published in *Chisla* in 1930–1932. Charchoune referred to himself as a "magic realist."

ANTON PAVLOVICH CHEKHOV (1860–1904). Acknowledged in Russia as in the West as one of the great short story writers and dramatists in world literature. His most famous plays are *The Sea Gull* (1899), *Uncle Vanya* (1899), *Three Sisters* (1901), and *The Cherry Orchard* (1903).

VIKTOR MIKHAILOVICH CHERNOV (1873–1952). Leader of the Socialist Revolutionary party from its inception in 1901. Chernov served as minister of agriculture in the Provisional Government and was elected chairman of the Constituent Assembly at its only meeting. During the Civil War, Chernov was head of a

Socialist Revolutionary government set up in Samara. After being arrested by the Bolsheviks and then freed by the forces of Admiral Kolchak, Chernov fled to the West, living out his life in Europe and later the United States.

NIKOLAI GAVRILOVICH CHERNYSHEVSKY (1828–1889). Influential "radical" critic, editor, and novelist. Chernyshevsky continued and more explicitly politicized the Russian critical tradition that began with Belinsky. He became coeditor of the "thick" journal *Sovremennik* in 1859. In 1862, the journal was closed, and Chernyshevsky was arrested. While imprisoned in the Peter and Paul Fortress in St. Petersburg, he wrote the novel, *What Is to Be Done?* (1863), which has had a lasting influence on Russian revolutionary literature. From 1864, Chernyshevsky spent the rest of his life in forced exile.

CHERTOK. Editor.

LYDIA DAVYDOVNA CHERVINSKAYA (1907–). Emigré poet. Chervinskaya's personal, diarylike lyrics exemplify the so-called Parisian note in emigré poetry.

KONSTANTIN ALEKSANDROVICH CHKHEIDZE (1897–?). Socialist Revolutionary political figure. Chkheidze was noted for his eloquence.

SASHA CHORNY (real name: Aleksandr Mikhailovich Glikberg) (1880–1932). Satirist, poet, and prose writer. Chorny, an active contributor to the Petersburg satirical journal *Satirikon,* was well known in Russia before the Revolution as a political satirist. In 1920, he emigrated first to Berlin and then to Paris. In emigration, Chorny published two books of satire as well as collections of lyrical poetry and childrens' verses.

JEAN COCTEAU (1889–1963). French film director, poet, novelist, actor, and painter.

CHARLOTTE CORDAY (1768–1793). Assassin of the French revolutionary Jean-Paul Marat.

VLADIMIR IVANOVICH DAHL (Dal) (1801–1872). Writer and collector of Russian folklore. Dahl's four-volume *Sensible Dictionary of the Living Russian Language* (1863–1866) and his *Proverbs of the Russian People* (1862) remain standard sources for students and scholars of the Russian language.

DOROTHY DAY (1897–1980). Journalist, writer. Together with Peter Mauria, founder of the Catholic Worker movement and publication and one of the greatest social-religious American figures.

ANTON ANTONOVICH DELVIG (1798–1831). Poet and editor. Delvig attended the Tsarskoe Selo Lycée with Pushkin, and the two remained close friends for life.

Delvig served as editor of the almanac *Northern Flowers* (1825–1831) and of the newspaper the *Literary Gazette* (1830–1831).

IGOR PLATONOVICH DEMIDOV. Journalist. Friend and assistant of the editor-in-chief of *Poslednie novosti*, Pavel Nikolaevich Milyukov.

YURY PETROVICH DENIKE (1887–1964). Menshevik publicist and editor. In the United States from 1940, he became a member of the editorial staff of the New York-based journal *Novy zhurnal*.

GENERAL ANTON IVANOVICH DENIKIN (1872–1947). Commander of the White Volunteer Army which fought against the Bolshevik forces in the Civil War.

GAVRILA ROMANOVICH DERZHAVIN (1743–1816). Major Russian poet of the pre-Pushkin period.

SERGEI PAVLOVICH DIAGHILEV (1872–1929). Russian impressario who played a leading role in introducing Russian culture to the West. Diaghilev was instrumental in founding the lavish illustrated journal the *World of Art* (1898–1904). After organizing the first, wildly successful performances of Russian ballet in Europe in 1909–1910, Diaghilev formed the permanent touring company of the Ballets russes in 1911. He is buried in Venice.

FYODOR MIKHAILOVICH DOSTOEVSKY (1821–1881). One of the world's great novelists. Less well-known in the West is the writer's journalistic activity. Founder and editor of the journals *Time* (1861–1863) and *Epoch* (1864), his most ambitious journalistic enterprise was the monthly *Diary of a Writer* (1876–1877, 1881), which he himself wrote and published.

VALERIAN FYODOROVICH DRYAKHLOV. Poet of the Paris school.

FELIKS EDMUNDOVICH DZERZHINSKY (1877–1926). Bolshevik leader. In 1917, appointed by Lenin the first head of the Cheka (Extraordinary Commission for Fighting the Counter-revolution, renamed OGPU in 1922), a post he held until his death.

SERGEI YAKOVLEVICH EFRON (1893–1940). Husband of Tsvetaeva. In Paris, Efron worked as an editor on the journal *Vyorsty* and became involved in the Union of Repatriates. After being exposed as an agent of the Cheka and implicated in a political assassination, Efron fled to Russia, where he was shot shortly after Tsvetaeva followed him there in 1939.

ILYA GRIGORIEVICH EHRENBURG (1891–1967). Soviet prose writer and journalist. Because his works so accurately mirror shifts in Soviet literary policy, Ehrenburg earned a reputation as a "barometer" of the official line.

ALEKSEI VLADIMIROVICH EISNER. Poet and prose writer. Eisner lived for a time in Prague, where he belonged to the *Skit poetov* group and published in the Prague-based journal *Volya Rossii*. He became involved with Sergei Efron and fled to the Soviet Union before World War II.

VIKTOR NIKOLAEVICH EMELIANOV (1899–1963). Prose writer. Published in *Krug*.

ALEKSANDR IVANOVICH ERTEL (1855–1908). Prose writer. His most notable work is a two-volume epic novel entitled *The Gardenins, Their Retainers, Their Friends, and Their Enemies* (1889), which was published with an introduction by Lev Tolstoi.

SERGEI ALEKSANDROVICH ESENIN (1895–1925). Soviet poet. Married to Isadora Duncan from 1923 to 1924. Esenin came from a peasant background, and village life supplied the central theme for his poetry. He committed suicide by hanging in a Leningrad hotel room and is viewed by many as an early martyr to the Soviet literary bureaucracy.

GEORGY EVANGULOV. Emigré poet and prose writer. Evangulov published two books of poetry in Paris in the 1920s, and his short stories appeared in *Sovremennye zapiski* in the 1930s.

KONSTANTIN ALEKSANDROVICH FEDIN (1892–1977). Soviet novelist. Fedin's first novel, *Cities and Years* (1924), is marked by formal experimentation. From the thirties on, however, he toed the Socialist Realist line in his works and, from 1959, served as general secretary of the Soviet Writers' Union.

GEORGY PETROVICH FEDOTOV (1886–1951). Russian religious thinker. Fedotov emigrated to France in 1925 and, in 1940, to the United States, where he taught at Union Theological Seminary and St. Vladimir's Theological Seminary until his death. Fedotov's most influential scholarly work is the two-volume *Russian Religious Mind* (1946–1966).

YURY FELSEN (Felzen) (real name: Nikolai Berngardovich Freidenshtein) (1895–1943?). Emigré prose writer and literary critic. Felsen was a member of the "younger" generation of emigré writers, and he wrote under the influence of Western European literature, especially the works of Proust. His novels—*Deception* (Obman, 1930), *Happiness* (Schastie, 1932), and *Letters about Lermontov* (Pisma o Lermontove, 1935–1936)—are formally complex and virtually plotless. His third book was published by the Paris Union of Writers. Felsen was killed by the Germans during World War II, on his way to Switzerland.

AFANASY AFANASIEVICH FET (1820–1892). Major poet. Fet published his first book of poetry in 1840, and two more collections followed in the 1850s. Although Fet's poetry was originally well received, he came under attack by the radical critics in the late fifties and early sixties for his conservative political and literary views and did not publish another book of poetry until 1883. Fet was influenced by the philosophy of Schopenhauer and was a close friend of Lev Tolstoi.

DMITRY VLADIMIROVICH FILOSOFOV (1872–1940). Editor and publicist. Close associate of the Merezhkovskys. Before the Revolution, Filosofov served as literary editor of the journal *World of Art* and aided the Merezhkovskys in founding the Religious-Philosophical Society of St. Petersburg in 1901. In emigration, he was editor of the Warsaw newspaper *Za svobodu*.

GEORGY VASILIEVICH FLOROVSKY (1893–). Priest and religious thinker. He served as a professor of Patristics in Paris from 1926 to 1939 and, from 1939 to 1955, he was a professor and dean of St. Vladimir's Seminary in New York. He also taught at Harvard and Princeton universities.

ILYA ISIDOROVICH FONDAMINSKY (pseud. I. Bunakov) (1888–1942). Socialist Revolutionary, editor and publicist. Fondaminsky was commissar of the Black Sea Fleet under Kerensky. In emigration, he served as a member of the editorial board of *Sovremennye zapiski* and, in the 1930s, as editor of the journal *Novy grad*. In 1935, Fondaminsky founded, in conjunction with *Novy grad,* the Circle literary society. He died in a concentration camp during the Second World War.

SEMYON LYUDVIGOVICH FRANK (1877–1950). Religious philosopher. Frank converted to Russian Orthodoxy in 1912. He taught philosophy at the universities of Saint Petersburg, Saratov, and Moscow until he was expelled from Russia by the Soviet Government in 1922. In emigration, he lived in Berlin, then in France, and after World War II he moved to London, where he died.

NIKOLAI FYODOROVICH FYODOROV (1828–1903). Religious philosopher and librarian of the Rumyantsev Museum in Moscow. In his *Philosophy of the Common Cause* (1906, 1913), which was compiled from his notes after his death, Fyodorov argued that mankind should unite in the common project of finding scientific means to raise the dead. Fyodorov was greatly admired by such major figures as Solovyov, Dostoevsky, and Tolstoi.

GEORGY (GAITO) IVANOVICH GAZDANOV (1903–1971). One of the young generation of emigré writers, he wrote under the influence of current trends in Western literature. Gazdanov's first novel, *An Evening at Claire's* (Vecher u Kler) was published in Paris in 1930. His short stories and novels appeared in *Volya Rossii, Chisla,* and *Sovremennye zapiski*. All five of Gazdanov's post–World War II novels were published in *Novy zhurnal*.

ANDRÉ GIDE (1869–1938). Major French writer.

ALEKSANDR SAMSONOVICH GINGER (1897–1965). Highly respected emigré poet. Husband of Anna Prismanova. Ginger's poems and short stories appeared in such Parisian emigré publications as *Chisla* and *Krug,* and he published five collections of poetry: *Svora vernykh* (1922), *Predannost* (1925), *Zhaloba i tvorchestvo* (1939), *Vest* (1957), and *Serdtse* (1965). He was also affiliated with the Kochevie literary group.

ZINAIDA NIKOLAEVNA GIPPIUS (pseud. Anton Krainy and Lev Pushchin) (1869–1945). Major symbolist poet and prose writer. Wife of Dmitry Merezhkovsky. The Merezhkovskys emigrated from Russia in 1919 and, after participating in a resistance organization against the Bolsheviks in Poland, settled in Paris in 1920. Gippius' writing is marked by a strong religious and philosophical bent. She played an active role in emigré literary and philosophical life, organizing with her husband in 1926 the Green Lamp Society, a philosophical and literary discussion group. Gippius stands with Akhmatova as one of the foremost women writers in modern Russian literature.

NIKOLAI VASILIEVICH GOGOL (1809–1852). Gogol is best known in the West for the play *The Inspector General* (1836), the short stories "The Nose" (1836) and "The Overcoat" (1842), and his masterpiece, the novel *Dead Souls* (1842).

ALLA SERGEEVNA GOLOVINA (1911–). Poet. Sister of Anatoly Steiger. A member for a time of the Prague literary group Skit poetov, Golovina later moved to France. Her only book of poetry, *Lebedinaya karusel,* was published in 1935.

NATALIA SERGEEVNA GONCHAROVA (1871–1962). Neoprimitivist painter. Wife of Larionov.

PAVEL GORGULOV (pseud. Pavel Bred). Russian emigré writer who assassinated the French president, Paul Doumer, in 1932.

MAKSIM GORKY (real name: Aleksei Maksimovich Peshkov) (1868–1936). Major Russian realist prose writer and dramatist. He was actively associated with the revolutionary intelligentsia. Between 1921 and 1931 he lived mainly at a villa in Sorrento which served as a gathering place for Soviet writers. He returned to the Soviet Union permanently in 1931 and died there under suspicious circumstances in 1936. Gorky has been canonized by the Soviet literary establishment as a founder of official Soviet literature.

ALEKSANDR SERGEEVICH GRIBOEDOV (1795–1829). Playwright. His satirical play, *Woe from Wit* (1823–1824) is a classic of the Russian theater. Griboedov was killed in a riot while serving as Russian minister to Persia.

IRINA GRJEBINA (Grzhebina) (1908–). Dancer, daughter of the well-known pre-revolutionary publisher Z. Grzhebin. Grjebina came to Paris when she was a child and studied dance under Olga Preobrazhenskaya. She danced for a time with the Opéra Russe and, in 1938, opened her own studio de danse on Boulevard Montparnasse. Since 1973 she has been teaching classes in character dancing at the Paris Opera.

ROMAN NIKOLAEVICH GRYNBERG (1897–196?). Businessman, editor, and publisher. Grynberg was one of the original editors of the journal *Opyty,* which began coming out in New York in 1935. Between 1960 and 1967, he published nine issues of the almanac *Vozdushnye puti.*

NIKOLAI SERGEEVICH GUMILYOV (1886–1921). Acmeist poet and theoretician. Husband of Anna Akhmatova from 1910 to 1918. Gumilyov played a leading role in defining the aesthetic principles of Acmeism and in organizing the Acmeists as a literary group in opposition to the fading influence of the Symbolists. The poet was executed by the Soviet authorities in 1921. A number of the most talented Parisian poets began writing under the influence of Gumilyov's *Tsekh poetov* and later broke away.

ALEKSANDR IVANOVICH HERZEN (1812–1870). Russian writer and liberal publicist. Herzen left Russia for Europe in 1847. In 1855, in collaboration with the poet Nikolai Ogaryov, he began publishing the journal *North Star* in London and, in 1857, the *Bell.* Despite the censorship, Herzen's emigré publications circulated widely in Russia in the years preceding the emancipation of the serfs in 1861. Herzen's memoirs, *My Past and Thoughts* (1852–1868), are a great literary achievement and a major historical document.

HIPPIUS. *See* Zinaida Nikolaevna Gippius.

PANAIT ISTRATI (1884–1935). Romanian and French novelist.

HELENE (ELENA ALEKSANDROVNA) ISWOLSKY (1896–1973). Her father was the diplomat A. P. Izvolsky, whose last appointment was as imperial ambassador to France. After the Revolution, her family remained in Paris, where she studied, converted to Catholicism, and became the friend of many outstanding French and Russian literary and religious figures. She wrote articles, did translations, and wrote a number of books, notably *Light before Dusk* and *Christ in Russia.* After coming to the United States in 1941, she taught Russian literature at Fordham University. She was the soul of the *Third Hour,* an ecumenical journal which she founded together with Irma de Manziarli, V. S. Yanovsky, and Arthur Lourié in New York in 1944.

IVAN I (Kalita). Grand prince of Moscow from 1328 until his death in 1341. Ivan Kalita began the "unification of the Russian lands," which led eventually to the Muscovite hegemony over all of Russia.

IVAN IV (the Terrible) (1530–1584). Grand prince of Moscow and, from 1547, tsar of Russia.

GEORGY VLADIMIROVICH IVANOV (1894–1958). Emigré poet and prose writer. Husband of I. Odoevtseva. His first book of poetry appeared in 1912. A member of the Acmeist Poets' Guild founded by Gumilyov. The Ivanovs emigrated to Paris in 1922. A leading poet of the emigration, Ivanov also wrote memoirs and a striking work of experimental fiction entitled *Disintegration of the Atom* (Raspad atoma, 1938). Ivanov's most important book of poetry is *Roses* (Rozy, 1931).

VSEVOLOD VYACHESLAVOVICH IVANOV (1895–1963). Soviet prose writer and dramatist. Ivanov's most famous work is *Armored Train No. 14-69* (novella, 1922; play, 1927).

VYACHESLAV IVANOVICH IVANOV (1866–1949). Major symbolist theoretician and poet and classical scholar. Host of the famous salon the Tower, which met in Ivanov's apartment in St. Petersburg from 1905 to 1910. Ivanov left Russia for Italy in 1924 and taught Russian literature at the University of Pavia from 1926 to 1934. He retired to Rome, where he converted to Catholicism.

YURY PAVLOVICH IVASK (1907–1986). Emigré poet and scholar. After the Revolution, Ivask lived in Estonia, where he published his first book of poetry, *Severny bereg*, in 1938. Displaced to Germany during the Second World War, he moved to the United States in 1949. His second book of verse, *Tsarskaya osen*, appeared in 1953; in 1954, he received his doctorate in Russian literature at Harvard University and taught at a number of American universities. He produced a body of critical studies on Russian writers.

JEAN JAURÈS (1859–1914). French socialist leader assassinated in 1914.

LEV BORISOVICH KAMENEV (real name: Rosenfeld) (1883–1936). Major Bolshevik political figure. A member of the Bolshevik party from its inception in 1903, after the October Revolution, he held a number of important posts in the Soviet government. In 1936, Kamenev fell victim to the Stalinist purges; sentenced to death at a show trial, he was executed.

MIKHAIL MIKHAILOVICH KARPOVICH (1888–1959). Historian. Karpovich came to the United States in 1917 as a secretary of the Russian embassy, and from 1927 he taught Russian history at Harvard University. From 1943 to his death he was an editor of the New York–based *Novy zhurnal* (chief editor from 1946).

ANTON VLADIMIROVICH KARTASHOV (1875–1961). Leading churchman and historian. Headed the church administration under the Provisional Government. Kartashov emigrated to France in 1919 and served as dean of the St. Sergius Theological Institute in Paris.

KASIANKINA. One of the early defectors from the USSR.

VALENTIN PETROVICH KATAEV (1897–). Soviet prose writer. Kataev's long career has spanned the entire history of Soviet literature, and the writer has changed the direction of his writing several times to conform to prevailing Soviet literary politics. Kataev's major works are the adventure novel *The Embezzlers* (1927), the socialist realist novel *Time, Forward!* (1932), and the semiautobiographical childhood memoir *The Lonely White Sail Is Gleaming* (1936).

ALEKSANDR LVOVICH KAZEM-BEK. Leader of the Mladorossy. Kazem-Bek founded the Mladorossy in Paris in 1930.

LAZAR IZRAILEVICH KELBERIN (1907–). Poet. Kelberin published in *Chisla* and served for a short time as secretary of the almanac. His collection of verse, entitled *Idol,* was published in 1930.

ALEKSANDR FYODOROVICH KERENSKY (1881–1970). Lawyer, statesman, editor, and political writer. Kerensky, a member of the Trudovik party, was elected to the Fourth State Duma in 1912. After the February Revolution, he served first as minister of justice and then, from June 1917, as president of the Provisional Government. After the Bolsheviks seized power, he emigrated to Europe. Living first in Berlin and later in Paris, Kerensky edited the newspaper *Golos Rossii* and the journals *Dni* and *Novaya Rossiya.* He died in New York.

VLADISLAV FELITSIANOVICH KHODASEVICH (1886–1939). Poet and critic. Khodasevich's works first began to appear in print in 1905, and he published three books of poetry—*Molodost* (1908), *Shchastlivy domik* (1914), and *Putem zerna* (1920)—in Russia before emigrating to Western Europe in 1922. His first collection of verse to be published abroad was *Tyazhelaya lira* (1923). His last collection, *Evropeiskaya noch,* was never published separately but appeared only in his collected works (1927). From 1927 until his death, he served as main literary critic of *Vozrozhdenie.*

ALEKSEI STEPANOVICH KHOMYAKOV (1804–1860). Leading Slavophile ideologist, theologian, and poet. Khomyakov argued the superiority of Russian culture, rooted in the Orthodox Church, over the "dying" civilization of the West. His concept of *sobornost* (the spiritual communion of believers) has had a lasting influence on Russian thought.

NIKITA SERGEEVICH KHRUSHCHEV (1894–1971). First secretary of the Communist party from 1953 to 1963.

VLADIMIR MIKHAILOVICH KIRSHON (1902–1938). Soviet dramatist, a leading member of RAPP (Russian Association of Proletarian Writers). His best known work is the play *Bread* (Khleb, 1930). Kirshon was executed during the purges of the thirties.

TATIANA KISELYOVA. Anthroposophist, disciple and friend of Rudolph Steiner.

NIKOLAI ANDREEVICH KLEPININ (?–1937). Emigré historian. Returned to the Soviet Union and vanished there.

IRINA NIKOLAEVNA KNORRING (1906–1943). Poet. Wife of Yury Bek-Sofiev. Influenced by Akhmatova, she published three collections of verse: *Stikhi o sebe* (1931), *Okna na sever* (1939), and *Posle vsego* (1949, posthumously).

DOVID KNUT (real name: David Mironovich Fiksman) (1900–1955). Emigré poet and prose writer. Last husband of Ariadna Scriabin. His first collection of poetry, *Moi tysyacheletiya*, appeared in 1925. He published in *Chisla* and was a member of the *Perekryostok* literary group. Knut was involved in the French Résistance during World War II. After the war, he emigrated to Israel.

DMITRY YURIEVICH KOBYAKOV. Emigré poet.

ALEKSANDR VASILIEVICH KOLCHAK (1873–1920). Admiral, commander of the Black Sea Fleet from 1916. Kolchak headed an anti-Bolshevik government in Omsk during the Civil War. He was captured by the Bolsheviks and shot on 7 February 1920.

KONDAUROV. Russian consul in Paris.

VLADIMIR GALAKTIONOVICH KOROLENKO (1853–1921). Popular prerevolutionary prose writer, began publishing in 1879. In 1881, he was exiled to Siberia for three years for his involvement with the Populists. In the late 1890s, he became literary editor of the "thick" journal *Russkoe bogatstvo*. Korolenko's best-known works are the story "Makar's Dream" (1885) and the autobiographical novel *The Story of My Contemporary* (1904–1918).

ZOYA KOSMODEMIANSKAYA. Soviet girl who perished fighting the German invaders during World War II.

SOFIA VASILIEVNA KOVALEVSKAYA (1850–1891). Mathematician and writer. Kovalevskaya first turned to literature and later became the first woman professor of mathematics in Sweden.

ILYA NIKOLAEVICH KOVARSKY. Physician and emigré publisher.

GENERAL PYOTR NIKOLAEVICH KRASNOV (1869–1947). Officer in the tsarist army and emigré novelist. In 1918, during the Civil War, Krasnov, a Cossack by birth, was elected ataman of the Don Region and led Cossack troops against the forces of the Bolsheviks. He resigned from this post in the spring of 1919 and left Russia. In emigration he wrote long, patriotic, nostalgic novels. In 1945, he joined a Cossack puppet state established by the Germans in the Italian Alps. The Allies surrendered him to the Soviets after the war, and he was returned to the Soviet Union and hanged.

VLADIMIR PIMENOVICH KRYMOV (1878–1968). Writer and businessman. Before the Revolution, Krymov worked as a journalist and editor and wrote books of travel impressions. In the early 1920s, he emigrated to Berlin and in the thirties, to Paris. In emigration, Krymov wrote novels which enjoyed success with the mass reader, although they were not taken seriously as literature by emigré critics. His most important work is the trilogy *Za millionami* (1933). His works were widely and successfully translated into English.

VERA KRYZHANOVSKAYA. Theosophist.

KUBA. Habitué of the Russian Montparnasse.

RINALDO KUEFFERLE. Russian-born Italian writer, poet, and translator.

ALEKSANDR IVANOVICH KUPRIN (1870–1938). Realistic prose writer. Kuprin's reputation as a writer reached its peak in the first decade of the twentieth century with his most important novel, *The Duel* (1905). He settled in Paris in 1920 and contributed to emigré newspapers and to the journal *Sovremennye zapiski*.. While in emigration, Kuprin wrote two novels, *Koleso vremeni* (1930) and *Yunkera* (1933). He returned to Russia in 1937, where he died of cancer.

EKATERINA DMITRIEVNA KUSKOVA (1870–1958). Liberal publicist, active in public affairs. Kuskova, a leader of the cooperative movement, was exiled from Russia in 1922, along with her husband, the economist Sergei N. Prokopovich. She published in a number of emigré publications—including *Sovremennye zapiski* and, during the postwar years, *Novoe russkoe slovo*—and wrote her memoirs, which appeared in *Novy zhurnal*. Kuskova died in Geneva.

GALINA NIKOLAEVNA KUZNETSOVA. Emigré poet, writer, and memoirist. A collection of her poems entitled *Olivkovy sad* was published in Paris by the Sovremennye Zapiski Publishing House in 1937, and a collection of her short stories, under the title *Utro,* was issued by the same publisher. Kuznetsova lived in Grasse with the Bunin family, and her *Grasse Diary* is a valuable document of those years.

ANTONIN PETROVICH LADINSKY (1896–1961). Poet and prose writer. Ladinsky was a member of *Kochevie;* and his works appeared in *Sovremennye zapiski,*

Chisla, and *Krug.* He published five books of poetry and two historical novels. After the Second World War, Ladinsky returned to the Soviet Union.

PÄR (FABIAN) LAGERKVIST (1891–1974). Swedish novelist, poet, and dramatist. Won the Nobel Prize for Literature in 1951.

MIKHAIL FYODOROVICH LARIONOV (1881–1964). Neoprimitivist artist. Husband of Natalia Goncharova.

LEONID MAKSIMOVICH LEONOV (1899–). Soviet prose writer. Leonov published his first short story in 1921 and his first novel, *The Badgers,* in 1924. He was a fellow traveler in the twenties, and it was then that he wrote what is probably his major novel, *The Thief* (1927), a work greatly influenced by Dostoevsky. Leonov turned to Socialist Realism in the 1930s.

KONSTANTIN NIKOLAEVICH LEONTIEV (1831–1891). Philosopher, critic, and writer. Although Leontiev wrote fiction, he is remembered today primarily for his philosophical essays, which were collected in two volumes and published under the title *The East, Russia, and Slavdom* (1885–1886). Leontiev propounded an organic theory of the development of civilizations and stressed the indebtedness of Russian culture to Byzantium.

MIKHAIL YURIEVICH LERMONTOV (1814–1841). Major poet and novelist. Lermontov's works stand as the most thoroughgoing expression of Byronic Romanticism in Russian literature. His most famous works are the long poem *The Demon* (1839) and the novel *A Hero of our Time* (1840), which is the beginning of the Russian psychological novel. Lermontov, like Pushkin, was killed in a duel.

NIKOLAI SEMYONOVICH LESKOV (1831–1895). Major short story writer. In 1860, Leskov moved to St. Petersburg to become a professional journalist and soon turned to fiction. Early, he incurred the ire of the radical critical establishment and, having gained a reputation as a reactionary, found it increasingly difficult to find publication outlets for his works. Although he wrote several longer works, Leskov's reputation rests primarily on his stories, most notably "Lady Macbeth of Mtsensk District" (1865), "The Enchanted Wanderer" (1873), and "The Steel Flea" (1881). In later years, Leskov fell under the influence of Tolstoyan philosophy.

ANATOLY LEVITSKY (1901–1942). Member of the resistance group based at the Musée de l'Homme. Executed together with Boris Vildé and others. Brother of the poet Yu. Rogalya-Levitsky.

SERGEI (SERGE) MIKHAILOVICH LIFAR (1905–). Emigré dancer, choreographer, and author of memoirs and books on dance. Lifar danced with Diaghilev's Ballets russes and later with the Paris Opera. He has staged numerous productions for the Opera ballet as well as for the Nouveau Ballet de Monte Carlo.

ARTUR SERGEEVICH (ARTHUR) LOURIÉ (1893–1966). Composer. After the Revolution, Lourié worked for a time as an assistant to Luncharsky, the commissar of education, then emigrated to Paris. In emigration, he published articles in *Chisla* and *Vozdushnye puti* and was active in the *Third Hour*. Lourié died in Princeton.

ANATOLY VASILIEVICH LUNACHARSKY (1875–1933). Marxist critic. Involved in the revolutionary movement from 1892, he was appointed people's commissar of education by Lenin in 1917. He was removed from his post by Stalin in 1929.

L. D. LYUBIMOV. Contributor to *Vozrozhdenie* who returned to the USSR and remained there after World War II.

VASILY ALEKSEEVICH MAKLAKOV (1869–1960). Lawyer and liberal politician. In 1906, he became a member of the Central Committee of the Constitutional Democratic (Kadet) party and served as deputy from Moscow to the third and fourth Dumas. Appointed Russian ambassador to France after the February Revolution, he remained in France after the Bolshevik takeover, assuming legal and administrative functions on behalf of the emigré community. Articles by Maklakov appeared in *Sovremennye zapiski* and, after the Second World War, he published his memoirs.

VIKTOR ANDREEVICH MAMCHENKO (1901–1982). Emigré poet, published in *Chisla* and *Krug*.

OSIP EMILIEVICH MANDELSHTAM (1891–1938). Major Acmeist poet. His first poems were published in 1910, and his first book of poetry, *Stone* (Kamen), appeared in 1913, followed by *Tristia* in 1922, and *Poems* in 1928. The majority of Mandelshtam's poetry was not published in the Soviet Union during the poet's lifetime and was preserved by his wife after his death. In the 1920s, he also turned to prose, producing a number of works, including *The Noise of Time*. Mandelshtam was arrested in 1938 and apparently perished in the camps. The official date of his death is given as 27 December 1938.

YURY VLADIMIROVICH MANDELSHTAM (1908–1943). Emigré poet and critic. A member of the Perekryostok group, also attended meetings of the Circle. Mandelshtam regularly wrote articles on literature for the newspaper *Vozrozhdenie*. He was arrested in 1942 and died in a concentration camp.

DR. I. I. MANUKHIN. Medical doctor specializing in radiology.

IRMA VLADIMIROVNA DE MANZIARLI. Editor and theosophist. Manziarli was born in Russia of German parents and lived for a time in India. She was a supporter of the first four issues of *Chisla* and published several short articles there. One of the founders of the journal the *Third Hour* in New York.

GABRIEL MARCEL (1889–1973). French Catholic Existential philosopher, dramatist, and critic.

MARCION. Early Christian heretic.

PAVEL IVANOVICH MELNIKOV (pseud. Andrei Pechersky) (1818–1883). Prose writer. His major works, the novel *In the Woods* (1871–1874) and its sequel *In the Hills* (1875–1881), chronicle the life of Old Believer communities in the Nizhny Novgorod region of Russia.

DMITRY SERGEEVICH MEREZHKOVSKY (1864–1941). Writer, poet, religious philosopher. Husband of Zinaida Gippius. Merezhkovsky began his career as a poet in the 1880s but turned primarily to criticism in the last decade of the nineteenth century. His works on such major writers as Pushkin, Tolstoy, Dostoevsky, and Gogol served as a forum for his own religious and philosophical ideas. His literary reputation rests primarily on his trilogy of historical novels, published between 1896 and 1905. The Merezhkovskys left Russia at the end of 1919 and, after attempting to organize an anti-Bolshevik movement in Poland, settled in Paris in November 1920. Merezhkovsky wrote two more historical novels, which appeared in *Sovremennye zapiski* in 1924 and 1925; but after 1926 he published exclusively works of philosophical prose. Merezhkovsky viewed bolshevism as an incarnation of absolute evil which had to be fought through any means available. This stance led him to sympathize with Mussolini in the 1920s and 1930s and with Hitler during World War II.

GEORGY ANDREEVICH MEYER (1894–1966). Emigré critic.

ADAM MICKIEWICZ (1798–1855). Polish poet of great stature and acclaim.

PAVEL NIKOLAEVICH MILYUKOV (1859–1943). Russian historian and major political figure. Milyukov was a founder of the Constitutional Democratic (Kadet) party in 1905 and served as main spokesman for the party in the third and fourth Dumas. From February to May of 1917, he was minister of foreign affairs in the Provisional Government. After the Bolshevik Revolution, Milyukov left Russia for London and then Paris, where he served as editor of the newspaper *Poslednie novosti* and as head of the RDO (Russian Democratic Organization).

V. MIRNY. Pseudonym under which V. S. Yanovsky contributed to *Illustrated Russia*.

KONSTANTIN VASILIEVICH MOCHULSKY (1892–1950). Literary scholar and philosopher. Mochulsky published in most of the major Parisian emigré journals.

His principal works are his five book-length studies: *Vladimir Solovyov* (1932), *Dukhovny put Gogolya* (1934), *Dostoevsky* (1947), *Aleksandr Blok* (1948), and *Andrei Bely* (1955).

MOTHER MARIE (religious name of Elizaveta Yurievna Pilenko; by first marriage Kuzmina-Karavaeva; by second marriage Skobtsova) (1891–1943). Poet and social activist. Before the Revolution, a book of her poetry, entitled *Skifskie cherepki*, was issued by the Acmeist publishing house Giperborei. In emigration, she became a "nun in the world," doing menial jobs for needy emigrants. She also participated actively in meetings of the Circle and, with Father Bulgakov, founded the Orthodox Cause. During the Second World War, Mother Marie was arrested by the Germans for helping to conceal Jews and died in a concentration camp.

NIKOLAI DMITRIEVICH NABOKOV (1903–197?). Composer and musicologist.

VLADIMIR VLADIMIROVICH NABOKOV (pseud. V. Sirin and Vasily Shishkov) (1899–1977). Major Russian and American writer. Nabokov left Russia with his family in 1919. He attended Cambridge University and, in 1922, settled in Berlin, where he lived until 1937. Nabokov began publishing verse in emigré publications as early as 1920. In Berlin he turned to prose, and all nine of his Russian novels were written there. Nabokov moved to France in 1937 and to the United States in 1940. All of his later works of fiction were written in English. From 1948 to 1959 Nabokov taught Russian literature at Cornell University. After the success of his novel *Lolita* (1955), the writer moved to Switzerland, where he lived until his death.

NARODNIKI. *See* Populists.

IVAN FYODOROVICH NAZHIVIN (1874–1940). Prose writer. His first novel appeared in 1907. He also produced two biographical works on Tolstoi, whose philosophy influenced him greatly. After emigrating to Riga in 1920, he wrote historical novels, most notably *Rasputin* (1923), and published his memoirs.

SERGEI GENNADIEVICH NECHAEV (1847–1882). Revolutionary extremist. In 1873, Nechaev was the defendant in a political murder trial which inspired the plot of Dostoevsky's novel *The Possessed*.

NIKOLAI ALEKSEEVICH NEKRASOV (1821–1878). Radical poet, journalist, and editor. In 1848, became editor of the journal *Sovremennik* and, in 1868, of *Otechestvennye zapiski*. His best-known works include *Frost the Red-Nosed* (1863), *Russian Women* (1871–1872), and *Who Is Happy in Russia?*

BORIS IVANOVICH NIKOLAEVSKY (1887–1966). Historian and journalist, brother-in-law of Rykov. Before the Revolution, Nikolaevsky served as an editor on a number of Menshevik newspapers, and after the Revolution he worked in historical archives. He was exiled from Russia in 1922. In emigration, Nikolaevsky contributed to the Menshevik publication *Sotsialistichesky vestnik* and to *Novy zhurnal;* he also published several historical studies. He sold his enormous archives to the Hoover Institute and moved to California, where he died.

NIKOLAI IVANOVICH NOVIKOV (1744–1818). Founder of Russian journalism and book trade. Novikov published a succession of four satirical journals from 1769 to 1774, in which he polemicized with Catherine the Great on the nature and limits of satire. In 1779, Novikov took over the Moscow University Press, where he undertook numerous publishing projects until his arrest in 1792. His imprisonment lasted until Catherine's death in 1796 and put an end to his career.

IRINA VLADIMIROVNA ODOEVTSEVA (real name: Iraida Gustavovna Ivanova; née Heinicke) (1901–). Emigré poet and novelist. Wife of Georgy Ivanov. Odoevtseva published her first book of poetry in Petersburg in 1921 before emigrating from Russia with Ivanov in 1922. In emigration, Odoevtseva turned to prose, publishing novels and short stories. She returned to poetry in the 1950s, with several collections appearing since 1951, and also wrote her memoirs.

ZOYA SERGEEVNA OLDENBURG (Zoé Oldenbourg) (1916–). Historical novelist. Although from a Russian emigré background, Oldenburg writes in French.

YURY KARLOVICH OLESHA (1899–1960). Major Soviet prose writer. Olesha was a fellow traveler in the twenties. His masterpiece is the novel *Envy* (1927). He produced virtually no original work during the Stalin years. His last notable literary achievement was the autobiographical *No Day without a Line,* published posthumously in 1965.

MIKHAIL ANDREEVICH OSORGIN (real name: Mikhail Andreevich Ilin) (1878–1943). Writer, journalist, and editor. From 1906 to 1916 Osorgin lived abroad, mainly in Italy, serving as a foreign correspondent for a number of Russian periodicals. He was exiled from the Soviet Union in 1922 and finally settled in Paris. He actively contributed to a number of emigré newspapers and journals, above all *Sovremennye zapiski,* in which he published both reviews and works of fiction. Osorgin's first novel, *Sivtsev Vrazhek,* which was later a Book-of-the-Month Club selection, originally appeared in *Sovremennye zapiski* (1926–1928) and was followed in the thirties by three others. He also published volumes of memoirs, sketches, and short stories and was founder of the New Writers Publishing House. Osorgin died in France during the German occupation.

NIKOLAI AVDEEVICH OTSUP (1894–1958). Poet and editor. A member of the Acmeist Poets' Guild, Otsup published his first book of poetry in 1921. He emigrated in 1922. A second collection of verse appeared in 1926, and subsequent poems appeared in a number of emigré periodicals. In the thirties, he served as editor of *Chisla*. During the Second World War, Otsup escaped after being arrested by the Germans and fought in the Italian resistance. After the war he received his doctorate and became a professor of Russian in Paris.

PYOTR DEMIANOVICH OUSPENSKY (Uspensky) (1878–1947). Philosopher, theosophist, associate of Gurdjieff.

NICHOLAS PALKIN (the "stick"). Nickname given to Nicholas I by Lev Tolstoi.

BORIS LEONIDOVICH PASTERNAK (1890–1960). Major Soviet poet, prose writer, and translator. Pasternak published his first book of poetry in 1914, and it was followed by a number of works of short prose and collections of verse, most notably *My Sister Life* (1922). When the Socialist Realist hegemony over Soviet literature was established in the early thirties, Pasternak's poetry came under attack for its "difficulty" and introspection, and the poet turned his hand to translations, including renderings of Shakespeare's major tragedies and Goethe's *Faust* into Russian. Pasternak's novel *Doctor Zhivago* was published in the West in 1957, and the writer was awarded the Nobel Prize for Literature in 1958.

LA PASIONARIA (real name: Dolores Ibarruri Gómez) (1895–1981). Leading Spanish Communist political activist and orator. Elected to the Central Committee of the Spanish Communist Party in 1930. On 18 July 1936, she made a famous radio speech calling for defense of the government against the fascists. In March 1939, after the end of the Spanish Civil War, she left Spain for the Soviet Union. In 1977, she returned to Spain, where she died.

(HENRI-) PHILIPPE PÉTAIN (1856–1951). Chief of state of the French government at Vichy during World War II. He died while serving a sentence of life imprisonment for collaboration with the Germans.

F. I. PIANOV. Friend and collaborator of Mother Marie.

BORIS PILNYAK (real name: Boris Andreevich Vogau) (1894–1937?). Soviet prose writer. The publication of his novel *The Naked Year* (1921) established him as a major Soviet writer. His other works include the novels *Machines and Wolves* (1924) and *The Volga Falls into the Caspian Sea* (1939) and the short story "The Tale of the Unextinguished Moon" (1926), which, it has been alleged, is a fictionalized account of the political assassination of M. V. Frunze. Pilnyak was arrested in 1937 and, according to the official report, died in the camps.

GEORGY VALENTINOVICH PLEKHANOV (1856–1918). Marxist ideologist and philosopher. After a brief period of involvement in revolutionary populism, Plekhanov left Russia in 1880 and lived abroad until the February Revolution. In Europe, Plekhanov became a propagandist for Marxism and spokesman for the Social Democratic movement. He opposed the Bolsheviks.

ALEKSANDR ABRAMOVICH POLYAKOV (1879–1971). Journalist. Did the page layouts for *Poslednie novosti* in Paris and later for *Novoe russkoe slovo* in New York.

SOLOMON LVOVICH POLYAKOV-LITOVTSEV (1875–1945). Prose writer and journalist. Worked as a correspondent for the newspaper *Rech* before the Revolution. In emigration, he published articles in *Sovremennye zapiski* and wrote a play, *Labirint* (1921), and a historical novel, *Sabbatai-Tsevi* (1923).

BORIS YULIANOVICH POPLAVSKY (pseud. Apollon Bezobrazov) (1903–1935). Leading Paris poet and prose writer. During his lifetime Poplavsky published only one book of poetry, *Flagi,* containing poems written between 1923 and 1930. Two other books—*Snezhy chas* and *V venke iz voska* appeared after his death. At his tragic death from an overdose of narcotics, he left two unfinished novels: *Apollon Bezobrazov* (published in *Chisla*) and *Domoi s nebes* (an excerpt was published posthumously in *Krug*).

POPULISTS *(narodniki)*. Adherents of agrarian socialism, most active from approximately 1860 to 1895. The Populists believed that the road to socialism for Russia lay through the traditional peasant commune. The Populist campaign of "going to the people" to propagandize the peasantry and incite them to revolt reached its height in the early 1870s before being quashed by the government in 1874. By the end of the 1870s, the more radical Populists had turned to terrorist methods, and the Populist organization the People's Will (*Narodnaya volya*) engineered the assassination of Alexander II on 1 March 1881.

STEPAN IVANOVICH PORTUGEIS (Pseud. St. Ivanovich and V. I. Talin) (1881–1944). Journalist, essayist, Social Democrat. Contributed to *Poslednie novosti* and *Sovremennye zapiski.*

MARFA POSADNITSA. Widow of "mayor" of Novgorod who led the fight for the city-state's independence against Ivan the Terrible.

BORIS PREGEL. Wealthy businessman, patron of the arts, semiprofessional opera singer. Brother of Sofia Pregel.

SOFIA YULIEVNA PREGEL (1904–1972). Emigré poet and editor. Pregel published four books of poetry—*Razgovor s pamyatyu* (1935), *Solnechny proizvol* (1937), *Polden* (194?), and *Berega* (1953)—and founded the New York–based journal *Novoselie* during the Second World War.

ANNA SEMYONOVA PRISMANOVA (18?–1962). Poet. Wife of Aleksandr Ginger. Prismanova published three collections of poetry: *Ten i telo* (1937), *Bliznetsy* (1946), and *Sol* (1949).

LEONID PROTSENKO. Friend and inspiration to many young emigré poets in Paris.

ALEKSANDR SERGEEVICH PUSHKIN (1799–1837). Widely held to have been Russia's greatest poet. Among Pushkin's best-known works are the novel in verse *Evgeny Onegin*, the play *Boris Godunov*, the long poem *The Bronze Horseman,* and the *Belkin Tales.*

SERGEI VASILIEVICH RACHMANINOV (1873–1943). Pianist and composer. Left Russia in 1917.

KARL BERNARDOVICH RADEK (real name: Sobelsohn) (1885–1947). Bolshevik. Radek arrived in Russia with Lenin on the "sealed train" through Germany. He held a number of Soviet political posts, in particular as head of the Third International. A defendant in Stalin's second large show trial in 1937, he was sentenced to ten years at hard labor and probably died in the camps.

ALEKSANDR NIKOLAEVICH RADISHCHEV (1749–1802). Writer, author of *Journey from Petersburg to Moscow* (1790), an exposé of the evils of serfdom cast in the form of a fictional journey through the Russian countryside. Catherine the Great considered the work seditious, and Radishchev was exiled to Siberia. He was allowed to return to European Russia after Catherine's death and, in 1802, committed suicide.

GEORGY RAEVSKY (real name: Georgy Avdeevich Otsup) (1897–1963). Poet. Brother of Nikolai Otsup. Raevsky published in *Chisla* and *Sovremennye zapiski* and was a member of *Perekryostok*.

FYODOR FYODOROVICH RASKOLNIKOV (1892–1939). Bolshevik. Appointed deputy people's commissar of the Soviet Navy in 1918. Served as Soviet envoy to Afghanistan in 1921–1922 and, from 1936, to Estonia, Denmark, and Bulgaria. Raskolnikov refused to return to the Soviet Union when recalled in 1938 and died under suspicious circumstances.

ALEKSEI MIKHAILOVICH REMIZOV (1877–1957). Major prose writer. An established writer before the Revolution, Remizov left Russia in 1921 and, in 1923, settled in Paris. Many of Remizov's works are creative adaptations of legends, fairy tales, and works of old Russian literature; dreams and the fantastic are distinguishing features of his writing.

SERAFIMA PAVLOVNA REMIZOVA-DOVGELLO (1876–1943). Wife of Remizov. Specialist in medieval paleography.

N. REZNIKOV. Young Paris poet.

YU. ROGALYA-LEVITSKY. Emigré poet.

N. ROSHCHIN (real name: Nikolai Yakovlevich Fyodorov; other pseud., Dneprovin). Prose writer. Roshchin, whose writing was greatly influenced by Bunin, published a book of stories entitled *Zhuravli* and two novels, *Gornoe solntse* (1928) and *Belaya siren* (1936). From the end of the twenties, he was a permanent contributor to *Vozrozhdenie*. Roshchin returned to Russia in 1946.

MIKHAIL IVANOVICH ROSTOVTSEV (1870–1952). Historian of classical antiquity. In the 1920s, Rostovtsev published in *Sovremennye zapiski* and headed the *Russky osvoboditelny komitet* in London. He later taught at Yale University.

VASILY VASILIEVICH ROZANOV (1856–1919). Philosopher, literary critic, writer. One of the most idiosyncratic and isolated figures in Russian philosophy, Rozanov oriented his views around a concern with Christianity, sexuality, individual happiness, and family life.

VADIM VIKTOROVICH RUDNEV (1879–1940). Physician, Socialist Revolutionary, editor and publicist. An active member of the Socialist Revolutionary Party, he became Mayor of Moscow after the February 1917 Revolution. He emigrated after the October Revolution and became a member of the editorial board of *Sovremennye zapiski*.

ANDREI DMITRIEVICH SAKHAROV (1921–). Leading Soviet physicist and dissident. In the 1970s, Sakharov became the leader of the dissident campaign for human rights in the Soviet Union, and, in 1975, he was awarded the Nobel Peace Prize. He is currently in exile in Gorky.

MIKHAIL EVGRAFOVICH SALTYKOV-SHCHEDRIN (pseud. N. Shchedrin) (1826–1889). Novelist, satirist, and radical journalist. His most famous work, *The Golovyov Family* (1875–1880), paints an unremittingly grim portrait of the life of a family in the Russian provinces.

A. SAVELIEV (real name: Savely Grigorievich Sherman). Emigré literary critic. Saveliev published reviews of contemporary emigre literature in *Sovremennye zapiski* and *Krug*.

BORIS VIKTOROVICH SAVINKOV (pseud. V. Ropshin) (1879–1925). Socialist Revolutionary terrorist, writer, and poet. Served as assistant minister of war in the Provisional Government until ousted on suspicion of involvement in the Kornilov revolt. Savinkov was arrested when he returned secretly to the Soviet Union in 1924, was sentenced to hard labor, and, according to the official report, committed suicide the following year. Before the Revolution, Savinkov, writing under the pseudonym Ropshin, published novels based on his experiences as a terrorist.

ALEKSANDR SCHMEMAN (1921–1983). Orthodox priest and theologian. Specialist in church history. Born in Estonia and educated in Paris, he moved to the United States in 1951. Taught church history and liturgics at St. Vladimir's Seminary and became dean of the seminary in the early 1960s.

ARIADNA SCRIABIN. Daughter of the composer and wife of Dovid Knut. Killed by the Germans while working for the French underground in the South of France during World War II.

ARTHUR SCHNITZLER (1862–1931). Austrian playwright and novelist.

ANDREI SEDYKH (real name: Yakov Moiseevich Zwibak) (1902–). Emigré writer and journalist. In 1920, emigrated first to Constantinople and then to Paris, where he worked as a reporter for *Poslednie novosti*. Moved to New York in 1942 and joined the staff of *Novoye russkoe slovo;* became its editor-in-chief in 1973 after the death of Mark Weinbaum, founder of the newspaper.

IGOR SEVERYANIN (real name: Igor Vasilievich Lotaryov) (1887–1942). Modernist poet very fashionable at one time. One of the founders, in 1911, of Russian ego-futurism. After the Revolution, he emigrated to Estonia, where he remained until his death.

GENERAL SHAPOSHNIKOV. Leading Soviet general of the Stalin era.

LEON SHESTOV (real name: Lev Isaakovich Shvartsman) (1866–1938). Philosopher. Shestov did his training in law and turned to philosophy only in 1895. Emigrated to Paris, where he died. Shestov is one of the originators of existentialism and a "discoverer" of Kierkegaard for European intellectuals.

TARAS GRIGOREVICH SHEVCHENKO (1814–1861)—Ukrainian national poet. Of peasant origin and a nationalist who opposed Russian domination of the Ukraine, he was arrested in 1847 and spent the years from 1850 to 1857 in internal exile.

EVGENIA IVANOVNA SHIRINSKY-SHIKHMATOV (d. 1940). Former Socialist Revolutionary. Wife of Boris Savinkov and mother of their son Lev. Last marriage to Yury Alekseevich Shirinsky-Shikhmatov.

PRINCE YURY ALEKSEEVICH SHIRINSKY-SHIKHMATOV. Son of the arch-conservative imperial official Aleksei Shirinsky-Shikhmatov, who served as chief procurator of the Holy Synod. A determined liberal and patriot, Yury Shirinsky-Shikhmatov founded the Post-Revolutionary Club and died in a German concentration camp during World War II.

IVAN SERGEEVICH SHMELYOV (1873–1950). Writer. Launched his reputation as a writer in the realist tradition in Russia before the Revolution. His best-known work from this early period is *The Man from the Restaurant* (Chelovek iz restorana, 1911). Shmelyov left Russia in 1922 and settled in France in 1923. His first major emigré work was *Sun of the Dead* (Solntse myortvykh, 1926), a collection of sketches describing his experiences in the Crimea after the Bolshevik takeover. His other major emigré works include three large novels and two volumes of sketches on pre-Revolutionary Russian life. During the Second World War, Shmelyov sympathized with the Germans.

MIKHAIL ALEKSANDROVICH SHOLOKHOV (1906–1984). Soviet prose writer. Sholokhov won the Nobel Prize for Literature in 1965, after the publication of his most famous work, the monumental four-volume *Quiet Flows the Don* (1928–1940). However, since the publication of the first volume in 1928, controversy has persisted over his authorship. In the last decades of his life, after Stalin's death, Sholokhov played a less than honorable role in Soviet literary politics, toeing the Party line and viciously attacking dissident writers.

SHUMSKY. Emigré, former colonel on the Russian General Staff.

SIRIN. *See* Vladimir Vladimirovich Nabokov.

GRIGORY SAVVICH SKOVORODA (1722–1794). Ukranian philosopher. His philosophical writings are most often cast in the form of dialogues, and he has been termed the Ukrainian Socrates.

MARC LVOVICH SLONIM (1894–1976). Literary critic, journalist, Socialist Revolutionary. From 1922 to 1932, served on the editorial board of the Socialist Revolutionary journal *Volya Rossii*, which was published in Prague. After World War II he taught at Sarah Lawrence College and authored a number of books on Russian literature.

R. SLOVTSOV (real name: Nikolai Viktorovich Kalishevich) (?–1941). Journalist. Published weekly feuilletons in the newspaper *Poslednie novosti*.

VLADIMIR ALEKSEEVICH SMOLENSKY (1901–1962). Emigré poet. Published two books of poetry: *Zakat* (1931) and *Naedine* (1938). Nazi sympathizer.

YURY SOFIEV (real name: Yury Borisovich Bek-Sofiev) (1899–1975). Poet. Husband of Irina Knorring. Sofiev, who began writing under the influence of Gumilyov, published one book of poetry, *Gody i kamni* (1936). He was several times elected president of the Union of Writers and Poets in Paris. A former officer in Denikin's anti-Bolshevik forces, he reemigrated to the Soviet Union after World War II.

FYODOR KUZMICH SOLOGUB (real name: Fyodor Teternikov) (1863–1927). Major symbolist writer, poet, and playwright. After the success of his best-known novel, *The Petty Demon* (1907), he retired from schoolteaching and devoted himself exclusively to literature. He remained in the Soviet Union after the Revolution.

IVAN LUKIANOVICH SOLONEVICH (1891–1954). Journalist. Solonevich escaped from a labor camp in the Solovetsky Islands with his family and fled to the West. His outstanding account of the Siberian camps was published in *Poslednie novosti* and was later issued separately in book form.

SOLOVEICHIK. Socialist Revolutionary. Kerensky's secretary.

VLADIMIR SERGEEVICH SOLOVYOV (1853–1900). Major philosopher, writer, and poet. The focal tenet of Solovyov's philosophy is "Godmanhood," an idea first developed in a series of public lectures delivered in 1878 and subsequently published under the title *Lectures on Godmanhood*. Central to Solovyov's religious thought is the idea of Sophia (Divine Wisdom). His ideas had a profound influence on the Symbolists and on the subsequent development of Russian religious philosophy.

BRONISLAV BRONISLAVOVICH SOSINSKY (1903–). Writer and literary critic. Sosinsky published in *Volya Rossii* and some emigré journals. He worked for a time at the United Nations in New York and later returned to the Soviet Union.

PERIKL STAVROVICH STAVROV (1895–1955). Poet and translator who contributed to various emigré publications.

ST. STEFAN OF PERM (?–1396). Missionary to the Permian lands whose *Life*, written by Epiphanius the Wise, is one of the most important works of medieval Russian hagiography.

BARON ANATOLY SERGEEVICH STEIGER (Shteiger) (1907–1944). Emigré poet. Steiger left Russia with his family after the Revolution, eventually settling in Paris, where he became one of the primary exponents of the Parisian note in poetry. He died of tuberculosis in Switzerland.

RUDOLPH STEINER (1861–1925). Founder of anthroposophy. Steiner had many disciples among Russian intellectuals, most notably poet Andrei Bely.

FYODOR AVGUSTOVICH STEPUN (1884–1965). Philosopher and writer. Stepun was exiled by the Soviet Government in 1922. In emigration in Germany, he regularly contributed critical articles and essays to *Sovremennye zapiski* and served as *de facto* editor of the literary section of the journal. Stepun's only novel, a "philosophical novel in letters" entitled *Nikolai Pereslegin*, was serialized in *Sovremennye zapiski* (1923–1925). His memoirs were issued in a separate edition by the Chekhov Publishing House in 1956.

MARGARITA STEPUN (1895–1972). Sister of Fyodor Stepun. Singer at the Dresden Opera. Close friend of Galina Kuznetsova.

PYOTR ARKADIEVICH STOLYPIN (1862–1911). Political figure. In 1906, Stolypin was appointed Nicholas II's minister of the interior and, later the same year, president of the Council of Ministers. His most notable achievement was the institution of agricultural reforms. Stolypin was notorious for his harsh repression of terrorists and rebellious peasants, and nooses were termed Stolypin neckties because of the hangings carried out by his military courts. He was assassinated by the double agent Dmitry Bogrov.

IGOR FYODOROVICH STRAVINSKY (1882–1971). Composer.

MIKHAIL ALEKSANDROVICH STRUVE (1890–1948?). Emigré poet. Emigrated to Paris. After World War II, he became involved in pro-Soviet emigré circles.

ILYA DMITRIEVICH SURGUCHOV (1881–1956). Prose writer and dramatist. His play *Osennie skripki* was produced by the Moscow Art Theater before the Revolution. In emigration, Surguchev published a book of stories entitled *Emigrantskie rasskazy* (1926) and a novel, *Rotonda* (1928). Surguchev was a German sympathizer during World War II.

TALIN. See Stepan Ivanovich Portugeis.

NADEZHDA ALEKSANDROVNA TEFFI (real name: Nadezhda Aleksandrovna Buchinskaya; née Lokhvitskaya) (1872–1952). Humorist, short story writer, and poet. In Russia before the Revolution, Teffi contributed most notably to the Petersburg satirical journal *Satirikon* and the Moscow newspaper *Russkoe slovo*. She settled in Paris in 1920 and, in the twenties and thirties, published her short works almost exclusively in Russian-language newspapers. While in emigration, Teffi also wrote a novel, *An Adventure Novel* (Avantyurny roman, 1932), and *Reminiscences* (1932).

BORIS TEMIRYAZEV. See Yury Annenkov.

YURY (GEORGY) KONSTANTINOVICH TERAPIANO (1896–1980). Emigré poet and critic. Allegedly served as a volunteer in the White Army during the Russian Civil

War and, after the war, settled in Paris. He was a member of Perekryostok and the founder of the Union of Young Writers. Terapiano published in *Sovremennye zapiski, Chisla,* and the almanac *Krug*. After the Second World War, he primarily wrote literary reviews and articles for emigré newspapers and served as a permanent contributor to the Paris-based paper *Russkaya mysl*. Terapiano's memoirs, entitled *Vstrechi* (1953), are a source of information on emigré literary life.

V. G. TERENTIEV. Worked as a translator at the United Nations.

NIKOLAI SEMYONOVICH TIKHONOV (1896–1979). Soviet poet and prose writer. In the 1920s, Tikhonov was a member of the Serapion Brothers. His first collection of verse was published in 1922. In later years, following the general movement of Soviet literature, his poetry became increasingly patriotic and propagandistic. He served as secretary of the executive board of the Soviet Writers' Union until he was forced to step down in the wake of Zhdanov's attack on the journals *Zvezda* and *Leningrad* in 1946. Tikhonov was awarded Stalin prizes in 1942, 1949, and 1952.

ALEKSEI NIKOLAEVICH TOLSTOI (1883–1945). Soviet writer. Tolstoi left Russia after the Revolution, settling first in Paris and then in Berlin. He returned to the Soviet Union in 1923. Among his works written abroad were the first book of his trilogy on the Revolution, *Road to Calvary* (1921–1940), and the science fiction novel *Aelita* (1922). Under Stalin Tolstoi became an official spokesman for the literary establishment. He was awarded Stalin prizes in 1941 for his novel *Peter the Great* and in 1942 for *Road to Calvary*.

LEV NIKOLAEVICH TOLSTOI (1828–1910). Tolstoi is best known for his novels *War and Peace* and *Anna Karenina*. After passing through a crisis of faith in 1878, Tolstoi turned increasingly to the propagation of his religious views, and the Tolstoyan tenet of nonresistance to evil found many followers both in Russia and abroad.

LEON TROTSKY (real name: Lev Davidovich Bronstein) (1879–1940). Bolshevik political figure. Active in the revolutionary movement from 1898, joined the Bolshevik Party in July 1917. As chairman of the Military Revolutionary Committee, played a leading role in the Bolshevik seizure of power in Petrograd. He served as commissar for foreign affairs in the first Soviet Government and was commissar of war from 1918 to 1925. After Lenin's death, Trotsky led the opposition to Stalin's takeover of power. He was expelled from the Party in 1927; and, in 1929, he was banished from the Soviet Union for life. Trotsky was murdered at his villa in Mexico City on 20 August 1940.

PRINCE SERGEI PETROVICH TRUBETSKOI (1790–1860). Decembrist. Exiled to Siberia after the failure of the Decembrist uprising.

MARINA IVANOVNA TSVETAEVA (1892–1941). One of the outstanding Russian poets of the twentieth century. Tsvetaeva's first collection of poetry was published in 1910. In 1922, she left Russia to join her husband, Sergei Efron, in the West. She settled with her family in Paris in 1925. Tsvetaeva was an alien and isolated figure in the emigration. Her poetry and prose appeared in a number of emigré journals, but not a single volume of her collected writing was published while she lived in Paris. In 1939, Tsvetaeva followed Efron (a Soviet agent) and their daughter back to the Soviet Union, and there, in 1941, she committed suicide.

IVAN SERGEEVICH TURGENEV (1818–1883). One of the great Russian prose writers of the nineteenth century. The novel *Fathers and Sons* (Ottsy i deti, 1862) is generally acknowledged as his masterpiece.

ASYA TURGENEVA. Common-law wife of Andrei Bely. Turgeneva accompanied Bely to Europe in 1912 and lived with him abroad until 1916, when Bely returned to Russia. She became an ardent disciple of Rudolf Steiner.

PAVEL TUTKOVSKY. Emigré prose writer, whose novels include *Marionetki nevedomogo* (1923) and *Deti komety* (1925).

FYODOR IVANOVICH TYUTCHEV (1803–1873). Major Russian poet. Not recognized as an important poet until 1850, he published his first book of verse in 1854. A career diplomat, he spent some two decades of his life in Germany, and his poetry shows the influence of Schelling. His poetry was greatly admired by the Russian symbolists.

DR. UNKOVSKY. Physician and journalist. Unkovsky lived for a time in equatorial Africa. He wrote novels and later was a frequent visitor of Remizov.

USPENSKY. *See* Pyotr Demianovich Ouspensky.

P. VAKAR. Reporter for *Poslednie novosti*.

VLADIMIR SERGEEVICH VARSHAVSKY (1906–1977). Emigré prose writer. Varshavsky moved from Prague to Paris at the end of the twenties. In the twenties and thirties, his works appeared in *Volya Rossii* and *Chisla*. During World War II, Varshavsky was a prisoner of war in Germany. After the war he moved to the United States and began to publish in *Novy zhurnal*. In 1950, his autobiographical novella *Sem let* appeared, and, in 1956, he published a study of emigre writers under the title *Nezamechannoe pokolenie*.

VEIDLÉ. *See* Vladimir Vasilievich Weidlé.

BORIS VLADIMIROVICH VILDÉ (pseud. Boris Dikoi) (1908–1942). Emigré writer and anthropologist. During World War II, he headed the resistance group based at the Musée de l'Homme in Paris and was executed by the Germans on 23 February 1942.

MAKSIM MOISEEVICH VINAVER (1862–1926). Political figure and editor. A founding member of the Constitutional Democratic (Kadet) party, Vinaver was elected a deputy to the First Duma. In 1918, he served briefly as minister of foreign affairs in an anti-Bolshevik government in the Crimea and soon after fled to the West. In emigration, he coedited with Milyukov the Parisian Russian-language newspaper *Zveno* (1923–1928).

MARK VENIAMINOVICH VISHNYAK (1883–1977). Professor of public law, publicist, editor. From 1905, a member of the Socialist Revolutionary party. At its only meeting, he was elected secretary of the Constituent Assembly. Visnyak emigrated to Paris in 1919, where he served as a member of the editorial board of *Sovremennye zapiski*. He moved to the United States in 1940.

LAZAR VOLOVICK (signed his paintings only with his last name) (1902–1977). Post-impressionist painter. Husband of the dancer Lya Grjebina (sister of Irina). Volovick arrived in Paris together with his friend K. Terechkovitch in 1921. His paintings are highly valued by connoisseurs, and he was considered one of the better Russian painters in Paris. However, he shunned publicity and was slow to establish himself.

KLEMENT EFREMOVICH VOROSHILOV (1881–1969). Major Soviet military figure. Voroshilov was elected to the Constituent Assembly as a Bolshevik representative in 1917. A supporter of Stalin in the power struggle after Lenin's death, he was appointed people's commissar of military and naval affairs in 1925 and held the post until 1940, playing a major role in the purges of the military in 1937 and 1938. Voroshilov also became a member of the Politburo in 1926. In 1935, he was made marshall of the Soviet Union, and from 1946 to 1953, served as chairman of the Council of Ministers. After Stalin's death in 1953, he became chairman of the Presidium of the Supreme Soviet. Voroshilov retired from public office in 1960.

BORIS PETROVICH VYSHESLAVTSEV (1862–?). Philosopher and theologian. Vysheslavtsev was expelled from Russia in 1922 and took up residence in Paris. Collaborated with the Germans and died in Switzerland.

VLADIMIR VASILIEVICH WEIDLÉ (Veidlé) (1895–1979). Emigré literary and art critic and essayist. Weidlé began contributing to *Russkie zapiski* in 1927, and his articles on literature and art appeared regularly in *Zveno, Sovremennye zapiski,* and later (under the pseudonym N. Dashkov) in *Vozrozhdenie*. Weidlé also published in *Chisla* and *Krug*. His major work, on the crisis of contemporary art, was published in French in 1936 under the title *Les Abeilles d'aristée* and, a year later, in Russian under the title *Umiranie iskusstva*. A collection of his literary essays, *Vecherny den,* was issued by the Chekhov publishing house in 1952.

SIMONE WEIL (1909–1943). French philosopher and mystic. Active in the French Résistance during World War II. Her major work is *La pesanteur et la grâce* (1947).

GENERAL BARON PYOTR NIKOLAEVICH WRANGEL (1878–1928). Commander of White forces during the Civil War. In 1920, Wrangel succeeded Denikin as commander of the White Volunteer Army in the south of Russia. Routed by the Red Army and, in November 1920, the general and what was left of his army were evacuated from the Crimea to Constantinople.

PAULINA YANOVSKY. First wife of V. S. Yanovsky. Mother of their daughter, Marie (Masha).

ALEKSANDR EVGENIEVICH YAKOVLEV (1887–1938). Emigré artist.

IRINA YASSEN. Poet.

BORIS ZAKOVICH. Emigré poet. Published in a number of emigré publications, including *Chisla* and *Krug*. A collection of his poetry, *Dozhd' idyot nad Cenoy*, appeared in Paris in 1984.

BORIS KONSTANTINOVICH ZAITSEV (1881–1972). Writer and critic. Zaitsev's first story was published in a Moscow newspaper in 1901. He emigrated to Paris in 1923. Zaitsev's major work is the autobiographical tetralogy *Puteshestvie Gleba* (1937), *Tishina* (1948), *Yunost* (1950), and *Drevo zhizni* (1953). In emigration Zaitsev also wrote saints' lives, accounts of his pilgrimages to Orthodox monasteries, and biographies of Turgenev, Zhukovsky, and Chekhov. He served as literary editor of the Paris-based Russian weekly *Russkaya mysl*.

EVGENY IVANOVICH ZAMYATIN (1884–1937). Prose writer and critic. Zamyatin joined the Bolshevik party before the 1905 Revolution and was imprisoned and exiled in 1905. One of the founders of the Serapion Brothers in 1921. Best known in the West for his pioneering dystopian novel *We*, which exerted an acknowledged influence on George Orwell's *1984*. Written in 1919 and 1920, the novel was first published abroad in English in 1924 and has never been published in the Soviet Union. In 1931, Zamyatin was allowed to emigrate to Western Europe, where he held aloof from emigré life and periodicals.

ILYA M. ZDANEVICH (1894–1975). Futurist poet and playwright. Zdanevich was a practitioner of *zaum* (trans-sense language). In the years between 1917 and 1920, he was active in the Futurist group "41°" in Tiflis, Georgia. In the early twenties, Zdanevich emigrated to Paris, where he became involved in the dadaist movement and in the writers' organization *Cherez*. The last and most famous of a series of *zaum* dramas which he began publishing in Tiflis appeared in Paris in 1923 under the title *Lidantyufaram*. His novel, *Voskhishchenie*, appeared in Paris in the thirties.

VLADIMIR FEOFILOVICH ZEELER (1874–1954). Emigré journalist. Served as the secretary of the Union of Writers and Journalists in Paris and was an editor of and contributor to *Russkaya mysl* from the newspaper's inception in 1947.

ZELYUK. Publisher and owner of his own typography shop.

VLADIMIR MIKHAILOVICH ZENZINOV (1880–1953). Political figure and publicist. A member of the Socialist Revolutionary party from 1900, Zenzinov spent much of the prerevolutionary period abroad or in exile in Russia. He was elected to the Constituent Assembly in 1917. Zenzinov took up residence in Paris in 1919 and, in 1940, moved to New York. After the Second World War, he published his memoirs. Zenzinov was a close friend of I. I. Fondaminsky.

MIKHAIL OSIPOVICH ZETLIN (TSETLIN) (pseud. Amari) (1882–1946). Writer, poet, and critic. Published in *Sovremennye zapiski* from the first issue and served as editor of the poetry section of the journal. He was also one of the most active contributors to the critical section of the journal. Moved to New York at the beginning of World War II and, in 1942, founded the quarterly journal *Novy zhurnal*, which he edited until his death. Tsetlin published *Pyatero i drugie* about "the Five" great Russian composers in New York in 1944.

MARIA SAMOILOVNA ZETLIN (TSETLINA) (1882–1977). Socialist revolutionary and publisher. Wife of M. O. Tsetlin. Tsetlina published, with her husband, the quarterly journal *Okno*, which came out in Paris in 1923. She was also the publisher of the New York–based literary journal *Opyty*, which began to appear in 1953. Her main activity was to preside over literary and political salons.

SERGEI P. ZHABA. Socialist revolutionary and historical writer.

VLADIMIR EVGENIEVICH ZHABOTINSKY (1880–1940). Zionist and emigré writer.

VLADIMIR ANANIEVICH ZLOBIN (1894–1967). Emigré critic, poet.

MIKHAIL MIKHAILOVICH ZOSHCHENKO (1895–1958). Soviet satirical prose writer. Zoshchenko began his career as a member of the Serapion Brothers, a group devoted to the idea of the writer's creative freedom. The rich colloquial language of his humorous and satirical short stories on Soviet everyday life made him one of the most popular writers among Soviet readers in the 1920s and into the 1930s. Zoshchenko wrote longer works of prose as well, notably the novel *Michel Sinyagin* (1930). In 1946, Zoshchenko, along with Anna Akhmatova, was singled out for attack by Stalin's chief literary bureaucrat, Andrei Zhdanov, and was expelled from the Soviet Writers' Union. Zoshchenko was rehabilitated after Stalin's death, and his long work, *Before Sunrise,* was published in full in the Soviet Union only in 1972. It was the first book inspired by Freud published in the Soviet Union.

COUNT VALENTIN P. ZUBOV (1884–). Professor. Wrote memoirs on the Revolution entitled *Stradnye gody Rossii* (1968).

LEONID FYODOROVICH ZUROV (1902–1971). Emigré prose writer. After the Revolution, Zurov lived in Estonia, where he began publishing his fiction. He moved to Paris only in the 1930s. Zurov's realistic prose style was heavily influenced by Bunin. His works include the story *Fatherland* (Otchina, 1929) and the novels *Ancient Road* (Drevny put, 1934) and *The Field* (Pole, 1938).

Nikolai Berdyaev, Paris, 1939.
(Courtesy of Silver Age
Publishing.)

Leon Shestov, Paris, 1934.
(Courtesy of Silver Age
Publishing.)

Pavel Milyukov, Paris, 1936.
(Courtesy Silver Age Publishing.)

Georgy Fedotov, New York,
1942.

Aleksandr Kerensky, Paris, 1932.

Evgenia Savinkova (later Shirinsky-
Shikhmatova). From the archives of
the tsarist Okhranka.

Ilya Fondaminsky. From
the archives of the
tsarist Okhranka.

Mother Marie.

Helene Iswolsky. New
York, 1961.

Ivan Bunin, Grasse, 1936.

Aleksei Remizov, Paris,
1931. (Courtesy Silver Age
Publishing.)

Vladislav Khodasevich,
Paris, 1934. (Courtesy Silver
Age Publishing.)

Marina Tsvetaeva, Paris, 1935.
(Courtesy Silver Age Publishing.)

Georgy Ivanov. (Courtesy Silver
Age Publishing.)

Georgy Adamovich, Paris, 1935.
(Courtesy Silver Age Publishing.)

Georgy Adamovich and
V. S. Yanovsky, New York, 1972.

Yury Felsen,
Georgy
Adamovich,
Anatoly Steiger,
Paris, 1936.
(Courtesy Silver
Age Publishing.)

Boris Poplavsky.

· Boris Vildé, Paris. This is the last
picture taken of Vildé, who was
executed by the Germans in 1942.

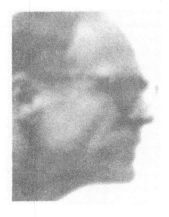

Vladimir Varshavsky, Long Island, 1953.

Galina Kuznetsova, Paris, 1934.

Lydia Chervinskaya, Paris, 1936.
(Courtesy Silver Age Publishing.)

V. S. Yanovsky, Marseilles, 1942.

V. S. Yanovsky, Long Island, 1951.

V. S. Yanovsky, New York, 1953.

Contributors to *Chisla* (Numbers), Paris, 1936. Standing: M. Larionov, B. Poplavsky, V. Mamchenko, V. Yanovsky, A. Roumanov, Yu. Felsen, Yu. Mandelshtam, N. Otsup, G. Raevsky, V. Smolensky, S. Stasin, Yu. Terapiano, A. Ginger, V. Varshavsky. Sitting: S. Charchoune, D. Knut, S. Pregel, E. Bakunina, L. Cherninckaya, I. Odoevtseva, D. Merezhkovsky, G. Adamovich, Z. Gippius, G. Ivanov. Bottom row: P. Stavrov, A. Alferov, Yu. Sofiev, B. Vildé, A. Burov, V. Zlobin, L. Kelberin.

"They Died for France." Plaque in the Musée de l'Homme in Paris, in memory of Boris Vildé and Anatoly Levitsky, who were on the staff of the museum and who also initiated one of the first cells of the Résistance. Both were executed by the Germans.

MORTS POUR LA FRANCE ET POUR LA LIBERTE
MUSEE DE L HOMME * INSTITUT D ETHNOLOGIE DE L UNIVERSITE DE PARIS

André ALEXOPOULOS	Deborah LIFCHITZ
Michel BOUSSION	Louis LIOTARD
Maurice BUHLER (fusillé)	Bernard MAUPOIL
Francois CUZIN (fusillé)	Louis MILLOT
Jean DENIKER	Georges PAPILLON
Patrick DESCAMPS	Yves PAVRET de la ROCHEFORDIERE
Guy DUBALEN	Jean RAGNET
Gilles FERRIER du CHATELET	Bernard RAUDOT
Charles LE CŒUR	Hubert SCHWAB
Valentin FELDMANN (fusillé)	Jean Pierre SET
Paul LE LAN	Colette STAUFFERT
Jean LEONI	Gilbert VIEILLARD
Anatole LEWITZKY (fusillé)	Boris VILDE (fusillé)
Yvonne PICARD	Paul NIZAN

"They Died for France and Freedom." Plaque in the Musée de l'Homme, commemorating the members of this center of the Résistance.

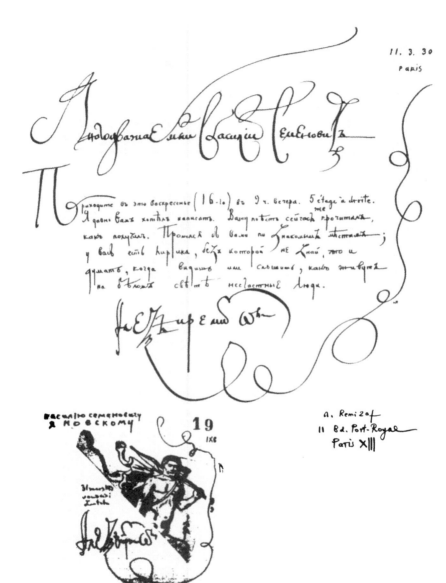

Letter from A. Remizov to Yanovsky, Paris, 1930.

The Consul-General for the U.S.A, Marseilles, France

Paul Milioukov, Hôtel de la Paix, Rue Lamartine,
Aix-les-Bains - France.

Sir,

I certify hereby that I know personnally Mr Basile
Yanovsky who was for many years my contributor to
the Russian daily paper "Posledniya Novosti" (The Last News")
edited in Paris. Mr Yanovsky is well known in Russian
literary circles as a talented author of fiction, whose novels were largely read and approved. Without occupying
himself with politics he shares democratic views represented by my newspaper. His morals are beyond any
question. Under present conditions his wish to leave the country
seems well founded.

Yours sincerely
Paul Milioukov,
June 9, Aix-les-Bains, Rue
Lamartine, Hôtel de la Paix, Savoie

Letter of recommendation from P. Milyukov to the US consul in Marseilles, May 1942. It was on the basis of this letter that Yanovsky was issued a US visa.

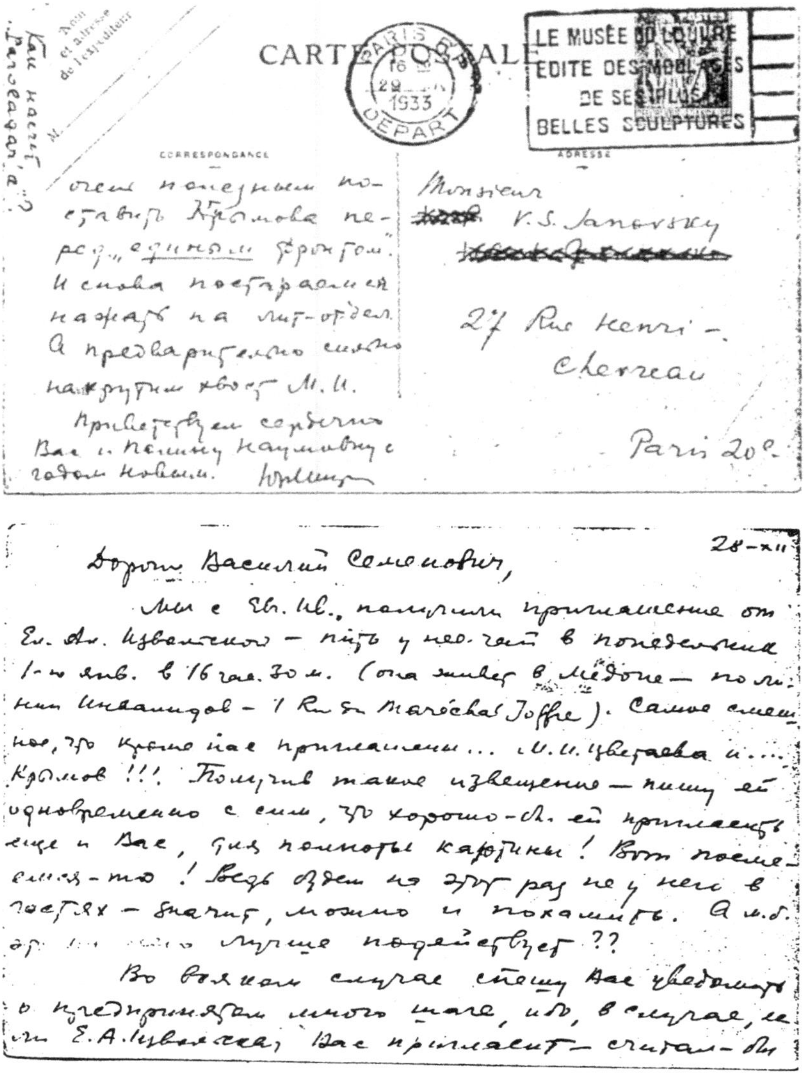
Как насчет Цветаевой?
Nom et adresse de l'expéditeur
CARTE POSTALE
PARIS
1933
DEPART
LE MUSÉE DU LOUVRE
EDITE DES MOULAGES
DE SES PLUS
BELLES SCULPTURES
CORRESPONDANCE
ADRESSE
очень полезным по-
ставить Крымова пе-
ред „единым фронтом".
И снова постарается
нажать на лит-отдел.
А предварительно сильно
накрутить хвост М. И.
Приветствуем сердечно
Вас и Полину Наумовну с
годом новым. Юрий Шир
Monsieur
V. S. Janovsky
27 Rue Henri-
Chevreau
Paris 20e
28-XII
Дорогой Василий Семенович,
Мы с Ев. Ив., получили приглашение от
Ел. Ал. Извольской — пить у нее чай в понедельник
1-го янв. в 16 час. 30 м. (она живет в Медоне — по ли-
нии Инвалидов — 1 Rue du Maréchal Joffre). Самое смеш-
ное, что кроме нас приглашены... М. И. Цветаева и....
Крымов!!! Получив такое извещение — пишу ей
одновременно с сим, что хорошо-де ей пригласить
еще и Вас, для полноты картины! Вот посме-
емся-то! Ведь здесь на этот раз не у него в
гостях — значит, можно и покаяться. А м. б.
это [illegible] [illegible] лучше подействует??
Во всяком случае спешу Вас уведомить
о [illegible] много шаге, и, в случае, если Е. А. Извольская Вас пригласит — считал-бы

Postcard from Yu. Shirinsky-Shikhmatov to Yanovsky, following their visit to V. Krymov, Paris, 1933, inviting Yanovsky to a meeting with Tsvetaeva "to talk some sense into her."

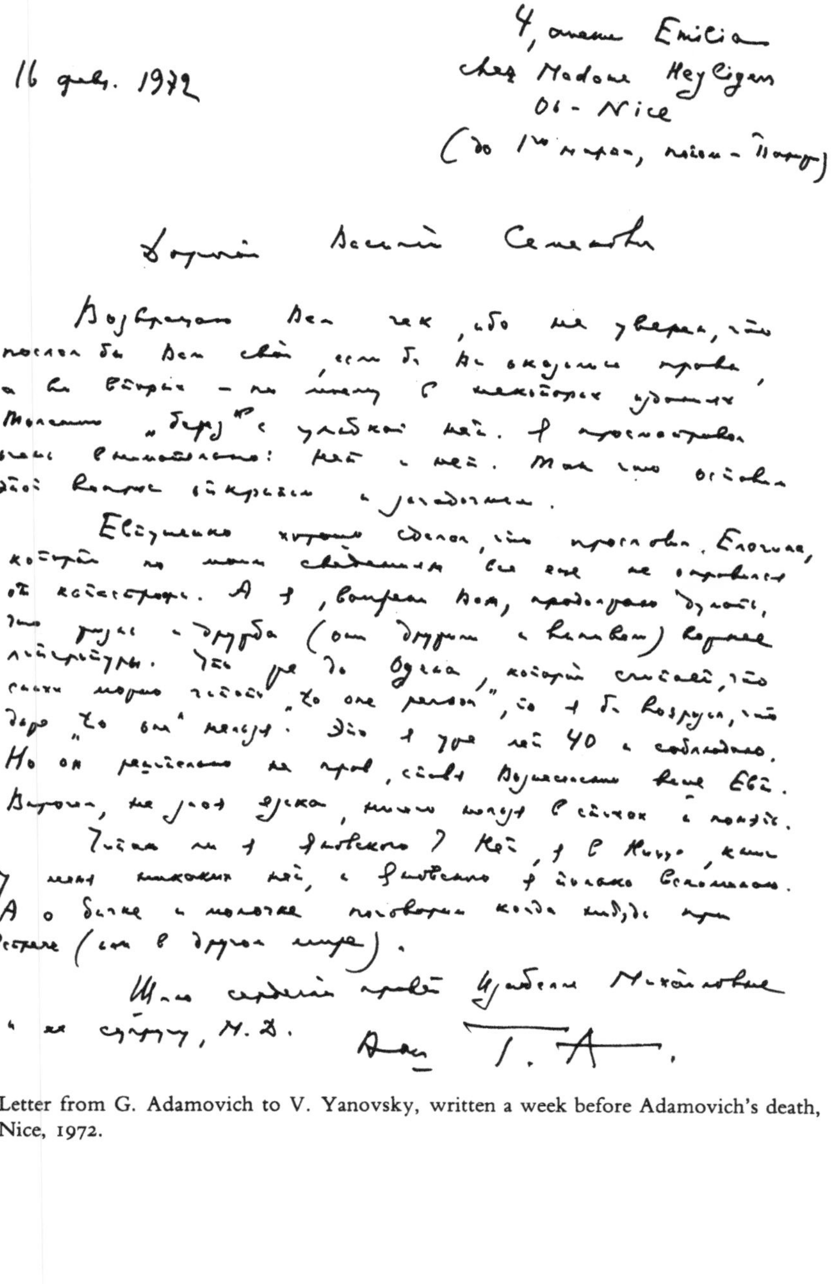
4, avenue Emilia
chez Madame Heyligen
06 - Nice
(до 1го марта, после – Париж)

16 фев. 1972

Дорогой Василий Семенович

Возвращаю Вам чек, ибо не уверен, что послал бы Вам свой, если бы Вы оказались правы, [illegible] Я просмотрел очень внимательно: нет и нет. Так что оставим этот вопрос открытым и загадочным.

Евтушенко хорошо сделал, что прогнал Елагина, который по моим сведениям все еще не оправился от катастрофы. [illegible]

[illegible]

Шлю сердечный привет Изабелле Михайловне [illegible]

Ваш Г. А.

Letter from G. Adamovich to V. Yanovsky, written a week before Adamovich's death, Nice, 1972.

Certificate issued by the Paris Préfecture de Police to the effect that in 1933 Yanovsky was elected secretary general of the Union of Writers and Poets.

FRANCE

PASSEPORT *NANSEN*

CERTIFICAT D'IDENTITÉ ET DE VOYAGE

Taxe : 38 francs

N° CS34615

TITULAIRE :

Nom : *Yanovsky,*

Prénoms : *Basile*

Ce certificat d'identité et de voyage comprend 18 pages non compris la couverture

Cover of passport introduced by the great humanitarian Friedtjof Nansen and accepted by the League of Nations. The Nansen Passport gave status to and legalized the life of millions of Russian emigrés after World War I.

Journals and Literary Groups of the Emigration

CHISLA (Numbers). Elegant literary journal. Ten issues came out in Paris between 1930 and 1934 under the editorship of Nikolai Otsup. Unlike most emigré publications of the period, *Chisla* shied away from politics, while publishing articles on painting, sculpture, music, and dance along with articles on and works of literature. Although a number of writers of the older generation—notably Gippius, Merezhkovsky, and Remizov—published in *Chisla,* the journal drew its contributors primarily from the ranks of those younger writers and poets who were just beginning their careers.

ESTAFETA (Relay). Anthology of Russian emigré poets published in Paris after World War II.

ILLYUSTRIROVANNAYA ROSSIYA (Illustrated Russia). Weekly magazine which appeared in Paris though published in Riga.

KOCHEVIE (Nomad Camp). Emigré literary group founded in Paris in 1928 under the leadership of Marc Slonim. Among its members were Aleksandr Ginger, Anna Prismanova, Boris Poplavsky, Antonin Ladinsky, and Vadim Andreev. The group disbanded in the mid-1930s after more than 100 meetings.

KRUG (The Circle). Literary society founded in Paris in 1935 by I. I. Fondaminsky to bring emigré writers of the "younger" generation together with religious thinkers of the "older" generation, including Berdyaev, Mother Marie, and Fedotov. Between 1936 and 1938, the society issued three almanacs, also titled *The Circle,* in which the works of many young prose writers and poets were represented. The Circle was closely affiliated with Fondaminsky's journal *Novy grad,* and the minutes of meetings of the Circle were published for a time in *Novy grad.*

NOVAYA ROSSIYA (New Russia). Biweekly journal published in Paris from 1936 to 1940 under the editorship of A. F. Kerensky.

NOVOE VREMYA (New Time). Major pre-Revolutionary Russian newspaper published in St. Petersburg; from 1876, under the control of the publisher Aleksei Sergeevich Survorin.

NOVOSELIE (New Abode). Journal published by Sofia Pregel in New York.

NOVOYE RUSSKOYE SLOVO (New Russian Word). Russian-language daily which has been appearing in New York since 1910.

NOVY GRAD (New City). Journal published in Paris from 1931 to 1939, under the editorship of I. I. Fondaminsky, Fyodor Stepun, and Georgy Fedotov. Among its contributors were the important emigré religious philosophers as Nikolai Berdyaev, Father Sergei Bulgakov, N. O. Lossky, and B. P. Vysheslavtsev. The journal condemned capitalist civilization as spiritually bankrupt and called for a "new city," based on "Christian socialism," to be constructed on the foundation of the old order. In 1935, Fondaminsky founded the Circle to bring together younger emigré writers with religious thinkers grouped around the *New City* to discuss political, philosophical, and literary issues.

NOVY KORABL (New Barque). Literary journal published in Paris (1927–1928) under the editorship of Vladimir Zlobin, Yury Terapiano, and Lev Engelgardt.

NOVY ZHURNAL (New Journal). Emigré journal published in New York since 1942, founded by M. A. Aldanov and M. O. Zetlin. After the death of the latter in 1945, it came out under the editorship of M. M. Karpovich until his death in 1959. *New Journal* was later edited by Roman Gul (died in 1986), who had served on the editorial board since 1959. During the course of its long history, *New Journal* has published works by many important emigré writers.

OBEDINENIE MOLODYKH PISATELEI I POETOV (Union of Young Writers and Poets). Writers' organization based in Paris. Drew its members from the "younger" generation of emigré writers.

PEREKRYOSTOK (Crossroads). Literary group which came into being among emigré poets in Paris in the mid-1930s. The group drew its literary orientation from Khodasevich. *Perekryostok* put out several literary anthologies and included among its members Yury Terapiano, Vladimir Smolensky, Georgy Raevsky, Dovid Knut, and Yury Mandelshtam.

POSLEDNIE NOVOSTI (Latest News). Russian-language daily published in Paris from 1920 to 1940. The newspaper was founded and edited by P. N. Milyukov.

RUL (Rudder). Russian language newspaper published in Berlin, 1920–1931.

RUSSKIE ZAPISKI (Russian Annals). Emigré "thick" journal published in Paris in 1937. Beginning with its fourth issue, the journal was edited by P. N. Milyukov.

RUSSKOE BOGATSTVO (Russian Wealth). "Thick" journal published monthly in St. Petersburg from 1876 to 1918.

SEGODNYA (Today). Emigré newspaper published in Riga.

SOVREMENNYE ZAPISKI (Contemporary Annals). Emigré "thick" journal published in Paris from 1920 through 1940. The original editorial board of *Contemporary Annals* consisted of five Socialist Revolutionaries: M. V. Vishnyak, A. I. Gukovsky, V. V. Rudnev, N. D. Avksentiev, and I. I. Fondaminsky. However, from the very beginning, it announced the intention of remaining outside party politics and attracting a diverse group of contributors. Following this policy, *Sovremennye zapiski* became the most prestigious journal of the emigration and, during the course of its existence, published works by virtually every major poet and prose writer in the emigration.

SOYUZ PISATELEI I ZHURNALISTOV (Union of Writers and Journalists). Emigré organization in Paris headed by P. N. Milyukov to provide material assistance to elderly writers in need. Drew its members from the "older" generation of emigré writers.

THE THIRD HOUR. Ecumenical journal edited by Helene Iswolsky, Irma de Manziarli, and Yanovsky. Ten issues of *The Third Hour* were published in New York between 1944 and the late 1960s.

UTVERZHDENIYA (Affirmations). Journal published in Paris in 1931–1932. Prince Yu. A. Shirinsky-Shikhmatov was the moving force behind the publication, which announced as its intention the unification of the various "post-Revolutionary" trends in emigré thought. Berdyaev was an active contributor to *Affirmations*, and the editorial slant of the journal was heavily influenced by his ideas.

VOLYA ROSSII (The Will of Russia). Socialist Revolutionary publication published in Prague from 1922 to 1932. *Volya Rossii* began as a weekly newspaper, but by 1925 it had become a monthly journal. The journal represented the views of the left wing of the Socialist Revolutionary party. Unlike *Sovremennye zapiski*, *Volya Rossii* kept up with the new developments in Soviet literature and favored emigré writers of the younger generation over older, more established authors.

VOZROZHDENIE (Renaissance). Russian-language daily of conservative orientation published in Paris from 1925 to 1936. Until 1927, the newspaper came out under the editorship of P. B. Struve.

YAKOR (Anchor). Anthology of Russian poets edited by Adamovich and published in Paris in the mid-1930s.

ZA SVOBODU (For Freedom). Daily newspaper published in Warsaw from 1921 through 1932, first under the editorship of D. V. Filosofov and M. P. Artsybashev and later edited by Filosofov alone.

ZELYONAYA LAMPA (Green Lamp). Literary and philosophical discussion group founded by Zinaida Gippius and Dmitry Merezhkovsky in Paris in 1927. The Green Lamp took its name from a well-known literary circle of Pushkin's day.

Index

à la Klyuch (The Key), 103
À la Recherche du temps perdu, 29
Abramovich, Aleksandr, 224
Adamovich, Georgy Viktorovich, 4,
  9, 11, 14, 22, 27, 33, 34, 37, 38,
  39, 41, 42, 67, 69, 72, 73–74, 85,
  88, 89, 90–92, 93, 94, 97, 106, 122,
  123, 134, 147, 153, 160, 176, 177,
  178, 186, 189, 191, 192, 194, 196,
  205, 208, 209, 212, 213, 214, 215,
  219, 224, 236, 239
Ageev, M., 20, 196, 239
Akhmatova, Anna Andreevna, 136,
  239
Aksakov, Ivan, 237
Aksakov, Konstantin, 237
Aldanov, Mark Aleksandrovich, 12–
  13, 39, 63, 70, 88, 90, 103, 104,
  113, 116, 121, 125, 126, 128, 129,
  130, 180, 181, 213, 219, 220, 226,
  239
Alekhin, A. A., 194, 218
Aleksandrova, Vera Aleksandrovna,
  213, 240
Aleksandrovich, Mark, 126, 129
Aleksandrovich, Valerian, 88
Alekseev, Nikolai Nikolaevich, 74,
  128, 240
Alekseevich, Ivan, 69, 121, 122, 123,
  126, 128, 194
Alekseevich, Yury, 71, 154, 155, 156
Alfyorov, Anatoly, 74, 176, 177
Altro amore, 113
Alyorhin, A. A., 240

Amerikansky opyt (American Experi-
  ence), 60, 108
Aminado, Don, 240
Anderson, 118
Andreev, 118, 119, 120, 165
Andreev, Leonid Nikolaevich, 240
Andreev, Vadim, 55, 56, 182
Andreevich, Mikhail, 162
Anna Karenina, 103, 155
Annenkov, Yury Pavlovich, 150–51,
  152, 240
Annensky, Innokenty Fyodorovich,
  92, 119, 209, 241
Apollon Bezobrazov, 9
Archives Internationales de Danse, 39
Aristotle, 139
Askoldov, 194, 241
Atlantis, 115–16
Auden, W. H., 5, 116, 183
Averchenko, Arkady Timofeevich, 5,
  241
Avksentiev, Nikolai Dmitrievich, 19,
  241
Avvakum, Archpriest, 81, 83, 241
Azef, Evno-Meyer, 241
Azev, 82, 236

Babel, Isaak Emmanuilovich, 170,
  171, 198, 200, 206, 241
Bakst, Father Andrei, 24–25, 192,
  242
Bakunin, Mikhail, 237
Balmont, Konstantin Dmitrievich,
  165, 182, 237, 242

Balmont, Mirra, 182
Barabbas, 84
Baum, Vicky, 206
"Beauty," 168
Beck, 15
Beginning of the End, The, 103
Bek-Sofiev, Colonel, 174
Belinsky, Vissarion Grigorievich, 98,
  137, 189, 242
Bely, Andrei, 20, 69, 87, 97, 112,
  119, 120, 148, 149, 197, 206, 207,
  237, 242
Bely, Asya, 87
Berberova, Nina Nikolaevna, 99, 242
Berdyaev, Nikolai Aleksandrovich, 3,
  47, 52–53, 59, 60, 63, 66, 67, 68,
  72, 91, 127, 131, 133, 134, 135,
  136, 141, 155, 156, 210, 220, 242
Bergson, Henri, 177
Berlinger Tageblatt, 126
Berngardovich, Nikolai, 31, 172
Bestuzhev Institute, 181, 238
Blavatsky, Helena Petrovna, 16, 87,
  242
Blok, Aleksandr Aleksandrovich, 69,
  118, 119, 150, 160, 165, 172, 206,
  207, 237, 242
Blokha (The Flea), 170, 171
Blum, Léon, 193, 226, 234, 243
Boldyrev, Ivan, 164, 165, 166, 243
Bollet, La, 9, 16, 183
Boris Gudunov, 159
Borov, Aleksandr, 244
Bozknev, Boris, 196, 197, 243
Brasserie des Lilas, 150
Bred, Pavel, 16, 175
Brothers Karamazov, The, 106, 141,
  237
Bryusov, Valery Yakovlevich, 101,
  118, 119, 165, 178, 237, 243
Bukharin, Nikolai Ivanovich, 69, 243
Bulgakov, Sergei Nikolaevich, 68,
  73, 160, 161, 243
Bulkin, A., 183, 243

Bunakov. *See* Fondaminsky, Ilya Isi-
  dorovich
Bunin, Ivan Alekseevich, 3, 5, 11, 29,
  39, 41, 69, 72, 79, 90, 91, 93, 99, 116,
  118–26, 129, 135, 163, 169–70, 194,
  205, 206, 219, 228, 243
Bunin, Vera Nikolaevna, 29, 122,
  123–24, 243
Burevesnik (Stormy Petrel), 69
Burov, Aleksandr, 31, 107, 201, 244
Butashevich-Petrashevsky, M., 235
Butrevich, Boris, 153, 244
"Bytovya yavleniya" (Everyday
  Occurrences), 227

Café du Dôme, 32
Café Murat, 34, 35, 38, 98, 102, 113,
  121, 225
Céline, Louis-Ferdinand, 134, 244
Central Terror, 82
Chaadaev, Pyotr Yarovlevich, 43, 81,
  244
Chaliapin, Fyodor Ivanovich, 66,
  218, 244
Chapsky, Count, 214, 244
Charchoune, Sergei Ivanovich, 6, 24,
  34, 40, 74, 76, 93, 196, 197, 213,
  244
Chartogon (Exorcism), 116
Châtelet, 15
Chekhov, Anton Pavlovich, 115,
  132, 198, 207, 244
Chekhov Publishing House, 213
Chelyust emigranta (Emigrant's Jaw),
  148, 189, 193
Chernov, Viktor Mikhailovich, 182,
  244–45
Chernyshevsky, Nikolai Gavrilovich,
  69, 81, 245
Chertok, 164–65, 245
Chervinskaya, Lydia Davydovna, 4,
  25, 31, 32, 41, 93, 147, 175, 184,
  186, 191–92, 194–96, 219, 236, 245
Chiappe, 231

Childhood, Boyhood, and Youth, 76–77
Chisla (Numbers), 15, 22, 25, 34, 86,
  95, 102, 106, 115, 150, 153, 168,
  176, 182, 184, 186, 197, 212, 213,
  214, 215, 216, 217, 218, 295
Chisla soirée, 218
Chkheidze, Konstantin Aleksandro-
  vich, 48, 245
"Chornaya Madonna" (The Black
  Madonna), 8
Chorny, Sasha, 219, 245
Christian Students' Movement, 61
Clara Milich, 204
Cocteau, Jean, 150, 245
Commentaries, 213
Congress of the Orthodox Cause,
  143
Corday, Charlotte, 139, 245

Dahl, Vladimir, 164, 238, 245
Dante, 113, 168, 216
Day, Dorothy, 158, 245
Dead Souls, 12, 21, 127, 128n, 129,
  236
de Gaulle, Charles, 56
Delvig, Anton Antonovich, 37, 245–
  46
Demidov, Igor Platonovich, 133,
  223, 224, 246
Denfert-Rochereau (Union of Young
  Writers), 27
Denike, Yury Petrovich, 177, 246
Denikin, Anton Ivanovich, 91, 161,
  246
Derzhavin, Gavrila Romanovich,
  127, 163, 246
Descartes, 91, 130
Despair, 205, 232
Diaghilev, Sergei Pavlovich, 215, 246
Diary of a Writer, 90, 177
Dikoi, Boris, 94, 183, 189
Diogenes, 133
Dnevnik moikh vstrech (Diary of My
  Encounters), 151

Dnevnik v stikhakh (Diary in Verse),
  215–16
Doctor Zhivago, 207
Dokhturov, 152
Dolgolikov, 197
Dominique, 11, 29, 31, 32, 40, 122,
  179
Domoi s Nebes (Home from Heaven),
  20
Don-Aminado, 219, 220
Dostoevsky, Fyodor Mikhailovich,
  11, 12, 39, 50, 80, 81, 89, 90, 91,
  98, 106, 107, 113, 122, 127, 132,
  138, 140, 144, 150, 156, 163, 171,
  177, 189, 199, 205, 232, 235, 236,
  246
Dostoevsky, Mikhail, 236
Double, 205
Dryakhlov, Valerian Dyodorovich,
  16, 23, 84, 85, 86–87, 88, 214, 246
"Durachie" (Fools), 176
Dvoinoi Nelson (Double Nelson), 21,
  22, 69, 98, 100
Dzerzhinsky, Feliks Edmundovich,
  60, 237, 246

Editeurs Réunis, 195
Efron, Sergei Yakovlevich, 200, 204,
  246
Ehrenburg, Ilya Griforievich, 160,
  171, 206, 246
Einstein, Albet, 79
Eisner, Aleksei Vladimirovich, 151,
  204, 247
Emelianov, Viktor Nikolaevich, 40,
  74, 76, 247
Enukidze, 151
Ertel, Aleksandr Ivanovich, 169, 247
Esenin, Sergei Aleksandrovich, 199,
  247
Esperienza americana, 113
Estafet (Relay), 180, 275
Eugene Onegin, 56n, 108
Evangulov, Georgy, 196, 247

Fedin, Konstantin Aleksandrovich,
171, 247
Fedotov, Georgy Petrovich, 3, 43–
61, 63, 67, 74, 82, 91, 109, 127,
134, 135, 136, 143, 145, 147, 188,
220, 247
Fedotov, Mrs., 47, 54, 57, 74
Fedotov, Nina (daughter), 50, 60
Felitsianovich, Vladislav, 97
Felsen, Yury, 4, 5, 6, 9, 12, 13, 19–
20, 26–42, 49, 73, 74, 95, 98, 102,
114, 115, 123, 142, 162, 172, 173,
195, 196, 197, 201, 203, 206, 215,
216, 228, 232, 247
Fet, Afanasy Afanasievich, 34, 105,
107, 108, 146, 238, 247–48
Filosofov, Dmitry Vladimirovich, 89,
114, 214, 248
Flagi (Flags), 190
Flaubert, 172
Florovsky, Georgy Vasilievich, 60,
61, 248
Foch, Marchal, 189
Fondaminsky, Ilya Isidorovich, 3, 20,
45, 47, 48, 49, 52, 53, 54, 56, 57,
62–83, 91, 100, 103, 109, 121,
127, 135, 143, 145, 147, 148, 149,
150, 159, 161–62, 177, 178, 180,
187, 188, 189, 206, 207, 209, 217,
223, 248
Fondaminsky-Bunakov, I. I., 73
Foujita, 151
Fourteen, 179, 190
Frank, Semyon Lyudvigovich, 248
Freidenstein, Nikolai Berngardovich.
See Felsen, Yuri
Freud, Sigmund, 79, 133
Front Populaire, 34
Fyodorov, Nikolai Fyodorovich, 81,
87, 248
Fyodorovich, Aleksandr, 110, 117
Fyodorovich, Leonid, 125
Fyodorovich, Valerian, 16, 86

Gaas, Dr., 236
Gagarin, Y., 203
Gavriliada, 37, 59
Gayana, 160
Gazdanov, Georgy (Gaito) Ivanovich,
164, 165, 248
Geibiner, Boris, 75
Geographical Society (Metro Solfer-
ino), 205
Georgievsky, M. A., 234
Gershenkron, 38, 55, 74, 111, 214
Gide, André, 114, 163, 184, 185, 187,
205, 248
Gift, The, 68, 103
Ginger, Aleksandr Samsonovich, 23,
95, 196, 249
Gioconda, 124
Gippius, Zinaida Nikolaevna, 27, 37,
85, 89, 97, 112, 114, 116, 123, 126,
142, 180, 186, 190, 191, 208, 219,
220, 233, 237, 249
Glinyanye cherepki (Pottery Shards),
73
Gogol, Nikolai Vasilievich, 17, 56,
111, 113, 114, 127, 128n, 165, 166,
199, 236, 249
Golovina, Alla Sergeevna, 93, 249
Golovlyov Family, The, 203, 236
Goncharova, Natalia Sergeevna, 203,
249
Gorgulov, Pavel, 16, 175, 249
Gorky, Maksim, 64, 69, 94, 99, 118,
119, 120, 165, 166, 224, 249
Gorky, Pavel, 249
Granovsky, Timothy, 237
Grassky zhurnal (Grasse Diary), 128
Griboedov, Aleksandr Sergeevich,
79n, 249
Grigoriev, Apollon, 236
Grinberg, R. N., 102
Grjebina, Irina, 94, 187, 249–50
Grjebine family, 55
Grynberg, Roman Nirolaevich, 250

Gumilyov, Nikolai Sergeevich, 12, 120, 174, 178, 189, 250

Hachette, 212
Hegel, Georg, 82, 139, 146, 227
Hemingway, Ernest, 12
Herzen, Aleksandr Ivanovich, 41, 43, 53, 66, 68, 99, 145, 166, 205, 237, 250
Hippius. *See* Gippius, Zinaida Nikolaevna
Homer, 199
Horizon Club, 181

Illyustrirovannaya Rossiya (Illustrated Russia), 101, 275
Institute of Eastern Languages, 142
In the Woods, 144
Isaakovich, Lev, 137
Isidorovich, Ilya, 52, 72
Istrati, Panait, 250
Iswolsky, Helene (Elena Aleksandrovna), 47, 60, 117, 136, 154, 180, 250
Ivan I, 250
Ivan IV, 78, 251
Ivanov, Georgy Vladimirovich, 4, 12, 31, 33, 34, 39, 42, 64–65, 69, 74, 78, 94, 95, 97, 105, 106, 107, 108, 109, 110, 114, 115, 120, 127, 137, 151, 178, 179, 190, 191, 194, 201, 209, 212, 213, 215, 251
Ivanov, Vsevolod Vyacheslavovich, 171, 206, 251
Ivanov, Vyacheslav Ivanovich, 146, 148, 165, 237, 251
Ivanovich, Konstantin, 54, 88, 115
Ivanovna, Evgenia, 71, 154, 155, 156–57
Ivanovna, Marya, 32, 179, 200
Ivask, Yury Pavolovich, 186, 251
Ivitation to a Beheading, 206
Izanov, 213
Izwolsky, Helene, 212

J'accuse, 170, 171
Jaurés, Jean, 251
Joyce, James, 99, 130, 163, 197, 199, 206

Kafka, Franz, 39, 120, 198, 206, 207
Kalita, Ivan, 175
Kamenev, Lev Borisovich, 71, 201, 235, 251
Karamazov, Alyosha, 143, 171, 237
Karataev, Platon, 143, 171, 237
Karlinsky, Simon, 231
Karpovich, Aleksandrova, 60, 61
Karpovich, Mikhail Mikhailovich, 60, 229, 251
Kartoashov, Anton Vladimirovich, 251
Kasiankina, 181, 252
Kataev, Valentin Petrovich, 198, 252
Katya, 177
Kazem-Bek, Aleksandr Lyovich, 47, 67, 208, 252
Kelberin, Lazar Izrailevich, 4, 13, 74, 109, 185, 191, 195, 252
Kennedy, 183
Kennedy, John, 116
Kerensky, Aleksandr Fyodorovich, 4, 48, 54, 74, 82, 110, 113, 116–17, 129, 183, 205, 217, 218, 252
Khodasevich, Vladislav Felitsianovich, 3, 7, 9, 22, 27, 31, 33, 34, 37, 39, 69, 85, 89–90, 94–104, 105, 107, 110, 123, 127, 135, 149, 164, 168, 175, 178, 179, 207, 215, 232, 252
"Kholstomer," 177
Khomyakov, Aleksei Stepanovich, 71, 237, 252
Khorosho zhili v Peterburge (We Lived Well in St. Petersburg), 201
Khrushchev, Nikita Sergeevich, 166, 252
Kierkegaard, Soren Aabye, 79, 140, 141, 142

Kireevsky, Ivan, 237
Kirshon, Vladimir Mikhailovich, 171, 206, 252–53
Kiselyova, Tatiana, 87, 253
Klepinin, Nikolai Andreevich, 204, 253
Klyuch, 126
Knorring, Irina Nirolaevna, 147, 174, 216, 219, 253
Knut, Ariadna, 210
Knut, Dovid, 24, 31, 69, 86, 175, 210, 253
Knut, Simkha, 210
Kobyakov, Dmity Yurievich, 166, 253
Kochevie (Nomads), 26, 198, 212, 295
Kolchak, Aleksandr Vasilievich, 253
Koleso (The Wheel), 150, 162, 164, 166, 167, 175
Komsomol, 80, 138
Kondaurov, 230, 253
Korolenko, Vladimir Galaktionovich, 227, 253
Kosmodemianskaya, Zoya, 138, 139, 253
Kovalevskaya, Sofia Vasilievna, 99, 253
Kovarsky, Ilya Nikolaevich, 195, 253
Krasin, L. B., 151
Krasnov, Pyotr Nikolaevich, 80, 91, 132, 156, 253–54
Krug (Circle), 20, 38, 44, 49, 52, 55, 64, 65, 68, 70, 73, 77, 78, 107, 109, 134, 135, 149, 159, 160, 161, 182, 191, 197, 200, 208, 209, 212, 221, 295
Krymov, Vladimir Pimenovich, 151, 200–4, 254
Kryzhanovskaya, Vera, 254
Kryzhanovsky, 87
Kuba, 31, 32, 254
Kuefferle, Rinaldo, 113, 254
Kuprin, Aleksandr Ivanovich, 69, 124, 135, 162, 254

Kuskova, Ekaterina Dmitrievna, 41, 254
Kutuzov, M. I., 234
Kuznetsova, Galina Nikolaevna, 121, 122, 124, 125, 128, 154, 254

Ladinsky, Antonin Petrovich, 69, 74, 175, 221, 222, 254–55
Lagerkvist, Par (Fabian), 84, 255
Land and Freedom Party, 65
Larionov, Mikhail Fyodorovich, 150, 186, 255
Lenin, V. I., 78, 81
Lenov, Leonid Maksimovich, 255
Lensky, 162
Leonardo da Vinci, 116
Leonidas, 182
Leonov, L. M., 198
Leontiev, Konstantin Nikolaevich, 71, 92, 255
Lermontov, Mikhail Yurievich, 35, 127, 255
Le Rouge et le noir, 186
"Les Batelliers de la Volga," 170
Leskov, Nikolai Semyonovich, 116, 170, 172, 255
Levi, Marc. *See* Ageev, M.
Levitsky, Anatoly, 189–90, 255
Lifar, Sergei (Serge) Mikhailovich, 151, 194, 255–56
Lindbergh, Charles, 116, 183
Lourié, Athur Sergeevich (Arthur), 47, 136, 212, 256
Lunacharsky, Anatoly Vasilievich, 151, 256
Lutèce, 52
Luxembourg Gardens, 51, 98
Lyubimov, L. D., 175, 256
Lyubov vtoraya (The Other Love), 20, 29, 75, 84

Maklakov, Vasily Alekseevich, 129, 136, 230–31, 256

Malchiki i devochki (Boys and Girls), 164
Malraux, 197
Mamchenko, Viktor Andreevich, 74, 84, 85, 88, 115, 141, 256
Mandelshtam, Alfyorov, 4, 6, 85, 170
Mandelshtam, Osip Emilievich, 256
Mandelshtam, Yury Vladimirovich, 4, 49, 74, 84, 97, 177, 178, 203, 256
Mansfield, Katherine, 64, 224
Manukhin, Dr. I. I., 64, 224, 256
Manziarli, Irma Vladimirovna de, 47, 136, 212, 256–57
Marcel, Gabriel, 52, 53, 232, 257
Marion, 6, 126, 257
Marianne, 132
Marquand, John, 130
Maupassant, Guy de, 120
Mayakovsky, Vladimir, 196, 199
"Mechtali Flagi" (The Flags Dreamed), 8
Melnikov, Pavel Ivanovich, 144, 172, 190, 257
Melnikov-Pechersky, 144, 172
Memoirs, 169
Memoirs of a Terrorist, 187
Mephisto, 98, 99, 183
Merezhkovsky, Dmitry Serfeevich, 4, 7, 41, 44, 59, 64, 77, 85, 89, 93, 105–30, 135, 136, 179, 186, 197, 205, 213, 218, 219, 233, 237, 257
Meyer, Georgy Andreevich, 129, 257
Mickiewicz, Adam, 82n, 198, 205, 257
Mikhailovich, Aleksei, 6, 7, 168, 172, 173
Milyukov, Pavel Nikolaevich, 22, 48, 90, 91, 96, 98, 111, 128, 135, 148, 156, 168, 218, 219, 220, 221, 224, 228, 229, 230, 257
Mir (The World), 9, 134, 140, 172, 175, 205

Mirny, V., 102, 257
"Mistika chelovekoobshcheniya" (Mystique of Human Relations), 159, 160
Mitina lyubov (Mitya's Love), 120
Mladoross, 139
Mladorossy, 218
Mochulsky, Konstantin Vasilievich, 55, 74, 81, 85, 143, 160, 172, 220, 257–58
Mogilevsky, 226
Monet, Claude, 139
Mother Marie, 6, 44, 49, 53, 55, 65, 73, 74, 81, 143, 153–73, 178, 235, 258
Mussolini, Benito, 77

Nabokov, Nikolai, 214
Nabokov, Vladimir Vladimirovich, 68, 70, 94, 163, 170, 206, 207, 231–32, 258
Nabokov-Wilson Letters, The, 231
Nachalo kontsa (The Beginning of the End), 102
Naked King, 118
Nakokov, Nikolai Dmitrievich, 102, 258
National Labor Union, 108
National Union of the New Generation, 234
National Union of the Working Generation, 106, 236
National Workers Union, 41–42, 234
Nazhivin, Ivan Fyodorovich, 75–76, 258
Nechaev, Sergei Gennadievich, 78, 258
Nekrasov, Nikolai Alekseevich, 98, 177, 258
Nekropol (Necropolis), 101
Ne mogu molchat' (I Cannot Be Silent), 227
Nietzsche, Friedrich, 78, 91, 142
Nikolaevich, Lev, 142

Nikolaevich, Pavel, 230
Nikolaevna, Vera, 121, 122, 124, 125
Nikolaevna, Zinaida, 114, 126
Nikolaevsky, Boris Ivanovich, 180, 258–59
Nina, 55
Notes from the Underground, 88
Notes of a Madman, 142
Novaya Rossiya (New Russia), 63, 65, 295
Novgorod, Nizhny, 192
Novikov, Nikolai Ivanovich, 81, 259
Novoe Russkoe Slovo (New Russian Word), 41, 147, 220, 224, 296
Novoe vremya (New Time), 96, 296
Novoselie (The New Abode), 217, 296
Novy grad (New City), 45, 48, 63, 65, 135, 145, 147, 296
Novy Korabl (New Barque), 26 296
Novy zhurnal (New Journal), 57, 60, 72, 108, 148, 296
Nozier, Violette, 112

Obedinenie molodykh pisatelei i poetov (Union of Young Writers and Poets), 124, 296
Oblonsky, Stiva, 214
Oboroncheskoe movement, 156
Odoevtseva, Irina Vladimirovna, 65, 180, 213–14, 259
Oldenburg, Zoya Sergeevna, 53, 259
Olesha, Yury Karlovich, 198, 259
Olsen, Regine, 140, 141
Orthodox Cause, 65, 82, 158, 235
Osennie skripki (Autumn Violins), 128
Osipovna, Amalia, 63–64, 72
Osorgin, Mikhail Andreevich, 12, 13, 19, 103, 150, 162, 164, 165, 166, 170, 224, 259
Osorgina, Tatiana Bakunina, 162, 242
Other Love, The, 123

Otsup, Nikolai Avdeevich, 31, 34, 35, 69, 97, 168, 175, 184, 191, 196, 209, 212, 213, 214, 215, 216, 217, 218, 259–60
Ouspensky, Pyotr Demianovich, 260

Palkin, Nicholas, 68, 260
Parabola, 165
Paris Association of Russian Writers and Poets, 17
Paris Minuit, 224
Paris Union of Writers and Poets, 217
Pascal, Blaise, 91, 109, 130
Pasionaria, La, 45, 260
Pasternak, Boris Leonidovich, 20, 127, 171, 200, 260
Pavlovna, Serafima, 7, 168, 170
Pecherin, Vladimir Sergeevich, 43, 186
Pechersky, 144, 172
Pensé Russe, 151
Perekrestok (Crossing), 175
Perekryostok (Crossroads), 296
Pétain, (Henri-) Philippe, 260
Pétain, Marshal, 70
Peterburgskie zimy (Petersburg Winters), 108
Peter the Great, 78
Petrashevsky Circle, 72, 235
Petrovich, Georgy. *See* Fedotov
Petty Demon, 172
Pianov, F. I., 158, 260
Picasso, Pablo, 151
Pilnyak, Boris, 146, 170, 260
Pisma o Lermontove (Letters from Lermontov), 20, 39
Plan Sviftsona (Swiftson's Plan), 135
Plato, 80
Plekhanov, Georgy Valentinovich, 69, 260–61
Podvig (Glory), 102
Poe, Edgar Allen, 120
Polyakov, Aleksandr Abramovich, 166, 224, 261

Polyakov-Litovtsev, Solomon Lvovich, 201, 261
Polyana, Yasnaya, 130
Poor Folk, 99
Poplavsky, Boris Yulianovich, 3–25, 27, 38, 44, 50, 64, 69, 85, 97, 102, 107, 116, 135, 175, 177, 185, 189–90, 198, 207, 209, 213, 215, 218, 219, 226, 236, 261
Poplavsky, Vsevolod, 15
Portativnoe bessmertie (Portable Immortality), 100
Porte de Versailles, 182
Portugeis, Stepan Ivanovich, 115, 261
Posadnitsa, Marfa, 138, 139, 158, 261
Poslednie novosti (Latest News), 14, 24, 34, 91, 96, 126, 132, 153, 154, 162, 168, 191, 213, 218, 219, 220, 221, 224, 226, 226, 228, 230, 296
Possessed, The, 93, 164
Post-Revolutionary Club, 30, 44, 65, 71, 155, 200, 234
Povest o sestre (Story of My Sister), 163
Pregel, Boris Yulievich, 142, 216, 217, 261
Pregel, Sofia Yulievna, 80, 203, 216, 217, 261
Preobrazhenie (The Transfiguration), 29
Prismanova, Anna Semyonova, 204, 262
Prospect, Nevsky, 137
Protsenko, Leonid, 10, 11, 13–14, 15, 23, 84, 86, 88, 193, 262
Proust, 6,̄26, 27, 29, 39, 99, 103, 112, 122, 129, 130, 139, 163, 187
Punshevaya vodka (The Vodka Punch), 125
Pushkin, Aleksandr Sergeevich, 37, 56, 59, 90, 91, 101, 108, 122, 127, 139, 149, 163, 176, 183, 189, 198, 262
Pusya, 18–19

Quiet Flows the Don, 170

Rachmaninov, Sergei Vasilievich, 262
Radek, Karl Bernardovich, 151, 262
Radishchev, Aleksandr Nikolaevich, 189, 262
Raevsky, Georgy, 175, 262
Rakovsky, 151
Raskolnikov, Fyodor Fyodorovich, 74, 262
Raspad atoma (The Disintegration of the Atom), 108
"Rasskaz o tryokh raspyatykh i mnogikh ostavshikhsyazhit," 84
Real Politik, 220
Reiss, 204
Remizov, Aleksei Mikhailovich, 6, 7, 79, 84, 132, 136, 140, 141, 160, 165, 167, 168, 169, 170, 171–72, 172, 173, 183, 197, 199, 206, 262
Remizova-Dovgello, Serafima Pavlovna, 167–68, 262
Repetition of the Past, 37
Resurrection, 177
Reznikov, N., 182, 263
Roerich, Nikolai Konstantinovich, 233
Roerich Museum, 19, 30
Rogalya-Levitsky, S., 189, 190
Rogalya-Levitsky, Yu., 263
Roman s kokainom (Novel with Cocaine), 20, 196
Roshchin, N., 124, 175, 263
Rostovtsev, Mikhail Ivanovich, 70, 263
Rotonde, 35
Round Table of the Mladoross, 65
Rozanov, Vasily Vasilievich, 24, 50, 92, 100, 109, 111, 213, 263
"Rozovye deti" (Rosy Children), 160
Rudnev, Mrs., 180–81
Rudnev, Vadim Viktorovich, 21, 22, 63, 68, 102, 127, 180, 263
Rudnev-Vishnyak, 159

Rul (Rudder), 296
Russia's Historical Ways, 65
Russkie zapiski (Russian Annals), 22, 65, 98, 100, 125, 135, 147, 148, 229, 297
Russkoe Bogatstvo (Russian Wealth), 227, 297

St. Augustine, 79
St. John of the Cross, 68, 106, 115
St. Stefan of Perm, 68, 266
St. Thomas Aquinas, 68
Sakharov, Andrei Dmitrievich, 110, 263
Salle Hoche, 194
Salle Lascaze, 41–42, 206, 232
Saltykov-Shchedrin, Mikhail Evgrafovich, 11, 18, 118, 163, 189, 203, 236, 263
Samarin, Yury, 237
Saveliev, A., 74, 76, 196, 263
Savinkov, Boris Viktorovich, 71, 113, 154, 157, 187, 208, 235, 263–64
Savinkov, Lev Borisovich, 156
Savinkova, Princess, 71, 154
Sazonov, 71, 235
Schiller, Johann, 82
Schmemann, Father Alexander, 61, 177, 264
Schnitzler, Arthur, 264
Schriabin, Ariadna, 210, 264
Seagull, 207
Sedykh, Andrei, 123, 166, 228, 264
Sedykh-Zwibak, A., 226
Segodnya (Today), 147, 220, 297
Select Café, 40, 165
Semyonovich, Vassily, 10, 102
Senior, Yerkhovensky, 164
Sergeevich, Dimitry, 7, 114, 126
Severyanin, Igor, 5, 183, 264
Shaposhnikov, General, 221, 264
Shestov, Leon, 59, 85, 136–37, 139, 141, 142, 264

Shevchenko, Taras Griforevich, 198, 264
Shevtov, Lev, 140, 143
Shevtov, Madame, 142
Shirinsky, 154, 160, 203, 208
Shirinsky-Shikhmatov, Evgenia Ivanovna, 153, 155, 264
Shirinsky-Shikhmatov, Prince Yuri Alekseevich, 30, 65, 71, 155, 157, 159, 200, 202, 234, 264–65
Shmelyov, Ivan Sergeevich, 5, 63, 69, 91, 162, 169, 265
Sholokhov, Mikhail Aleksandrovich, 265
Shumsky, 225, 265
Sidorovo uchenie (Sidorov's Education), 201
Sirin, 183, 207. *See also* Nabokov, Vladimir Vladimirovich
Sirin-Nabokov, Vladimir, 15, 17, 67, 69, 74, 90, 102, 106, 116, 170, 197, 205, 207, 214, 231, 232
Skovoroda, Grigory Savvich, 133, 265
Slonim, Marc Lvovich, 62, 147, 156, 198, 212, 265
Slovtsov, R., 224–25, 265
"Sluzhitel kulta" (Servant of the Cult, A), 143
Smerdyakov, 42
Smolensky, Vladimir Alekseevich, 13, 32, 80, 97, 105, 175, 178, 179, 190, 192, 193–94, 265
Smotr (Parade), 191
Sobakevich, 129
Socrates, 133
Sofiev, Yury, 19, 49, 174, 175, 178, 216, 222, 265–66
Soglyadatai (The Eye), 205
Sologub, Fyodor Kuzmich, 165, 172, 237, 266
Solonevich, Ivan Lukianovich, 54, 66, 195, 266
Solovyov, Vladimir Sergeevich, 43, 50, 133, 237, 266

Soplovyov, 144
Sosinsky, Bronislav Bronislavovich, 56, 182, 266
Sovremennye zapiski (Contemporary Annals), 21, 22, 24, 29, 48, 62, 63, 65, 68, 69, 70, 98, 100, 103, 119, 125, 137, 147, 150, 170, 180, 206, 218, 223
Soyuz pistelei i zhurnalistov (Union of Writers and Journalists), 12, 128, 297
Spellman, Cardinal, 136
Spinoza, Batuch, 140, 141
Stavrov, Parikl Stavrovich, 32, 39, 69, 86, 94, 108, 121, 179, 266
Steiger, Baron Anatoly Sergeevich, 69, 93, 147, 207–8, 209, 236, 266
Steiner, Rudolph, 87, 148, 149, 266
Stendhal, 186, 189
Stepun, Fyodor Avgustovich, 45, 133, 145, 146, 147, 148, 149, 267
Stepun, Margarita, 67, 121, 133, 267
Stillman, Tatiana, 178
Stolpyin, Pyotr Arkadievich, 226–27, 267
"Story of the False Coupon, The," 177
Strakhov, Nikolai, 236
Stravinsky, Igor Fyodorovich, 177, 267
Strider, 177
Struve, Kobyakov, 166
Struve, Mikhail Alleksandrovich, 166, 267
Surguchov, I. D., 128

Talin. See Portugeis, Stepan Ivanovich
Taproot of Soviet Society, 226, 227–28
Taras Bulbs, 17
Teffi, Nadezhda Aleksandrovna, 5, 220, 267
Temiryazev, Boris, 150. See also Annenkov, Yury

Tent, The, 180
Terapiano, Yury (Georgy) Konstantinovich, 19, 38, 74, 84, 85, 97, 175, 178, 219, 267–68
Terentiev, V. G., 61, 268
Teresa of Avila, 158
Terrible Vengeance, 114
Theresa of Lisieux, 115
Third Hour, 47, 117, 136, 212, 277
Thirteen, 179
Tikhonov, Nikolai Semyonovich, 200, 206, 222, 268
Tolstoi, 34, 39, 68, 76, 88, 99, 103, 105, 119, 127, 133, 138, 139, 142, 152, 163–64, 176, 177, 199, 205, 214, 227
Tolstoi, Aleksandra, 154, 181
Tolstoi, Aleksei Nikolaevich, 71, 125, 146, 148, 151, 160, 171, 268
Tolstoi, Lev Nikolaevich, 83, 125, 129, 233, 132–33, 268
Trocadero (Musé de l'Homme), 82, 185
Trotsky, Leon, 150, 268
Troubadours, 118
Trubetskoi, Madame, 124, 237
Trubetskoi, Prince Sergei Petrovich, 268
"Tsar and Soviets" movement, 67
Tsetlin, Maria Samoilovna, 192
Tsetlin, Mikahil, 217, 218
Tsvetaeva, Alya, 200, 204
Tsvetaeva, Efron, 151
Tsvetaeva, Marina Ivanovna, 68, 69, 97, 101, 107, 151, 169, 198–99, 200, 202, 203, 204, 208, 209, 268–69
Tukhachevsky, M. I., 151
Turgenev, Ivan Sergeevich, 56, 119, 137, 139, 145, 157, 163–64, 166, 199, 204, 209, 269
Turgeneva, Asya, 269
Turgeneva, Natalia, 87
Tutkovsky, Pavel, 32, 269

Tyazholaya lira (The Heavy Lyre), 97
Tyutchev, Fyodor Ivanovich, 144, 269

Underwood to the USSR, 71
Union of Soviet Patriots, 107, 236
Union of Soviet Repatriates, 151, 237–38
Union of Students from the Soviet Union, 200, 238
Union of Writers and Journalists, 12, 128, 297
Union of Writers and Poets, 30, 129, 174–90
Union of Young Writers and Poets, 124, 296
Union Theological Seminary, 59, 61
Unkovsky, Dr., 84, 168, 269
Uspensky, 87
Utverzhdeniya (Affirmations), 71, 200, 203, 297

Vakar, Nicholas P., 226, 227–28
Vakar, P., 269
Valerian, 194
Vanichka, 94
Varshavsky, Vladimir Sergeevich, 39, 106, 176, 177, 187, 269
Vasilievna, Inna, 122
Vecher u Kler (Evening at Claire), 164
Veidlé. *See* Weidlé, Vladimir Vasilievich
Verlaine, 16
Vildé, Boris Vladimirovich, 4, 21, 39, 49, 82, 94, 116, 165, 177, 183, 184, 185, 186, 187, 188, 189, 269–70
Vinaver, Maksim Moiseevich, 153, 270
Vishnyak, Mark Veniaminovich, 22, 63, 68, 69, 100, 127, 148, 159, 180, 181, 229, 270
Vishnyak, Rudnev, 62, 147
Vnutrenny Krug (Inner Circle), 21, 38, 44, 46, 47, 174, 175, 187, 217

Volkonsky, Mrs., 124, 237
Volno-Amerikanskaya (Catch-as-Catch-Can), 103
Volovick, Lazar, 217, 270
Volya Rossii (The Will of Russia), 62, 297
Voroshilov, K. E., 151
Voyage au bout de la nuit, 134
Voyoshilov, Klement Ehremovich, 270
Vozrozhdenie (Renaissance), 22, 34, 96, 98, 102, 124, 128, 175, 178, 190, 220, 224, 297
Vysheslavtsev, Boris Petrovich, 149, 270

Wallenrod, Konrad, 82
War and Peace, 38, 52, 121, 129, 144, 152, 171, 222, 232, 237
Weidlé, Vladimir Vasilievich, 27, 37, 73, 74, 123, 144–45, 270
Weil, Simone, 130, 271
What Is to Be Done, 69
Wilde, Oscar, 16
Winter Palace, 121
Woe from Wit, 79n
Wolfe, Thomas, 197, 199, 207
Wrangel, General Baron Pyotr Nikolaevich, 271
Writer's Union, 165, 203, 216

Yakor (Anchor), 190, 278
Yanovsky, Paulina, 135, 271
Yanovsky, V. S., 33, 39, 60, 73, 78, 88, 101, 117, 136, 148, 160, 164, 166, 215, 231
Yarovlev, Aleksandr, 271
Yassen, Irina, 217, 271
Yulievna, Sofia, 217
Yury, 55, 143

"Zadanie-vypolnenie" (Task and Realization), 231

Zadovich, B., 4
Zaitsev, Boris Konstantinovich, 5,
    39, 69, 122, 129, 162, 169, 192,
    271
Zakovich, Boris, 18–19, 86, 115,
    214, 271
Zamyatin, Evgeny Ivanovich, 170,
    171, 271
Za Svobodu (For Freedom), 84, 89,
    298
Zdanevich, Ilya M., 196, 271
Zeeler, Vladimir Feofilovich, 12, 129,
    194, 272
Zeitlin, M., 21, 60
Zelyonaya Lampa (Green Lamp), 7,
    110, 115, 195, 212, 218, 233, 278
Zelyuk, 216, 272
Zemgor, 24, 233–34
Zenzinov, Vladimir Mikhailovich,

    63, 64, 70, 71, 72, 74, 82, 103,
    127, 147, 148, 180, 181, 229, 272
Zetlin, Maria Samoilovna Avksenti-
    eva, 60, 70, 71, 80, 100, 113, 116,
    147, 181, 272
Zetlin, Mikhail Osipovich, 272
Zhaba, Sergei P., 46, 74, 272
Zhabotinsky, Vladimir Evgenievich,
    70, 206, 272
Zinoviev, G. E., 151
Zlobin, Vladimir Ananievich, 77, 78,
    105, 109, 110, 112, 114, 178, 179,
    180, 190, 191, 272
Zoshchenko, Mikhail Mikhailovich,
    6, 39, 170, 198, 272
Zosima, Father, 171
Zubov, Count Valentin P., 61, 273
Zurov, Leonid Fyodorovich, 29, 69,
    74, 119, 121, 122, 124, 194, 273

Lightning Source UK Ltd.
Milton Keynes UK
UKHW040744290919
350631UK00003B/155/P

9 780875 801193